CW00548874

LIBRARY OF SECOND T
85

Formerly Journal for the Study of the Pseudepigrapha Supplement Series

THE BODY IN BIBLICAL, CHRISTIAN AND JEWISH TEXTS

Edited by

Joan E. Taylor

Bloomsbury T&T Clark
An imprint of Bloomsbury Publishing Plc

B L O O M S B U R Y
LONDON • OXFORD • NEW YORK • NEW DELHI • SYDNEY

Bloomsbury T&T Clark
An imprint of Bloomsbury Publishing Plc

Imprint previously known as T&T Clark

50 Bedford Square   1385 Broadway
London   New York
WC1B 3DP   NY 10018
UK   USA

www.bloomsbury.com

**BLOOMSBURY, T&T CLARK and the Diana logo are trademarks
of Bloomsbury Publishing Plc**

First published 2014
Paperback edition first published 2015

British Library Cataloguing-in-Publication Data
A catalogue record for this book is available from the British Library.

ISBN: HB: 978-0-56725-426-9
PB: 978-0-56766-607-9
ePDF: 978-0-56731-222-8

Library of Congress Cataloging-in-Publication Data
Taylor, Joan E.
The Body in Biblical, Christian and Jewish Texts / Joan E. Taylor p.cm
Includes bibliographic references and index.
ISBN 978-0-5672-5426-9 (hardcover)

Series: The Library of Second Temple Studies

Typeset by Forthcoming Publications Ltd (www.forthpub.com)

CONTENTS

LIST OF FIGURES

LIST OF ABBREVIATIONS

AAA	*Apocryphal Acts of the Apostles*
AB	The Anchor Bible
AfO	*Archiv für Orientforschung*
AJU	Des Antiken Judentums und des Urchristentums
APTh	*The Acts of Paul and Thecla*
AUU	Acta Universitatis Upsaliensis
b.	Babylonian Talmud
BASOR	*Bulletin of the American Schools of Oriental Research*
BDAG	Bauer, W., F. W. Danker, W. F. Arndt, and F. W. Gingrich. *A Greek–English Lexicon of the New Testament and Other Early Christian Literature*. 3rd ed. Based on the 6th ed. of Walter Bauer's *Griechisch-deutsches Wörterbuch zu den Schriften des Neuen Testaments und der übrigen urchristlichen Literatur* (ed. Kurt Aland and Barbara Aland, with Viktor Reichmann, 1988), and on previous editions of William F. Arndt, F. Wilbur Gingrich and F. W. Danker (Chicago, 2000).
BDB	Francis Brown, Samuel Rolles Driver and Charles A Briggs, *The Brown–Driver–Briggs Hebrew and English Lexicon of the Old Testament* (Pcabody, MA, 2000)
BETL	Bibliotheca Ephemeridum Theologicarum Louvaniensium
BNTC	Black's New Testament Commentaries
BZAW	Beihefte zur Zeitschrift für die Alttesamentliche Wissenschaft
CAD	*The Assyrian Dictionary of the Oriental Institute of the University of Chicago* (ed. Ignace J. Gelb et al.; Glückstadt and Chicago, 1956–2011)
CBC	The Cambridge Bible Commentary
CBET	Contributions to Biblical Exegesis and Theology
CBQ	*Catholic Biblical Quarterly*
CEJL	Commentaries on Early Jewish Literature
ClQ	*Classical Quarterly*
CSRT	Cambridge Studies in Religious Traditions
DJBA	Michael Sokoloff, *Dictionary of Jewish Babylonian Aramaic of the Talmudic and Geonic Periods* (Ramat Gan, 2002)
EBib	*Études Bibliques*
ET	*Expository Times*
GCS	Die Griechischen Christlichen Schriftsteller der ersten Jahrhunderte
GLAJJ	Menaham Stern, *Greek and Latin Authors on Jews and Judaism* (2 vols.; Jerusalem, 1974)
HSS	Harvard Semitic Studies
HTR	*Harvard Theological Review*
HTS	Harvard Theological Studies

HUCA	*Hebrew Union College Annual*
IVP	Inter-Varsity Press
JANES	*Journal of the Ancient Near Eastern Society*
JAOS	*Journal of the American Oriental Society*
JBL	*Journal of Biblical Literature*
JECS	*Journal of Early Christian Studies*
JJS	*Journal of Jewish Studies*
JJSSup	Journal of Jewish Studies: Supplement Series
JNES	*Journal of Northwest Semitic Languages*
JPS	Jewish Publication Society
JQR	*Jewish Quarterly Review*
JRS	*Journal of Roman Studies*
JSJ	*Journal for the Study of Judaism in the Persian, Hellenistic, and Roman Period*
JSJSup	Journal for the Study of Judaism: Supplement Series
JSOT	*Journal for the Study of the Old Testament*
JSOTSup	Journal for the Study of the Old Testament: Supplement Series
JSPSup	Journal for the Study of the Pseudepigrapha: Supplement Series
LHBOTS	Library of Hebrew Bible/Old Testament Studies
LSJ	Henry George Liddell and Robert Scott, *A Greek–English Lexicon*, revised and augmented throughout by Sir Henry Stuart Jones, with the assistance of Roderick McKenzie (Oxford, 1940)
m.	Mishnah
NICOT	New International Commentary on the Old Testament
NJPS	*JPS Hebrew–English Tanakh: The Traditional Hebrew Text and the New JPS Translation* (2nd ed.; Philadelphia, 1999)
NRSV	New Revised Standard Version
NTS	*New Testament Studies*
OTP	*The Old Testament Pseudepigrapha* (ed. James H. Charlesworth; 2 vols.; London, 1983–85)
PVTG	Pseudepigrapha veteris testamenti graece
REN	*Records from Erech: From the Time of Nabonidus* (ed. Raymond P. Doughtery; New Haven, 1920)
RQ	*Revue de Qumran*
SBL	Society of Biblical Literature
SBLDS	Society of Biblical Literature Dissertation Series
SC	Sources chrétiennes
SHG	Subsidia Hagiographica
STDJ	Studies in the Texts of the Desert of Judah
SVTP	Studia in Veteris Testamenti Pseudepigrapha
TDNT	*Theological Dictionary of the New Testament* (ed. Gerhard Kittel; trans. Geoffrey W. Bromiley; Grand Rapids, 1965)
TynBul	*The Tyndale Bulletin*
USQR	*Union Seminary Quarterly Review*
VT	*Vetus Testamentum*
WBC	Word Bible Commentary
WUNT	Wissenschaftliche Untersuchungen zum Neuen Testament
y.	Jerusalem Talmud
YBT	Yale Oriental Series: Babylonian Texts, Volumes I–V
ZA	*Zeitschrift für Assyriologie*
ZAW	*Zeitschrift für die Alttestamentliche Wissenschaft*

NOTES ON CONTRIBUTORS

Laliv Clenman is Lecturer in Rabbinic Literature at Leo Baeck College and Visiting Lecturer in the Department of Theology and Religious Studies at King's College London. She holds a PhD in Hebrew and Aramaic Language and Literature (Rabbinics) from the University of Toronto. She is particularly interested in the multiplicity, diversity and development of rabbinic law and the complex relationship between *halakhah* and *aggadah*. Her research explores the nature of rabbinic discourse and hermeneutics focusing on the areas of authority, identity and status, including intermarriage, gender, sexuality, the construction of Jewishness and the impact of *halakhah* on the individual.

Michelle Fletcher read English as an undergraduate at Cambridge University. She has an MA in Biblical Studies from King's College London, where she is currently in her final year of doctoral research on the use of the Hebrew Bible in the book of Revelation. Her research interests include feminist hermeneutics, literary and film theory, and textual imitation. Her publications and conference papers cover the topics of violence in the Apocalypse, feminist reinterpretation of Mark's Gospel and Revelation's literary composition.

Davina Grojnowski completed her doctoral thesis on Josephus's *Vita* at King's College London. She holds a degree in Classics, also from King's, and a Master's degree in Jewish Studies from the University of Oxford. Her research interests lie in the development of autobiography as a literary genre, proselytism in antiquity, and the classical historical background to Judaea. She currently teaches New Testament Greek at King's College London and has previously taught in the Department of Theology at the University of Bielefeld, Germany.

Rebecca Harrocks is currently working on her doctoral thesis on self-identity in the Jewish community at Alexandria at King's College London. She holds an undergraduate degree in Theology from the University of Nottingham, as well as a Master's degree in Theology and Religious Studies, also from Nottingham, which was completed under the supervision of Roland Deines. Her interests lie in Gentile inclusion in the early church, the relationship between Jesus and Paul, and Jesus' healing miracles.

Daniel Hayter holds a BA in Theology and an MA in Biblical Studies from King's College London. His MA dissertation explored the various views on resurrection as an eschatological mode of existence that emerge in Jewish texts of the Second Temple period. He is particularly interested in the Jewish background of early Christianity, the eschatology of the New Testament and the New Testament's interpretation of the Old Testament/Hebrew Bible.

Sandra Jacobs is a Visiting Researcher in the Theology and Religious Studies Department at King's College London. Her doctoral thesis, *The Body as Property: Physical Disfigurement in Biblical Law*, is published by Bloomsbury Press and she is also the Reviews Editor for *Strata: The Bulletin of the Anglo-Israel Archaeology Society*. Her research interests include: the pre-history of biblical law, representations of the body and physical disfigurement in biblical and Second Temple tradition, the treatment of women in post-biblical and rabbinic literature.

Steffan Mathias is a final-year doctoral student in the Department of Theology and Religious Studies at King's College London. He is working on a thesis entitled 'Paternity, Progeny and Perpetuation: Creating Lives after Death in the Hebrew Bible', looking at biblical responses to childlessness. His research interests include anthropological approaches to biblical texts; queer negativity the anti-social turn in queer theory; death, dying and tombs in the ancient Near East; and using Foucauldian methodologies with ancient texts.

Rosie Ratcliffe is currently finalising her doctoral thesis on the *Acts of Paul and Thecla* at King's College London. Rosie read Theology as an undergraduate and also completed a postgraduate Masters in Biblical Studies at King's College, before she was ordained in 2001. Previously Rosie worked as a part-time lecturer at King's College London and was also Mental Health Chaplain for the South London and Maudsley NHS Trust. She has recently been appointed as Trust Chaplain and Mental Health Lead at Imperial College Healthcare Trust. Her research interests include gender studies, women in early Christianity, martyrdom literature and representations of violence. She publishes in the areas of biblical studies, contemporary spirituality and chaplaincy.

C. A. Strine is Vice-Chancellor's Fellow and Lecturer in Hebrew Bible at the University of Sheffield. Previously, he spent 2012–13 at King's College London as Early Career Research Fellow in the Arts and Humanities Research Institute. Strine specializes in social scientific approaches to historical reconstruction of the ancient Near East, focusing on how the experience of forced migration influences the development of ethnic, national, and religious identity. His first monograph—*Sworn Enemies: The Divine Oath, the Book of Ezekiel, and the Polemics of Exile*—demonstrates that Ezekiel contains both a 'public' transcript of an intra-ethnic debate among two Judahite communities and a disguised transcript of an inter-national resistance against the Babylonian empire. Now, Strine is exploring ways that the study of forced migration can illumine the themes and diachronic growth of the Pentateuch, beginning his work here with a monograph on the patriarchal narrative (Gen 12–36).

Joan E. Taylor is Professor of Christian Origins and Second Temple Judaism at King's College London. She completed postgraduate studies at the University of Otago, New Zealand, majoring in New Testament, and then went to the British School of Archaeology in Jerusalem (Kenyon Institute) as Annual Scholar in 1986. She undertook a PhD in early Christian archaeology and Jewish-Christianity at New College, Edinburgh University, and was appointed in 1992 to a position of lecturer (subsequently senior lecturer) at the University of Waikato, New Zealand, in the departments of both Religious Studies and History. In 1995 she won an Irene Levi-Sala Award in Israel's archaeology, for the book version of her PhD thesis, *Christians and the Holy Places* (1993, rev. 2003). In 1996–97 she was Visiting Lecturer and Research Associate in Women's Studies in New Testament at Harvard Divinity School, a position she held in association with a Fulbright Award. She publishes in the fields of biblical studies, Second Temple Judaism and early Christianity, with a special focus on women and gender, history, archaeology and context. Her most recent book is *The Essenes, the Scrolls and the Dead Sea* (2012).

Katie Turner is currently undertaking doctoral research at King's College London, studying the cultural impact of Passion plays: specifically, how they present and have created misconceptions of first-century Judaea. She has previously completed a BA in History at Stony Brook University, New York, an MA in History at Royal Holloway, University of London, and an MA in Biblical Studies, also undertaken at King's. Her research interests include the historical Jesus and the development of the early Christian community, the development of ritual and cultural practice, the development and perpetuation of beliefs and traditions, as well as, more generally, heritage studies and cultural history. Complementary to her studies, she has worked in museum/heritage education at the National Trust, Historic Royal Palaces, and the Science Museum.

INTRODUCTION

The chapters contained in this book arose out of a one-day symposium at King's College London in which scholars and doctoral students of the Department of Theology and Religious Studies joined together to celebrate common interests in aspects of the body. Such was the response to the event—hailed as innovative and ground-breaking—that the decision to collect these papers together followed. We discovered at the symposium that a focus on the body reconfigures religious discourse, and creates striking connections across cultures, places and times that have wide-ranging impacts today. What began as a focused King's event is now shared with the wider scholarly community. That many of the voices in this collection are at the beginning of their academic careers means that there is an overall youthful and fresh style to this collection, with innovative and provocative perspectives.

Why the body? The importance of this focus lies in the fact that the body is an entity on which religious ideology is printed, both as a single artefact and in relation to other bodies. Thus it is frequently a subject of interest, anxiety, prescription and regulation in biblical law, the New Testament or early Christian and Jewish writings. Issues such as the body's age, disability, purity, sickness, vulnerability, gender, sexual activity, modesty, activities and placements can revolve around what the body is and is not supposed to do or be. The body can be the locus of future expectation as the site of resurrection and hope, but the body can also be banned from spaces and activities on account of its sex.

The body appears within texts from specific times and places, reflecting embedded cultural notions, and yet regulations and ideas about the body from past times and places affect how the body is seen today, because of the situation of such regulations and ideas within religious works deemed authoritative. At the present time, the body is at the centre of issues of church leadership and marriage; questions hinge on whether roles are appropriate to the male or female body. Its sexual actions are considered 'religious' issues. For those within religious communities, one's own body is configured by means of a range of textual, traditional and interpretational notions that define appearance, conduct, placement and status.

In putting the body at the centre of discussion this book aims to provide inter-disciplinary and creative explorations of the body as it is described and defined in texts. This cannot be comprehensive, but only begins probings that will, it is hoped, be developed further by others. While the body can, in academic discourse, be viewed anthropologically and sociologically, sexually or theoretically, it can function in specific ways within religious texts that ultimately point to essential features of religious ideology. The body is both a symbolic surface as well as an actual one that defines proper 'religious' boundaries, both in terms of the self and the wider community in which that self belongs. There is so much work still to be done.

Already in biblical, early Jewish and Christian studies many under-standings of the limitations and uses of the body have been explored within the fields of women's, gender and queer studies. These have refined varieties of thinking about the body as an entity that religious texts absorb within ideological and theological programmes. In the same way that a focus on women as a distinct category has created new ways of seeing and new hermeneutics of interpretation, a focus on the body—male or female, damaged or whole, sick or well, sexual or celibate, fed or hungry—can change the way we look at texts.

This book seeks to create a new perspective of body-centred readings that will enable previously unseen patterns of relationship and meaning to come to the fore. It provides a timely and contemporary discussion, exploring the dance of religion and culture as it is played out on the body. It is also a celebration not of one distinct hermeneutic but of multiple strategies for understanding the body and the role of religious texts in defining it. In the end, the contributors collectively provide a fascinating and challenging study of several critical biblical texts, as well as early Christian and Jewish material, that will I hope be referred to in a broad range of future studies.

To summarize what is contained here, in Chapter 1 Sandra Jacobs argues that the body was a visible, inscriptional surface in the Hebrew Bible and related literature. Despite the explicit prohibition against body marking in Lev. 19.28, it is evident that marking acts were, nevertheless, symbolically understood as expressions of devotion and piety, with language reflecting cultural practices known in ancient Israel, both in terms of slavery and temple devotion. The Priestly language used to describe body marking in the Holiness Code reflects Neo-Babylonian consecratory formulae, indicating close cross-cultural connections, and perhaps also practices within Israel not entirely consistent with legal formulae.

In Chapter 2, Steffan Mathias provides an innovative reading of Lev. 18.22, 20.13, and Deut. 22.5: gay 'texts of terror'. Such texts prohibit certain sexual acts between men, acts categorized at different times as 'abominations'. Mathias notes how Daniel Boyarin and Saul Olyan have made huge strides forward in understanding the origins of the law and in divorcing it from contemporary discourses of (homo)sexuality. He explores the bodily dimensions of the laws, arguing they are specifically concerned with the act of male–male penetration, guarding the male body from 'feminization'. Bringing Lev. 18.22 into dialogue with Deut. 22.5, it is apparent that there is a general concern with both maintaining boundaries of gender and a valorization of patriarchal, phallocentric culture. Mathias asks: What happens to the contemporary (gay male) reader when we consider these bodily aspects of the text? Using Foucault's understanding of knowledge and power, and its affect on understanding and regulating our bodies, both ancient and contemporary bodies (male/female, gay/straight) are deconstructed and shown to be contingent on the effects of certain kinds of knowledge. Mathias suggests the work of Leo Bersani, which builds on Foucault and Freud, has offered a way to tackle both homophobia and misogyny through a queer embrace of powerlessness. This can be further developed by reference to Pauline theology, read as rejecting worldly power structures in a kenotic strategy, and as suggesting new avenues for sexual ethics around the embrace of powerlessness. This shows ways of reading the text that may offer new modes of resistance, not through circumventing texts and arguing for their irrelevance, but by tackling them head on.

In Chapter 3 Casey Strine explores Ezek. 37.1-14, a vision in which dry bones in a valley assemble into bodies and come to life. Strine observes that scholars have given little attention to the bodies that dominate this vision, nor have they explored the ritualized actions those bodies perform. Strine notes, for instance, that the prophet's first action upon arriving in the valley is to circumambulate it, demarcating the space and creating an inside–outside group dynamic that structures the subsequent events. Utilizing Catherine Bell's observation that such simple movements mark off space and time, defining even the most complex ritual environments as a matrix of oppositional schemes, Strine explores how the prophet and the reconstituted bodies consisting of the dry bones construct the ritual space with their bodily movements. These ritualized actions enable the passage to tap into a non-conscious, visceral logic possessed by its audience that increases the possibility it can persuade the audience to maintain their ethnic identity and resist the strong temptation to assimilate into Babylonian culture.

In my own essay, in Chapter 4, I focus on 'the Twelve', as described as being appointed by Jesus in Mark 6, and question whether we should assume that twelve male bodies are indicated exclusively, using a hermeneutic of suspicion and historical reconstruction indebted to the work of Elisabeth Schüssler Fiorenza. The Marcan reference to the Twelve being sent out 'two by two' (Mk 6.7) is suggestive of archetypal male–female partners going into the ark (Gen. 6.21), so that 'the Twelve' historically might have been a shorthand for twelve apostolic pairs authorized by Jesus to act in his place, as servants like him. If so, this group would have included women with their own distinctive service (cf. Mk 15.40-41), especially in terms of healing. This hidden model finds endorsement not only within the New Testament (cf. 1 Cor. 9.6), but also within the writings of the early church, where female apostolic companions and co-leaders are widely attested.

Rebecca Harrocks, in Chapter 5, discusses the healings of Gentile bodies by Jesus, and provides a careful survey of commentators' discussions of these. Harrocks notes how the canonical Gospels depict Jesus' favoured modes of healing as direct spoken words and touch, as a means to channel the healing force. However, in the case of the two key Gentile healings—the Syrophoenician woman's daughter and the centurion's boy (Mt. 15.21-28/Mk 7.24-30; Mt. 8.5-13/Lk. 7.1-10, cf. Jn 4.46-54)—these are carried out without physical contact: there is a strong emphasis on the requirement of faith. This essay considers the context of the early church in which the place of Gentiles demanded that the healing stories provide an inclusive message to Gentiles that would strike at the heart of the Christian message.

In Chapter 6 Katie Turner tackles the cultural issues involved in the eucharistic proclamation of bread and wine being the body and blood of Jesus, particularly the instruction by Jesus to drink the wine as his blood, an especially shocking symbol given the prohibition on consuming any blood in biblical Law. She considers the history of the blessing itself, including its cultural origins, focusing on questions that have arisen, and asks ultimately whether the blessing could even originate with Jesus. Might there have been a 'Passoverization' that explains the wording we have in the New Testament, resulting from a conservation of the story of Jesus' last meal as heritage rather than history?

With a view to better awareness of the resurrection narratives of the New Testament, the context of Second Temple Judaism is explored in the essay by Daniel Hayter, in Chapter 7. Hayter seeks to find more clarity than has hitherto been discovered on the question of the resurrection of the body in a range of extant texts. The idea of resurrection as an eschatological phenomenon in early Judaism has received much scholarly attention over the last few decades. However, some disagreement still persists over whether resurrection necessarily entailed a belief in the raising of a body, or whether the concept could refer to the raising of a disembodied soul or spirit. Hayter contends that such disagreements can stem from an *a priori* view of what constitutes the human body. By offering a brief survey of the most salient references to resurrection from non-canonical early Jewish writings, Hayter suggests that if we avoid importing anachronistic assumptions on the nature of the body into an ancient text, the evidence from Second Temple Jewish writings suggests that resurrection was, in fact, always thought of as a bodily event, and not a way of speaking of disembodied immortality.

In the book of Revelation (Rev. 17) the 'whore of Babylon' is most often read as a figurative female who symbolizes a city. In Chapter 8 Michelle Fletcher notes how her textual body is examined by scholars attempting to discover which Hebrew Bible source texts she is constructed from, in order to explain her symbolic properties. However, this process leads to an abandonment of the very thing being presented: Babylon's body. Fletcher sets out to reconstruct this overlooked body and to do this she takes an innovative reanimation approach by carrying out a comparative analysis with Frankenstein's monsters. By using different filmic portrayals of these textual monsters, Fletcher explores how Babylon has been envisioned by the scholars reading her. She asks: what has been inscribed onto Babylon's body, what has been overlooked in readings and what threats Revelation's own animated female monster offers in the narrative of the text? In doing so she demonstrates that Babylon is presented in the text of Revelation 17 as a multiply penetrated prostitute who offers a significant fleshly threat to the lamb and its followers. Ultimately, Fletcher argues that, like Frankenstein's female monster, it is her bodily destruction that reveals why she is so threatening and shows that she is as much a literal woman as she is a figurative female.

In Chapter 9, Davina Grojnowski examines Josephus's attitude to circumcision, both forced and voluntary, within the context of conversion to Judaism, using a meticulous literary approach. She stresses that all Josephus's circumcision/conversion episodes need to be read within their respective literary contexts within his works, focusing on terminology and literary setting, before attempting a holistic conclusion as to Josephus's personal opinion of circumcision. It is argued that Josephus neither emphasized nor concealed the requirement of circumcision. Rather, Josephus used the mark of circumcision to define his own, private understanding of conversion.

Moving on to the world of the early church, Rosie Ratcliffe discusses in Chapter 10 the body of the 'not-quite' martyr Thecla, in the narrative of *The Acts of Paul and Thecla*, questioning whether this is a text that can be read positively for female empowerment. Rather, this text is highly androcentric. Despite repeated efforts to end the life of this troublesome woman, Thecla survives extreme torments without any harm to her body. She climbs out of fires unharmed and is protected against wild beasts, her limbs remain intact despite efforts to tear her apart and there are no traces of wounds upon her chaste and beautiful body. In surviving and transcending the physical torments within the arena, however, Thecla as a real woman is also sexualized and degraded, subjected to what appears to be a male gaze. In this text there is almost nothing to indicate that Thecla is a noted teacher and leader, despite this being known in the wider Thecla tradition. In the *Acts of Paul and Thecla*, the real hero is Paul, and Thecla is no longer a real woman but an embodied symbol of Christian resistance and resilience which speaks back to the Roman Empire. Thecla's spectacular acts of endurance and courage answer Rome's might—a bodily form of witness to God's transforming power.

Finally, Laliv Clenman, in Chapter 11, turns to the question of the talmudic discourse on male bodies as sexual objects. It is seen that the comparative analysis of talmudic narratives involves the rare motif of the self-destruction of male genitalia. The story in *b. Kid.* 81b deals with the notion of male sexual self-control. It tells of a Rabbi Charuta or Rav Chiya bar Ashi, who is fastidious regarding such self-control to the point of avoiding all sexual contact, even with his own wife. He brings about his own destruction and death in a fire after an apparent moment of weakness. The narrative relies on the hermeneutical device of destruction of the sexual body leading to death, not only as a complex commentary on the extremes of sexual abandon and celibacy, demonstrating the futility and fatality of each, but also as a narrative means for the solution of intractable legal problems: killing the person in whom the problem is embodied.

With these wide-ranging explorations, it is hoped that this collection will stimulate scholarly debates and provide a provocative and innovative assemblage of readings that can be used as a basis for student discussions in the classroom, at both undergraduate and postgraduate level. These essays overall contribute young and fresh perspectives on old issues, and strategies that point the way forward to further enterprise that situates the body at the centre of academic study in religion, just as the body has become central in contemporary public discourse on religious questions. I am very grateful to the editors and readers of Bloomsbury T&T Clark for making this publication possible, especially Alinda Damsma, and to my friends and colleagues Laliv Clenman and Sandra Jacobs, with whom I birthed the idea of the symposium in the first place.

Joan Taylor

1

THE BODY INSCRIBED:
A PRIESTLY INITIATIVE?*

Sandra Jacobs

The body appears as an inscriptive surface in the Hebrew Bible,[1] where its construction, 'like clay in the hands of the potter',[2] recalled the conventional writing surface of ancient Near Eastern antiquity: the clay tablet, upon which signs were inscribed with a reed stylus. The individual body is also the surface that must be cut (in the case of male circumcision) and pierced (as the ear of the permanent Israelite slave).[3] Yet, notwithstanding these situations, body marking is largely forbidden in the Holiness Code (Lev. 19.28; 21.5), and in Deuteronomic Law (Deut. 14.1).[4] This, then, raises the question: how can the inscriptive

*   I wish to thank Paul Joyce for his response to an earlier draft of this study, which was delivered as a paper at "The Body" symposium in May 2012, together with Michelle Fletcher, Laliv Clenman and Joan Taylor. Unless otherwise noted, all translations of the Hebrew Bible in this chapter are from the NJPS.

1.   See Elizabeth Grosz's chapter, 'The Body as Inscriptive Surface', in her book *Volatile Bodies: Toward a Corporeal Feminism* (Theories of Representation and Difference; Bloomington: Indiana University Press, 1994), pp. 138-59, and also Sandra Jacobs, *The Body as Object: Physical Disfigurement in Biblical Law* (LHBOTS 582; London: Bloomsbury T&T Clark, 2014).

2.   As represented in Jer. 18.5-6: 'Then the word of the Lord came to me: O House of Israel, can I not deal with you like this potter?—says the Lord. Just as clay in the hands of the potter, so are you in My hands'. See further Isa. 29.16; Job 10.9-10; Ben Sira 33.13; and Rom. 9.19-21.

3.   The need for Abraham's circumcision is first mentioned in Gen. 17.1-21 (cf. also Lev. 12.3 and 19.23). The instruction to the Moses regarding the piercing of the Israelite slave's ear is found in Exod. 21.6 and Deut. 15.16.

4.   The Holiness Code refers to Priestly law found in Lev. 19–26, whereas Deuteronomic law refers to the collection presented in Deut. 12–26.

nature of the human body be reconciled with these prohibitions?[5] This issue becomes all the more challenging since the idea of marking or tattooing the body evoked notions of faithful devotion and piety, with such acts simultaneously perceived as a sign which activated divine protection.

Such signs are fascinating also from an anthropological perspective. Wade Davis explains their significance in the context of pre-literate societies:

> The human body was seen as yet another feature of the landscape, a sensual geography upon which might be written and inscribed the hopes and fears of a people. To mark the body electric was to record mystical events, give credence to established patterns of order and hierarchy, make sense of sensation, and secure through artistic expression the place of the individual in the collective.[6]

This desire to give 'credence to established patterns of order and hierarchy' can be traced, likewise, in Priestly and prophetic texts, where 'the place of the individual in the collective', is highlighted by a number of divinely instructed body markings. In this context important parallels exist between the formal consecration of Levites and Israelites, and the marking of temple oblates (*širku, širkutu*) in cuneiform records[7] from the

---

5.   While these prohibitions are restricted to Priestly and Deuteronomic law, it is notable that Lev. 19.28 and Deut. 14.1 do not proscribe the identical body markings, despite the fact that both are presented as a unified tradition at the Temple Scroll at Qumran (11Q19 48.7-9). It is not appropriate to retroject the rabbinic requirement, ועשו סיג לתורה, 'to make a fence for the law' (*m. Avot* 1.1), onto the early reception of the biblical laws. Thus, while all forms of tattooing were subsequently prohibited in Jewish law, this does not negate the semantic meaning of the biblical texts. For reference to the Hellenistic origins of the rabbinic principle, see Siegfried Stein, 'The Concept of the "Fence": Observations on Its Origin and Development', in Siegfried Stein and Raphael Loewe (eds.), *Studies in Jewish Religious and Intellectual History: Presented to Alexander Altmann on the Occasion of his Seventieth Birthday* (Alabama: Published with the Institute of Jewish Studies, London, by the University of Alabama Press, 1979), pp. 301-29.

6.   Wade Davis, 'Foreword', in Chris Rainier (ed.), *Ancient Marks: The Sacred Origins of Tattoos and Body Marking* (San Rafael: Earth Aware Editions, 2004), p. 14. See also Mary Douglas, *Purity and Danger: An Analysis of Concepts of Pollution and Taboo* (London: Routledge & Kegan Paul, 1966; repr. London: Routledge Classics, 2006), p. 5.

7.   Cuneiform writing (from the Latin, *cuneus*, meaning 'wedge') was for nearly 3,000 years the principal media of recorded communication throughout the ancient Near East, where the earliest signs were scratched onto damp clay using a reed stylus. These signs were initially pictographic, so that (for example) an ox, fish, or

Neo-Babylonian period.⁸ These relationships are additionally relevant to our emerging knowledge of the satellite exilic communities in the Babylonian-Borsippa regions of āl-Yāhūdu and Našar,⁹ from where evidence of the early Judaean diaspora is only just coming to light.¹⁰

bird was intentionally recognizable in its earliest written form. In order to express more complex ideas, a syllabic system evolved in the early dynastic era (c. 2800 BCE in Ur and Jemdet Nasr) from which Sumerian (the oldest known written language) and Akkadian subsequently developed. The dialects of Semitic Akkadian preserved in cuneiform script include Babylonian (Iraq), Elamite (Iran), Hittite (Turkey) and Hurrian (Syria).

8. The focus on texts from the Neo-Babylonian period (626–539 BCE), rather than the Neo-Assyrian (934–609 BCE), is because the earlier texts are much less well-documented, with no more than two or three examples published; see J. Nicholas Postgate, *Fifty Neo-Assyrian Legal Documents* (Warminster: Aris & Philips, 1976). Furthermore, the Neo-Babylonian texts have been extensively examined in scholarship since their publication by Raymond P. Dougherty, *The Shirkûtu of Babylonian Deities* (New Haven: Yale University Press, 1923).

9. Laurie Pearce uses the acronym TAYN (Texts from āl-Yāhūdu and Našar) to describe the cuneiform texts from this corpus, in 'New Evidence for Judeans in Babylonia', in Oded Lipschits and Manfred Oeming (eds.), *Judah and the Judeans in the Persian Period: Conference Proceedings Held Jointly by the University of Heidelberg, the Hochschule für Jüdische Studien Heidelberg and Tel Aviv University, 15–18 July 2003* (Winona Lake: Eisenbrauns, 2006), pp. 399-411. See further: Edwin M. Yamauchi, 'The Eastern Jewish Diaspora under the Babylonians', in Mark W. Chavalas and K. Lawson Younger Jr (eds.), *Mesopotamia and the Bible: Comparative Explorations* (JSOTSup 341; London: Sheffield Academic Press, 2002), pp. 356-77, and David S. Vanderhooft, 'New Evidence Pertaining to the Transition from Neo-Babylonian to Achaemenid Administration in Palestine', in Rainer Albertz and Bob Becking (eds.), *Yahwism after the Exile: Perspectives on Israelite Religion in the Persian Era. Papers Read at the First Meeting of the European Association for Biblical Studies, Utrecht, 6–9 August 2000* (Assen: Van Gorcum, 2003), pp. 219-35.

10. Estimates of the number of tablets extant in this corpus have ranged from 80 to 120, although at the recent Schweich Lectures (held at the British Academy, 25–27 June 2013, which included a discussion of 'West Semitic Epigraphy and the Judean Diaspora during the Achaemenid Period: Babylonia, Egypt, Cyprus'), André Lemaire indicated that there were as many as 200 in total. Those published to date include Kathleen Abraham, 'West Semitic and Judean Brides in Cuneiform Sources from the Sixth Century BCE: New Evidence from a Marriage Contract from Al-Yahudu', *Archiv für Orientfurschung* 51 (2005/2006), pp. 198-219, and Francis Joannès and André Lemaire, 'Trois tablettes cunéiformes à onomastique ouest-sémitique (Collection S. Moussaieff)', *Transeuphratène* 17 (1999), pp. 17-34. Anticipated future publications include: Laurie F. Pearce and Cornelia Wunsch, *Into the Hands of Many Peoples: Judean and West Semitic Exiles in Mesopotamia* (Bethesda: CDL Press, forthcoming), and Cornelia Wunsch, *Judeans by the Waters*

The present chapter will therefore explore the fundamental attitudes to the marking of the individual body within the diverse memories preserved by the biblical scribes, with attention to relevant analogues from cuneiform texts of the Neo-Babylonian period.

First, however, what exact physical markings were prohibited in the Holiness Code? Leviticus 19.28 prohibits the 'gashing of flesh', where שרט לנפש (literally 'gashing for life' or 'gashing for a person')[11] is forbidden. Such injuries were conventionally incurred as part of the rites during mourning ceremonies, and Saul Olyan thus asks: 'Why is Yhwh offended by the presence of a priest at his altar with a permanent or long-lasting mourning marker?'[12] The text of Lev. 19.28 reads:

You shall not make any gashes	ושרט לנפש לא תתנו
in your flesh [for the dead],	בבשרכם
or incise any marks on yourselves:[13]	וכתבת קעקע לא תתנו

Here the translation 'for the dead' are included in square brackets to make the mourning relationship clearer, although למת is not present in the Hebrew. It has been inferred by relating this passage to the law in Deut. 14.1, where reference to the cult of the dead is explicit:

You shall not gash yourselves	לא תתגדדו
or shave the front of your heads	ולא תשימו קרחה בין עיניכם
because of the dead.	למת

The prohibition is reiterated again in Lev. 21.5, where it is limited to the priesthood, for whom additional shaving restrictions are itemized:

of Babylon: New Historical Evidence in Sources from Rural Babylonia: Texts from the Schoyen Collection (Dresden: Islet Verlag, forthcoming). I am grateful to Alan Millard for bringing these last two items to my attention.

11. See BDB, p. 976, שרט, where its use as an infinitive absolute in Zech. 12.3 is noted. Here, however, שרוט ישרטו is translated as '[they] shall injure themselves' in the following verse: 'Behold, I will make Jerusalem a bowl of reeling for the peoples all around. Judah shall be caught up in the siege of Jerusalem, when all the nations of the earth gather against her. In that day I will make Jerusalem a stone for all the peoples to lift; all who lift it shall injure themselves'. In addition, the verbal form of שרט, meaning 'to incise' or 'to scratch', is also related to its cognates in Aramaic (סרט) and Akkadian (*šarātu*, 'to slit up' or 'rend'). See *CAD*, 'Š', Part Two, p. 59, '*šarātu*'.

12. Saul M. Olyan, *Biblical Mourning: Ritual and Social Dimensions* (Oxford/ New York: Oxford University Press, 2004), p. 118.

13. קעקע (BDB, p. 891) is an 'incision, imprintment, tattoo', as noted by Naftali Tur-Sinai, 'תכבת קעקע', in *Enṣiqlopedya Miqra'it* 4:378–80.

They shall not shave smooth any part of their heads,[14]	לא יקרחו קרחה בראשם
or cut the side-growth of their beards,	ופאת זקנים לא יגלחו
or make gashes in their flesh.[15]	ובבשרם לא ישרטו שרטת

This association with mourning is supported by comparative affinities to Canaanite, if not also Egyptian, practices, where ancestor cult worship was prevalent.[16] Here Olyan suggests that other factors need to be taken into account, where the temporal effects between tattooing and incising flesh are significant.[17] He distinguishes between the permanence of the tattoo, which typically are 'not easily or rapidly reversible',[18] and laceration scratches or scars, which would (often, but not always) disappear. These distinctions invariably recall the requirement for a priest's blemish-free male physique, stipulated in Lev. 21.16-23, where even physical disabilities (including blindness or lameness) would disqualify his participation in the cult.[19] Accordingly, Olyan concludes that the under-lying rationale of Lev. 21.5-6 is based on the fact that the body marks are self-inflicted, and therefore were preventable. In addition, the presence

14. Cf. Ezek. 44.20: 'They shall neither shave their heads nor let their hair go untrimmed; they shall keep their hair trimmed'. In contrast, there are the divine instructions to 'take a sharp knife, use it as a barber's razor and pass it over your head and beard' in Ezek. 5.1. This passage is explored in E. J. Smit, 'The Concepts of Obliteration in Ezekiel 5.1-4', *JNSL* 1 (1971), pp. 46-50. Together with the separate traditions in Isa. 15.2c ('On every head is baldness, every head is shorn'), Jer. 41.4-5 and Ezra 9.3, these prophetic sources do not present a unified or con-sistent rationale for prohibiting facial hair and head shaving, and the question of genital shaving does not appear to be relevant. It is not possible to make any viable connection between these prophetic traditions and the shaving of the slave's head, to provide an *abbuttu(m)*, or hair-lock, known from Sumerian and Old Babylonian sources.

15. For further discussion of the reception of these laws in rabbinic tradition, see *m. Mak.* 3.6, *b. Mak.* 21a and *y. Ned.* 21a.

16. See Brian B. Schmidt, *Israel's Beneficent Dead: Ancestor Cult and Necro-mancy in Ancient Israelite Religion and Tradition* (Winona Lake: Eisenbrauns, 1996), pp.166-78; Jacob Milgrom, *Leviticus 17–22: A New Translation with Introduction and Commentary* (AB 3A; New York: Doubleday, 2000), pp. 1840-41 ('Mourning Customs in the Biblical World').

17. Olyan, *Biblical Mourning*, p. 114.

18. *Ibid.*, pp. 115-16.

19. See Sarah J. Melcher, 'Visualizing the Perfect Cult: The Priestly Rationale for Exclusion', in Nancy L. Eiesland and Don E. Saliers (eds.), *Human Disability and the Service of God: Reassessing Religious Practice* (Nashville: Abingdon Press, 1998), pp. 55-71.

of a priest 'marked as a mourner in the sacrificial context of rejoicing',[20] could threaten, or even endanger, the cultic process. Admittedly, Olyan's explanation has not been evaluated by John Huehnergard and Harold Liebowitz, in their discussion of 'Morning Practices in Ancient Israel',[21] who prefer that 'the biblical prohibition of tattooing should not necessarily be viewed in connection with mourning'.[22]

Beyond mourning, there was also the widespread use of tattooing (and branding) for the marking of slaves throughout antiquity, which was an additionally significant factor underlying the biblical prohibitions. By the first millennium BCE, the common method of inscribing text onto the skin was by means of tattooing, using ink and a reed stylus, unlike branding, which was attested primarily in second-millennium sources for both slaves and livestock. Sources identifying the marking of slaves, prisoners and oblates (devotees of gods formally donated to a temple), are preserved in Neo-Assyrian and Neo-Babylonian cuneiform sources, Aramaic legal records in Achaemenid Egypt, in addition to Greek and Latin texts.[23] In its Mesopotamian context, the cultic marking of temple slaves, or oblates (*širkû*), is particularly informative, where the sign of the god (e.g. a star for those at the Eanna temple, a spade and stylus for the god Nabû at the Ezida temple in Borsippa, etc.) was inscribed either on the hand or wrist of the individual slave.[24] As Mathew Stolper

20.   Olyan, *Biblical Mourning*, p. 119.

21.   John Huehnergard and Harold Liebowitz, 'The Biblical Prohibition against Tattooing', *VT* 63 (2013), pp. 59-77 (62-64).

22.   *Ibid.*, p. 70.

23.   There is also a rare example from the Seleucid period which has been published by Timothy Doty, 'A Cuneiform Tablet from Tell 'Umar', *Mesopotamia* 13–14 (1978–79), pp. 91-98; see also Beatrice A. Brooks, 'The Babylonian Practice of Marking Slaves', *JAOS* 42 (1922), pp. 80-90; Mathew Stolper, 'Registration and Taxation of Sale Slaves in Achaemenid Babylonia', *ZA* 79 (1989), pp. 80-101; *idem*, 'Inscribed in Egyptian', in Maria Brosius and Amélie Kuhrt (eds.), *Studies in Persian History: Essays in Memory of David M. Lewis* (Achaemenid History 11; Leiden: Nederlands Instituut voor het Nabije Oosten, 1998), pp. 133-43; Erica Reiner, 'Runaway—Seize Him', in Jan G. Derckson (ed.), *Assyria and Beyond: Studies Presented to Mogens Trolle Larsen* (Leiden: Nederlands Instituut voor het Nabije Oosten, 2004), pp. 475-82; Nili S. Fox, 'Marked for Servitude: Mesopotamia and the Bible', in G. Frame *et al.* (eds.), *A Common Cultural Heritage: Studies on Mesopotamia and the Biblical World in Honor of Barry L. Eichler* (Bethesda: CDL Press, 2011), pp. 267-78; Christopher P. Jones, 'Stigma: Tattooing and Branding in Graeco-Roman Antiquity', *JRS* 77 (1987), pp. 139-55.

24.   See further A. Leo Oppenheim, 'Assyriological Gleanings II', *BASOR* 93 (1944), pp. 14-17 (15-16); Muhammad Dandamaev, *Slavery in Babylonia from Nabopolassar to Alexander the Great: 626–331 B.C.* (DeKalb: Northern Illinois

explains, 'these marks were not simple indications of ownership, and not simple marks of reduction to servitude; they were cited in records of dispute as legal evidence of a juridical status that was protected against sale and purchase by ordinary citizens, hence fundamentally distinct from the status of slaves'.[25]

Evidence of Judaeans branding their own slaves is additionally available in a Neo-Babylonian promissory note from Adabil—a location which is assumed to be in the vicinity of āl-Yāhūdu—where the female slave is tattooed on her wrist with the name of her owner (Kalbaya, son of Ammâ). Rachel Magdalene and Cornelia Wunsch explain that 'this wrist inscription is mentioned in the contract because it is important for the creditor to prove his rightful possession of the slave, should the previous owner, or someone else in, or of, his name, attempt to claim the slave woman as his own, or should she herself assert belonging to someone else'.[26] During the subsequent Persian period (529–335 BCE), the branding of Egyptian slaves by their Jewish owners (attested in the Elephantine papyri) is also notable, as in the following case:

Branded on his right hand	שנית על ידה בימן
(with) a brand reading (in) Aramaic, like this	שניתת מקרא ארמית כזנה
(Belonging) to Mibtahiah.[27]	למבטחיה

In this document (dated to 10 February 410 BCE), Mibtahiah's two sons (namely, Mahseiah and Jedaniah) acquire two Egyptian slaves, previously belonging to their late mother, who are identified as Petosiri and Belle, both of whom were sons of the slave Tabi, and who were marked with Mibtahiah's name in Aramaic.[28] Quite separate to these traditions

University Press, 1984), p. 469; and Cornelia Wunsch, 'Sklave, Sklaverei', in Michael P. Streck (eds.), *Reallexikon der Assyriologie*, vol. 2 (Berlin: W. de Gruyter, 2011), p. 593.

25. Stolper, 'Inscribed in Egyptian', p. 135.

26. Rachel F. Magdalene and Cornelia Wunsch, 'Slavery Between Judah and Babylon: The Exilic Experience', in Laura Culbertson (ed.), with contributions by Indrani Chatterjee *et al.*, *Slaves and Households in the Near East: Papers from the Oriental Institute Seminar 'Slaves and Households in the Near East' Held at the Oriental Institute of the University of Chicago, 5–6 March 2010* (OIS 7; Chicago: The Oriental Institute, 2011), p. 120.

27. This translation from 'B33: Apportionment of Slaves' is from Bezalel Porten *et al.*, *The Elephantine Papyri in English: Three Millennia of Cross-cultural Continuity and Change* (2nd rev. ed.; Documenta et Monumenta Orientis Antiqui 2; Atlanta: SBL, 2011), p. 201.

28. What is also extremely interesting in this case is that Mibtahiah's wealth was inherited directly from her father, in contradiction to the directives of biblical law. For an informed account of the biblical restrictions, see Judith Hauptman's

are the slave records found among the Samaritan documents at Wadi Daliyeh (14 km north of Jericho) which follow Neo-Babylonian legal formulations, and where use of the Aramaic רושם, 'tattoo', is also attested for slaves.[29] This is extremely interesting in view of the fact that these papyri are clearly dated from the thirtieth to thirty-ninth years of Artaxerxes II (375–365 BCE), a time when the Neo-Babylonian legal traditions appear normative, even in this significantly later period.

Undoubtedly the presence of such marks would visibly contravene the exclusive worship of the God of Israel, and this would be all the more unacceptable in the case of a priest officiating in the sacrificial cult, who could presumably not be marked as one who was consecrated to a foreign deity. While there is little to indicate precisely what constituted a 'gashing of your flesh', it is reasonable to assume that the prohibition not to 'incise any mark on yourselves', would have included (at least) some form of slave mark, the very presence of which would have functioned as a public sign of subservience to another human master or alternative deity. The marking of bodies has substantial implications also for questions of ethnicity, identity and familial status, aside of its significance to constructions of ritual purity. For example, in the Neo-Babylonian context it is apparent that the status of descendants of a *širkû* was affected to at least the third generation. In one particular case, the absence of the star mark (testified by witnesses) freed the woman's grandson from potential life-long obligations of service, in this case, to the cult of the goddess Bêlit of Erech.[30] Such physical disfigurements would explain the Priestly prohibition in Lev. 19.28, given that 'the very permanence of the markings is a statement of commitment'.[31]

---

discussion in her *Rereading the Rabbis: A Woman's Voice* (Boulder, Colo.: Westview Press, 1998), pp. 177-95, together also with Zafrira Ben-Barak, *Inheritance by Daughters in Israel and the Ancient Near East: A Social, Legal and Ideological Revolution* (trans. B. Sigler Rozen; Jaffa: Tel Aviv Archaeological Center Publications, 2006).

29. See further Jan Dušek, *Les manuscrits araméens du Wadi Daliyeh et la Samarie vers 450–332 av. j.-c.* (Culture and History of the Ancient Near East 30; Leiden: Brill, 2007). I must thank also Dr Dušek his time and attention in answering my questions when we met in Vienna.

30. *REN* 224, lines 1-26, translated in Dougherty, *The Shirkûtu*, pp. 36-37. In somewhat different circumstances, this appears evident in a separate case from the Persian period from Uruk. See the details in Martha T. Roth, 'A Case of Contested Status', in H. Behrens *et al.* (eds.), *DUMU-E2-DUB-BA-A: Studies in Honor of Åke W. Sjöberg* (Occasional Publications of the Samuel Noah Kramer Fund 11; Philadelphia: University Museum, 1989), pp. 481-89.

31. Huehnergard and Liebowitz, 'The Biblical Prohibition', p. 61.

This perception of permanence informs the divinely instructed physical inscriptions which are recorded in the Hebrew Bible, particularly in Gen. 4.1, where the indeterminate mark of Cain appears:[32]

| And the Lord put a mark on Cain, | וישם יהוה לקין אות |
| lest anyone who met him should kill him | לבלתי הכות־אתו כל־מצאו |

In this instance, the mark is made in response to the exclusive rights of the blood redeemer to avenge the death of his brother (Abel), but, more importantly, it protects Cain from the biblically sanctioned administration of the death penalty. In prophetic literature, however, the description of body inscription evokes a rather more positive association, where it represents a mark of personal virtue and devotion, denoting those who are set apart for divine protection. This context reflects, again, a general knowledge of Mesopotamian cult practices, with regard to those who are marked as being under God's care, given also that the *širkû* were not classed as slaves, *per se*, but rather as a protected class of individuals who were maintained and supported by the Temple authorities. In more dramatic terms, however, for the prophet Ezekiel (9.4-6) such protection was ultimately life-saving: 'And the Lord said to him, "Pass through the city, through Jerusalem and put a mark on the foreheads,[33] of the men who moan and groan because of all the abominations that are committed in it"'. This instruction concludes: 'To the others he said in my hearing, "Follow him, through the city and strike; show no pity or compassion. Kill off greybeard, youth and maiden, women and children; but do not touch any person who bears the mark"'.

While the benefits of divine protection are commonly restricted to those who display active righteousness, in Hag. 2.23 it is the servant himself who constitutes the divine signature: 'On that day declares the Lord of Hosts, "I will take you, O My servant Zerubbabel son of

---

32. See Claus Westermann, *Genesis 1–11: A Continental Commentary* (trans. John J. Scullion; Minneapolis: Fortress Press, 1994), p. 312, and also R. Walter L. Moberly, 'The Mark of Cain—Revealed at Last?', *HTR* 100 (2007), pp. 11-28.

33. The phrasing והתוית תו מצחות, literally 'mark a *tav* on the foreheads', might represent the verb תוה, reflecting the last letter of the Hebrew alphabet, ת, which orthographically was written as a cross. See Walter Zimmerli, *Ezekiel: A Commentary on the Book of the Prophet Ezekiel, Chapters 1–24* (trans. Ronald E. Clements; Hermeneia 1; Philadelphia: Fortress Press, 1979), p. 247 n. 61. Compare this to הן־תוי שדי יענני in Job 31.35, 'O that Shaddai would reply to my writ', where the NRSV provides: 'Here is my signature! Let the Almighty answer me!'; note also the translation in *The Holy Scriptures* תורה נביאים כתובים (Jerusalem: Koren Publishers, 1998), p. 847: 'Here is my mark! Let the Almighty answer me!'

Shealtiel", declares the Lord "and make you as a signet;[34] for I have chosen you", declares the Lord'.[35] This recalls also the inscribing of God's faithful in Isa. 44.5, which provides:

One shall say, 'I am the Lord's',	זה יאמר ליהוה אני
Another shall use the name of 'Jacob',	וזה יקרא בשם יעקב
Another shall mark his arm 'of the Lord',[36]	וזה יכתב ידו ליהוה
and adopt the name of 'Israel'.	ובשם ישראל יכנה

For Isaiah it is clear that the name (or mark) of the Lord was to be engraved on the hand (or arm, in the above translation) of the Israelite, precisely in the same place that an owner could mark or brand their slave. In addition, there is also the corresponding engraving of the individual name of the faithful devotee (or even Israel?) upon God's palm, as recorded in Isa. 49.16—'See, I have engraved you on the palms of My hands,[37] your walls are ever before Me'—though such reciprocity is exceptional. Here the emphasis on mutual commitment is highlighted by the immediate association with a betrothal, where Zion's children will assemble and 'you shall don them all like jewels, deck yourself with them like a bride'.[38]

In describing such markings it may have been that these prophet visionaries were oblivious of the restrictions in Priestly law as enshrined in Lev. 19.28 and 21.5, given that the redaction (i.e. its consolidation of

---

34. See Carol L. Meyers and Eric Meyers, *Haggai, Zechariah 1–8: A New Translation with Commentary* (AB 25B; New York: Doubleday, 1987), p. 69.

35. In palaeographic terms, David Vanderhooft observes: 'To indulge in a bit of fancy, we may imagine that when Haggai records an oracle about God's intention to transform Zerubbabel into his חותם, "seal", at the time of the rebuilding of the temple in the late sixth century (Hag 2.23), that seal would have been cut to the formal specifications of the old Judean model but inscribed with Aramaic script'. David S. Vanderhooft, ' *'el-mĕdînâ ûmĕdînâ kiktābāh*: Scribes and Scripts in Yehud and in Achaemenid Transeuphratene', in Oded Lipschits and Manfred Oeming (eds.), *Judah and the Judeans in the Achaemenid Period: Negotiating Identity in an International Context* (Winona Lake: Eisenbrauns, 2011), pp. 529-44 (539 n. 15).

36. כתב ידו (Isa. 44.5c) is literally, '[he] will write on his hand'. NRSV offers 'another will write on the hand'; see also John L. McKenzie, *Second Isaiah: Introduction, Translation and Notes* (AB 20; New York: Doubleday, 1968), p. 62. Here the Akkadian, *rittu šataru* (indicative of an owner inscribing his own name on his slave's hand), corresponds to the term יכתב יד; as Dougherty (*The Shirkûtu*, p. 82) notes: 'the placing of an incised or branded mark upon a slave or devotee's hand could well be expressed by the verb *šataru*, "to write" in view of the nature of cuneiform script'.

37. Note that this terminological distinction הן על כפים־חקתיך, denoting the palm (rather than the whole hand) was employed.

38. The significance of Isa. 49.18 was pointed out to me by Joan Taylor.

sources and editing) of the Holiness Code is generally presumed to have taken place in the late sixth or early fifth centuries BCE. This would apply, likewise, to those prophets who were active prior to this time and also to those writing in later generations, given the suggestion of Israel Knohl, namely, that in the Neo-Babylonian and Persian periods the Priestly writings were restricted to a scribal elite who controlled access to, and management of, the cult.[39] If this was the case, the Priestly writings, including the Holiness Code, would not have been accessible to other literate groups—rather in the same way that today the conventions of Freemasons are restricted to the male members of their society.

Having examined how the divine presence makes its mark on the body in prophetic sources, it is by no means certain that these were perceived exclusively in physical terms, but may also have been understood as abstract or metaphorical conceptions. Such distinctions are relevant also to the description of physical markings apparently placed upon the body of the individual worshipper in other Priestly sources. In all of the above prophetic texts, including the description of Zerubbabel in Hag. 2.3, both loyalty to God and protection by him are key elements in the divine choice of subject: the two elements, likewise, vital to the ideological construction of Priestly ritual. In this respect, the instruction which followed the Priestly blessing in Num. 6.22-26 is extremely informative; the blessing states: 'The Lord spoke to Moses: Speak to Aaron and his sons: Thus shall you bless the people of Israel. Say to them: The Lord bless you and protect you! The Lord deal kindly and graciously with you! The Lord bestow His favor upon you and grant you peace!'[40] The blessing then concludes with the following instruction:

6.27a	Thus they shall link My name	ושמו את־שמי
6.27b	with the people of Israel	על־בני ישראל
6.27c	and I will bless them	ואני אברכם

---

39. Israel Knohl, *The Sanctuary of Silence: The Priestly Torah and the Holiness School* (Minneapolis: Fortress Press, 1995), and also *The Divine Symphony: The Bible's Many Voices* (Philadelphia: Jewish Publication Society, 2003), esp. pp. 1-8. This need not preclude the possibility that earliest strata of Priestly writings originated in the eight century (as suggested by Knohl), even though this is not the scholarly consensus.

40. The sectarian expansion of this blessing in 1QS has been published by Bilha Nitzan, *Qumran Prayer and Religious Poetry* (STDJ 12; Leiden: Brill, 1994), pp. 145-71, and discussed further by Shani Tzoref, 'The Use of Scripture in the Community Rule', in Matthias Henze (ed.), *A Companion to Biblical Interpretation in Early Judaism* (Grand Rapids: Eerdmans, 2012), pp. 203-34 (218-22).

This NJPS translation of ושמו את־שמי, 'they shall link my name', is at best misleading, if not also erroneous, given that the verb שים is translated elsewhere as 'to put, place, or to set',[41] as in Gen. 4.15: וישם יהוה לקין אות, 'the Lord put a mark on Cain'.[42] The instruction is correctly rendered by the NRSV, which reads: 'so they shall put my name on the Israelites and I will bless them'.[43] Such usage recalls also to the cognate Akkadian verb *šamâtu*, which denoted placing the brand upon the *širku*, where the interchangeable use of the idiom *kakkabtu šamâtu* and *kakkabtu nadû*, both meaning to 'mark with a star', was witnessed.[44] Thus both the relevant active verbs, namely שום or שים, meaning 'to place, put', together with נתן, meaning 'to give', recall their Neo-Babylonian equivalents (*šamâtu* and *nadû*) that designate the marking, or inscribing, of the name (or emblem) of a deity upon the body of the individual devotee to the temple cult.

These linguistic parallels provide substantial support for the interpretation of Meir Bar-Ilan, who proposes that the phrase ושמו את־שמי, 'so they shall put my name' (NRSV translation), is to be understood specifically in physical (rather than metaphorical) terms, and accordingly that the Priestly requirement was 'literal and actual'.[45] Accordingly, Bar-Ilan asserts that the name of God was written or placed directly on the hand, palm or forehead of the Israelite as primarily an apotropaic rite, as was

---

41. See BDB's entry for שים/שום, 'to put, place, set', where its relationship to the Assyrian *šâmu* 'to fix, or to determine', is identified. See also G. Vanoni, 'שים *śîm*; תשומה *teśûmâ*', in *TDOT*, XIV, pp. 89-112.

42. Compare also the description of Solomon's consecration of the temple in 1 Kgs 9.3—'I have heard the prayer and supplication which you have offered to Me. I consecrate this House which you have built and I set my name there forever'— where the infinitive occurs: לשום־שמי שם. See also 2 Chron. 33.7, which provides: אשים את־שמי לעולם, 'I will establish my name forever'. For the use of this formula in Deut. 12.5. See also Sandra L. Richter, *The Deuteronomic History and Name Theology: lešakkēn šemô šām in the Bible and the Ancient Near East* (BZAW 318; Berlin/New York: W. de Gruyter, 2002).

43. Robert Alter, *The Five Books of Moses: A Translation with Commentary* (New York: W. W. Norton, 2004), however, provides: 'And they shall set my name over the Israelites and I myself shall bless them'.

44. Dougherty, *The Shirkutu*, p. 83, suggests that the Akkadian *nadû* corresponded to the Priestly use of נתן, meaning 'to give', and that *šamâtu* was the terminological equivalent to the verb שים, meaning 'to place'.

45. Meir Bar-Ilan, 'So Shall They Put My Name Upon the People of Israel (Numbers 6.27)', *HUCA* 60 (1989), pp. 19-31 (Hebrew), and also *idem*, 'Jewish Magical Body-Inscription in the First and Second Centuries', *Tarbiz* 57 (1988), pp. 37-50 (Hebrew), translation by Menachem Sheinberger http://faculty.biu.ac.il/~testsm/tatoos.html, accessed 15 February 2008, pp. 1-22 (2-3).

apparent in Gen. 4.15; Ezek. 9.4; Isa. 44.5, and Job 31.35. Here the use of the Priestly blessing of Num. 6.22-25a etched in (or engraved upon) a silver amulet in the form of two metal strips, dated to the seventh century BCE and discovered Ketef Hinnom in Jerusalem, is significant. The fact that these amulets also contain the Tetragrammaton would suggest additionally that the inscription of the divine name upon the body was potentially transferred to an amulet carried on the body at this time.

Both practices, namely, placing the name of God inside an amulet worn on the body and physically marking the divine name on the hand or forehead, need not have been mutually exclusive acts, as the tradition in Num. 11.24-25 indicates. Here God transfers his spirit upon the seventy Israelite elders, where the text clarifies: 'And two men remained in the camp. The name of the one was Eldad and the name of the other was Medad. And the spirit rested upon them, and *they were among those inscribed* (והמה בכתבים), but they did not go out from the tent and they prophesied within the camp.' In this case, the phrase והמה בכתבים, literally meaning 'they were inscribed', provides inner-biblical support for their physical (rather than metaphorical) marking. In this instance the NRSV translation, 'they were among those registered', affords the additional option of explaining this verse in accordance with the rabbinic notion of depicting God inscribing each individual Jew in 'the book of life' (ספר החיים) where, as Carol Meyers notes, 'the idea of God record-ing the names of people in a book is part of a general Near Eastern belief in heavenly ledgers. The popular conception of such records is rooted in the practices of record keeping in the political and economic realms.'[46] This is clearly not a case of superimposing later rabbinic interpretations on the earlier biblical sources, given that the association is explicit in the Hebrew Bible itself. For example, in Exod. 32.32-33, after the Israelites worship the golden calf, Moses declares: '"Now if you will forgive their sin [well and good]; but if not, erase me from the record which You have written!" But the Lord said to Moses, "He who sinned against Me, him only will I erase from my record".'[47]

---

46. Carol Meyers, *Exodus: The New Cambridge Bible Commentary* (Cambridge: Cambridge University Press, 2005), p. 261.

47. See also Mal. 3.16; Ps. 139.16, etc. Shalom M. Paul, 'Heavenly Tablets and the Book of Life', *JANES* 5 (1975), pp. 345-53, separately traces this notion from early Sumerian sources to pseudepigraphal literature, to include *Jub.* 30.19-23, *1 En.* 47.3, the *Apoc. Zeph.* 3.15–4.13 and 14.5—and further in the Dead Sea Scrolls, the New Testament, the Babylonian Talmud and formal rabbinic liturgy. From a pedagogic perspective see also Jonathan Sacks, 'What Chapter Will We Write in the Book of Life', in *The Yom Kippur Koren Maḥzor* מחזור קורן ליום הכיפורים (Jerusalem: Koren Publishers, 2012), pp. lxxvii-lxxxi.

The case of the נתינים (*netînîm*) may also bear upon this discussion. The term literally means 'given ones', and is variously translated as 'devoted ones' or 'temple slaves'. They appear in the framework of cultic service, and are associated with the Levites. Accordingly, the relevant consecratory formulas—where the Levites are 'assigned' to the service of Aaron—are highly significant:

Num. 3.9	You shall assign the Levites	ונתתה את־הלוים
	to Aaron and to his sons:	לאהרן ולבניו
	they are formally assigned to him	נתונם נתונם המה לו
	from among the Israelites.	מאת בני ישראל
Num. 8.16	For they are formally assigned to Me	כי נתונם נתונם המה לי
	from among the Israelites.	מתוך בני ישראל
Num. 8.19	I formally assign the Levites	ואתנה את־הלוים
	to Aaron and his sons	לאהרן ולבניו
Num. 18.6	I hereby take	ואני הנה לקחתי
	your fellow Levites	את־אחיכם הלוים
	from among the Israelites;	מתוך בני ישראל
	they are assigned to you	לכם מתנה
	to do the work of the Tent of Meeting[48]	לעבד את־עבדת אהל מועד

In his Anchor Bible commentary to the book of Numbers, Baruch Levine maintains that the cultic servitors known as נתינים (*netînîm*) correspond in practical terms to the *širku/širkûtu*.[49] Furthermore, the terminology is not restricted exclusively to Priestly literature, as Hannah's vow in 1 Sam. 1.11 indicates:

If you will grant your maidservant a male child,	ונתתה לאמתך זרע אנשים
I will dedicate him to the Lord for all the days of his life.[50]	ונתתיו ליהוה כל־ימי חייו

48. As also 1 Chron. 6.33:

And their kinsmen the Levites were appointed	ואחיהם הלוים נתונים
for all the service of the Tabernacle	לכל־עבודת המשכן
of the House of God.	בית האלהים

49. Baruch A. Levine, *Numbers 1–20: A New Translation with Commentary* (AB 4A; New York: Doubleday, 1993), p. 278: 'In Akkadian, the verb *šarāku*, "to donate, hand over, devote", is used in the same way, and the Neo-Babylonian documents actually speak of temple servants called *širkûtu* "devotees"'. Levine provides further discussion of the consignment of Gibeonites in Josh. 9.27.

50. With the following variant witnessed in 1 Sam. 1.27-28:

And the Lord granted me	ויתן יהוה לי
what I asked of him.	את־שאלתי אשר שאלתי מעמו
I, in turn, hereby lend him to the Lord.	וגם אנכי השאלתהו ליהוה
For as long as he lives he is lent	כל־הימים אשר היה הוא שאול
to the Lord.	ליהוה

The correspondence between these נתנים (*netînîm*) is demonstrated by the technical language used to formalize the Neo-Babylonian individual consecrations, where the terminology *ana širkūti ana* [DN] *nadānu*,[51] 'to give to [DN] for oblate temple service',[52] was employed: *[m]Aḫiddin qalla šunu ana balât napšati[meš]–šunu ana [d]Ištar iddinu*, 'Aḫ-iddin, their slave, for the preservation of their lives to Ishtar [they] gave'.[53] Here Edward Lipiński maintains that this was a formula that was familiar to the Priestly redactor a follows: '*nātan* [PN] *netîn(â)* *l[e]YHWH*,[54] "give [PN] to Yahweh as a consecrated one"'.[55] It is this cultic convention which illuminates the objectives of both the Priestly consecration formula of Levites and the purpose of physically marking Israelites, since it is in this context that the branding or tattooing of the mark of the deity (or temple) onto the bodies of the dedicated servants is attested in cuneiform records from the Neo-Babylonian period.

In conclusion, despite explicit prohibitions in biblical law, it is evident that both Priestly and prophetic scribes did commend the bodily marking of Israelites. This is reasonably apparent despite the effects of contemporary English translations which obscure the precise meaning of the Hebrew biblical text. Such marks also conveyed positive values and attributes: those inscribed could be assigned to, and protected by, God, as was the case even in the description of temporary body markers, where the consecration of the Aaronid Priests, 'as Yahweh's chattel',[56] required the application of blood to the right ear, thumb of the right hand and

51. Superscript [DN] stands for 'Deity Name'.

52. As Edward Lipiński, 'נתן *nātan*', in *TDOT*, X, pp. 90-108 (106), with further variations in Dandamaev, *Slavery in Babylonia*, p. 469. See also Magen Broshi and Ada Yardeni, 'On Netinim and False Prophets', *Tarbiz* 62 (1993), pp. 45-54 (Hebrew).

53. *YBT* VII, 17 (lines 6-9). Lines 1-9 are translated as follows: 'Nabû-aḫê-bulliṭ, the son of Nabû-shum-ukîn, son of the Priest of Enurta and Bulṭâ, the daughter of Bêl-ushallim, son of Kurî, his wife, of their own free will, Aḫ-iddin, their slave, for the preservation of their lives to Ishtar gave' (Dougherty, *The Shirkûtu*, p. 40).

54. Superscript [PN] stands for 'Personal Name'.

55. Lipiński, 'נתן *nātan*', p. 106. Levine states: 'Hebrew *nātan* may, in certain contexts, specifically connote compulsory assignment to cultic service, where the recipient is a deity or a religious establishment. Thus Joshua "consigned" the Gibeonites (Hebrew *wayyittenēm*, "he consigned them") to cultic service (Josh 9.27). Cultic servitors are known as *netînîm*, "devoted cultic servitors", in Ezra 2.43. In Akkadian, the verb *šarāku*, "to donate, hand over, devote", is used in the same way, and the Neo-Babylonian documents actually speak of temple servants called *širkûtu*, "devotees"' (Levine, *Numbers 1–20*, p. 278).

56. William H. C. Propp, *Exodus 19–40: A New Translation with Introduction and Commentary* (AB 2A; New York: Doubleday, 2006), p. 195.

toes.[57] What is all the more notable is that such visible markers are accepted in Priestly sources, whereas gashings, lacerations and shavings were concomitantly prohibited. And it is also here that the normative Neo-Babylonian convention of consecrating *širku* to cultic service has been integrated (almost seamlessly) into the remembered biblical land-scape, despite its obvious adaptation from its normative foreign context, and where the cuneiform requirement *ana širkūti ana* [DN] *nadānu*, 'to give to [DN] for oblate temple service', is equated to *nātan* [PN] *netîn(â) le YHWH*, meaning to 'give [PN] to Yahweh as a consecrated one' as suggested by Edward Lipiński.

In this vein, 'for many of the ancients, body marks were thought to have brought the spirit world into existence. Each subsequent generation that reproduced the marks reaffirmed the original "ancient mark". In doing so, an individual also forged a sacred connection to his ancestors while substantiating his own identity in the present.'[58] Such markings forged far more than a sacred connection to an idealized past for the prophetic and priestly scribes. While regularizing their national identity in an uncertain present, these signs offered their audiences the assurance of ongoing divine protection and, ultimately, the confidence with which to rebuild new lives, homes and families—not least of all in the Persian province of Yehud, but earlier also in the Babylonian districts of āl-Yāhūdu, Našar and Adabil. Both in Judea and beyond, 'the human body was seen as yet another feature of the landscape, a sensual geography upon which might be written and inscribed the hopes and fears of a people'[59]—hopes and fears which were saturated with the memory of their national God and in his visibly emblematic demands for their exclusive service.

---

57. As specified in Exod. 29.20; Lev. 8.23-24; 14.14.
58. Rainier (ed.), *Ancient Marks*, p. 182.
59. Davis, 'Foreword', p. 14.

QUEERING THE BODY:
UN-DESIRING SEX IN LEVITICUS

Steffan Mathias

In March of this year, a twenty-year-old man was jailed for murdering openly gay, autistic teenager Steven Simpson at his eighteenth birthday party. Jordan Sheard had scrawled homophobic slurs over Simpson's body before covering him in tanning oil and setting him alight, resulting in severe burns from which he died the next day.[1] Amnesty International recognizes seven states where male same-sex intercourse may (and in several cases does) result in the death penalty, and legislators in Uganda have been working to add their number to this list.[2] It is clear that queer bodies can face additional levels of damage, in comparison to others: bullying, torture, violence and even state-sanctioned death. While these stories may seem shocking, there is an uncomfortable resonance between them and the 'queer texts of terror'[3] of the Bible, texts in which some same-sex act(s) appear to warrant death. In dealing with passages such as Lev. 18.22 and 20.13 we often, in attempting to resist or critique them, circumvent the texts, arguing for their irrelevance, given that they are part of an historical cultural context that seems alien now.[4] Alternatively,

---

1. Http://www.bbc.co.uk/news/uk-england-south-yorkshire-21887535 (accessed 28 June 2013). Between 2010 and 2011, of the 4252 reported hate crimes against lesbian, gay, bisexual and 315 against transgender people in England and Wales, 81% and 67% respectively were classed as 'violence against the person'. An estimated three out of four people fail to report hate crime (https://www.gov.uk/government/publications/hate-crimes-england-and-wales-2011-to-2012--2/hate-crimes-england-and-wales-2011-to-2012 [accessed 28 June 2013]).

2. Amnesty International, *Love, Hate and the Law: Decriminalizing Homosexuality* (London: Amnesty International Publications, 2008).

3. To borrow from Phyllis Trible, *Texts of Terror: Literary-Feminist Readings of Biblical Narratives* (Minneapolis: Fortress Press, 1984).

4. Martti Nissinen, *Homoeroticism in the Biblical World: A Historical Perspective* (trans. Kirsi Stjerna; Minneapolis: Fortress Press, 1998), p. 42.

we attempt to mute their impact by emphasizing what is not mentioned in terms of a relationship: concepts such as love, permanence, fidelity or stability.[5] My intent here is not to critique these valuable approaches, but rather to offer a reflection on what happens when we refocus our attentions on bodies. I ask what happens when both the body of the text and the body of the queer[6] reader are emphasized instead of sexuality or desire. What problems arise in mapping these bodies onto each other, and what new modes of resistance and ethics might this offer?

In the act of reading, the gay male body or subject attempts to read itself onto the bodies presented in biblical texts. However, this reading is by no means linear. I will argue, following a line of queer theory, that these bodies (ancient and modern) are not biologically constituted, but discursively made (through conceptions of sex, penetration, gender, adornment, desire and kinship) in different ways and around different principles. Therefore, when the reader attempts to map their constructed bodies onto the constructed bodies of the text, a kind of awkward meshing takes place, resulting in a dissonance between the different conceptions of bodies. Deborah Sawyer suggests that the biblical text *pre-empts all existence:* 'any space we might think to negotiate has already been anticipated and occupied',[7] so when we read texts like Lev. 18.22 and 20.13, they appear to prohibit something analogous to contemporary conceptions of homosexuality.

We presume all bodies, whether in the Bible or those we live in, are the same, that gender and sexuality follow biology in similar ways. Through this we allow the Bible, as Loughlin states, to write 'our flesh, its meanings and possibilities'.[8] This writing takes place in different contexts, from attempts to legislate the death penalty for sodomy in Uganda[9] (the most severe form of writing on the body) or as a justification for

5. See, for example, Jeffery John, *Permanent, Faithful, Stable: Christian Same-Sex Partnerships* (2nd rev. ed.; London: Darton, Longman & Todd, 2000).

6. This essay is from the position of a gay male reader, though with a queer twist, as it focuses on Lev. 18.22/20.13 and the interaction between text and reader as the text goes through the process of deconstruction, as I hope will become apparent. Any failure to acknowledge women/trans/intersex perspectives, or any other, is due either constraints of space or an unintentional omission.

7. Deborah Sawyer, *God, Gender and the Bible* (London/New York: Routledge, 2002), p. 7.

8. Gerard Loughlin, 'The Body', in John F. A. Sawyer (ed.), *The Blackwell Companion to the Bible and Culture* (London: John Wiley & Sons, 2012), pp. 381-96 (381).

9. Joanna Sadgrove *et al.*, 'Morality Plays and Money Matters: Towards a Situated Understanding of the Politics of Homosexuality in Uganda', *Journal of Modern African Studies* 50, no. 1 (2012), pp. 103-29.

reparative therapies which attempt to 'cure' homosexuality[10] (where our bodily desires and actions are written as a form of psychology). However, Loughlin suggests that because this always involves us in *reading* the text, there is a 'space for movement, for a field of energy'.[11]

Thus, through understanding the biblical text as discursive and constructed, as opposed to absolute and fixed, this chapter will attempt *deconstruction in exegesis*. By paying very close attention to the two dialoguing bodies, the reader and the text that is read, 'one may watch and document meaning undoing itself', as Beal puts it.[12] Through engaging with Michel Foucault and Queer Theory, particularly the work of Judith Butler and Leo Bersani, I hope to suggest news ways of thinking about our own bodies and the bodies presented by the text, and to suggest how this may offer new modes of relating to one another. By bringing these tragic stories of homophobic hate crime into dialogue with these texts of terror, new modes of resistance to the texts will be sought, and by dialoguing with Pauline theology I will suggest an alternative Christian sexual ethic which attempts to take the use of power into account, and not simply sexually differentiated bodies.

I. *Thinking About Bodies, Queering Bodies*

Foucault, famously, attempted to reverse the normal understanding that knowledge is power. Instead of a kind of 'top down' power, owned by oppressive governments, Foucault conceptualizes power as everywhere, exercised through relationships, a power which is *productive*, producing knowledge, whether knowledge about medicine, or psychiatry, or knowledge about bodies.[13] This relationship between knowledge and power manifests as *discourses*, which are the traces left behind of particular structures and modes of understanding. Discourses are not linear, developing over time, but can more be seen as reorganizations of ways of thinking, known as epistemes, in particular time periods. So, in modernity, our knowledge of bodies is the product of power exercised by

---

10. Ariel Shidlo, Michael Schroeder and Jack Drescher, *Sexual Conversion Therapy: Ethical, Clinical, and Research Perspectives* (Philadelphia: Haworth Press, 2001).

11. Loughlin, 'The Body', p. 381.

12. Timothy K. Beal, 'Opening: Cracking the Binding', in Timothy K. Beal and David Gunn (eds.), *Reading Bibles, Writing Bodies: Identity and The Book* (London: Routledge, 1997), p. 2.

13. Michel Foucault, *The History of Sexuality*. I, *An Introduction* (trans. Robert Hurley; 5th ed.; New York: Vintage, 1990), p. 59.

disciplines such as psychiatry, criminology or sexuality, which teach us how to monitor and regulate our own bodies. Knowledge and power 'mark [the body], train it, torture it, force it to carry out tasks, to perform certain ceremonies, to emit signs',[14] and, through the body, power creates a kind of *interiority*, such as the notion of the soul or the psyche.[15]

Judith Butler takes this notion of the body a step further, and suggests the very materiality of the body, its fixity, contours and movements, is an effect of power; sexual difference, rather than being produced by materiality, *creates* the materiality of the body, which is marked and formed by discursive practices.[16] In our discourse, sex is what 'qualifies a body for life within the domain of cultural intelligibility', since there is no way to exist culturally without your body being materialized through reference to its sex, which 'produces the bodies it governs'.[17]

For Foucault, the emergence of confession in the early Christian period established desire as central to an understanding of sexuality; this was taken up by psychology, which transformed desire into a scientific organizing principle around which the subject and their body could be categorized into self-regulating groups such as 'homosexual' and 'hetero-sexual'. What were previously seen as 'perversions', acts cohering with certain 'abominations' of the Bible, now became a 'specification of individuals':

> The nineteenth-century homosexual became a personage, a past, a case history, and a childhood, in addition to being a type of life, a life form, and a morphology, with an indiscreet anatomy and possibly a mysterious physiology. Nothing that went into his total composition was unaffected by his sexuality. It was everywhere present in him: at the root of all his actions because it was their insidious and indefinitely active principle; written immodestly on his face and body because it was a secret that always gave itself away. It was a consubstantial with him, less as a habitual sin than as a singular nature.[18]

A new category of person had been created through a refocusing on their desire as constitutive of their subject, and the subject dictating the body. Foucault continues:

---

14. Michel Foucault, *Discipline and Punish: The Birth of the Prison* (trans. A. Sheridan; New York: Random House, 1977), p. 25.

15. Margaret A. McLaren, *Feminism, Foucault, and Embodied Subjectivity* (Albany: SUNY Press, 2002), p. 84.

16. Judith Butler, *Bodies That Matter* (New York/London: Routledge, 1993), pp. 1-2.

17. *Ibid.*

18. Foucault, *The History of Sexuality*, I, pp. 42-43.

The psychological, psychiatric, medical category of homosexuality was constituted from the moment it was characterized—Westphal's famous article of 1870 on 'contrary sexual sensations' can stand as its date of birth—less by a type of sexual relations than by a certain quality of sexual sensibility, a certain way of inverting the masculine and the feminine in oneself. Homosexuality appeared as one of the forms of sexuality when it was transposed from the practice of sodomy into a kind of interior androgyny, a hermaphrodism of the soul. The sodomite had been a temporary aberration; the homosexual was now a species.[19]

Foucault forcefully argues that, by identifying desires, subjects are taught to identify their 'essence' (for example homosexual/heterosexual), which becomes tied up with their psyche and body, through which an individual learns self-regulation. This regulation, according to Butler, is a kind of *performance*, a reiteration of repeated acts, which 'congeal over time to produce the appearance of a substance, of a natural sort of being',[20] though these are kinds of *fabrications*.[21] Butler argues that the failure to repeat a performance 'exposes the phantasmatic effect of abiding identity as a politically tenuous construction';[22] it demonstrates that our ideas of sexed bodies are contingent, and thus this failure to repeat performance is threatening and is punished.[23]

If power exercising itself on the body creates certain types of knowledge in the form of ideas around gender or sexuality, what are the consequences? Some have argued that Foucault's work can only produce submissive bodies, which lack agency.[24] However, the relational aspect of power suggests that where there is power 'there is resistance'.[25] For Foucault, in being *relational* instead of top down, power can be normally *political*, offering modes of resistance. However, when one gains total control over another's body, power stops being political; under total domination 'you can be knocked down and stripped naked in a heartbeat... Your body is their playground and their laboratory.'[26]

---

19. *Ibid.*, p. 43.

20. Judith Butler, *Gender Trouble: Feminism and the Subversion of Identity* (New York/London: Routledge, 2006), p. 33.

21. *Ibid.*, p. 136.

22. *Ibid.*, p. 176.

23. *Ibid.*, p. 140.

24. For example, see Nancy Hartsock, 'Foucault on Power: A Theory for Women?' in Linda Nicholson (ed.), *Feminism/Postmodernism* (New York/London: Routledge, 1990), pp. 157-75.

25. Foucault, *The History of Sexuality*, I, pp. 94-95.

26. Ladelle McWhorter, *Bodies and Pleasures: Foucault and the Politics of Sexual Normalization* (Bloomington: Indiana University Press, 1999), p. 146.

II. *Gay Male Bodies*

These particular dynamics of gender, sexuality and sexed bodies have created particular discourses that act on gay male bodies, discourses which will be contrasted to those in Lev. 18.22, 20.13, read with Deut. 22.5. In order to understand how we construct terms like 'gay' or 'straight', and how this affects the reader as they read biblical bodies, it will be necessary briefly to explore contemporary conceptions of gay bodies, and through doing this begin to understand how these bodies, ancient and modern, are constructed.

Unrealistic ideals of body image, complex relationships to gender-presentation and dynamics of being in and out of the closet have created specific factors in how gay males relate to their bodies. For Bersani, the increasing visibility of sexual minorities is not an act of liberation but a form of social regulation:

> The social project inherent in the nineteenth-century invention of 'the homosexual' can perhaps now be realized: visibility is a precondition of surveillance, disciplinary intervention, and, at the limit, gender-cleansing… Psychology in this argument *discovered* nothing; the questions it asked created the answers necessary to the social strategies that produced the questionnaire. Confession is a form of ventriloquism.[27]

The knowledge formed in the 'identification' of sexual identities was actually the creation of knowledge *about* homosexuals by disciplines, which formed certain kinds of scripts to be followed.

In the UK, around the time of the Oscar Wilde trials in 1895, this newly created category of the homosexual became associated with effeminacy, and so homosexual men began regulating their gendered bodies to avoid detection. Some identified with types of effeminate behaviour, which was seen as subverting ideas of masculinity,[28] while others opted for hyper-masculine presentations, culminating in the stereotypes of the 'macho-clones' in 1970s gay subcultures.[29] Even the hyper-masculine presentation, of large, buff, hairy bodies adorned in 'masculine' clothing (think *The Village People*) has been seen as both enforcing and subverting heterosexual ideas of masculinity.[30] The centrality of

27. Leo Bersani, *Homos* (Cambridge, MA: Harvard University Press, 1996), pp. 12-13.

28. For example, Quentin Crisp, *The Naked Civil Servant* (rev. ed.; London: Flamingo, 1985). Crisp's writings draws on a self-understanding similar to Foucault's description of a hermaphrodism of the soul.

29. Mitchel J. Wood, 'The Gay Male Gaze', *Journal of Gay and Lesbian Social Services* 17 (2004), pp. 43-62 (54).

30. *Ibid.*, p. 56 For an example of the ambiguity of machismo in the gay community, see Bersani's critique of Richard Dyer's suggestion that machismo subverts

2. MATHIAS *Queering the Body*

desire to identities such as homosexuality had been organized around whom desire was directed towards in terms of the sexed body.

With the emergence of gay subcultures, and the way masculinity and femininity was used and manipulated, gender became subsumed in the discourse of sexuality. Through the 1980s, with the advent of the AIDS crisis, the gay male body came to be examined for signs of AIDS, heightening the appeal of young, healthy, muscled gay bodies within gay subcultures. Death, disease and effeminacy became especially associated with the passive sexual position, and therefore masculine body types were adopted as guards 'against both actual and symbolic signs of wasting syndrome and disease'.[31] A gay vernacular developed to delineate gender/sex roles: twink, bear, jock, top, bottom, versatile,[32] straight-acting, camp, fem, fat, muscle-mary, bisexual, transsexual, transvestite, drag queen, transgender, queer (the list goes on), which all came to stand for who-has-sex-with-whom, who-is-attracted-to-whom, how-sex-is-to-take-place. Going beyond simple categories of gay or straight, attempts to negotiate power coalesced around conceptions of desire, gender, sexual-role and relationality, and created specific types of knowledge of gay bodies.[33] This is mainly uncritically absorbed, as Wood suggests, since gay men lack a tradition of critical-analysis of power relations:

> This lack of self-critical analysis has persisted because many gay men are still deeply identified with the gendered hierarchies endemic to patriarchal culture. On the one hand, many gay men derive their sense of power from the stigmatization of female traits, while many others are still too constrained by self-stigmatization and shame to confront their own gender oppression.[34]

traditional relations of gender and power; Leo Bersani, *Is the Rectum a Grave? And Other Essays* (Chicago: University of Chicago Press, 2009), pp. 13-15.

31. Wood, 'The Gay Male Gaze', p. 54. The film *Beyond the Candelabra* (2013), for example, explores Liberace's (ultimately vain) attempts to hide his dying from AIDS related illnesses, in order to maintain his heterosexual presentation and, therefore (in his eyes), reputation.

32. 'Top' is the insertive partner, 'bottom' the receptive, whereas 'versatile' suggests either both, or a desire to be discrete about preference.

33. Eve Sedgwick suggests: 'of the many dimensions along which the genital activity of one person can be differentiated from that of another (...preference for certain acts, certain zones or sensations, certain physical types, a certain frequency, certain symbolic investments, certain relations of age or power, a certain species, a certain number of participants, etc. etc. etc.), precisely one, the gender of the object of choice, emerged from the turn of the century, and has remained, as *the* dimension denoted by the now ubiquitous category of "sexual orientation"'; Eve K. Sedgwick, *Epistemology of the Closet* (Berkeley: University of California Press, 1990), p. 8.

34. Wood, 'The Gay Male Gaze', p. 57.

Following Foucault, this can be seen as a demonstration of how power reaches 'into the very grain of individuals, touches their bodies and inserts itself into their actions and attitudes, their discourses, learning processes and everyday lives'.[35] Because of the association between homosexuality and effeminacy, disease and stigma, the body learns to discipline itself to perform as masculine or feminine in different social contexts. The body, organized around an internal psyche which has particular desires, becomes subject to knowledge about itself, and learns to understand itself and its relation to others. By uncovering the genealogy of our modern bodies, we can start to see how they differ from ancient ones articulated within different cultural constructs; it is to these ancient ones we now turn.

III. *Biblical Bodies: Leviticus 18.22, 20.13 and Deuteronomy 22.5*

Genesis 2.21-22 recounts the creation of woman from the צלעת, or side/rib of first created person. This bodily sexual differentiation has been explored by Emmanuel Levinas who imagines a kind of androgynous two faced being which becomes sexually differentiated through a created act.[36] This sexual differentiation takes places on the body throughout subsequent narratives. For example, Eilberg-Schwartz argues for the 'fruitful cut' of circumcision in Genesis 21, as being subsumed in the symbolic relationship between the male and his penis, progeny and masculinity, rather than as being an innocuous bodily marking.[37] Crushed male genitalia prohibit animals from being sacrificed and men from entering the political-religious community (Deut. 23.1; see also Lev. 21.20; 22.24).[38] Inability to penetrate and procreate is conceptualized as being not 'whole', and is compensated for in prophetic texts with strong phallic imagery.[39] The Hebrew term נקבה, 'female', because of its

35. Michel Foucault, *Power/Knowledge: Selected Interviews and Other Writings, 1972–1977* (ed. Colin Gordon; Knopf Doubleday Publishing, 1980), p. 39.

36. Emmanuel Levinas, *Nine Talmudic Readings* (trans. Anette Aronowicz; Bloomington: Indiana University Press, 1994), pp. 168-72.

37. Howard Eilberg-Schwartz, *The Savage in Judaism: An Anthropology of Israelite Religion and Ancient Judaism* (Bloomington: Indiana University Press, 1990).

38. Gen. 24.2-9 and 47.27-31 both have promises regarding marriage and descent made through one man placing his hands on the others genitals. Roland Boer, *The Earthy Nature of the Bible: Fleshly Readings of Sex, Masculinity, and Carnality* (London: Palgrave Macmillan, 2012), pp. 54-55.

39. Isaiah 56.5-6 promises a יד ושם, 'a monument and a name', to the eunuch; יד, meaning both 'hand' and 'monument', is used here instead of מצבה, 'standing stone', and suggests a pun is being played, with יד being euphemistic for the phallus.

relationship with the word נקב 'subterranean passage' (Ezek. 28.13), carries semantic overtones of an orifice bearer, pierced one,[40] defining the woman as one whose body is to be penetrated and receptive, where as זכר, 'male', carries overtones of remembrance, perpetuation, associated with the verb, זכר, 'remember'.[41] A male is, correspondingly, a remembrance bearer, with the locus of remembrance in male genitalia that contain and implant the memorializing 'seed'. The central orifice of a woman, the womb, רחם, is the site of compassion,[42] רחמים, and yet the female body is constituted as violable and penetrable, rooted in narratives that continuously reinforce male virility/dominance and female passivity/subjugation, especially through legal material which enforces boundaries and sexual dominance by men over women.[43]

With a strong textual focus on the body, it appears that acts of transgression of gender roles have the ability to destabilize the body and society, and so are tightly regulated.[44] Within this discourse, the sexual household is formed around the penetrative sovereignty of the father, which in turn forms the boundaries and embodiments of the household.[45] In the narratives of Sodom and Gomorrah (Gen. 19) and the Levite's concubine (Judg. 19) the righteous male actor, through preventing the

40. For example, the verbal form of נקב in the *Qal* means to pierce or bore a hole (2 Kgs 18.21; Job 40.24) See BDB, נקב.

41. Athalya Brenner, *The Intercourse of Knowledge: On Gendering Desire and 'Sexuality' in the Hebrew Bible* (New York: Brill, 1997), p. 13, who states: 'A "female" is sexed rather than gendered: she is an "orifice"; orifices and holes require that they be filled. A "male" is gendered: he is the carrier of memory, the one "to be remembered", thus a social agent.'

42. BDB, רחם.

43. For an overview of sexual politics and the construction of gendered bodies in the Hebrew Bible, see the following: Esther Fuchs, *Sexual Politics in the Biblical Narrative: Reading the Hebrew Bible as a Woman* (JSOTSup 310; London: Sheffield Academic Press, 2000); Brenner, *The Intercourse of Knowledge*; Deborah L. Ellens, *Women in the Sex Texts of Leviticus and Deuteronomy: A Comparative Conceptual Analysis* (LHBOTS 458; London: T&T Clark International, 2008); Carolyn Pressler, *The View of Women Found in the Deuteronomic Family Laws* (Berlin: W. de Gruyter, 1993).

44. Howard Eilberg-Schwartz, 'Problem of the Body for the People of the Book', in Howard Eilberg-Schwartz (ed.), *People of the Body: Jews and Judaism from an Embodied Perspective* (Albany: SUNY Press, 1992), pp. 17-46 (20). Eilberg-Schwartz follows the emphasis of Mary Douglas, *Purity and Danger: An Analysis of Concepts of Pollution and Taboo* (London: Routledge, 1966) with the focus on the body as the first symbol of society, and so its management corresponds to the regulation of society.

45. Jon L. Berquist, *Controlling Corporeality: The Body and the Household in Ancient Israel* (New Brunswick: Rutgers University Press, 2002), p. 85.

men of the town knowing (ידע) the male visitors, protects the ideally impenetrable male body, as that which exercises power and is not subject to it, *and* exercises sexual control over the women of the household, valorizing certain power relations between men and women.[46] It is within this area of the regulation of sexual relationships (incest and others), in which the boundaries of power within the household are regulated and delineated, that Lev. 18.22 appears.[47] The text reads:

ואת־זכר לא תשכב משכבי אשה תועבה הוא

> And with a male you shall not lie the lying down of a woman; it is a *to'eva*[48]

The debate around Lev. 18.22 has been impacted by the work of Saul Olyan and Daniel Boyarin, who both significantly inform our discussion here. Olyan compares the unattested term משכבי אשה, 'the lyings down of a woman' (actually plural in the Hebrew), with the more common term משכב זכר ('the lying down of a male'), arguing that the idiom משכב זכר refers to male vaginal penetration. For example, Judg. 21.11-12 defines a young virgin, נערה בתולה, as one who 'has not known a man with respect to the lying down of a male' (לא־ידעה איש למשכב זכר).[49] The non-virgin 'knows the lying down of a male' (אשה ידעת משכב־זכר). With 'the lyings down of a male' referring to male vaginal penetration,[50] Olyan suggests משכבי אשה implies something like 'the act or condition of a woman's being penetrated'.[51] Leviticus 18.22 and 22.5, therefore,

> [s]eem to refer specifically to intercourse and suggest that anal penetra-
> tion was seen as analogous to vaginal penetration on some level, since
> 'the lying down of a woman' seems to mean vaginal receptivity.[52]

It is penetration that defines and genders the act, and constitutes the vagina as penetrated and passive, and the male body as the one which

---

46.   The cutting up of the concubine's body in Judg. 19, having been subjected to multiple rape, further emphasizes the disturbing power relations within the household.

47.   Ellens, *Women in the Sex Texts of Leviticus and Deuteronomy*, pp. 73-74.

48.   This translation is taken from Saul M. Olyan, '"And with a Male You Shall Not Lie the Lying Down of a Woman": On the Meaning and Significance of Leviticus 18.22 and 20.13', *Journal of the History of Sexuality* 5 (1994), pp. 179-206 (180). For a definition of *to'eva*, see below.

49.   Olyan also draws on Num. 31.17, 18, 35.

50.   Olyan states that '*mishkab neqeba*' would be the expected companion of '*mishkab zkr*', and that it is not at all clear why the pairing that occurs takes place.

51.   Olyan, p. 185.

52.   *Ibid.*

should remain impenetrable and penetrating. The command is addressed to him as 'you', לא תשכב, 'you (sing. masc.) shall not lie' or 'do not lie', though there has been some debate as to which male the legislation is directed towards.[53]

The text also fails to prohibit non-penetrative forms of sex, either heterosexual or homosexual, which would suggest the text does not aim at prohibiting non-reproductive forms of intercourse, but is discussing something more specific. Leviticus 18.22 and Deut. 22.5 appear loosely in the context of mixing laws, and the only attempt at explanation of the laws is that they are תועבה, often translated 'abomination' or 'abhorrent', representing revulsion at an act. It is suggested the term implies something which 'offends one's ritual or moral order', for example the Egyptians finding shepherding or eating with foreigners repugnant (Gen. 46.34; 43.32).[54] In the context of Leviticus and Deuteronomy it may express a covenantal backdrop of practices which threaten Israel's stability with YHWH or with the land, for example idolatry or cult prostitution (Lev. 18.26, 27, 29, 39), deceit or corruption (Deut. 25.16) or the offering of imperfect sacrificial animals (Deut. 15.19-23). Within Prophetic texts the majority of occurrences refer to idolatry, whereas in Proverbs the covenantal backdrop is lacking. However, the term expresses a kind of personal loathing. While there are certain cultic emphases in texts such as the Holiness Code or Ezekiel that frequently use the term, its use in these texts never appears wholly cultic, and its occurrence in Proverbs should warn us against too narrow a definition.[55] Boyarin argues that the term has a broader meaning in referring to the transgression of boundaries; the prohibition in Lev. 18.22 immediately precedes the legislation against human–animal intercourse, which is described as a תבל, a mixing or confusion of things. These acts of cross-dressing and male–male intercourse transgress the discursively formed bodies of the Hebrew Bible, and are thus acts which fail to reiterate specific types of sexually differentiated bodies. Within the Holiness Code there is the continuous retort not to commit certain acts or the land will vomit the inhabitants out. Leviticus 18.25-28 reads:

53. Olyan, '"And with a Male You Shall Not Lie the Lying Down of a Woman"', p. 186, argues that the law addresses the penetrator not the penetrated, as '*mishkebe issa*' is 'what a male experiences in vaginal intercourse, and the law stipulates that 'you' [male, singular] shall not experience it with a male'. However, Walsh, who essentially accepts the dynamics of Olyan's argument, suggests that the receptive partner is addressed. Jerome T. Walsh, 'Leviticus 18:22 and 20:13: Who Is Doing What to Whom?', *JBL* 120, no. 2 (2001), pp. 201-9.

54. Michael A. Grisanti, 'תועבה', in *NIDOTTE*, IX, pp. 314-18.

55. *Ibid.*, p. 317.

> Thus the land became defiled…and the land vomited out its inhabitants.
> But you shall…commit none of these abominations, neither the citizen or
> the alien who resides among you (for the inhabitants of the land, who
> were before you, committed all of these abominations, and the land
> became defiled); otherwise the land will vomit you out for defiling it, as it
> vomited out the nation that was before you.

Here, despite certain themes throughout the Holiness Code, the 'covenantal' aspect of 'abominations' are undermined. It is not exclusively a case
of certain acts being repulsive to YHWH-worship, but the very acts are
too much for the land itself to handle. Rather than simply Israelite, these
abominations are to be avoided by all residing in the land. The threat of
the acts, and responsibility for dealing with them, are taken from the
personal to the communal.

While the lack of a parallel law for women–women sex may be taken
as a disregard for female sexuality, the control of women's sexual bodies
is emphasized by other texts:

> You shall not have sexual relations with any animal and defile yourself
> with it, nor shall any woman give herself to an animal to have sexual
> relations with it: it is perversion. (Lev. 18.23)

In Leviticus 20 the prohibitions of Leviticus 18 are given an expanded
treatment, and specific punishments are defined for transgressions. The
punishments in 20.15-16 are that the man who has sex with the animal
(יתן שכבתו בבהמה) is to be put to death, whereas the same punishment is
meted out to the woman who simply 'approaches (תקרב) in order to lie
down stretched out (לרבעה) *before* (לפני)' the animal. The verb תקרב,
'approaches', indicates that the woman has intent, and its combination
with her 'stretching out' suggests the animal, as the penetrator, is cast in
the position of being the actual sexual actor, regardless of whether the
animal does act. In both cases the animal is also put to death.

Women–women 'sexual' acts are not just simply ignored, they are,
arguably, *precluded as a possibility*, in terms of the definition of acceptable or non-acceptable sex, through a lack of penetration. Bestiality is
interesting to the writers of the Holiness Code precisely because it
involves a male penis, even if this is not a human one. Daniel Boyarin
demonstrates Talmudic understandings of sexual legislation that likewise
defines sexual acts primarily in terms of penetration—thus intercrural sex
between men is classed in a different category from anal penetration, and
sexual contact between women is in places barely acknowledged.[56]

---

56.   Daniel Boyarin looks at *b. Yeb.* 76a and *b. Shab.* 65a-b where there are prohibitions against same-sex activity between women as minor misdemeanours, being
acts which may potentially lead them to sleep with men. Elsewhere, *b. Nidd.* 13b

Leviticus 18.22 presumes the inviolability of the male body, and seals its borders, drawing on misogynistic discourse which situates the sexual act as something that moves a male body into a female body. In the case of a male body taking on the role of the female body, essential categories are eroded. While the male body has a penetrable orifice, and can behave, then, like a female body, this behaviour must be rejected. Such a prohibition is primarily concerned with issues of classification, with ontology;[57] so the text makes clear that male-anal receptivity is not an acceptable analogue to female-vaginal receptivity. The 'lyings down of a woman' is to be experienced by women only. In contrast to Athens and Rome where status is important in defining the penetrator/penetrated dyad, here the gendered body is the organizing principle around which sexual difference is constituted.[58]

In terms of the specific punishment defined in Lev. 20.13, it empha-sizes the bodily aspects and, as in the case of the animals who are (with-out intent) subject to punishment for their participation in transgressive penetrative sex, both parties are to be killed. In particular, it parallels the wording of the punishment for the woman who approaches the animal for penetration:

> You shall kill the woman and the animal, they shall be put to death; their blood is upon them. (Lev. 20.16)

> They—the two of them—have committed a *to'eva*; they shall be put to death; their blood is upon them. (Lev. 20.13)

While the form of execution of the bodies is not specified, the double use of the verb in מות יומתו emphasizes the certainty of death. Both bodies have transgressed something. Whereas in Lev. 18.20 and 20.16 the

distinguishes between male intercourse '*miškāb zākor*' and intercrural intercourse '*děrěk 'ēbārim*', likening the latter to masturbation. He concludes that the Tannaitic statements understood 'the Torah's interdiction to be limited only to the practice of male anal intercourse, the use of the male as a female', and that it is counter-intuitive to presume that the biblical period had a category of homosexuality, which was then lost by the Palestinian and Babylonian period. See Daniel Boyarin, 'Are There Any Jews in "The History of Sexuality"?', *Journal of the History of Sexuality* 5 (1995), pp. 333-55 (131-33).

57. Ellens, *Women in the Sex Texts of Leviticus and Deuteronomy*, p. 79.

58. David Halperin, analysing Graeco-Roman discourse on sex, rejects a notion of sexual orientation, instead suggesting sex was primarily constructed in terms of power-relations within the bedroom, with free male adult citizens as penetrator, and women/male or female slaves as penetrated. A reversal of this was a transgression of status and power. His approach is drawn upon by both Boyarin and Olyan. David M. Halperin, *One Hundred Years of Homosexuality: And Other Essays on Greek Love* (New York/London: Routledge, 1990).

woman is cast as 'other', the third person feminine that must behave in certain ways, in 18.22 the act is addressed to 'you' (masc. sing); however, in the punishment of 20.13 the two men are referred to in the third person. While 18.22 is only addressed to one, as the party who has chosen to act in a certain way, the double punishment can be compared to 20.15-16, which emphasizes that both animal and human are to die. The reason for this is that these transgressions are directly polluting to the land, and the land will vomit the entire nation out (18.28). The materiality of the body becomes related to the materiality of the land and the materiality of the community. In contrast to discourses Foucault outlined which posit desire as substantiating the subject's body, the body here is constituted by its *physical use* in relation to its materialization as sexed, the male being required to penetrate, and the female being required to be penetrated (by being categorized as orifice bearing). A penetrated male body confuses the categories. The body rather than an internal desire is the site at which power is exercised and produces knowledge.

Moving from the Holiness Code to Deuteronomy, there is no specific definition of abhorrent acts, but there is a similar distinction between the gendered body in terms of categorization. Deuteronomy 22.5 states:

> There shall not be (לא יהיה) on a woman (אשה) an object of a man (גבר כלי) nor shall a man wear (ילבש) a garment (שמלת) of a woman, for whoever does such things is abominable (תועבה) to the Lord your God.[59]

The second section relates to the wearing of a שמלה, a garment.[60] The first section, however, while clearly a parallel, states there should not be a כלי גבר on a woman. The term כלי, while including clothing, extends to imply tool, implement or weapon, with the use of גבר rather than איש, for 'man', carrying heightened overtones of masculinity, valour and strength. Deuteronomy 22.5 appears in the context of laws relating to clothing and to the mixing of things: do not plough an ox and donkey together, do not mix two seeds in a field, do not wear clothes made of wool and linen woven together, and make tassels on the four corners of your cloak.[61]

---

59. My translation.

60. Harold T. Vedeler, 'Reconstructing Meaning in Deuteronomy 22.5: Gender, Society, and Transvestitism in Israel and the Ancient Near East', *JBL* 127 (2008), pp. 459-76 (461).

61. Explanations have been offered (Jeffery H. Tigay, *Torah Commentary: Deuteronomy* [JPS Torah Commentary; Philadelphia: Jewish Publication Society, 1996], p. 100), from fear that cross-dressing facilitates mingling with the opposite sex, to that it encourages homosexual acts; however, there is little sexual context, and it fails to address *why* this is a problem. Often suggested is that it reflects an

According to Athalya Brenner, clothing 'supplies visual parameters for the sexual identity of males and females';[62] in other words, 'the anxiety is about *male* sexual and social identity'.[63] A woman is prohibited from wearing anything that allows her to perform as a man—clothes, weapons, tools; the law acts to limit her chance to imitate the opposite gender; she is unable to dress like a man, take part in male economic production with tools or to penetrate a man with a weapon. The fact that a man is only prohibited from wearing the clothing of a woman may be because the objects of a woman would be located primarily within the private domestic sphere, which the man dominates. According to Boyarin, the man does not transgress the gender boundary by performing most of the tasks of a woman; however, by placing on the clothes of a woman, he crosses over in the act of *being* a woman.[64] For Boyarin, there is a connection between Lev. 18.22 and Deut. 22.5, through the semantic/syntactic parallelism of 'a woman's garment', שמלת אשה, and 'a woman's lyings', משכבי אשה.[65] Boyarin is explicit that it is not the mere mixing of two things together that is the issue, which would make homoerotic relations *more* appropriate than heterosexual, but it is the *use* of a male as a female, a crossing over and confusion of the boundaries, that is at stake.[66]

In the Holiness Code the laws are specifically associated also with the prohibitions against various forms of incest. Such a connection is most understandable when the potential of the legislation to regulate forms of kinship is taken into account. However, the immediate sentence preceding Lev. 18.22 concerns the worship of Molech: 'You shall not give your offspring to pass them over to Molech and profane the name of your

---

ancient Near Eastern rite or Canaanite cultic sex act (see Anthony Phillips, *Deuteronomy* [Cambridge: Cambridge University Press, 1973], p. 145) though why the text would conceal this is not apparent, neither is the rationale behind its particular rejection. Military explanations, that due to the importance of military might in the creation of masculinity the idea of women holding weapons was transgressive, would have resonance with the argument made in here; however, the overall context does not appear to emphasize a military concern. Harry A. Hoffner, 'Symbols for Masculinity and Femininity: Their Use in Ancient near Eastern Sympathetic Magic Rituals', *JBL* 85 (1966), pp. 326-34.

62. *Ibid.*, p. 144.

63. *Ibid.*, p. 145.

64. 2 Sam. 3.28-29 has a curse that Joab's descendants will forever be holding 'the spindle'—an object repeatedly associated throughout the ancient Near East with femininity (see Hoffner, 'Symbols for Masculinity and Femininity', pp. 331-34).

65. Boyarin, 'Are There Any Jews in "The History of Sexuality"?', pp. 342-43.

66. *Ibid.*, p. 343.

God: I am YHWH'. The 'you' addressed by the commandment has the authority to organize the sexual practices of his household. If sexual knowledge/power is constituted around penetration, and who penetrates whom endorses relationships within the household, then, even more than prohibiting the feminization of the body, the text seeks to prohibit the male 'you' being placed in a subjugated position, having the same status as the women of the household. Men are constructed to be men, dominant, and thus there cannot be any exception, for the sake of the nation in the land. The possibility cannot be entertained that the male can become feminized, in terms of power, or that the feminizing/subjugating act of being penetrated can be tolerated. For a male to be penetrated is to reject discourses of male power. The cohesiveness of the male subject itself comes into question and is exposed as a fabrication, in that it is made and must be defended. However, we can choose to reject the underlying misogynistic premise regarding power relationships. It is this rejection of discourses of power that brings biblical bodies and the way gay men view their bodies, as discussed above, back into dialogue. Bersani, for example, draws on various social taboos and regulations on the receptive position in male anal sex through time to suggest a general fear that, drawing on Freud, passivity relates to an *abdication* of power:[67]

> Phallocentrism is…not primarily the denial of power to women (although it has obviously also led to that, everywhere and at all times), but above all the denial of the value of powerlessness in both men and women. I don't mean the value of gentleness, or nonaggressiveness, or even of passivity, but rather of a more radical disintegration and humiliation of the self.[68]

For Bersani, the fear of passive male-anal sex is more than just parodying dominant power relations—it is a site at which the very value of power itself is questioned. Whether biblical insistence that men's control of the household is exercised through penetration, or gay men's responses to AIDs is made through gendered displays of their bodies, the rejection of power, and the way it constitutes the person in relation to others, is seen as threatening; it leads to a kind of self-shattering, a disintegration of the self that has been constructed, in the mind of the observer. It is this association of sex with disintegration of the self that we will now turn to, exploring ways of resisting homophobia through engaging with the work of Foucault and Bersani.

---

67. Bersani, *Is the Rectum a Grave?*, pp. 17-19.
68. *Ibid.*, p. 24.

IV. *Resistant Bodies*

In the House of Commons debate on the Equal Marriage Bill, on the thirteenth of February 2013, David Simpson, MP for Upper Bann (Democratic Unionist Party), objected to the governments 'redefinition' of marriage by stating, 'in the Garden of Eden it was Adam and Eve, not Adam and Steve'.[69] Simpson's somewhat unsophisticated appeal to creation theology for sexual ethics has a long tradition in Christian theologies of sexuality, but even the creation narrative itself is not quite so straightforward. God declares in Gen. 2.18, before the creation of the first woman, that, 'It is not good that man be alone', which should cause us to at least question whether there are other opportunities for sexuality to flourish for those who don't have the same reaction to the opposite sex as *haadam* in Gen. 2.23.

What follows here is an attempt at a response to biblical and ecclesiastical homophobia from the location of a young, gay, Christian reader. What may appear as an overly political approach comes from a place of urgency to tackle homophobia in the Church and wider society. From attempts to 'cure' homosexuality through psychotherapy or exorcisms (which I myself was subject to, during my teens), to damaging attempts to enforce celibacy, to horrific instances of hate crimes, prejudice emerges at all levels of society. By taking into account relations of power, I now hope both to challenge homophobic readings and offer wider suggestions for a Christian theology of sexuality.

As we have seen, despite its power, no discourse can fully map itself onto the bodies and desires it has formed and created, which, following Butler, undermines regimes of gender. But what happens when a reader attempts to merge two separate discourses, ancient and modern, onto each other through reading their bodies into the biblical text? When done in a certain manner, a gay male reader may rationalize in the following way: 'Lev. 18.22 prohibits homosexuality; my impulses towards same-sex bodies means I'm a homosexual; therefore Lev. 18.22 prohibits my desires and sexual pleasure'.

However, as Foucault makes clear, relations of power offer opportunities for resistance, and I would like to suggest these can happen in the space between the reader and the biblical text. Foucault suggested the first point of counter-attack against the discourse of sex/desire—that we are constituted through our sexed bodies and how these sexed bodies

69. Proceedings of the House of Commons. Online: http://www.publications. parliament.uk/pa/cm201213/cmhansrd/cm130205/debtext/130205-0003.htm (accessed 26 July 2013).

desire other sexed bodies—is to shift the focus onto what he elusively terms bodies/pleasure. While this has not been received uncritically,[70] it can provide a useful starting point with which to resist aspects of certain restrictive readings of the text. Compared to desire, for Foucault:

> The term 'pleasure'…is free of use, almost devoid of meaning. There is no 'pathology' of pleasure, no 'abnormal' pleasure. It is an event 'outside the subject', or at the limit of the subject, in that something which is neither of the body nor of the soul, which is neither inside nor outside, in short, a notion not assigned and not assignable.[71]

For Foucault, pleasure is useful precisely because it is so vague; it cannot be subsumed under the discourse of sex or desire. So by moving towards pleasure, something undifferentiated and undefined, we can find ways of understanding erotic relations that can escape talking about gender or penetration, and so can find ways of living 'that produce alternatives to subjection within the modern regime of sexuality'.[72] We can find ways of expressing sexuality that cannot be contained or categorized according to regulatory regimes. By being at the 'limit of the subject', the ways the subject is organized and categorized by knowledge (such as gender performance or a sexed body), pleasure is something which escapes categorization according to sex, desire, soul or psyche, and so critiques ways of relating to each other constituted, for example, around penetration.

  The biblical texts of Leviticus, with their focus on penetrating or penetrated bodies rather than desires, can begin to refocus our attention away from our desires as being formative of embodied sexuality. If there is no confessional desire in Lev. 18.22, only certain bodily actions, we can break the identification of the text with discourses of homosexuality, which as we have seen are modern categories centred around conceptions like desire, and so we can avoid reading 'homosexuality' into the text of Lev. 18.22 at all. Where desire does occur in the Hebrew Bible, it is capable of being constructed in a positive same-sex way: for example in

---

70. Judith Butler, 'Revisiting Bodies and Pleasures', *Theory, Culture and Society* 16, no. 2 (1999), pp. 11-20, for example, problematizes aspects of Foucault that suggest a pre-discursive body. For positive responses, see Jana Sawicki, 'Foucault, Queer Theory, and the Discourse of Desire', in Timothy O'Leary and Christopher Falzon (eds.), *Foucault and Philosophy* (Oxford: Wiley-Blackwell, 2010); McWhorter, *Bodies and Pleasures*.

71. From an interview, quoted in Arnold I. Davidson, *The Emergence of Sexuality: Historical Epistemology and the Formation of Concepts* (Cambridge, MA: Harvard University Press, 2001), p. 213.

72. Sawicki, 'Foucault, Queer Theory, and the Discourse of Desire', p. 200.

Isa. 53.2, where the servant of God is defined as having 'no appearance that we should desire him', as if desire is a natural reaction to male beauty.[73] Beyond penetrative sex, even Lev. 15.16-17 regulates the purity laws for emissions of semen, with the same purity requirements: while in the case of (male–female) penetrative sex the woman who receives the semen and the man will bathe in water and be unclean until the evening (the end of the day), in regard to non-penetrative sex involving emissions of semen the object on which the semen falls is equivalent to the penetrated woman, in that the cloth or skin should be washed and both this and the man will be unclean until evening (Lev. 15–16). There is no moral condemnation of such emissions, and no requirement is made on the nature of the non-penetrative desire or pleasure involved.[74] In reading Lev. 18.22 and 20.13 as being about power relationships within the household within a particular ancient cultural context, our reading becomes resistant to attempts to define our own relationality based on sexual difference or sexed bodies, and as such becomes an attempt to resist those manifestations of knowledge/power that attempt to read and inscribe female bodies or gay male bodies as having particular roles in relation to other bodies.

In the gaps the texts leave—the forms of pleasure it fails to include within its discourse centred around penetration (or in Deut. 22.5, the clothing and objects it fails to specify)—we can begin to think of ourselves outside of the social project referred to by Bersani, that of surveillance and discipline, of certain regulatory forms of sexuality. In a queer turn, a focus on pleasures over desires mutes the ventriloquist who dictates our modern conceptions of sexuality, of our confessions, our psychology and our identities, who attempts to identify us as male, female, gay, straight, effeminate or butch, and demonstrates that the text deals with neither, but instead is concerned with bodies. We become unwritten and undone, but not annihilated.

But what of the central restriction on male penetrative sex? How can we take this on, without completely circumventing the text itself, while not colluding with its ancient cultural values, with its restrictive and

73. See David J. A. Clines, *Interested Parties: The Ideology of Writers and Readers of the Hebrew Bible* (JSOTSup 143; Gender, Culture, Theory 1; Sheffield: Sheffield Academic Press, 1995), p. 224: 'it is implied that ordinarily one would expect a high-ranking "servant of Yahweh" to be beautiful in form and face, and to be sexually attractive...to "us" (? males)'.

74. The sin of Onan (Gen. 38.8-10), which has been constructed as banning non-procreative sex, or masturbation (cf. *b. Nid.* 13a), actually regulates against the failure of a man to fulfil his duty in levirate marriage, by engaging in *coitus interruptus*.

oppressive prohibitions? Through critiquing his rejection of psycho-analysis, Bersani attempts an ambitious move to go beyond Foucault by integrating him with Freud. Drawing on psychoanalytical understanding of the human move to both master power and renounce it for the sake of pleasure, Bersani invokes the notion of *jouissance*. If pleasure is at the limit of the subject, *jouissance*, in the mode used by Lacan (usually left untranslated due to his elusiveness in defining it), is a kind of *going beyond* pleasure, to something which Bersani characterizes as a form of 'self-shattering'.[75] Pleasure is something that happens within structures, whereas *jouissance* is a breaking of those structures, a going beyond them, neither entirely enjoyment nor entirely pain, but often appearing as aspects of both. *Jouissance* is precisely so pleasurable and so painful because it breaks the categories we usually organize our world about. In this way, it is a form of disintegration of the subject, 'in that it disrupts the ego's coherence and dissolves its boundaries',[76] suggesting psycho-analysis 'challenges us to imagine *a nonsuicidal disappearance of the subject*',[77] 'a defeat of power in which the subject is momentarily undone'.[78] Desire 'is a defence against *jouissance*, in that it introduces a limit to the person's lustful self-erasure'.[79] Unlike Foucault's suggestion of reaching the edge of the subject, this is not just a testing of the borders, but a kind of shattering of the self, a resistant move which accepts a divestment of power. Using Freud, Bersani wants to see how the male body can reject its agency, and experience 'a man's most intense experience of his body's vulnerability'.[80]

Whereas we can effectively 'unread' desire from Lev. 18.22, the bodily aspects remain; both discourses (biblical, gay) are tied up in the act of penetration and power and so the biblical text still inscribes contemporary bodies. What Bersani suggests, in his now seminal essay *Is the Rectum a Grave?*, is not a rejection of the homophobic, misogynistic discourse that accompanies the passive sexual position (here written at the height of the AIDs scare in the United States), but a kind of queer

---

75. Roland Barthes 'distinguishes between *plaisir*, which is comfortable, ego-assuring, recognized and legitimated as culture, and "*jouissance*", which is shocking, ego-disruptive, and in conflict with the canons of culture'. Jane Gallop, 'Beyond the Jouissance Principle', *Representations* 7 (1984), pp. 110-15 (111).

76. Bersani, *Homos*, p. 101.

77. *Ibid.*, p. 99.

78. *Ibid.*, p. 100.

79. Jeanne W. Bernstein, 'Love, Desire, Jouissance: Two out of Three Ain't Bad', *Psychoanalytical Dialogues* 16 (2007), pp. 711-24 (719).

80. Bersani, *Homos*, p. 102.

embrace, while fully rejecting *complicity* with the misogyny and homophobia:

> But if the rectum is the grave in which the masculine ideal (an ideal shared—differently—by men *and* women) of proud subjectivity is buried, then it should be celebrated for its very potential for death... Gay men's 'obsession' with sex, far from being denied, should be celebrated—not because of its communal virtues, not because of its subversive potential for parodies of machismo...but rather because it never stops re-presenting the internalized phallic male as an infinitely loved object of sacrifice. Male homosexuality advertizes the risk of the sexual itself as the risk of self-dismissal, of *losing sight* of the self, and in so doing it proposes and dangerously represents *jouissance* as a mode of ascesis.[81]

If Lev. 18.22 is a fear of a disavowal of male phallic power, then an embrace of the rhetoric of the text and of the actual act it prohibits in order to control offers a kind of self-shattering, a rejection of the self, the self which the text and the reader constantly try and protect to regulate and control their relations to others. Through an embrace of *jouissance* the male reader can take himself out of the patriarchal economy in which he finds himself and recognize the vulnerability of his body, an ethical turn which forms a kind of solidarity with those others the text or societies designate as powerless or dangerous. By embracing the constraints the text places on the body, the misogynistic discourse it associates with certain kinds of sex, the reader is offered a deliberate choice to shatter the way the text writes onto their body.

How may this be related to a specifically theological sexual ethic? I would like to turn to the Christ-Hymn of Philippians (2.5-8). After exhorting the community to reject ambition and conceit and embrace humility in relation to one another, Paul writes:

> Let the same mind be in you that was in Christ Jesus, who, though he was in the form (μορφῇ) of God, did not regard equality with God as something to be exploited (ἁρπαγμὸν), but emptied himself (ἑαυτὸν ἐκένωσεν), taking the form of a slave (μορφὴν δούλου), being born in human likeness. And being found in human form (σχήματι), he humbled himself and became obedient to the point of death—even death on a cross.

In exhorting the community to be in the same mind as Christ, the hymn becomes an ethical instruction to incorporate Christ's humility into the life of the community, specifically in the context of their relations with one another.[82] Through *kenosis*, by *emptying himself*,[83] the form of Christ

81. Bersani, *Is the Rectum a Grave?*, p. 30.
82. For a discussion of the text and its relation to the theological notion of kenosis, see Sarah Coakley, *Powers and Submissions: Spirituality, Philosophy and*

transmutes from the form of God to the form of a slave. Christ rejects a grasping at hierarchy, which the community at Phillipi should also reject. In our mimetic response to Christ our attempt to grasp our bodily form (μορφή) becomes mute while we undergo kenosis and positively reject power. While resisting an erasure of difference, Paul's theology allows for moments in which hierarchical differences appear collapsed and the normal preference for power within hierarchy is reversed (2 Cor. 12.9; Gal. 3.28). Paul states in 1 Cor. 1.27-28:

> But God chose what is foolish in the world to shame the wise; God chose what is weak in the world to shame the strong; God chose what is low and despised in the world, things that are not, to reduce to nothing things that are.

Once we begin to account for Lev. 18.22 not as a moral teaching on sexual ethics but as mediation of familial and communal power, we can begin to undermine it through a self-reflective ethical kenosis. The common division of moral and ritual or ceremonial law in Leviticus and the Torah[84] more widely fails to stand up to scrutiny, with the text itself failing to make any form of distinction and in fact inserting what would generally be taken as moral laws (Lev. 19.18, 'You shall not take vengeance or bear a grudge') into ritual laws (Lev. 19.19, 'You shall not sow your field with two kinds of seed'). Considering Paul's marginalization of the law for those 'in Christ',[85] by divorcing Lev. 18.22 from 'moral' law Paul's admonition against 'sexual immorality' such as that reported in Acts 15.29 (πορνεία) can no longer be automatically identified with same-sex acts and becomes decontextualized. This therefore requires the community of readers to find a new way of responding. By forming a Christian sexual ethics based around a Pauline rejection of worldly power and not around an exegesis of sexual difference in the creation account, we can begin to integrate Bersani's call for an embrace of powerlessness in relations to each other.

Gender (Oxford: Blackwell, 2002), pp. 3-39. Coakley's discussion is specifically concerned with whether kenosis can be a useful feminist tool or not. As part of this, she covers a wide range of exegetical and theological opinions on the passage, placing an emphasis on the ethical as opposed to 'incarnational' modes of reading the hymn.

83. For a discussion of the term see *TDNT*, III, p. 661. The verb κενόω only appears in the form ἐκένωσεν in the New Testament. The same form is used in the LXX version of Jer. 14.2 to mean 'desolation'.

84. For example, the title in the NRSV translation to Lev. 19 is 'Ritual and Moral Holiness'.

85. For example Rom. 7.4-8.

Here the avoidance of certain same-sex acts because they inscribe misogynistic imaginations of feminization on the male body can be embraced through an active assertion of powerlessness, a kind of self-emptying of the internalized phallic male Bersani calls on us to sacrifice. The ethics of sexual relations based on a form of self-sacrifice and self-emptying can coalesce around a giving of one's body wholly to the other, a giving which involves the renunciation of power over the other. This form of Christian sexual ethics based on an *undermining* of discourses of power can speak to a reflective Christian sexual ethic which has wider implications than same-sex relations, invoking a stricter ethic than one based on sexual complementarity. A constant questioning of a sexual actors' power in relation to their partner in terms of age, social and economic class, emotional dominance can speak to a Church which is in constant turmoil over how to articulate sexual ethics in a contemporary age, and a society which is plagued by continual stories of those in positions of power and dominance sexually exploiting or abusing others.

Conclusions

I have offered here two attempts to resist the mapping of bodies in ways that create restrictive and oppressive readings of texts, by noting the absence of reference to desire, going from desire to pleasure, beyond pleasure to *jouissance*, and finally suggesting new avenues for sexual ethics around the embrace of powerlessness. However, an acceptance of the bodily aspects of the text, both literary and physical, may offer a final form of resistance, albeit a limited, contingent one. By acknowledging the punishments meted out in the text in association with the horrors of the hate crimes discussed in the introduction, it may, in certain contexts where the revulsion is strong enough, cause an ethical intervention in the reader. When the true horror of the pain and torture of queer bodies in different contexts—scriptural, criminal and state-sanctioned—is acknowledged, it may force the reader to confront any potential writability of the text, rejecting its attempts to impose its discursive bodies onto our discursive bodies, and forcing a contextualisation of the text itself so strong that the reader can begin to formulate new ways of relating to the text and its bodies.

It is contingent as it ultimately relies on the perspective of the reader. The horrific homophobic murder of Matthew Shepherd in Laramie, Wyoming (1998)—tortured and hung up crucifix-like to die on a fence in a field—evoked widespread condemnation. However, it was also the beginning of the infamous *God Hates Fags* protests of the Westboro

Baptist Church, with signs such as 'No Tears for Queers'. They knew the punishment called upon in Lev. 20.13, and so any show of pity or sadness was tantamount to a rejection of the Bible.

Ultimately, no hermeneutical strategy, bar a radical revision, can undo the horrors of the text—that certain forms of bodily interactions between people, which may take place out of consensual love, are to result in the death of the people involved—but by struggling to increase acceptance of queer ways of being in the world, there are small avenues for resisting the discourse of the text and its attempts to inscribe itself upon our bodies. This may be through an engagement with a close reading of the text, or a critique of contemporary discourses of sexuality. However, where these fail it may be an ethical challenge to re-evaluate the bodily reality of the text, that the text does not just disapprove of male same-sex acts, but actively despises them to the point of death, and ask to what extent it can continue to write itself onto queer bodies at all.

RITUALIZED BODIES IN THE VALLEY OF DRY BONES (EZEKIEL 37.1-14)

C. A. Strine

Ezekiel 37.1-14, the oracle concerning the valley of dry bones, is about bodies. It is an unavoidable observation: the text describes a collection of bones scattered about on the ground that assemble into skeletons, which are subsequently covered with sinews, flesh, and skin prior to receiving breath. At the end, these bodies stand on their feet.

The *prima facie* nature of this observation has not impacted on the secondary literature.[1] There is almost no discussion of why this bodily image is selected and how its embodied character helps it to function.[2] Rather, there is keen interest in redactional questions and the role of this passage in the development of Jewish concepts of resurrection.[3] True, those questions deserve attention, but not at the exclusion of inquiring about the importance of the peculiar bodily images.

Michael Fox grasped this imbalance and went some ways towards redressing it with his 1980 article, 'The Rhetoric of Ezekiel's Vision of the Valley of the Bones'. Fox provides a lucid definition of what

1. Among the limited prior discussion, Jacqueline Lapsley, 'Body Piercings: The Priestly Body and the "Body" of the Temple in Ezekiel', *Hebrew Bible and Ancient Israel* 1 (2012), pp. 231-45, is the most relevant; cf. Julie Galambush, *Jerusalem in the Book of Ezekiel: The City as Yahweh's Wife* (SBLDS 130; Atlanta: SBL, 1992). Yvonne M. Sherwood, 'Prophetic Scatology: Prophecy and the Art of Sensation', *Semeia* 82 (1998), pp. 183-224, includes some noteworthy points on Ezekiel, especially the sign-act in ch. 4.

2. For a discussion of the ways in which Ezekiel's metaphors work, see Carol Newsom, 'A Maker of Metaphors: Ezekiel's Oracles Against Tyre', *Interpretation* 38 (1984), pp. 151-64.

3. For details of this development, see the discussions and references in M. Greenberg, *Ezekiel 21–37: A New Translation with Introduction and Commentary* (AB 22A; New York: Doubleday, 1997), pp. 749-51, and Daniel I. Block, *The Book of Ezekiel: Chapters 1–24* (NICOT; Grand Rapids: Eerdmans, 1997), pp. 388-92.

rhetorical criticism is, explains how it enhances biblical interpretation, and outlines how biblical scholars might offer insights for rhetorical theory in general,[4] while he also demonstrates how the imagery (vv. 1-10) and its interpretation (vv. 11-14) provide the necessary hope for the Babylonian exiles, hope that 'has become essential for keeping the people together until the time comes to return' to Israel.[5]

The imminent challenge for the community is not the horror of exile; far from it. 'Ezekiel sees the situation as intolerable', observes Fox, because in its relatively benign and livable nature 'it could so easily become permanent, and that would mean the end of Israel as a people'.[6] Fox recognizes that this is a formidable task for which the prophet must craft 'a response to a rhetorical situation, a situation felt to need change of the sort that discourse may accomplish'.[7] The audience must be disoriented, confronted with something that would supersede the immediate impression that a life of assimilation in Babylonia is acceptable. The prophet must supply a reason why the Judahite exiles should be ardently nationalistic when their external circumstances suggest that choice is futile. Fox contends that 'Ezekiel's primary strategy is boldly to affirm the absurd'[8] with an image that 'will restructure their view of reality…to make them expect the unexpectable'.[9]

'To bring about such a conviction', writes Fox, 'the rhetor must go *deeper than conscious reason.* He must find a shortcut *to the subconscious* and implant there a new perspective on reality strong enough to overcome the vision of reality that usually imposes itself on the conscious.'[10] This is a prescient statement, though Fox does not fully grasp its ramifications. He spends the remainder of his article dissecting Ezek. 37.1-14 as an exhortation, a rhetorical strategy that stirs the emotions in a way that might produce belief. Though he recognizes that the text uses primarily concrete and sensual imagery (vv. 1-10) and only partially argument that is abstract and cognitive (vv. 11-14),[11] he never considers

4. Michael V. Fox, 'The Rhetoric of Ezekiel's Vision of the Valley of the Bones', *HUCA* 51 (1980), pp. 1-15 (1-5).
5. *Ibid.*, p. 6.
6. *Ibid.*
7. *Ibid.*, p. 5.
8. *Ibid.*, p. 10.
9. *Ibid.*
10. *Ibid.*, p. 7. Emphasis added.
11. *Ibid.*, p. 13. Leslie C. Allen, *Ezekiel 20–48* (WBC 29; Dallas: Word Books, 1990), pp. 181-84, gives a succinct statement on the issue and lists the relevant secondary literature. Anja Klein, *Schriftauslegung im Ezechielbuch: Redaktionsgeschichtliche Untersuchungen zu Ez 34–39* (BZAW 391; Berlin: W. de Gruyter,

how something other than words might grasp the audience's attention, stir their affections, and transform their perception of reality. Despite his positive contributions, Fox fails to consider why the passage foregrounds bodies and how this choice might support the goal of reaching beyond conscious reason.

In this chapter, I take up that question. In order to complement Fox's insight that Ezek. 37.1-14 reaches deeper than conscious reason, I draw on Catherine Bell's model of ritual practice to argue that the bodily imagery of the passage engages a non-cognitive logic that enables it to reach a deeper, visceral understanding in its audience. The bodily movements of YHWH, Ezekiel, and the assembled dry bones structure and orient the environment into a series of binary oppositions and engage a non-conscious logic to assert that an inside–outside or Us–Them social structure is part of the created order of the world and cannot be ignored. Ezekiel 37.1-14 suggests that abandoning national identity is not a matter of choice; it is inscribed in the structure of reality.

My case will progress in three stages. First, I will aim to show that Ezek. 37.1-14 signals its ritual context by alluding to other texts within Ezekiel and also to the Mesopotamian cult statue induction ritual. Secondly, I will utilize Bell's concept of ritualization to explain how the bodily movements of YHWH, Ezekiel, and the multitude constituted from the dry bones mark off the activities in the passage as intrinsically differ-ent and indicative of a cosmology in which differentiated national identity is foundational. Thirdly, I will consider how this embodied, ritualized approach suits the aim of the passage, which, as Fox correctly ascertains, is to encourage the Babylonian exiles to retain their ethnic particularity.

I. *The Ritual Context of Ezekiel 37*

If it is self-evident that Ezek. 37.1-14 focuses on bodies, it is not obvious that it envisions these bodies participating in ritualized actions, or more

---

2008), pp. 270-300, is the most recent and thorough discussion of its redaction. Klein, even though she stratifies the passage into three strata, regards it as one of the earliest passages in the book. I treat the passage as a unity because my argument is based largely on evidence internal to the final form of Ezekiel. The lone exception is my contention that Ezek. 37.1-14 alludes to the Mesopotamian cult statue induction ritual, but the argument can stand without this point. Moreover, though those allu-sions are most helpful to my argument if they occur in the Neo-Babylonian period, they still add to my cumulative case for signaling ritualization in Ezek. 37.1-14, even if they date to the Persian period. Since it is unlikely that the people's complaint in 37.11 dates to long after 539 BCE, when a return to the land was possible, my view is supported by all but the most radical diachronic models as well.

precisely that the passage alludes both to other rituals in the book and also to the Mesopotamian cult statue induction ritual. Examining shared concepts and vocabulary across the book of Ezekiel itself, as well as with the larger cultural context which informs it, shows this to be true.

a. *Allusions to Ritual Activity within Ezekiel*

The references to other rituals begin immediately in 37.1: the 'hand of YHWH' seizes the prophet and sets him in the midst of 'the valley' (הבקה). The hand of YHWH is mentioned six times in Ezekiel, with the largest cluster coming in the prophet's call narrative in chs. 1 to 3 (1.3; 3.14, 22; cf. 33.22; 37.1, 2; 40.1). This image then recalls that account: YHWH transports the prophet to 'the valley'. This unspecified locale appears five times in Ezekiel: twice in the call narrative (3.22-23), once in a reference back to that narrative (8.4), and twice in Ezek. 37.1-14 (vv. 1-2). The combined effect of YHWH's transporting hand and the unnamed valley is to build a link between Ezekiel 1–3 and Ezek. 37.1-14.[12]

The call narrative is noteworthy because it describes a process of individual transformation: specifically, Ezekiel encounters the divine presence and undergoes a process of initiation into his role as prophet. It is important to stress that this is both a *process* and an *initiation rite*. The former is explicit in the text, which notes the passage of time (Ezek. 3.16). The time lapse of the process is also implied by the delay until the prophet says anything publicly. Margaret Odell observes that the initiation process begins in the fifth year of the exile (1.2), yet 'Ezekiel does not receive instructions to prophesy until ch. 6, and he does not have an audience until ch. 8',[13] which is dated in the sixth year of the exile (8.1).

For Odell, this is one way that Ezek. 1.1–3.24 shows that it is about an initiation process, a rite of passage in which Ezekiel transitions from his role as priest to the role of special messenger of YHWH to the Judahites exiled in Babylonia.[14] The theophanic vision of Ezekiel 1 ushers the prophet into a liminal state in which this initiation rite can occur.

12. Cf., for instance, Allen, *Ezekiel 20–48*, p. 184; Walther Zimmerli, *Ezekiel: A Commentary on the Book of the Prophet of Ezekiel, Chapters 25–48* (trans. James D. Martin; Hermeneia 2; Philadelphia: Fortress Press, 1983), p. 256.

13. Margaret S. Odell, *Ezekiel* (Smith & Helwys Bible Commentary; Macon: Smith & Helwys, 2005), p. 41.

14. Odell draws on the basic ideas of Arnold van Gennep (esp. *The Rites of Passage* [trans. Monika B. Vizedom and Gabrielle L. Caffee; Chicago: University of Chicago Press, 1960]) and Victor Turner (esp. *The Ritual Process: Structure and Anti-Structure* [New Brunswick: Aldine Transaction, 1969]) in her argument. Odell

After the initial vision, the hand of YHWH takes Ezekiel to a place of silent waiting (Ezek. 3.16), equivalent to the liminal period that frequently characterizes such rites of passage.[15] Then, the hand of YHWH transports him to the valley, where his tongue is bound[16] prior to him performing symbolic depictions of his message about Jerusalem's siege, famine, and destruction to come (3.25–5.17). These acts herald the crucial role the body plays in the book. In what follows, the embodied imagery persists; for instance, the prophet spends time lying on both his sides, shaves off his hair, and symbolizes the remnant that will survive Jerusalem's destruction by hiding some of that hair in his robe.[17] The initiation process ends with him uniquely prepared to carry out his task of mediating the divine word to the people (6.1–7.27). This ritualized process transforms Ezekiel's social role from merely priest dislocated from the temple to divinely appointed messenger to the exiles.[18]

When Ezek. 37.1 specifies that the hand of YHWH again transports Ezekiel to 'the valley' it constitutes an internal cross-reference that indicates the setting is ripe for ritualized actions. The text uses this self-indexing to alert the audience that the prophet is in a liminal location, a place where transformative actions may occur, an ideal locale for the astonishing events that follow.

b. *Allusions to Ritual Activity Outside Ezekiel*
To appreciate the full significance of the reference to the valley it is necessary to recognize that both Ezek. 1.1–3.27 and 37.1-14 allude to another ritual text: the Mesopotamian ritual for the induction of cult

contends that Ezekiel leaves his priestly identity behind. This is probably incorrect, and surely unnecessary. It is more likely that the initiation process marks Ezekiel out for an additional role; cf. the priestly figures of Samuel (1 Sam. 3) and Jeremiah (Jer. 1), who have a similar experience.

15. Van Gennep, *Rites of Passage*, pp. 65-115, esp. 81 and 114; Turner, *Ritual Process*, pp. 94-130, esp. 129; cf. Jacob Milgrom, *Leviticus 1–16: A New Translation with Introduction and Commentary* (AB 3; New York: Doubleday, 1991), pp. 566-69, on the priestly induction as a rite of passage.

16. On the meaning of this image, see Robert R. Wilson, 'An Interpretation of Ezekiel's Dumbness', *VT* 22 (1972), pp. 91-104.

17. Cf. Lapsley, 'Body Piercings', pp. 236-39.

18. Though it lies beyond the scope of this essay, it is clear that Ezek. 1.1–3.27 contains numerous signals that generate the perception that these activities are both intrinsically different from other acts and privileged in their significance and ramifications (Bell's definition of ritualization). One need look no farther than Ezek. 1, where the theophanic vision immediately connotes that something extraordinary and significant is underway.

statues.[19] This ritual, known as the mouth washing or *mīs pî* ritual, transformed a new or restored cult statue from a lifeless, humanly fashioned object into a vivified, powerful representation of the deity in the earthly realm. 'The ritual', concludes Angelika Berlejung, 'thus enabled [the statue] to become the pure epiphany of its god and to be a fully interacting and communicating partner for the king, the priests and the faithful'.[20] Andreas Schüle condenses the myriad activities into a four-stage process by grouping events that happen in the same locale.[21] His summary highlights that ritualized actions occur in four locations with processions between them that allow the cult statue, ritual personnel, and other necessary items to move among these places. Of greatest significance to the present question, Berlejung observes that the transformation from inert statue to vibrant divine mediator occurs in the steppe (Akkadian *ṣērum*), which is not so much a physical location as a mythical space, a 'free landscape' where all impurities could be removed from the image and left in an area 'where they could harm no one'.[22] The steppe 'represents chaos and the uncreated';[23] it is a prototypical liminal space, thus the ideal location for ritualized actions.

Elsewhere, I have demonstrated that there is a sustained parallel between the *mīs pî* ritual and Ezekiel in which the valley (הבקה) corresponds to the steppe (*ṣērum*).[24] Just as the steppe is a mysterious, barren space, so too is the valley. The undeveloped nature of both spaces is important, and Daniel Block captures its role in Ezekiel, remarking that 'this region was wasteland, an appropriate place for a private meeting with God'.[25] This unrefined character makes these places suitable for

19.   For a more detailed argument that the authors of Ezekiel know this text and allude to it in the book, see C. A. Strine, 'Ezekiel's Image Problem: The Mesopotamian Cult Statue Induction Ritual and the *Imago Dei* Anthropology in the Book of Ezekiel', *CBQ* 76 (2014), pp. 252-72.

20.   Angelika Berlejung, 'Washing the Mouth: The Consecration of Divine Images in Mesopotamia', in Karel van der Toorn (ed.), *The Image and the Book: Iconic Cults, Aniconism, and the Rise of Book Religion in Israel and the Ancient Near East* (CBET 21; Leuven: Peeters, 1997), pp. 45-72 (72).

21.   Andreas Schüle, 'Made in the "Image of God": The Concepts of Divine Images in Gen. 1–3', *ZAW* 117 (2005), pp. 1-20 (12-13).

22.   Berlejung, 'Washing the Mouth', p. 54

23.   Christopher Walker and Michael B. Dick, *The Induction of the Cult Image in Ancient Mesopotamia: The Mesopotamian Mīs Pî Ritual: Transliteration, Translation, and Commentary* (State Archives of Assyria Literary Texts; Helsinki: The Neo-Assyrian Text Corpus Project, 2001), p. 52 n. 36; cf. Berlejung, 'Washing the Mouth', pp. 53-54.

24.   For details, see Strine, 'Ezekiel's Image Problem'.

25.   Block, *Ezekiel*, p. 153; cf. Odell, *Ezekiel*, p. 53.

transforming the humanly crafted cult statue into the pure bodily epiphany of its god and also for initiating Ezekiel in chs. 1–3 into his role as the unique mediator of YHWH's word. James Kennedy apprehended how the Mesopotamian ritual that 'dedicated the sacred image for liturgical use, transforming it from a lifeless statue into a sacred image fit for the dwelling of the spirit of the god whom it represented'[26] paralleled Ezekiel's call narrative. He shows that when YHWH causes the prophet's tongue to cling to the roof of his mouth so that he cannot serve as an intercessor for the people and concurrently declares that the prophet's mouth will be opened (אפתח את פיך, 'I will open your mouth') when there is a divine word for the people, '[t]he startling effect' of YHWH's statement 'is to portray Ezekiel as a kind of living idol'.[27]

Ezekiel 37.1-14 builds further on this link, something that John Kutsko identified in his discussion of the ways that Ezekiel 36–37 adopts and adapts the Mesopotamian practice of refurbishing cult statues. Ezekiel, he shows, employs 'the categories of exile and return of *cult statues*, adopted from his exilic hosts' in order to depict 'the restoration of the *people of Israel*' in Ezek. 37.1-14.[28] Still, Kutsko omits at least one other connection between Ezek. 37.1-14 and the cult statue induction ritual: in a similar fashion to the way that Ezekiel's dry bones connect, receive sinews, and are covered in flesh and skin, the cult images' wooden cores are built and subsequently overlayed with precious metals and fine clothing.[29] At this stage, both the cult statues and Ezekiel's assembled bodies remain lifeless; it is only a further series of ritual actions that vivifies these vessels.[30]

The combined effect of depicting YHWH's hand seizing the prophet and transporting him to the locale where both his initiation rite and also the Mesopotamian cult statue induction ritual occurred is to prepare the audience for a series of ritualized actions. It is necessary to provide a theoretical foundation for interpreting those ritualized actions now.

26. James M. Kennedy, 'Hebrew *pithôn peh* in the Book of Ezekiel', *VT* 41 (1991), pp. 233-35 (233).

27. *Ibid.*, p. 235.

28. John F. Kutsko, *Between Heaven and Earth: Divine Presence and Absence in the Book of Ezekiel* (Biblical and Judaic Studies from the University of California, San Diego; Winona Lake: Eisenbrauns, 2000), p. 147, italics original. Cf. *ibid.*, p. 137.

29. Kutsko recognizes the parallel, but goes no further (*ibid.*); Ezek. 16.17-18 supports the point: personified Jerusalem uses the gold, silver, and fine clothes YHWH has given her to craft and clothe 'male images', צלמי זכר.

30. See Nineveh recension of the *mīs pî* text, lines 160-68; Babylonian recension of the *mīs pî* text, lines 49-52; and Ezek. 37.9-10.

II. *Catherine Bell and Ritualization*

Ritual is a topic that has grown in prominence and generated an enormous secondary literature.[31] Perhaps the most significant treatment of the issue in the last twenty-five years belongs to Catherine Bell, who synthesizes a wide range of philosophical, sociological, and anthropological material to support her paradigm-changing approach to ritual. Bell denies the possibility of reifying ritual—that is to say, she establishes that ritual is not an objective category that functions merely as an interpretive tool. That perspective presupposes a thought–action dichotomy that is no longer a sufficient epistemological position, leads to 'a discourse in which the concerns of [the] theorist take center stage',[32] and falls prey to the false notion that a 'thinking observer' has primacy over a 'non-thinking participant'. Ritual is not 'a natural category of human practice', argues Bell, but an activity, or perhaps more precisely a series of actions and practices, that are differentiated from the mundane. She concludes that one must speak of ritualization not ritual, of a process that 'involves the differentiation and privileging of particular activities'[33] in culturally relevant ways rather than a category with identifiable members.

Bell demonstrates that 'some activities are performed in culturally relevant ways to generate the perception that these activities are both *intrinsically different* from other acts and *privileged in their significance and ramifications*'.[34] To be sure, certain means of differentiation cross cultures, which explains why people may identify an unfamiliar practice as a ritual straight away. Bell enumerates a few of the more common strategies of ritualization, into which I have interspersed some features of Ezek. 37.1-14:

---

31. For a selection of important pieces, see Ronald L. Grimes, *Readings in Ritual Studies* (Upper Saddle River: Prentice–Hall, 1996). Within biblical studies, important work includes Mary Douglas's classic *Purity and Danger* (London: Routledge, 2003), along with her various other writings on Leviticus. Leviticus has remained the epicenter of ritual studies in the Hebrew Bible. J. W. Watts, *Ritual and Rhetoric in Leviticus: From Sacrifice to Scripture* (Cambridge: Cambridge University Press, 2007) and Michael B. Hundley, *Keeping Heaven on Earth: Safeguarding the Divine Presence in the Priestly Tabernacle* (Tübingen: Mohr Siebeck, 2011) are just two examples of the range of ways ritual studies can inform biblical interpretation and historical reconstruction.

32. Catherine Bell, *Ritual Theory, Ritual Practice* (Oxford: Oxford University Press), p. 54.

33. *Ibid.*, p. 204.

34. *Ibid.*, p. 219. Emphasis added.

...delineated and structured space to which access is restricted [e.g., 'the valley']; a special periodicity for the occurrence...; restricted codes of communication to heighten the formality of movement and speech [e.g., a conversation between YHWH and Ezekiel]; distinct and specialized personnel [perhaps Ezekiel's priestly and prophetic roles fit here]; objects, texts, and dress designated for use in these activities alone; verbal and gestural combinations that evoke or purport to be the way things have always been done [perhaps YHWH placing the רוח[35] in the bodies; cf. Gen. 2]; preparations that demand particular physical or mental states [e.g., the hand of YHWH grasping the prophet]; and the involvement of a particular constituency not necessarily assembled for any other activities [e.g., dry bones representing all Israel].[36]

More must be said about these aspects of Ezekiel 37, and shall be in due course, but the main point is evident: some of the most common strategies Bell identifies are discernible in Ezek. 37.1-14, so that it is reasonable to conclude that the text is describing a series of strategic actions that intend to demarcate its contents as both intrinsically different and privileged in their ramifications. Ezekiel 37.1-14 depicts ritualized activity.

Bell explains as well that ritualized actions create the so-called categories that scholars from Émile Durkheim to Claude Lévi-Strauss to Jonathan Z. Smith have asserted are the core of ritual.[37] Perhaps the paradigmatic example of these binary opposite categories is Durkheim's distinction between the sacred and the profane. Durkheim defined religion and ritual as that which is addressed to the sacred; however, Bell demonstrates that it is the strategic deployment of embodied actions that demarcate a time, place, or thing as intrinsically different, or sacred. Ritualized actions—kneeling in front of a totem after a highly structured bathing process, for instance—communicate without words to both participants and observers that they are in the presence of something sacred.[38] Bell inverts Durkheim's scheme and goes beyond it at the same time: '[t]hrough a series of physical movements ritual practices spatially and temporally construct an environment organized according to schemes of privileged opposition'.[39]

35. On the various uses and meanings of this term, see James Robson, *Word and Spirit in Ezekiel* (LHBOTS 477; London: T&T Clark International, 2006), pp. 79-94.
36. *Ibid.*, pp. 204-5.
37. *Ibid.*, p. 102.
38. *Ibid.*, pp. 88-93, esp. 91.
39. *Ibid.*, p. 98

Where does a person learn that certain actions create these distinctions? How does one grasp this abstruse concept that ritualization is capable of producing these hierarchical contrasts? Here Bell draws heavily on the work of Pierre Bourdieu.[40] She speaks of 'ritual mastery', of bodies that gain a cultural 'sense of ritual',[41] and of the ability of any 'moderately socialized person'[42] to deploy culturally relevant strategies to ritualize an activity. She argues that when a socialized body moves in space and time to create these oppositions it is simultaneously impressing and imprinting these schemes upon the bodies of other participants.[43] As a person participates in ritualized activities—a necessity in the socialization process—they internalize the principles and acquire a sense of how to reproduce similar schemes in other settings. Bell terms this ritual mastery, a 'practical mastery of the schemes of ritualization as an embodied knowing, as the sense of ritual seen in its exercise'.[44] To say it as Bourdieu does, the socialized body learns that 'practice has a logic which is not that of logic'.[45] Ritualization is not the realm of syllogisms and the principle of non-contradiction; it is a realm where there is a logic of kneeling, a practice that not only expresses the concept of subordination by symbolizing a higher–lower binary opposition, but one that actually 'produces a subordinated kneeler in and through the act itself'.[46]

The entirely tacit nature of this 'ritual mastery' makes it exceptionally powerful. The socialized body recognizes that a 'ritual' engages its cognitive faculties and provides a culturally relevant way to respond to a situation or problem; yet, it fails to see that 'ritual' simultaneously engages a visceral, affective level of comprehension that allows ritualized activities to 'reorder and reinterpret the circumstances so as to afford the sense of a fit among the main spheres of experience—body, community, and cosmos'.[47] It is the capacity of ritualization to engage a

---

40. In doing so, Bell is open to many if not all of the same critiques that have been advanced against Bourdieu. For a succinct summary of Bourdieu's model and a trenchant critique of it, see Richard Jenkins, *Pierre Bourdieu* (rev. ed.; Key Sociologists; London: Routledge, 2002).

41. Bell, *Ritual Theory*, p. 107.

42. *Ibid.*, p. 206.

43. Elsewhere Bell argues that the goal of ritualization is the 'production of a "ritualized body"…a body invested with a "sense" of ritual' (*ibid.*, p. 98).

44. *Ibid.*, p. 107.

45. Pierre Bourdieu, *Outline of a Theory of Practice* (trans Richard Nice; Cambridge Studies in Social Anthropology 16; Cambridge: Cambridge University Press, 1977), p. 109.

46. Bell, *Ritual Theory*, p. 100.

47. *Ibid.*, p. 109.

person in this way that makes it such an effective means of going beyond conscious reason, which Fox recognized was necessary to persuade the audience of the radical message of Ezek. 37.1-14.

'At best, ritualization can be described only as "a way of acting" that makes distinctions...by means of culturally and situationally relevant categories and nuances',[48] remarks Bell. The book of Ezekiel takes its eponymous figure, a Zadokite priest with a better than average proficiency in ritualization, and heightens his ritual mastery through his unique encounters with YHWH. The prophet becomes a supra-socialized body with a 'sense' of ritualization in both the human and divine realm.[49] When Ezekiel moves in a peculiar way through the valley in Ezek. 37.1-14 it is clear that something extraordinary is happening.

III. *The Ritualized Body Environment in Ezekiel 37*

With the enhanced perspective of Bell's model, it is possible to examine how Ezekiel 37 deploys the socialized bodies of YHWH, Ezekiel, and the assembled dry bones in order to create a series of related hierarchical oppositions that define and interpret the circumstances of the Babylonian exile in a way that supports a durable nationalism. I will highlight four strategies.

The oracle begins with YHWH's hand seizing the prophet to transport him out into 'the valley' (הבקה). This location, as suggested above, not only signals that ritualized actions are appropriate, but also connotes distance from the urban center and lack of development. It represents chaos and the uncreated. This is the first strategy, specifically, to create a contrast between urban and remote, between carefully structured space and disorder, by supernaturally transporting the prophet there. The valley is not reached by normal means; perhaps it cannot be accessed conventionally. Regardless, this centrifugal movement conveys an asymmetric relationship between urban and remote, where order evokes the dominant group and disorder conjures up the subordinate community.[50] Left unsaid in v. 1, this dichotomy receives voice in the lament of v. 11.

---

48. *Ibid.*, p. 205.

49. For instance, the account of YHWH's destruction of Jerusalem through a coterie of divine figures in Ezek. 8–11 is ritualized. Through participating in that ritualized event, Ezekiel learns what actions are culturally relevant in the divine realm for ritualizing an event. Ezekiel gains a 'ritual mastery' that surpasses just this world.

50. On the ways in which the binary opposites created in ritualization gain relations to others, see Bell, *Ritual Theory*, pp. 101-7.

Ezekiel immediately recognizes that the valley is full of bones (v. 1b), so when YHWH causes the prophet to go around them ('round and round', סביב סביב) in v. 2 this cannot be just about observing that the bones are there. By circumambulating the bones, Ezekiel's body effects another privileged opposition: his promenade creates an inside–outside contrast. Recall how Bell explained that kneeling does not only communicate subordination, it produces a subordinated kneeler. *Mutatis mutandis*, Ezekiel circumambulating the bones not only communicates that there is an inside–outside distinction, it literally produces the two groups. His movement constructs an Us–Them distinction in the environment and inscribes it onto the dissembled bodies lying in the valley. It is not those fictional bodies alone, but also the audience, represented by the bones, that apprehends this concept. The narrative activates the imperceptible ritual mastery of the socialized bodies in the audience. In doing so, the text asserts that the notion of ethnic differentiation is not merely the prophet's or author's preference; the Us–Them contrast is a divinely fixed feature of the cosmos.

These two strategies combat Ezekiel's chief conceptual opponent, namely, the temptation to view the exile as a relatively liveable context in which the people may come to regard ethnic differentiation as unnecessary, even cumbersome. As Ezekiel's bodily movements ritualize the space, they engage the visceral logic of the audience and, therefore, go beyond the potential power of words or rational arguments. The description engages the audience's sense of ritual, the non-conscious practical logic of the socialized bodies that hear this narrative, to persuade them that the insider–outsider distinction between Israel and the Babylonians is essential, not merely a temporary or inconsequential notion that can be disregarded when no longer convenient.

Fox, though focused on verbal and rhetorical features, underscores the centrality of bodily movement in the text by his inability to explain its meaning without reference to performance. '[Ezekiel's] part in the event is similar to that of a spectator invited up from the audience to "help" a stage magician by waving a wand over the magician's hat',[51] he writes. Fox cannot elucidate the text without reference to a set of familiar actions that have a similar communicative power. Indeed, at one point he describes vv. 1-10 as a 'dramatic movement'. Fox underscores that the prophet's bodily movements structure the text and convey its message, albeit unwittingly.

---

51.   Fox, 'The Rhetoric of Ezekiel's Vision of the Valley of the Bones', p. 9.

Locating YHWH in the valley with the prophet is another way that the passage employs the hierarchical relationships that the prophet's body generates. Just as YHWH meets Ezekiel, himself an exile, in the valley in Ezekiel 3, the presence of the deity in the valley filled with dry bones indicates a willingness to align with the subaltern rather than the dominant (cf. Ezek. 11.14-16).

This passage tells its audience that YHWH chooses the valley, the place of disorder, and the marginalized community represented by its lifeless inhabitants. To affiliate with the prophet and people in this way, to reverse the typical nexus between the deity and the dominant, powerful, ruling class adumbrates the other inversions that Ezek. 37.1-14 describes.

To summarize these first two strategies, the relocation of the prophet to the valley along with his walk around the bones tacitly communicates that there is an inside–outside distinction in the cosmos; the world contains two groups of people, Us and Them. Establishing this distinction is imperative for the attempt to persuade the exiles not to assimilate into Babylonian culture. The exiles must first be convinced that the loss of Israelite identity is problematic. 'To bring about such a conviction', observes Fox, 'the rhetor obviously must go deeper than conscious reason'. Ezekiel's ritualized actions are well suited to this task because they engage the non-conscious, practical logic that all socialized people possess. Whether they recognize it or not, the passage 37.1-2 portrays a ritualized body structuring its environment, engaging its audience's practical logic, grasping them at a visceral level.

A third strategy appears in the conversation between YHWH and Ezekiel (vv. 3-9), where YHWH asks 'Can these bones live?'. This question makes explicit and underscores the already implied opposition between dead and living. When the prophet specifies that the bones are very dry (v. 2bβ), this familiar metaphor, used elsewhere in Ezekiel (cf. 17.1-10, 22-24) and in the Hebrew Bible (Prov. 17.22),[52] presents the situation as dire. Simultaneously, the statement contrasts the dry, scattered bones with the living, moving prophet.

YHWH again subverts the typical asymmetric power relationship by identifying with the dead, lifeless, powerless, and marginalized group: the dry bones. The third strategy combines with the first two to create this perception: YHWH comes, with the prophet, to a remote place and aligns with the lifeless group demarcated by the prophet's walk around them. It is noteworthy that YHWH does not propose abandoning the dry bones to identify only with the living prophet (cf. YHWH's statement of

---

52. See Greenberg, *Ezekiel 21–37*, p. 745, for more on this metaphor.

intention to do so with Moses in Exod. 32 and Num. 14),[53] nor disavow-
ing a relationship with the dry bones in favor of the living, dominant
Babylonians (as might be feared from the way YHWH utilizes the king of
Babylon in Ezek. 17). No, YHWH transforms the typical asymmetric
inside–outside relationship by vivifying the dry bones.

Here, it is necessary to recognize the way in which the two-stage
nature of this life-giving process is culturally relevant. The progression
from scattered, dry bones to skeletons, with a subsequent introduction of
breath, may derive from the Mesopotamian cult statue induction ritual.
Recall that Ezekiel 37 locates these events in 'the valley', an analogous
locale to the steppe (*ṣērum*) where the cult statue goes to be vivified as
well, and narrates a very similar two-stage vivification process.[54] Even if
that is not the source of this idea, the two-stage creation of humanity in
Gen. 2.7 indicates that this process represents an Israelite belief about the
origins of human life, as if containers are made, and then life is breathed
into them.[55] In this respect, it is notable that Bell regards a common
strategy of ritualization to be 'verbal and gestural combinations that
evoke or purport to be the way things have always been done'.[56] Perhaps
YHWH putting breath into the assembled but lifeless bodies is a ritualized
action too.

The final embodied strategy of differentiation concludes the first
section of the passage, stating that the vivified multitude stand on their
feet (v. 10b). Now the reconstituted bodies create oppositions with their
movements. When the newly vivified bodies stand it distinguishes that
posture from lying on the ground, the transition the dry bones undergo
from the beginning of the passage (v. 2, they are 'on the surface of the
valley', על פני הבקה) to the end (v. 10, 'they stood on their feet', ויעמדו
על רגליהם). It goes almost without saying that the standing–lying contrast
triggers a larger taxonomy of up-down and high–low oppositions where
up/high are the dominant, powerful constituents. In fact, one of the most

---

53. On the similarities between Moses and Ezekiel, which suggest this potential
course of action, see Henry McKeating, 'Ezekiel the "Prophet Like Moses"', *JSOT*
61 (1994), pp. 97-109.

54. See above, section I.b.

55. Commentators frequently draw a connection between Ezek. 37.9-10 and
Gen. 2.7. Though there is a similarity between the two passages, there are substantial
differences that militate against seeing either one as dependent on the other (e.g.,
Ezek. 37 uses רוח, 'spirit', and Gen. 2 uses נשמת חיים, 'breath of life'). Perhaps the
two passages independently draw on an ancient Near Eastern tradition that deities
vivify inanimate things in this way.

56. Bell, *Ritual Theory*, p. 205.

often quoted and most incisive parts of Bourdieu's own discussion about embodied logic is that a whole cosmology is expressed in even the banal injunction: 'Stand up straight!'.[57] This command invokes the non-conscious practical logic, which senses that the erect, outward focused body 'expresses strength and resolution' and is honored and respected by others.[58] Describing the assembled bodies as erect, focused outward, and assured in their posture evokes a whole system of asymmetric contrasts that portrays this once-dead-now-living Israel as no longer weak, powerless, and subordinate, but instead as sturdy, robust, and resilient. No wonder this multitude is called 'a very great army' (חיל גדול מאד מאד; v. 10): they represent a community that will not go quietly into oblivion.

The hierarchical contrast between up and down also segues into the interpretation that follows in 37.11-14, so that YHWH's promise to 'bring up' (עלה) the whole house of Israel from their graves further expresses the transition from the powerless categories of dead and low (even underground) to the empowered categories of living and standing on their own land.[59]

IV. *Why Ritualization in Ezekiel 37?*

To conclude this discussion, it seems appropriate to ask: Why does Ezek. 37.1-14 select bodily movements to ritualize its contents? Or, perhaps more straightforwardly: What does Ezekiel 37 gain from narrating these ritualized actions?

Catherine Bell contends that ritualization 'is a way of acting that sees itself as responding to a place, event, force, problem, or tradition. It tends to see itself as the natural or appropriate thing to do in the circumstances'.[60] Those circumstances are, as noted, the relatively favourable quality of life in the Babylonian exile and the potential benefits of assimilation into the dominant, imperial culture; together these circumstances create a real and present danger that these Judahite Yahwists would

57. Bourdieu, *Outline*, pp. 87-95, esp. 93-95.
58. *Ibid.*, p. 94.
59. The latter is implied in the verb נוח 'set': this verb describes how YHWH sets the prophet down in the valley at the beginning of this passage (v. 1; cf. 40.2). It is an inference that Ezekiel was standing at that point, but one that is supported both by the lack of a command for the prophet to stand afterwards, a comment that does appear when the prophet encounters YHWH and finds himself no longer standing (i.e., 2.1), and also by the contrast between the living prophet who stands and the dead bones that lie on the ground (i.e., 37.1-3).
60. Bell, *Ritual Theory*, p. 109.

dissolve into Babylonian culture and become indistinguishable from this foreign group. Far from irrational, the disappearance of the Israelite northern kingdom and other ancient Near Eastern societies in precisely this fashion proves that this was a legitimate concern.

'Ritualization does not see how it actively creates place, force, event, and tradition', observes Bell, nor 'how it redefines or generates the circumstances to which it is responding'.[61] As highlighted earlier, the text uses the ritualized bodily movements of the prophet to claim that an Us–Them communal distinction is real and foundational to understanding the cosmos. On this foundation, the passage builds its argument that a dry, lifeless subaltern group abandoned to the barren valley should patiently wait for YHWH, who remains aligned with them. Depicting the transformation of the scattered bones from lifeless to living through a series of ritualized actions engages the 'sense of ritual' shared by the audience to convey the radical message that resilient nationalism can result in future restoration at a non-conscious, visceral level. By choosing words rich in imagery and foregrounding the bodily movements of its characters, the text guides its audience to imaginatively experience the ritual. The text exploits this cultural sixth sense of its audience to make its case.[62]

Bell also describes how ritualization 'does not see how its own actions reorder and reinterpret the circumstances so as to afford the sense of fit among the main spheres of experience—body, community, and cosmos'.[63] This is pertinent because it is impossible to say whether the author of Ezek. 37.1-14 deployed these strategies knowingly. Regardless of the debate that might be had about authorial intention, Bell's observation emphasizes that even the people who are ritualizing a situation do so instinctively. It is entirely possible, then, that whoever wrote this passage, whoever selected bodies and bodily motion to guide its imagery, did so because the idea 'just seemed to work'. Bell's model allows for a spectrum of possibilities, including an author that could write this text and yet could not articulate why this imagery seemed so well suited to the aim of persuading the audience to resist assimilation. Ultimately, it is the non-cognitive power of ritualization for those choosing the ritualizing strategy and those engaging with it, that makes ritualized actions so influential.

Expanding on this point, Bell remarks that 'in seeing itself as responding to an environment, ritualization interprets its own schemes as impressed upon the actors from a more authoritative source, usually from

61. *Ibid.*, p. 109.
62. *Ibid.*, p. 116.
63. *Ibid.*, p. 109.

well beyond the immediate human community itself'. Her point illuminates why the text depicts YHWH orchestrating all that happens in Ezek.
37.1-14. YHWH seizes the prophet, brings him to the valley, causes him
to circumambulate the bones (note the Hiphil form of עבר in v. 2: 'he
caused me to pass'); though the prophet pronounces the words that vivify
the bones, he does so under divine guidance, merely giving an occasion
for divine direction of the winds to vivify the bodies. Ezekiel 37.1-14
employs the dynamic of divine authorization in support of its aims just as
Bell predicts.

Finally, Bell explains that ritualized activities provide the correct
course of action 'when the relationships of power being negotiated are
based not on direct claims but on indirect claims of power conferred…
For example, *ritualization is the way to construct power relations when
the power is claimed to be from God*, not from military might or
economic superiority; it is also the way for people to experience *a vision
of a community order that is personally empowering.*'[64] Neither the
author(s) of Ezekiel 37 nor anyone else among the Judahite exiles had
the authority to back up any claim that resilient nationalism and a refusal
to assimilate into Babylonian culture would result in the positive
outcome it predicts. So, Ezekiel employed a strategy that circumvented
that problem by working not with its audience's rational faculties *per se*,
but with its ritual mastery, its embodied sense of how the hierarchical
oppositions in ritualization work. It unabashedly claimed that divine
power made its implausible viewpoint possible in the hope that it might
motivate enough individuals to adopt its perspective and bond together
into a community empowered to preserve their distinct identity.

Whether intentional or not, utilizing bodies and the embodied logic of
ritual in this way is consistent with Ezekiel's radically theocentric perspective and strident Judahite nationalism.[65] One might conclude, based
on the survival of the Yahwistic faith among the Judahite exiles who
returned from Babylon, that this passage successfully employed this
strategy to support its aims.

---

64. *Ibid.*, p. 116. Emphasis added.
65. For more on this, see C. A. Strine, *Sworn Enemies: The Divine Oath, the
Book of Ezekiel, and the Polemics of Exile* (BZAW 436; Berlin: W. de Gruyter,
2013), pp. 228-68.

4

'TWO BY TWO':
THE ARK-ETYPAL LANGUAGE OF MARK'S
APOSTOLIC PAIRINGS

Joan E. Taylor

> And he called to him the Twelve, and began to send them out two by two
> (δύο δύο), and gave them authority over the unclean spirits. (Mk 6.7)

> Of all winged birds according to kind, and of all cattle according to kind,
> and of all reptiles creeping upon the earth according to their kind, two by
> two (δύο δύο) from all [these] will enter towards you, to be fed with you,
> male and female. (Gen. 6.21 [LXX])

Bodies, as defined in biblical texts, have had a long after-life. In particular, sexed bodies within these texts have informed the 'correct'
understanding of sexed bodies over the centuries. Positions of leadership
within religious communities are assigned on the basis of whether a person is male or female, with male bodies being a requirement for various
roles. In the Vatican document, *Inter Insigniores*, issued in 1976 by the
Congregation for the Teaching of the Faith, it states that 'Jesus did not
call any woman to become part of the Twelve',[1] with the underlying
assumption that the Twelve are the primary model for Christian ministry.
Thus, the fact that there were no women among this group means that no
women can become priests. Other aspects of Twelveship (being Jewish,
working within Israel, the job of healing and exorcism, the necessity of
total poverty) are sidelined, while the sexed body is made paradigmatic
for roles that are now very different. As a Quaker, my own tradition is
not one that embraces an ordained ministry, but the relationship between
bodies within biblical texts and our bodies now remains one of critical
concern to me, given the way that some contemporary readings can reify
systems that alienate, marginalize and exclude.

---

1. Leonard Swidler and Arlene Swidler (eds.), *Women Priests: A Catholic
Commentary on the Vatican Declaration* (New York: Paulist Press, 1977), p. 10.

I would like here to reflect on the question of the sexed body both within the category of the Twelve and within apostolic missionizing among the first disciples of Jesus, focusing primarily on the Gospel of Mark, with reference also to what Paul writes in 1 Cor. 9.1-6. I will suggest that historically the Twelve were probably not a band of single men, but a set of Twelve pairs of men and women working together. Read with Pauline attestations of apostolic women, it appears that such pairs did not necessarily always function in accordance with patterns of normative male leadership. In this study, I would like to acknowledge my debt to the work of Elisabeth Schüssler Fiorenza,[2] who has questioned accepted notions of why Jesus chose the Twelve and what they were supposed to do, and also her hermeneutical method.[3]

I. *Witnesses*

In Mk 6.7, when Jesus sends the Twelve out 'two by two' (δύο δύο), it is usually assumed that this indicates a simple pair of male companions, with the assumption that pairs of men were required for witnesses in testimony (Deut. 19.15). After all, in Mk 6.11 the apostles are required to shake off the dust from the soles of their feet in unwelcome villages 'for a testimony to them'.[4] Deuteronomy 19.15 requires 'two or three' witnesses for a legal charge against someone (as in Mt. 18.15). The double confirmation indeed becomes a trope for credibility in Jn 8.13-14, where Jesus claims it is not only he who bears witness of himself but also the 'the Father who sent me'.

However, a single person can also witness multiple times: Paul states in 2 Cor. 13.1 that the fact that he is arriving for a third time in Corinth indicates a third testimony. Likewise, in Mark, disciples of Jesus will be delivered up to courts and be flogged in the synagogues and stand before governors and kings—a sequence of three actions—'for a testimony to them' (Mk 13.9). Such μάρτυρες, literally 'those who testify/witness',

2. Elisabeth Schüssler Fiorenza, 'The Twelve and the Discipleship of Equals', in *eadem*, *Discipleship of Equals: A Critical Feminist Ekklesia-logy of Liberation* (New York: Crossroad, 1993), pp. 104-16; *eadem*, 'The Twelve', and 'The Apostleship of Women in Early Christianity', in Swidler and Swidler (eds.), *Women Priests*, pp. 114-22 and 135-40.

3. Elisabeth Schüssler Fiorenza, 'Text and Reality—Reality as Text: The Problem of a Feminist Historical and Social Reconstruction Based on Texts', *Studia Theologica* 43 (1989), pp. 19-34.

4. John Donahue and Daniel Harrington, *The Gospel of Mark* (Sacra Pagina; Collegeville: Liturgical Press, 2002), p. 190.

were from the earliest time of the Church, both men and women (Acts 9.2; 22.4). Moreover, the 'testimony' in Mk 6.11 is an act of dust-shaking rather than proclamation of the Kingdom.

Deuteronomy 17.6 requires the witnesses of two or three men before someone can be put to death, as does Num. 35.30, and we see this play-ing out when people give false testimony in Jesus' interrogation (Mk 14.55-60); the key legal point is that there required to be two or three in agreement for a charge deserving death. When Jesus states that he is the Christ, Son of God, the High Priest tears his garment and declares: 'Why do we still need witnesses?' Nevertheless, legitimate evidence in capital trials is a separate matter. Overall in Mark the need for two or three male witnesses is not a *sine qua non* for credible witness: a healed leper is singly sent to a priest 'for a testimony to them' (Mk 1.44). As such, Mark does not assume that male pairs are necessarily needed for credible testimony.

It also needs to be noted that women's testimony or witness was by no means unrecognized in Second Temple Judaism. Josephus states that they could not be legal witnesses in court 'because of the levity and temerity of their sex' (*Ant.* 4.219). However, the same Josephus in *War* 4.81 and 7.399 uses women's reports for his historical evidence. In rabbinic law, the testimony of two or more men is required in certain circumstances in courts of law for a criminal charge to be brought or a certain sentence to be passed, but this does not invalidate all testimony or the credibility of women. For example, in determining whether some-one is alive or dead, or in ascertaining a credible statement of truth or in matters of purity, women were indeed valid witnesses, even if single, in a court.[5] Indeed, in the Gospel of Mark the proclamation of the

---

5. Moshe Mieselman, *Jewish Woman in Jewish Law* (New York: Ktav, 1978), pp. 75-76, and 'the disqualification of women is a technical rule, rather than an expression lack of credibility' (p. 79). Judith Hauptman, *Re-reading the Rabbis: A Woman's Voice* (Boulder: Westview Press, 1998), p. 196, suggests that despite the many affirmations of women's credibility the issue of testifying in criminal or civic cases was not allowed because they were, when married, 'beholden to their husbands and likely to be influenced by them in how they reported what they saw', since a woman's 'subordinate status was likely to compromise her ability to tell the truth' (p. 197). However, 'women as women were reliable'. Hauptman cites *m. Yeb.* 15.1-3, the case of a woman testifying about her marital status, debated by the Houses of Hillel and Shammai in the first century BCE (pp. 198-99). In *m. Yeb.* 16.7 there is 'a halakhic history of the rule of allowing one witness to establish the fact of a man's death and, moreover, allowing that one witness to be a woman', which reaches a consensus agreement that a woman could remarry on the basis of one testimony— including that of a woman—but the passage also preserves objection to this, *against*

Kingdom is not a testimony in a criminal or civil court, and women's witness was therefore valid. The requirement that the Twelve were historically male because they needed to be valid legal witnesses is then not correct.

II. *Two by Two*

It has long been noticed that the reference to Jesus sending out his Twelve 'two by two' (δύο δύο), in Mk 6.7, uses an expression found distinctively and repeatedly in Gen. 6.20, 21; 7.2, 3, 9, 15 (LXX) for the pairing of male and female animals going into Noah's ark.[6] In Genesis the pairing is clearly about sexed bodies, male and female bodies furnishing the physical requirements for procreation.

The normal Greek expressions for being 'in pairs' is εἰς δύο or ἀνα δύο, and 'two together' is σὺν δύο.[7] Perhaps it is for this reason that Matthew drops the expression from his version of the sending out of the Twelve, and instead links the named male apostles, fittingly in pairs, with the conjunction καὶ (Mt. 10.2-4),[8] while Luke uses the proper expression ἀνα δύο, with an additional δύο, following Mark, and transports pairing to a wider group of seventy (or seventy-two) apostles sent out ahead of Jesus (Lk. 10.1).

> After this the Lord appointed seventy [or: seventy-two] others, and sent them on ahead of him, two by two (ἀνα δύο δύο) into every city and place where he himself was about to go.

Mark's language is often considered a Semitism. So, for example, Zerwick and Grosvenor's *Grammatical Analysis of the Greek New Testament* comments on Mk 6.7: 'δύο δύο repetition, a colloquial form

the idea that one witness is all that is needed (Rabbi Eliezer and Rabbi Joshua) or that this one witness could be a woman (Rabbi Akiba), and often the final objection, by Akiba (in the second century CE), is quoted as the only standard practice.

6. See, for example, Eugene Boring, *Mark: A Commentary* (Louisville: Westminster John Knox Press, 2006), p. 174: 'this probably indicated that his representatives were not solitary individualists but represented a community, and it was in accord with the biblical precept that the testimony of one witness is inadequate', and also Richard T. France, *The Gospel of Mark* (The New International Greek Testament Commentary; Grand Rapids: Eerdmans, 2002), p. 247: '[t]he practice of sending them out in pairs…is a sensible policy, providing mutual support and companionship'.

7. See LSJ 453.

8. The pairs are: (i) Simon and Andrew; (ii) James and John; (iii) Philip and Bartholomew; (iv) Thomas and Matthew; (v) James son of Alphaeus and Thaddaeus/Lebbaeus; (vi) Simon the Cananaean and Judas Iscariot.

of distributive, *two by two*',[9] while the expression in Lk. 10.1, ἀνα δύο δύο, if correct, 'is a mixture of Gk ἀνα δύο, *in twos* and Hebr. δύο δύο, *two by two* (Gen. 6.19)'.[10]

The implication of there being two sexes of the body indicated in Genesis is passed over rather lightly in this analysis. In fact, the 'Semitism' is quite specific. In Hebrew the duplication שנים שנים, 'two [and] two', is not actually an expression found generally or emphatically. The normal Hebrew word for 'pairs' is זוגות.[11] The term שנים שנים, has a technical usage, in referring to male–female mates. This is clearly seen in the Damascus Document (CD 5.1), where Gen. 7.9, 'two by two they came into the ark', is used to draw a definitive conclusion that bigamy is not permitted: one husband and one wife is a divine law.[12] Marriage is conceptualized as being for conception: male and female bodies are necessary.

In the Hebrew text of the Flood narrative the duplication of the word for 'two', שנים, is actually found less often than in the Greek translation of the Septuagint (LXX). It occurs three times, in Gen. 6.19, 20, 7.2, in Hebrew, whereas in the Greek text of Gen. 6.19-20 MT = Gen. 6.20-21 (LXX: 𝕲) it is duplicated, and found twice further on in 7.9, 15, where its use seems to indicate a continuing sequence of pairings. Thus in the LXX there are double the number of uses of the expression 'two by two' than in the Hebrew, a usage six times in a short passage, stamping δύο δύο as a resoundingly distinctive term for male and female bodies.

If we seek for further Semitisms, the Syriac might normally help, but indeed the Peshitta version of Mk 6.7 does not give us a normal expression for 'in pairs' and uses the distinctive language of male–female pairings of the Flood narrative, though the *Compendius Syriac Dictionary* by Payne Smith translates *tryn tryn* as 'two each'.[13]

9.   Max Zerwick and Mary Grosvenor, *A Grammatical Analysis of the Greek New Testament* (3rd rev. ed.; Rome: Editrice Pontificio Istituto Biblico, 1988), p. 121.

10.   *Ibid.*, 217. With the strong weight of normal Greek expression to guide copyists, it is no wonder that the second δύο is omitted in A, C, D, L. W, Ξ, Ψ, 0181, *f*1, M.

11.   This was also a formal name for the 'pairs' of scholars heading the court as described in *m. Abot* 1.2, 4 *et al.*; see Marcus Jastrow, *Dictionary of the Targumim, the Talmud Babli, and Yerushalmi, and the Midrashic Literature* (New York: Title, 1943), p. 383.

12.   Timothy Lim, 'A New Solution to the Exegetical Crux (CD IV 20-21)', *RQ* 102.26 (2013), pp. 275-84.

13.   Robert Payne Smith, *A Syriac English Dictionary* (Oxford: Clarendon Press, 1903), p. 620.

The duplication of שנים does occur in Hebrew as a kind of short-hand in 1 Chronicles in relation to a distribution of Levites at gates within the Temple complex. It does not refer to going anywhere in pairs, but refers to numbers of guards in relation to numbers of gates; thus, while at 'the Parbar on the west four at the highway and two at the Parbar' (1 Chron. 26.17), on the east 'six Levites', on the north and south 'four daily' (1 Chron. 26.16), and at the 'storehouse' there were positioned 'two two'. This note-like list in this case indicates a spatial arrangement of two guards by two different entrances to the storehouse. Therefore, the LXX—rather than rendering the Hebrew as δύο δύο—ensures that the specific entrances are clarified and named as the 'Esephim', thus καὶ Εσεφὶμ δύο.

Danker's third edition of Bauer's *Lexicon*, BDAG, is, therefore, slightly less convinced of the attribution of a simple Semitism in the expression δύο δύο in Mk 6.7. In Greek it can occur for particular emphasis, perhaps best rendered with italics as 'two, *two*' (Aeschylus, *Pers.* 981) and it turns up like this in a third-century magical papyri (POxy 886, 19) as κατὰ δύο δύο, 'at a time two, *two*',[14] but such rare examples of intensification in Greek texts actually only serve to throw into sharper focus how odd the expression is in Mark, since in Mk 6.7 (and Lk. 10.1) intensification is simply not what is needed.

It is assumed that as there were pairings of the Twelve (Peter and Andrew, James and John and so on),[15] there were other apostolic male pairs, though the pairings could change (Peter and John, Acts 3.1-11; 8.14-25; Paul and Barnabas, Acts 9.27; 13.42–15.12; Paul and Silas, Acts 15.40; Timothy and Erastus, Acts 19.22).[16] Pairs of disciples do turn up at other places: John the Baptist sends two disciples to Jesus (Mt. 11.2); two disciples are walking to Emmaus (Lk. 24.13). However, these are not referred to as going out 'two by two', and pairings are by no means uninterrupted in the narrative of Acts: the deacon Philip appears to act singularly (Acts 8.4-8, 26-40) and Peter seems to be on his own in Joppa and Caesarea (Acts 10.1–11.18); Barnabas apparently goes to Antioch and Tarsus alone (Acts 11.19-26), and when the apostles Barnabas and Paul split up, they work as apostles with male assistants (ὑπηρέται, Acts 13.5): John Mark with Barnabas and Silas with Paul (Acts 15.40–17.15; cf. Titus and 'the brother' in 2 Cor. 12.18).

14. BGAD, p. 264.
15. Eugene Boring notes that the fact that Jesus calls his first disciples in pairs already anticipates them being sent out two by two; Boring, *Mark*, p. 59. But this only works for the two sets of brothers.
16. *Ibid.*, p. 175.

There is a simple, but admittedly radical, solution to this linguistic feature in Mark: if this reflects historical actuality, then Jesus sent out the Twelve as pairs of male and female disciples, and Mark has recorded only the male as the defining person within the category of Twelveship. Male and female pairing is something that may very rapidly have been fudged as awkward by the Church, especially one post-64 CE hoping to minimize its counter-cultural image under threat of persecution. Nevertheless, it may explain certain intractable issues in New Testament interpretation, if we approach the texts with a careful hermeneutics of suspicion, and probe beyond the androcentric texts to the historical situation of the Twelve.[17]

III. *The Twelve and the Women on the Road with Jesus*

The reference to the Twelve being sent out 'two by two' in Mark appears without any explicit indication that there were any women in Jesus' party at all. Yet this picture changes at the end of the story, where women appear suddenly at a critical moment:

> And there were also some women watching from a distance. Among them were Mary the Magdalene, Mary the mother of James the small and Joset, and Salome—when he was in Galilee, these women followed him and served him[18]—and many others who had come up to Jerusalem with him. (Mk 15.40-41)

This is a surprising inclusion of women, just at the moment when readers are distracted by other things, and we need to push the image of women following and serving back to the scenario of Galilee in order to situate the sending out of the Twelve within the whole picture Mark actually draws.[19] Women who serve are present in the story. Mark has already set

---

17. Along with most modern scholars on the historical Jesus, I accept that the 'Twelve' were a historical group, though John Crossan has doubted their historical existence; see *The Historical Jesus: The Life of a Mediterranean Jewish Peasant* (New York: HarperOne, 1991), pp. 72-90, 338-41. Crossan has a precedent in an older generation of biblical scholars, following Julius Wellhausen, *Einleitung in den drei ersten Evangelien* (Berlin: Georg Reimer, 1911), pp. 138-47 and Rudolf Bultmann, *Theology of the New Testament*, I (trans. Kendrick Grobel; London: SCM Press, 1952), p. 37. Nevertheless, the Twelve are attested in many diverse traditions, and this multiple attestation, along with the later instability of their naming (see below), suggests an ancient historical core.

18. Note the singular 'him' here.

19. For a careful analysis of this and the other corresponding passages about the role of women in Jesus' group, see Carla Ricci, *Mary Magdalene and Many Others: Women Who Followed Jesus* (Minneapolis: Fortress Press, 1994).

a serving paradigm right at the very start, with Simon's mother-in-law: after she is cured by Jesus, 'she served them' (Mk 1.31), as the angels had just 'served' Jesus in the wilderness (Mk 1.13). Thus, a woman takes on the role defined by angels, which would make someone 'first' in the Kingdom of God (Mk 9.35): '[i]f anyone wishes to be first let them be last of all and server (διάκονος) of all.' Women disciples are included as Jesus' true 'mother and sisters' when they do the will of God (Mk 3.31-35), but they are consistently veiled in the Marcan narrative in Galilee.

When it comes to the Twelve, the picture Mark presents as he tells the story is highly masculine, despite the curious expression δύο δύο; yet, viewed along with Mk 15.40-41, it appears that the Twelve go out 'two by two' from a mixed-sex body of disciples: a group who followed Jesus on the road from village to village.

If it is only men that go out, leaving Jesus behind, then Mark seems in danger of presenting an image of Jesus remaining on the road with a rather large group of women who are only concerned with serving him. But the verb 'serve', διακονέω, is always going to be a clanging one within the New Testament. If the women's service indicated only one of traditional women's work, one would have to wonder how much laundering and meal-preparation Jesus himself required in transit. Surely it would be better to read this as indicating that the women somehow did Jesus' bidding.

Interestingly Mark avoids explicitly stating that the Twelve 'serve', but rather indicates that they are advised to so, in imitating Jesus: '[f]or the son of humanity came not to be served but to serve' (Mk 10.45). The women, in serving the server, are then configured as being engaged in the replication of Jesus' service back to him, in some way that is undefined. They are the model that the Twelve are supposed to follow.

The Twelve are equated with 'apostles', though Mark in fact only uses this term of the Twelve once (6.30), leaving Twelveship and apostleship as a slightly loose association. There may be more apostles but there is one set of the Twelve.[20]

Pairing of males is suggested initially, in that there are callings to two pairs of brothers to come and follow, Simon and Andrew, James and John (Mk 1.16-20), and yet this pairing breaks down with the single call of Levi (2.14). We then have the passage describing the appointment of the Twelve:

20. Boring, *Mark*, p. 170 notes how in Mark they are usually just 'the Twelve', even when they are described as apostles. They are never 'the Twelve apostles' (contrast Mt. 10.2; Lk. 6.13; 9.10-12; Rev. 21.14), or 'the Twelve disciples' (contrast Mt. 10.1; 11.1; 20.17).

> And he went up to the mountain and called together those whom he himself wanted, and they came to him. And he made Twelve,[21] that they might be with him, and that he might send them out to proclaim [the Kingdom of God] and to have authority to cast out the demons: namely Simon, to whom he gave the name 'Rock' (=*Petros*), and James son of Zebedee and John the brother of James—and to them he gave the name Boanerges, which is 'the sons of thunder'—and Andrew, and Philip, and Bartholomew, and Matthew, and Thomas, and James the son of Alphaeus, and Thaddaeus, and Simon the Cananaean, and Judas Iscariot, the one who betrayed him. (Mk 3.13-19)

Two things are interesting here in this list: first, that the initial firm pair of brothers Simon and Andrew are separated; James and John appear sandwiched between them (Matthew puts them together again: Mt. 10.2), and, secondly, that Levi—having been called as a disciple to follow Jesus—does not appear as one of the Twelve. Following Jesus as a disciple—even with a call—and Twelveship are therefore differentiated. 'Thaddaeus' is an unstable name in the synoptic lists of the Twelve. In the Bezae (D) version and Old Italian of Mk 3.18 and Mt. 10.3 there is 'Lebbaeus', a form of the name 'Levi'.[22] Luke replaces the name with 'Judas the son of James', and situates him in between Simon Zelotes and Judas Iscariot (Lk. 6.15-16). In the Gospel of John this instability of naming is even more apparent: there is mention of 'the Twelve' (6.67-71; 20.24), but it is not clear which named disciples are included, apart from those specifically mentioned as being so, namely Simon Peter (1.40-44; 6.8, 68; 12.21; 21.2, 11, 15-19), Judas son of Simon, Iscariot (6.71; 12.4; 13.2, 26) and Thomas/Didymus (11.16; 20.24-29; 21.2), though there is mention of disciples as including the sons of Zebedee (21.2); Andrew (1.35-42; 6.8-9; 12.20-22), Philip (1.43-48; 6.5, 7; 12.21) and Judas (not Iscariot, 14.22). However, there is also mention of a Nathaniel (1.45-49; 21.2) and an unnamed disciple Jesus loved (13.23; 19.26; 20.2; 21.7, 20), but they are not defined as necessarily being among the Twelve. If Nathaniel is equated with Bartholomew and the disciple whom Jesus loved with John, we still have only nine men mentioned, and Mary Magdalene is a more important character than most of them (Jn 19.25-26; 20.1-2, 11-18).

In regard to their roles in Mark, the requirement for the Twelve 'that they might be with him' is curious when it is not exclusively men who are with Jesus, since Mk 15.40-41 indicates that there are women who

---

21. Some manuscripts add: 'whom he named "apostles"'.
22. 'Lebbaeus called Thaddaeus' in a variety of manuscripts including the Syriac Peshitta.

are with Jesus, serving him. The Twelve are more significant than others who have been called as followers (like Levi) and disciples, such as the blind beggar who addresses Jesus as 'Rabbouni', 'my teacher', and follows Jesus along the way (Mk 10.46-52; cf. 8.34).[23] But a simple equation in Mark between the Twelve and disciples in general, though sometimes suggested, is simply wrong.[24] The general disciples/followers and the Twelve remain distinct; and the named women of Mk 15.40-41 are also distinct, since Jesus' followers are not otherwise defined as serving him.

The Twelve are differentiated also by special renunciation. When Peter states, 'Look, we have left everything and followed you', Jesus replies, 'Amen I say to you, there is no one who has left households or brothers or sisters or mother or father or children or farms for my sake and for the good news...' who will not receive replacements 'in this time' (Mk 10.28-30). Jesus appears to indicate actual replacements; brothers and sisters are those within the community of disciples (Mk 3.3-35), the household of this community is what is established and the farm is probably the propagation of the good news, in just the same way as 'fishing' is conceptualized as hauling people into the community (Mk 1.17).[25] However, 'wives' or 'husbands' are not mentioned as being left in the Marcan list. It is in Luke that there is an alteration of the saying to masculinize those addressed: the specific reference to sisters is dropped and a reference to 'wives' is added (Lk. 22.29-30).[26] Instead, Mark asserts strongly the wrongness of any separation of husbands and wives (Mk 10.2-12):

> And Pharisees came up and asked him, 'Is it acceptable for a man ($\dot{\alpha}\nu\delta\rho\grave{\iota}$) to release his wife?' He answered and said to them, 'What did Moses command you?' They said, 'Moses permitted [that] he write a certificate of divorce and release [her]'. Jesus said to them, 'He wrote this commandment for you because of your hard-heartedness ($\sigma\kappa\lambda\eta\rho\kappa\alpha\rho\delta\acute{\iota}\alpha\nu$), but at the beginning of creation, "He made them male and female", and "for this reason a man ($\ddot{\alpha}\nu\theta\rho\omega\pi\circ\varsigma$) will leave his father and mother and

23. A rich young man cannot dispense with his wealth, and does not follow, despite being invited (Mk 10.17-22).

24. Esther de Boer, *The Gospel of Mary: Beyond a Gnostic and a Biblical Mary Magdalene* (London: T&T Clark International, 2004), p. 108.

25. France, *Mark*, pp. 406-9 also notes that Peter has not entirely left his family, and his home in Capernaum was used as a base.

26. 'There is no man who has left house or wife or brothers or parents or children for the sake of the Kingdom of God who will not receive much more in this time and in the age of come eternal life'.

be stuck (προσκολληθήσεται) to his woman[27] and the two will become one flesh". So they are no longer two but one flesh. What God has yoked together (συνέζευξεν) a man (ἄνθρωπος) must not then detach (χωριζέτω).'

In this teaching the word used for 'man' is ἄνθρωπος, translating Hebrew/Aramaic אדם, *'adam*, which is either a male human being or a human being generically; the former sense is used since only a man had the right to write the divorce document under Mosaic law (Deut. 24.1-4). The issue is that this right is actually an allowance for hard-heartedness (σκληροκαρδία), the opposite of compassion, which should be the principle that governs law. This is then explained by Mark: '[i]f a man divorces his woman and marries another he commits adultery against her, and if she divorces her man and marries another, she commits adultery' (Mk 10.11-12).[28] Since in Jewish law a woman could not technically divorce her husband, it is often thought the reference to a woman divorcing her 'man' is designed for Mark's Roman readers,[29] but this also serves the equalize the two sexes. The very strong focus on the body here is striking. They are one male body and one female body, and yet paradoxically they combine to create a single 'flesh' in which οὐκέτι εἰσὶν δύο, 'they are no longer two', but a two-in-one unit. This is not sexual language; the word προσκολληθήσεται is literally 'be glued on' (πρός + κολλάω) and is the opposite of a man being stuck with his father and mother; God has 'yoked together', συνέζευξεν, in a collaboration.

As is often noted, this refers to a pre-Fall scenario of marriage (Gen. 1.27; 2.24),[30] not requiring female subordination (3.16). This does not sit well with any notion of wife-abandoning male apostles going off in male pairs, careless of all spousal yoking. Peter, who has a mother-in-law at the beginning of the story, after he is called by Jesus (Mk 1.29-31), is an interesting case. No children are mentioned. It could be his wife is no

27. Καὶ προσκολληθήσεται πρὸς τὴν γυναῖκα ἀυτοῦ continues the quote from the LXX but is not found in the earliest manuscripts א, B, Ψ, Sinaitic Syriac and Gothic.
28. I use 'man' and 'woman' here to retain the Adam- focused bodily connection of the language.
29. Ernest Best, *Mark: The Gospel as Story* (Edinburgh: T. & T. Clark, 1983), p. 63. However, as pointed out by Craig Keener, *And Marries Another: Divorce and Remarriage in the Teaching of the New Testament* (Peabody: Hendrickson, 1991), p. 164, women could divorce their husbands under Hellenistic law. This would have been familiar to Jesus given the proximity of the Decapolis, where many Jews lived. Keener persuasively argues that Jesus accepts infidelity/adultery as severing the marriage, meaning that valid divorce would follow, but does not accept other reasons; see Keener, *And Marries Another*, pp. 21-49.
30. France, *Mark*, p. 392.

longer alive, but what if Peter's 'wife' is a woman erased not by death, but by a kind of androcentrism in which she would only be mentioned if she played some vital role in the story Mark wished to tell about Jesus? It just so happened that she was not the one who was healed. The 'one flesh' concept of a marital union does nevertheless raise the issue of how many hidden wives there might have been.

In Mark, when Jesus eventually sends out the Twelve 'two by two' they are engaged in entering new physical spaces of homes, as the animals enter the new physical space of the ark, with a role of proclaiming the Kingdom of God, exorcizing and healing:

> And he called together the Twelve, and began to send them out two by two, and he gave them authority over the unclean spirits. And he instructed them that they should take nothing on the way except a walking stick—no bread, no bag, no money in the belt. They should wear sandals and [have] no spare tunic. And he said to them, 'Wherever you enter into a house, remain there until you leave the region, and if ever a place does not welcome you or listen to you shake off the dust from under your feet for a testimony to them'. So they went off to proclaim for repentance, and they cast out many demons, and anointed many sick people with oil and cured them. (Mk 6.7-13)

Just as they are sent out, so they return:

> And the apostles gathered together with Jesus, and they reported to him all that they had done and taught. (Mk 6.30)

In going out 'two by two' and proclaiming the Kingdom, the Twelve are propagating, planting and nurturing seed (4.3-20, 26-32), by means of the 'authority' (ἐξουσία) of Jesus, which is the Holy Spirit (3.28-30); they are doing what Jesus is described as doing (e.g. 1.9-12, 22-27, 39).[31]

While it looks as if Mark points to a historical reality in which twelve named men go out in Jesus' place in Galilee, replicating his male body in their own bodies, we need to embody the apostles in real contexts in order to flesh out the possibilities. In entering a house, in first-century Galilee, a man might well have expected to be received by a male head of the house, and yet there are in Mark's narrative also 'widow's houses' (Mk 12.40). The job of the Twelve is very much one of healing, but, in the case of sick women, who required 'anointing with oil'—as the Twelve are instructed to do specifically—a pair of two strange men

---

31. For further discussion of Jesus' healing and exorcizing ministry in Galilee, see Joan E. Taylor and Federico Adinolfi, 'John the Baptist and Jesus the Baptist: A Narrative Critical Approach', *Journal for the Study of the Historical Jesus* 10 (2012), pp. 247-84.

arriving to undertake this method of healing by bodily contact likewise seems slightly improper. It is hard to imagine that a male head of house would freely allow such close physical contact with women, or that a lone widow would welcome it.

Elaine Wainwright has shown how concepts of healing women lie behind the Marcan text; in particular healing oil or ointment was a pointer to the activity of women. In Mk 14.3-9 a woman disciple pours out healing ointment within the house of 'Simon the Leper'. The house is a frequent locus of healing (1.29; 2.1, 15), and the woman is not defined as a family member, while nard has a medicinal use.[32] In the face of Jesus' knowledge of his imminent fate (and the distress he would exhibit in 14.32-42), she pours healing ointment on his head, and he acknowledges 'good work' that has been done 'in me' (καλὸν ἔργον ἐν ἐμοί),[33] though ironically her healing action is also a kind of pre-anointing for burial (14.8).[34] Women appear again with aromatic substances to anoint Jesus at the tomb (16.1).

If it were the case that Jesus sent out apostolic 'mates', δύο δύο—male and female—configured as 'one flesh' yoked together to heal and teach, then the situation of women healing presents itself. We might draw the female 'mates' from that body of 'many' women mentioned in Mk 15.40-41, or from the hidden wives of the named men. In the traditional image we have, the women around Jesus and on the road with him are remarkably silent and inactive: the male apostles go out and do all the healing, exorcizing and talking. The women are kept in the distance in the narrative; we catch only a fleeting glimpse of them, and they are configured as muted in their service roles. Yet, the very fact that they are on the road with Jesus and not in the household destabilizes that picture.

This situation of road women, serving Jesus (a man who is not actually a father, husband or brother, though conceptualized as both a brother and master) is anything but normal. For a woman to call Jesus 'master' (κύριος) creates a dissonance in a cultural context in which the Hebrew and Aramaic word *ba'al* (בעל), meaning 'possessor' or 'master', also meant 'husband', and an appropriate address of a wife to her husband was 'my lord', *'adoni* (אדוני; Gen. 18.12; 1 Kgs 1.17), in Greek

---

32. Elaine Wainwright, *Women Healing/Healing Women: The Genderization of Healing in Early Christianity* (London: Equinox, 2006), pp. 132-34.

33. *Ibid.*, p. 135.

34. *Ibid.*, p. 136. Note that she is a disciple whose nard was a common resource in that it could have been sold for money that other disciples could collectively give to the poor, and Jesus replies to them that they would always have the poor, but they would not always have him (14.6).

κυριός μου (see also 1 Pet. 3.6).[35] If a teacher used a pre-Fall concept of marriage, and had women live with him in a peripatetic band of followers on the roads of Galilee, rejecting the protected family locus of a woman's life, then quite frankly this teacher could have done anything in terms of overturning the usual gender stereotyping of men and women in his age.

As such, it is possible that Jesus himself—in turning to a pre-Fall concept of marriage—could also have turned to a pre-sex concept for an idea of marriage as a glued and yoked partnership. Sex is not actually mentioned until Gen. 4.1, after the eviction from Eden, and is connected immediately with procreation. Josephus thus defines childbirth itself as being one of Eve's punishments (*Ant.* 1.49). Mark 10.2-12 imagines cohabitation, after severing a primary gluing to father and mother (whose home might not even have been left, in the case of a son), not necessarily sex. Such encratism is already found in the Matthaean addition to the divorce saying, where the male disciples suggest that Jesus' ruling on divorce was so strict that 'it is better not to marry', to which Jesus provides the example of a castrated male body, saying:

> there are some eunuchs who were born such from their mother's womb, and there are some eunuchs made eunuchs by human beings, and there are some eunuchs who have made themselves eunuchs because of the Kingdom of Heaven; the one able to accommodate it, let him accommodate it. (Mt. 19.12)

In the context of Matthew's narrative this picture of the male body is read conceptually, not (presumably) physically, as a recommendation for celibacy, counterpointing marriage. Those who have (already) made themselves eunuchs for the Kingdom of God would seem to be both Jesus himself and John the Baptist, both of whom proclaim the Kingdom (Mt. 11.7-19), and indeed prophets were often expected to be celibate, even Moses (Philo, *Mos.* 2.68-69; *b. Shab.* 67a), who was married. Celibacy was a feature of highly admired groups in Second Temple Judaism (the Essenes and the Therapeutae) who embraced this asceticism both outside and within marriage.[36] Jesus' prohibition on divorce, then, does not necessarily assume that married couples continued sexual relations, and the Matthaean addition assumes that eschewing marriage was

35. Jastrow, *Dictionary*, p. 182.
36. For an extensive discussion of celibacy, see Joan E. Taylor, *Jewish Women Philosophers in First-Century Alexandria: Philo's 'Therapeutae' Reconsidered* (Oxford: Oxford University Press, 2003), pp. 248-64; *eadem*, 'Women, Children and Celibate Men in the *Serekh* Texts', *HTR* 104 (2011), pp. 171-90.

a valid choice. Thus, an unmarried male 'eunuch' (celibate man) may have joined with a female companion for the practical reasons outlined above, in terms of ministry to women in the cultural context of first-century Galilee. In Jesus' group of women disciples and the early churches there were those designated as 'widows' who did 'good works' (Acts 9.36-43),[37] and who could have acted alongside 'eunuch' men.

It is hard, then, not to think of the independent 'Mary the Magdalene' of Mk 15.40[38] as someone who could have acted as a female companion in regard to the teaching and healing of women. Mary is particularly attached to Jesus at the time of his crucifixion and burial.[39] The epithet may indicate her home village, since there is a small place called Migdal Nunaya just north of Tiberias mentioned in later rabbinic literature, though a town actually just called 'Magdala' by itself is unattested, and should not be confused with Tarichaea (Josephus, *War* 2.21).[40] Since the word in Aramaic means 'tower', there is a double-entendre that fits with the type of nicknames Jesus called his male apostles: Simon, given the name 'Kepha', *Petros*; James and John named 'Boanerges, or 'the sons of thunder' (Mk 3.16-17); Simon 'the Cananaean' or 'striver' (cf. 'called the *Zelotes*' in Lk. 6.15; cf. Acts 1.12); Judas 'Iscariot' which in Aramaic meant 'the choker' (Mk 3.19).[41] The fact that Mary the Magdalene is a very significant disciple of Jesus is thus indicated simply by her special name: 'Mary the Tower-ess'.

Mary Magdalene appears as one of the Twelve in the *Pistis Sophia* (1.9) and other Gnostic texts: the *Gospel of Mary*, the *Sophia of Jesus Christ* and the *Gospel of Thomas* (114).[42] In the circles of the *Gospel of Philip* (59.9; 63.33–64.5), Mary was considered to have been the

37. Bonnie Bowman Thurston, *The Widows: A Woman's Ministry in the Early Church* (Minneapolis: Fortress Press, 1989), pp. 30-34.

38. Luke likewise notes that she is 'called the Magdalene' (8.2) and she is thus named in a distinctive way; which is very curious, as otherwise only Jesus' apostles are 'called' by nicknames that he gives them.

39. See Joan E. Taylor, 'The Name Iskarioth (Iscariot)', *JBL* 129 (2010), pp. 369-85 (381-82).

40. Michael Avi-Yonah, *Gazetteer of Roman Palestine* (Qedem; Jerusalem: Institute of Archaeology, Hebrew University of Jerusalem, 1976), p. 99. See Joan E. Taylor, 'Missing Magdala and the Name of Mary "Magdalene"', *Palestine Exploration Quarterly* (forthcoming).

41. Taylor, 'Iskarioth', pp. 380-84.

42. Jane Schaberg, *The Resurrection of Mary Magdalene: Legends, Apocrypha and the Christian Testament* (New York: Continuum, 2004), p. 134; Antti Marjanen, *The Woman Jesus Loved: Mary Magdalene in the Nag Hammadi Library and Related Documents* (Leiden: Brill, 1996).

'companion' of Jesus.[43]. If we consider these texts as having some histori-cal credibility—combined with vagueness in the Gospel of John[44]—then this provides us with an historical possibility of Mary being Jesus' companion as a helper and co-worker or one of the Twelve, replacing perhaps the unstable name of Thaddeus.

The notion of helper is indeed built into the cultural concept of 'wife' at this time; in Genesis Eve is created as a 'helper corresponding to him' (עזר כנגדו), one who helps alongside Adam (Gen. 2.8).[45] While there is no suggestion of male authority and female subordination in the 'marriage' model Jesus provides in Mk 10.2-12, the practice as played out may have suggested to some a more subordinate serving role for women. It is this very role, however, that Jesus defines as superior in the Kingdom. The ramifications of women's service have already been discussed above in terms of Mk 9.35 and 10.45: Jesus is one who serves, and so are the Twelve.

Hidden women disciples can be read in various places in the Gospel of Mark. In Mk 6.39-44 'disciples' of unspecified gender serve the huge crowd with loaves and fishes. In Mk 14.12 disciples ask Jesus where they should prepare the Passover meal, and he sends 'two' (14.12-16).[46] These two are not configured as being among the Twelve, since he comes 'with the Twelve' (14.17) to the room. Gender is strikingly skewed in this passage; the two disciples are met by a *man* carrying a jar of water: a distinctively 'other' action since carrying water was women's work (14.13). That the Twelve themselves at the last supper are not simply twelve men is also indicated from Jesus' identification of the person who

43. This does not indicate she was the wife of Jesus, though this may be sug-gested in the newly discovered 'Gospel of Jesus' Wife', if genuine, for which see the article by Karen King online: www.hds.harvard.edu/faculty-research/research-projects/the-gospel-of-jesuss-wife. The only other explicit mention of an earthly 'wife' to Jesus, in our extant literature, is in Epiphanius, *Panarion* 26.8, when Epiphanius refers to a work called the 'Questions of Mary' in which at one point Jesus pulls a 'wife/woman' out of his side, has sex with her and then eats his semen, in front of a fainting Mary Magdalene: this is clearly a bizarre visionary experience.

44. Ann Graham Brock, *Mary Magdalene, the First Apostle: The Struggle for Authority* (Harvard Theological Studies; Cambridge, MA: Harvard University Press, 2003).

45. David Clines, *What Does Eve Do to Help? And Other Readerly Questions to the Old Testament* (Sheffield: JSOT Press, 1994), pp. 25-37, notes that this probably indicates necessary help in procreation, in terms of its original meaning. I am grateful to Sandra Jacobs for this reference.

46. In Mk 11.1-2 Jesus sends two of his disciples to Bethphage to get a colt for him to sit on. In Mk 16.12 Jesus appears to two disciples as they are walking along the road.

will betray him; when asked, Jesus announces dramatically that it is 'one of the Twelve, who is dipping into the same dish as me' (14.20). As Quentin Quesnell pointed out this would be semantically odd if only the Twelve were there.[47] At Passover it is required that those who prepare the meal sit together at the table: men, women and children, so the two disciples who have prepared the meal should be present. When Jesus leaves with this group to spend the night in Gethsemane (14.32) out from the group goes a young man wearing nothing but a linen cloth (14.51), and he is not one of the Twelve. We do not just have Twelve, we have a 'Twelve and co.' in both the last supper and Gethsemane, with no explanation given.

This is not to say that Mark himself did not primarily wish to imply rhetorically that the Twelve was a set of twelve men, a view we find embraced in Matthew and Luke–Acts, but rather that there are ways of reading behind the text to an historical reconstruction in which there are twelve pairs rather than twelve men, with the expression 'two by two' understood as one that destabilizes the dominant androcentrism. The notion that there were twelve men is easily read in Mk 10.32-45, which re-iterates the point of 9.30-37 where the 'disciples' in general are discussing who is the greatest. 'Sitting down', Jesus then calls 'the Twelve' to him, states that whoever wants to be the first shall be the last of all and stands an otherwise unnoticed child in the midst of them; taking the child in his arms, Jesus states that anyone who 'receives'[48] a child 'in my name' receives me. In Mk 10.32-45, Jesus takes 'the Twelve' aside and explains what will happen to him in Jerusalem. James and John, the sons of Zebedee, 'come forward' and ask to sit at the right and left hand of Jesus 'in your glory' (cf. Mk 13.26).[49] This seems to presume knowledge of a saying found in Mt. 19.28 (cf. Lk. 22.28-30) in which Jesus states that when the son of humanity sits on 'his throne of glory, you will sit on twelve thrones judging the twelve tribes of Israel', though this statement is not placed in Matthew (or Luke) in association with the Twelve.[50] In

47. Quentin Quesnell, 'The Women at Luke's Supper', in Richard J. Cassidy and Philip J. Scharper (eds.), *Political Issues in Luke–Acts* (Maryknoll: Orbis, 1983), pp. 59-79.

48. The word δέχομαι is used to 'receive' someone under your roof and look after them; the Twelve are supposed to be 'received' on their mission (Mk. 6.11).

49. In Mt. 20.20-28 the unflattering question is transferred to the ambitious mother of James and John.

50. Elisabeth Schüssler Fiorenza, *Discipleship of Equals*, p. 109, therefore sees the Twelve itself as a symbolic rather than an actual number, inclusive of women, though see John P. Meier, 'Jesus, the Twelve and the Restoration of Israel', in James M. Scott (ed.), *Restoration: Old Testament, Jewish and Christian Perspectives*

Mark, Jesus says to James and John that the seating arrangement is 'for those for whom it has been prepared' (10.40). Then 'the ten' hear of the question and are annoyed with James and John, and Jesus calls them together to explain. In other words, it is precisely in response to this question that Jesus insists on the pre-eminence of service, and the total antithesis of worldly notions of power in God's Kingdom. Whoever is the lowliest servant of all will sit next to him in glory. It is therefore necessary for the meaning of this story that the questioners be men who anticipate their own glory, so that Jesus can overturn the notion completely.

Historically, if Jesus chose twelve pairs (men and women), who went out without money, food or so much as a change of clothing in order to heal people and proclaim the Kingdom, this is a deeply ironic construction, created as a kind of embodied witness to show up ethical shortcomings and the wrongness of worldly ideas of success and power. This group was made up, we know, of a fair component of poor fishermen. Status is inherently challenged by this choice: it is the Holy Spirit that is the authority. Moreover, their task is to be with Jesus, living rough on the road, travelling off from the main group of disciples with no resources, helping the population of Galilee and hoping for subsistence in return. This is not a model of sacramental priesthood; this is a model of total service and humility for the benefit of humanity.

IV. *The Sister Wives*

The clearest resonance of a hidden situation of male–female apostolic pairings that may be alluded to in Mark's language of the ark is found in 1 Cor. 9.1-6, written over a decade before the Gospel. Paul responds to those who attack him by stating:

> Am I not free? Am I not an apostle? Have I not seen Jesus, our Lord? Are you not my work in the Lord? If to others I am not an apostle, surely I am to you; for you are the seal of my apostleship in the Lord. My defence to those who examine me is this:
>
> Do we not have a right to eat and drink? Do we not have a right to lead around a sister wife (ἀδελφήν γυναῖκα), like the rest of the apostles, and the brothers of the Lord, and Cephas? Or do only Barnabas and I not have the right to stop working?

(JSJSup 72; Leiden: Brill, 2001), pp. 365-404. For the concept of twelve tribes Gen. 35.22; 42.13, 32; 49.28; Exod. 24.4 *et al.* This led to a notion of 'twelve' signifying completeness, see: Gen. 14.4; 17.20; Exod. 15.27; Lev. 24.5; Num. 1.44; 7.84-87; 17.2; Deut. 1.23; Josh. 3.12; 4.1-9, 20; 2 Sam. 2.14; 1 Kgs 4.7; 7.25; 10.20; 11.30; 18.31; 19.19; 2 Chron. 4.15; 9.19; Ezra 8.25.

In the context of this statement, Paul is mounting a defence against the accusation that he has exploited the congregation. Paul provides a list of entitlements:
1. to eat and drink;
2. to take along a sister wife;
3. to stop working.

There is then in this sequence a sudden and unexpected picture of 'women' who are connected to male apostles. The male apostles, brothers of the Lord and Cephas that Paul points to as being like himself, each have a 'sister wife'. There is no indication that Paul and Barnabas have rejected this right, but rather they claim it here, as they also claim the fundamental right to eat and drink or to rest from working, as apostles.[51] It is considered completely normative and quite absolute. Paul elsewhere notes Cephas, the brothers of the Lord and the apostles as being groups in Jerusalem (Gal. 1.18-19; 1 Cor. 15.3-8) though he does not wholly equate them with the Twelve.[52] Rather, the Twelve are most likely a subgroup of the larger category 'apostles', or Paul's co-workers (2 Cor. 6.1).

As Anthony Thiselton notes, nearly all modern translations use the term 'Christian' or 'believing' for ἀδελφήν. But losing 'sister' for such translations is a serious omission, because it is women's independent sisterhood within the 'family' of the disciples of Jesus that is critically important to remember (cf. 1 Cor. 7.15; Rom. 16.1; Philem. 1). As Jesus said, in Marcan tradition: 'whoever does the will of my Father in Heaven is my mother, my brother and my sister' (Mk 3.35).

As Thiselton also notes, the dominant interpretation currently is that Paul (rather randomly) validates the right of the male apostles, brothers of the Lord, to marry, and to take their wives as companions on their missionary journeys, with both being supported by host churches.[53] But, in the text, with this reading, the woman has no meaningful role other than to be taken around by a male apostle as his wife. There is no mention of children here, which is odd if we are to imagine any kind of normal married couple in antiquity. Rather, it is the word γυναῖκα that

---

51. Paul claims to be an apostle frequently in his writings (e.g. Gal. 1–2; Rom. 1.1; 11.13). In Acts both Paul and Barnabas are made apostles through the commissioning of the church in Antioch (Acts 13.1-3; cf. 14.4).

52. See Gunter Klein, *Die zwolf Apostel: Ursprung und Gehatt einer Idee* (Göttingen: Vandenhoeck & Ruprecht, 1961), pp. 38-43, who rejects the notion that the Twelve should be classified as the only apostles.

53. Antony C. Thiselton, *The First Epistle to the Corinthians: Commentary on the Greek Text* (Grand Rapids: Eerdmans, 2000), pp. 679-81.

seems most problematic in terms of a translation, since while it might mean an actual wife, we may well here have something idiosyncratic. It is not a wife who is treated as a 'sister' because of her belief, for Paul; it is a believing sister who is in some way treated as a 'wife'.

Allo has noted that the patristic reading of this passage was that Paul was stressing that he and Barnabas had the right to a female assistant (Tertullian, *On Monogamy* 8; Clement, *Stromata* 4.3; Jerome, *Adversus Jovinianum* 1.26; Augustine, *De opera monachorum* 4.5).[54] Against this, Héring has stated that if only an assistant was meant then there would be no reason to include the word γυναῖκα (woman/wife) with ἀδελφήν.[55] But that is not true; a 'sister' is not necessarily an assistant or 'helper', but a wife should be, and the verb ἀγώ, 'lead', is standard language here for the action of a husband in regard to a wife (cf. Philo, *Hypoth.* 11.14). A male apostle has the right to 'lead around' (περιάγειν) a wife as he travels; a brother does not 'lead around' a sister. Given what has been explored above in terms of healing and teaching, male and female pairings were important for there to be a reach to both men and women in a gendered world. If we imagine the criticism against Paul here, it seems that in being accused of being taxing to the community, he counters the accusation with the fact that a 'sister-wife' is a necessity rather than a bonus, just as are his eating and drinking or stopping working at times: he is a duo.

In the later Pauline traditions of the second century onwards, the woman who is considered to be a kind of companion to Paul is Thecla.[56] Paul himself nowhere else indicates that he had a wife in any normal way, as he does not have a home (1 Cor. 4.9-14). Paul is clearly celibate, as in 1 Cor. 7.1: '[n]ow concerning the things abut which you wrote, it is good for a man not to touch a woman', and: '[y]et I wish all people were even as I myself am' (1 Cor. 7.7). In this passage, he 'allows' sexual relations in normal marriage, but reluctantly. As such, the term 'sister' in

---

54. Ernst B. Allo, *Saint Paul: Épitres aux Corinthiens* (Paris: Lecoffre, 1956), pp. 212-14. Thiselton, however, notes that the meaning of these patristic texts is not simply read, and Clement considers that wives accompanying apostles would have been treated as sisters, in that the relationship was celibate.

55. Jean Héring, *The First Epistle of Saint Paul to the Corinthians* (trans. A. W. Heathcote and P. J. Allcock; New York: Wipf & Stock, 2009), p. 77.

56. She is most famously described in the *Acts of Paul and Thecla*, though in fact in this text Paul and Thecla do not work as a team: Jeremy W. Barrier, *The Acts of Paul and Thecla; A Critical Introduction and Commentary* (Tübingen: Mohr Siebeck, 2009), pp. 52-53. However, this is likely to minimize the wider Thecla tradition; see the discussion by Rosie Ratcliffe in Chapter 9 of this volume.

ἀδελφήν γυναῖκα (1 Cor. 9.5) must imply much more than 'believing' or 'Christian'; it also indicates a woman he is not relating to sexually, as the Church Fathers also understood. To combine the two concepts of 'sister' and 'wife' would have been as odd in antiquity as today, creating a different category of relationship: a celibate team, conceptualized as a human pair bond, a marriage.

A hidden female companion of Paul undisclosed in either Acts or the Pauline letters also may yet explain one of its most intractable mysteries: the 'we' passages (Acts 16.10-17; 20.5-15; 21.1-18; 27.1-29; 28.1-16). While tradition has seized upon Luke (Philem. 24; Col. 4.14; 2 Tim. 4.11) as the author of these, there are really no easily identifiable male candidates for a narrator.[57] This is not the place for a detailed examination of these passages of sections written in the first person plural, but suffice to say that the persuasive examination by Stanley Porter has argued against the view that these are a literary device, preferring again the notion that these come from an earlier source redacted and integrated by the author of Luke–Acts, though the identity of the writer remains obscure.[58] They are distinctive in that they suddenly appear, without the author being identified.[59] It is particularly a problem in the final chapters, where Paul is sent in captivity to Rome, and shipwrecked in Malta, and yet the story is told as a 'we' account, with the companion avoiding the punishment inflicted on Paul.

One of the most intriguing proposals has been made by Randel McCraw Helms, who has suggested that the Gospel of Luke and the Acts of the Apostles were written by a woman, and that the 'we-passages' are designed inclusively by referencing as part of the 'we' 'a female member of Paul's party'.[60] Building on this and the tradition of Paul's companion being Thecla, it seems fair to ask whether these passages originated with her. The 'we-passages' begin after Paul and Silas have visited Cilicia, specifically Derbe, Lystra and Iconium, just after going on to Phrygia

57. Susan Marie Praeder, 'The Problem of First Person Narration in Acts', *Novum Testamentum* 29 (1987), pp. 193-218.
58. Stanley Porter, *Paul in Acts: Essays in Literary Criticism, Rhetoric and Theology* (Tübingen: J. C. B. Mohr/Paul Siebeck, 1999), pp. 10-46, and on their theology see pp. 48-65, though for a further defence of a literary approach, see William Sanger Campbell, *The 'We' Passages in the Acts of the Apostles: The Narrator as Narrative Character* (SBL Studies in Biblical Literature; Atlanta: SBL; Leiden: Brill, 2007).
59. Porter, *Paul in Acts*, p. 28.
60. Randall McCraw Helms, *Who Wrote the Gospels?* (Altadena: Millennium, 1997), p. 88.

and Galatia, Mysia and Troas (16.1-10), and it is Iconium that is the city of Thecla (*Acts of Paul and Thecla* 3.1). Early on these passages include a story where 'we' spoke to women in Philippi, including Lydia, and a slave girl (Acts 16.11-18), a very female audience, and there are a number of sea journeys where the narrator is travelling with Paul. A sea journey of the two together is indicated strongly in a fourth-century sarcophagus lid, where the names 'Paulus' and 'Thecla' are found together on a boat relief.[61] The name 'Thecla' is on the boat, and 'Paulus' next to a man (Paul?) steering it. If the 'we-passages' were authored by Paul's female companion, then the mystifying anonymity might be accounted for; but she is veiled in the way that other female bodies are veiled in androcentric texts.

In addition, it appears that the model of a lead male apostle and female companion as a helper 'wife' was not the universal norm, but there could be equal apostolic partners. At the end of the letter to the Romans Paul writes of 'Andronicus and Junia my relatives and fellow prisoners, who are outstanding among the apostles, who also before me were in Christ' (Rom. 16.7).[62] In Philemon, Paul addresses a pair, 'Apphia the sister, and Archippus our fellow soldier and to the church in your (sing.) house' (Philem. 1). While the house belongs to Archippus, Apphia is mentioned first. There is the model of Prisca/Priscilla and Aquila (Acts 18.2-3, 18-19, 26; Rom. 16.3-4; 1 Cor. 16.19; 2 Tim. 4.19), a team that Paul refers to as 'fellow workers' (συνέργοι) (2 Cor. 6.1), with Priscilla named first. Such equal or female-prioritizing terminology is hard to imagine as arising from nowhere, in an unprecedented way, without comment. This makes the understanding of 1 Cor. 9.1-6 more complex. A woman apostle might well have asked whether *she* had the right to eat and drink, have a brother husband like the rest of the women apostles, and stop working.

Furthermore, if a woman could be the lead apostle, with a husband/ male partner taking the role of an assistant, then it is possible also that roles of mates in general could be configured against sexed embodiment. The apostle and the assistant going off 'two by two' could be a man and

---

61. See illustration in Barrier, *Paul and Thecla*, pp. 51, 60, Figure 11.

62. Bernadette Brooten, 'Junia... Outstanding among the Apostles', in Swidler and Swidler (eds.), *Women Priests*, pp. 141-44; John Thorley, 'Junia, a Woman Apostle', *Novum Testamentum* 38 (1996), pp. 18-19; Ute Eisen, *Women Officehold-ers in Early Christianity: Epigraphy and Literary Studies* (trans. Linda Maloney; Collegeville: Liturgical Press, 1996), pp. 47-49.

a woman, a woman and a man, two men or two women,[63] if the circumstances sometimes required this in the early churches, despite the
advantages and precedent of there being two sexes. By suggesting this I
do not wish to return to the concept of male pairings among the Twelve,
but only to suggest that on the pattern of 'mates' there may yet have been
fluidity in terms of embodiments. Perhaps Titus and 'the brother' in
2 Cor. 12.18 indicates this male-pairing situation. Moreover, while in
actual marriage there is an indissoluble union, in accordance with Jesus'
teaching, in partnerships for apostolic 'seeding' these could presumably
be more flexible.

V. *The Second Century*

Given that we see male and female pairings in apostolic work in the
genuine Pauline corpus, and that we glimpse the same in terms of the
Twelve as portrayed in the Gospel of Mark, why were such pairings
written out of the Gospel record? This appears most likely to be the
result of a conscious attempt to ensure that Christianity was not viewed
as the notions of hysterical women, so Celsus (Origen, *Contra Celsum*
2.55; 3.55).[64]

In the second century we find the male–female pairing of apostolic
and leadership roles not so much in the proto-orthodox churches but as a
frequent trope in regard to the earliest heresiarchs, as they are defined by
the proto-orthodox. It seems that a male heresiarch often acted in a
pairing with a named woman: the very authority of this woman seems a
mark of heretical leanings. Simon Magus (Acts 8.9-24) had a female
co-worker and companion named Helen (Justin Martyr, *1 Apol.* 26.3;
Irenaeus, *Adversus Haer.* 1.23.2), perhaps understood as the Samaritan
woman of Jn 4.5-30.[65] Carpocrates was associated with a woman named
Marcellina, leader of the group in Rome (Irenaeus, *Adv. Haer.* 1.25.6;
Origen, *Contra Celsum* 5.62; Epiphanius, *Panarion* 27.6.1). Montanus
famously worked with two women associates: Priscilla and Maximilla.

63. In Philippi, Paul refers by name to two women, Syntyche and Euodia, who
have 'shared in the good message with me, with Clement also, and the rest of my
fellow-workers whose names are written in the book of life' (Phil. 4.3). Syntyche
and Euodia are linked in needing to be of one mind again, as a team.

64. Margaret Y. MacDonald, *Early Christian Women and Pagan Opinion: The
Power of the Hysterical Woman* (Cambridge: Cambridge University Press, 1996),
p. 1.

65. However, see Eisen, *Women Officeholders*, p. 50, for the celebration of the
Samaritan woman as an apostle among the Church Fathers.

Marcion sent a female associate to Rome ahead of his arrival (Jerome, *Adv. Ctesiphum* 4). As Virginia Burrus has noted, the construction of 'a heretic and his female co-worker(s)' is part of the anti-heresy rhetoric of the Church Fathers.[66] Given this, would there have been some careful pruning of statements indicating male–female pairings among the tradition claimed by the proto-orthodox?

It is hard to explain why just so many diverse heretics of the early second century are united by this one thing of male and female pairs if this model were not found somewhere in the common tradition that predated them. The problem is that what we may see as positive evidence of women's leadership and independence would have been configured by those within a patriarchal society as troubling. In other words, we struggle to find women in the texts of the New Testament because of some very significant erasures. The Gospel writers seem to have wished to acknowledge the existence of women as prominent disciples of Jesus, while not drawing great attention to this fact.

Conclusions

This chapter began with the observation that the language of the Twelve going off 'two by two' is odd in relation to male pairs, but rather fits better with an idea of male and female couples, of 'mates' going into the ark to repopulate the earth, as in Genesis 6–7. The possibility of apostolic pairings being configured along the lines of the normative leader-led marriage model of antiquity has been explored, with the 'wife' defined as 'helper' on the basis of Gen. 2.8. This explains the 'sister–wife' mentioned in 1 Cor. 9.1-6 as being a vital associate of the male apostles. Nevertheless, I have suggested that this model creates a gender presentation not necessarily always embodied historically in male apostles and female assistants, as we see in the Pauline correspondence, where there are equal male and female apostles, female apostles with male assistants/husbands and same-sex pairs. This raises the wider issue of a simple correspondence between gendered language and sexed embodiments overall within the New Testament, and whether the Twelve (pairs) were composed of Twelve lead men entirely may be questioned, especially given the instability of the name 'Thaddaeus' in the tradition, the vagueness of the Gospel of John and Mary Magdalene's prominent role.

66. Virginia Burrus, 'The Heretical Woman as Symbol', *HTR* 84 (1991), pp. 229-48. I am grateful to Piotr Ashwin-Siejkowski for this reference and observation.

If Twelve pairs were chosen to send a message to Galilee, Jesus' new world order was not about status or masculine authority, but appears fundamentally ironic. Some of the Twelve were poor fishermen. The concept of the Twelve would point to a collective inner core in which marginalized men and women participated together as those who serve, by living rough with Jesus on the road, and by being sent out with the Holy Spirit and nothing else to resource them at all, receiving subsistence from the villages. Their role was to proclaim the Kingdom, heal and exorcise, anointing bodies with oil. In this, Jesus would radically overturn notions of superiority, and stress that the greatest is the one who serves, as he himself serves, like the women.

JESUS' GENTILE HEALINGS:
THE ABSENCE OF BODILY CONTACT
AND THE REQUIREMENT OF FAITH

Rebecca Harrocks

Jesus was strongly associated with the body, in that he was renowned as someone who healed it. Exactly how he healed remains elusive, and there are reports of different methods.[1] Out of the twenty-two detailed healings/exorcisms across the Synoptic Gospels, twelve are reportedly effected through physical contact,[2] a healing mode second only to that of the spoken word (fifteen accounts).[3] Overall, Jesus' healings cure Jews. However, among them there are four non-Jewish healing stories: that of the Gerasene demoniac (Mk 5.1-20; Mt. 8.28-34; Lk. 8.26-37), the Syrophoenician woman's daughter (Mk 7.24-30; Mt. 15.21-28), the ten lepers (Lk. 17.11-19) and the centurion's boy (Mt. 8.5-13; Lk. 7.1-10). These healings are all carried out *without* bodily contact, and, in the first three of these cases, there is additional emphasis on Jesus' desire for his

1. E.g. Stevan Davies, *Jesus The Healer: Possession, Trance and the Origins of Christianity* (London: SCM Press, 1995), pp. 70-73, understands all of Jesus' healings as psychosomatic.

2. Simon's mother-in-law (Mt. 8.15; Mk 1.31); the leper (Mt. 8.3; Mk 1.41; Lk. 5.13); Jairus's daughter (Mt. 9.18b, 25; Mk 5.23, 41; Lk. 8.54); the haemorrhaging woman (Mt. 9.20-21; Mk 5.27-28, 30-31; Lk. 8.44, 45-47); the deaf-mute (Mk 7.32-33); the blind man of Bethsaida (Mk 8.22-25); the two blind men in Capernaum (Mt. 9.29); the blind men/man of Jericho (Mt. 20.34 against Mark and Luke); the widow's son at Nain (Lk. 7.14; Jesus touched the funeral bier, not the corpse); the bent woman (Lk. 13.13); the dropsical man (Lk. 14.4); and the high-priest's servant's ear (Lk. 22.51).

3. These figures do not consider parallels and are only approximate, particularly since the healing mode is sometimes only implied, not explicit. Also, some of the 'touch' healings involve word as well.

own body to be physically kept apart.[4] The latter three also place an unusually strong emphasis on the requirement of faith. In light of these observations I would like to explore here why the writers of the Synoptic Gospels may have depicted Jesus as deliberately avoiding physical contact in the healings of non-Jews, specifically Gentiles, and discuss the role of faith, given that in Acts Peter is shown as stating that it is 'unlawful' for a Jew to associate or visit a foreigner (Acts 10.29). In the present discussion my focus is on two key texts: the healings of the centurion's boy (Mt. 8.5-13; Lk. 7.1-10/cf. Jn 4.46-54) and the Canaanite/Syrophoenician woman's daughter (Mt. 15.21-28/Mk 7.24-30). I will review the engagement of commentators with these passages, and consider the central question of why these healings are included in the gospels and what they may tell us about the attitude of the historical Jesus to the healing of Gentile bodies.

I. *Healing Gentiles: The Discussion*

It was David Friedrich Strauss who began the modern age of historical study of Jesus' miracles, with the publication of his two-volume work *Das Leben Jesu kritisch bearbeitet* (1835–36).[5] His controversial conclusion was that the miracles were purely mythical, with only some of them having any historical nucleus, and he saw Jesus' ventures into Gentile territory as consequential of Jewish rejection. Another key figure is Rudolf Bultmann who, in his 1921 book, *Die Geschichte der synoptischen Tradition*,[6] theorized that the miracle stories had originated in actual events in which Jesus was perceived to have healed sick bodies, but that these stories were shaped by and even adopted from some Hellenistic sources; miracles in fact did not happen, since they would be contrary to the laws of nature. He considered the accounts of both the centurion's boy and the Syrophoenician woman's daughter to be different versions of the same source, originating in the early Church.[7]

---

4. In Mk 5.19/Lk. 8.38 Jesus does not allow the cured demoniac to accompany him; in Mt. 15.23 Jesus does not answer; in Lk. 17.12 the lepers stand at a distance from Jesus.

5. David F. Strauss, *Das Leben Jesu kritisch bearbeitet* (2 vols.; Tübingen: Osiander, 1935–36), published in English as *The Life of Jesus, Critically Examined* (trans. George Eliot; 3 vols.; London: Chapman Brothers, 1846).

6. Rudolf Bultmann, *Die Geschichte der synoptischen Tradition* (Göttingen: Vandenhoeck & Ruprecht, 1921), appearing in English as *The History of the Synoptic Tradition* (trans. John Marsh: New York: Harper & Row, 1963).

7. *Ibid.*, pp. 38-39.

Against this backdrop, scholars over the last fifty years have had diverse understandings of what the miracles of Jesus demonstrate, though not a great amount of focus has been on their repercussions for Jesus' relationship with Gentiles. Geza Vermes, who published *Jesus the Jew* in 1973, argued that the Jesus of the Gospels was a Jewish charismatic in the tradition of Honi the Circle Drawer and Hanina ben Dosa, and thus, for Vermes, the purpose of Jesus' healings was little more than to provide evidence of this designation, and his purely Jewish concerns; he describes Jesus' 'antipathy' in the accounts of the Gerasene demoniac and the Syrophoenician woman's daughter.[8] In 1978 Morton Smith put forward the case for *Jesus the Magician*,[9] defining exorcisms as 'the blackest sort of magic',[10] attributing other cures to the relief of hysteria, and branding revivifications historically false.[11] Smith made no distinction between Jew and Gentile in his observations on bodily healing.

In 1985, E. P. Sanders published *Jesus and Judaism*, arguing that there was insufficient evidence for the conclusions presented by Smith and Vermes.[12] Sanders speculates that as the Gentile healings are the only 'solid evidence'[13] for Jesus' contact with Gentiles, and given debates in early Christianity about their inclusion criteria, 'we need not think that Jesus imparted to his disciples any view at all about the Gentiles and the kingdom'.[14] In the 1990s, volume two of John P. Meier's *A Marginal Jew* allocated a large section to Jesus' miracles, addressing each healing account individually in order to build up a picture of the historical Jesus. Meier deems the general framework of the distance-healing of the centurion's boy as historically probable, though thinks it unlikely that the petitioner's ethnicity was specified in the Q form.[15] By contrast, despite the accounts of the Syrophoenician woman's daughter containing 'a number of unusual concrete details' suggestive of historicity, its theological resemblance to Paul (e.g. Rom. 1.16; 2.9-10) leads Meier to conclude it is more likely a 'creation by first-generation Christians'.[16]

---

8. Geza Vermes, *Jesus the Jew: A Historian's Reading of the Gospels* (London: Collins, 1973), p. 31.

9. Morton Smith, *Jesus the Magician* (New York: Harper & Row, 1978).

10. *Ibid.*, p. 110.

11. *Ibid.*, p. 118.

12. E. P. Sanders, *Jesus and Judaism* (London: SCM Press, 1985), p. 170.

13. *Ibid.*, p. 219.

14. *Ibid.*, p. 221.

15. John P. Meier, *A Marginal Jew: Rethinking the Historical Jesus*, II (London: Doubleday, 1994), pp. 718-27.

16. *Ibid.*, pp. 659-61.

Graham H. Twelftree responded to Meier in his book, *Jesus the Miracle Worker* (1999),[17] which similarly explored the relevance of the healings in the quest for the historical Jesus, but also how they were understood and presented in each Gospel. He concluded that Bultmann's position 'is not to be taken seriously',[18] and, in contrast to Meier, considers that both of the Gentile healing accounts we will look at here resulted from real events in the historical Jesus' life.[19]

The subject of Jesus' attitudes to Gentiles is not at the focus of any of these scholarly discussions, and is mentioned only in passing. An important recent work focusing on this topic specifically is Michael F. Bird's *Jesus and the Origins of the Gentile Mission.*[20] Bird argues the case strongly, and not always convincingly, that it is possible (through the Israel-centric focus of Jesus' work and the concept of eschatological pilgrimage—wherein the Gentiles would make pilgrimage to Mt Zion in the final days as a consequence of seeing Israel's redemption and glorification of Yahweh)[21] to 'identify…in Jesus' aims and intentions the germinal roots of a Gentile mission',[22] and Gentile inclusion, even in Jesus' lifetime. As such, Bird makes much of the healings of the Syrophoenician woman's daughter and the centurion's boy, seeing them as 'essentially authentic in outline' despite 'being overlaid with the theology of the evangelists',[23] and interpreting them as 'visible demonstrations' that since 'Israel's restoration was gradually becoming a reality, it was becoming possible for outsiders such as Gentiles to participate in it'.[24] He sees this, for example, in the detail that the centurion does not

17.   Graham Twelftree, *Jesus the Miracle Worker: A Historical and Theological Study* (Downers Grove: InterVarsity Press, 1999), and see also his earlier work, *Jesus the Exorcist* (Tübingen: Mohr Siebeck, 1993). For a detailed survey of the scholarship on Jesus as healer, see Barry L. Blackburn, 'The Miracles of Jesus', in Bruce Chilton and Craig Evans (eds.), *Studying the Historical Jesus: Evaluations of the State of Current Research* (Leiden: Brill, 1994), pp. 353-94.

18.   Twelftree, *Miracle Worker*, p. 296.

19.   *Ibid.*, pp. 289-90, 295-96.

20.   Michael F. Bird, *Jesus and the Origins of the Gentile Mission* (London: Continuum, 2007).

21.   Pss. 47.6-9; 68.30-32; Isa. 2.2-5; 18.7; 19.19-25; 45.14, 20-25; 56.7; 60.11, 14; 66.18-24; Jer. 3.17; 16.19; Mic. 4.1-3; 7.17; Hag. 2.7; Zech. 8.20-21; 14.16; Tob. 13.11-13; 14.6-7; *1 En.* 10.21; 48.5; 53.1; 90.33; *T. Ben.* 9.2; *2 Bar.* 68.5; *Sib. Or.* 3.702-31, 772-75; *Pss. Sol.* 17.31; *4 Ezra* 13.12-13; 1QS 12.13-14; 1QM 12.13-14; *Tg. Isa.* 16.1. Jews also believed that righteous Gentiles who kept the Noahide laws of Gen. 9.1-17 would be welcomed in the eschatological age.

22.   Bird, *Mission*, p. 173.

23.   *Ibid.*, p. 95.

24.   *Ibid.*, p. 123.

'convert',[25] despite conversion to Christianity being a concept outside of Jesus' lifetime and conversion to Judaism not being a concern of the Synoptic Jesus, as well as in the present nature of the dogs eating in the accounts of the Syrophoenician woman's daughter.[26]

Lastly, it has often been noted that it was only Jesus' *Gentile* healings which were carried out across distance.[27] To build on this culturally aware approach, I would like to explore the healings as taking place within a milieu with certain presuppositions about illness and the nature of the body in order to ascertain what can be gleaned of Jesus' overarching attitude towards Gentiles—or, more specifically, Gentile bodies—as portrayed in the Synoptic Gospels. I will focus particularly on how the Gospel-writers develop the theme of faith as overcoming the fundamental separation between Jewish and Gentile bodies.

Before advancing any further, it is necessary to address why there have been several exclusions from this discussion. Of the four non-Jewish healing stories mentioned at the outset—that of the Gerasene demoniac (Mk 5.1-20; Mt. 8.28-34; Lk. 8.26-37), the Syrophoenician woman's daughter (Mk 7.24-30; Mt. 15.21-28), the ten lepers (Lk. 17.11-19) and the centurion's boy (Mt. 8.5-13; Lk. 7.1-10), two are not examined. In the first place, the exorcism of the Gerasene demoniac is omitted because, although the man was almost certainly a Gentile, and his exorcism was performed with a saying and without physical contact, the motif of faith is not explicit. Although a degree of faith is to be assumed in *all* the healing accounts in which Jesus is approached to perform a cure,[28] in the case of the Gerasene demoniac, it was not *he* but the demons who appealed to Jesus, and thus the healed man cannot be commended for his faith.[29] Since this does not fit my focus, and due to word limitations, it will not feature.

25. *Ibid.*, p. 118.

26. *Ibid.*, p. 116: 'As the children of Israel are being fed, crumbs are *now* falling for the dogs…'

27. *Ibid.*, p. 122; Craig S. Keener, *The Gospel of Matthew: A Socio-Rhetorical Commentary* (Grand Rapids: Eerdmans, 2009), pp. 263-70; Robert A. Guelich, *Mark 1–8:26* (WBC 34a; Dallas: Word Books, 1989), p. 382; Eduard Schweizer, *The Good News According to Matthew* (London: SPCK, 1976), p. 213; and Donald A. Hagner, *Matthew 1–13* (WBC 33a; Nashville: Nelson, 1993), p. 206.

28. Davies, *Jesus the Healer*, p. 77: 'Of course, those who came to him to be healed were self-selected to have faith in him… Faith in physicians…plays an important role in all healing systems.'

29. Richard Bell, *Deliver Us From Evil: Interpreting the Redemption from the Power of Satan in New Testament Theology* (Tübingen: Mohr Siebeck, 2007), pp. 331-32: 'Faith is not prior to release from Satan but subsequent. We see this in

Secondly, the story of the ten lepers (Lk. 17.11-19) is not one that concerns Gentiles as such. Although it is carried out from a (short) distance[30] and the faith of the tenth leper is central to the account,[31] his Samaritan status makes him ἀλλογενής, 'other-born', but not actually Gentile. Therefore, whilst my observations will be relevant to the tenth leper, this narrative requires its own in-depth analysis which is unfortunately outside of the bounds of this study.

Another, briefer, omission is a healing summary at Mt. 12.15-21; Mk 3.7-12; Lk. 6.17-19, in which Jesus heals multitudes by the sea. This may involve both Jewish and Gentile bodies, but this is only possibly implied by Mt. 12.18-21 by means of the insertion of a quote from Isa. 42.1-4 (particularly, 'and in his name the nations will hope'), and is not explicit. The healings seem to be initiated by the crowds who have sought Jesus out, and although Jesus apparently acquiesced, both Mark and Luke depict the crowds taking the initiative for healing by pressing to make physical contact against Jesus' body.

Lastly, the case of the deaf-mute man (Mk 7.31-37) is a little more complex, and is highly distinctive in its use of touch, saliva and word. However, although seemingly situated in the Decapolis, the geographical description which lays the scene for the healing is extremely muddled and does not describe a straightforward journey,[32] and there is also divergence in the ancient sources on v. 31, with manuscript 𝔓45, along with others, providing a more geographically logical reading which has Jesus going *out from* the area of Tyre and Sidon, into the Decapolis region, where he is situated in Mk 8.1-10; however, this is usually rejected in favour of the *lectio difficilior* reading of *through* the area of Tyre and Sidon. Furthermore, at no point is it indicated that the man was Gentile, and he might well have been a Jew living in this region.[33]

---

the case of exorcisms: Jesus does not expect the afflicted person to have faith (and in this respect exorcisms are quite different to "healings").'

30.   Meier, *Marginal Jew*, p. 719: 'All ten lepers (unlike the centurion's servant, the official's son, or the Syrophoenician woman's daughter) do speak to Jesus face to face (though naturally at a distance) and do not employ an intermediary or intercessor'.

31.   Howard Marshall, *The Gospel of Luke: A Commentary on the Greek Text* (Exeter: Paternoster Press, 1978), p. 651: 'The command to go to the priests is a test of faith and obedience'.

32.   Guelich, *Mark*, p. 391: It 'describes what is at best an improbable if not nonsensical route'. So Joel Marcus, *Mark 1–8* (AB 27; London: Doubleday, 2005), p. 472.

33.   William Lane, *The Gospel According to Mark* (Grand Rapids: Eerdmans, 1974), p. 157: 'The location of the episode in the Decapolis proves nothing as to the participants since there were sizeable colonies of Jews in nearly all of the cities'. Cf. Bird, *Mission*, p. 110.

With these exclusions explained, it remains to turn to the two healings: the centurion's boy and the Syrophoenician woman's daughter. From these accounts of Gentile healings, I will endeavour to make some simple deductions regarding how the absence of bodily contact and the requirement of faith are presented. This is not intended as (nor can it be) a comprehensive analysis; it is hoped, simply, that it will draw attention to some basic conclusions as well as to topics for further discussion.

III. *The Centurion's Boy: Matthew 8.5-13 (par. Luke 7.1-10; cf. John 4.46-54)*

> [5]As he entered into Capernaum, a centurion (ἑκατόνταρχος) came up to him and begged him, [6]saying, 'Lord, my boy (ὁ παῖς μου)[34] lies at home, paralysed and suffering dreadfully'. [7]And he replied to him, 'I will come and heal him'. [8]And the centurion answered, 'Lord, I am not worthy to have you enter under my roof; but merely say the word and my boy (ὁ παῖς μου) will be healed. [9]Because also I am a man under authority, having soldiers under me. And I say to this one, 'Go', and he goes; and to another, 'Come', and he comes, and to my slave, 'Do this', and he does it. [10]When he heard this, Jesus marvelled (ἐθαύμασεν), and said to those who were following him, 'Amen, I say to you, I have not found such faith among anyone in Israel (παρ' οὐδενὶ τοσαύτην πίστιν ἐν τῷ Ἰσραὴλ εὗρον). [11]I tell you, many will come from the east and from the west and recline with Abraham and Isaac and Jacob in the kingdom of heaven, [12]but the sons/children of the kingdom (υἱοὶ τῆς βασιλείας) will be cast out in to the outer darkness; there will be weeping and gnashing of teeth. [13]And Jesus said to the centurion, 'Go, as you have had faith, let it be for you (Ὕπαγε, ὡς ἐπίστευσας γενηθήτω σοι)'. And his boy was healed at that very hour.

The version in Luke is very similar, but Luke has the word δοῦλος, 'slave' (Lk. 7.2) for παῖς, 'boy, servant' (Mt. 8.6), who is 'sick at the point of death' rather than paralysed, and the centurion sends 'elders of the Jews' who beseech Jesus on his behalf, who commend him because 'he loves our nation and he built our synagogue for us' (Lk. 7.3-4). As Jesus approaches the house, the centurion now sends a second delegation, of 'friends' (Lk. 7.6-8) with a message of humility, and when Jesus hears it he states that 'not even (οὐδὲ) in Israel have I found such faith'.

---

34. As noted by William D. Davies and Dale C. Allison, *A Critical and Exegetical Commentary on the Gospel According to St Matthew* (3 vols.; London: T&T Clark International, 2004), p. 21: 'Only once in the NT does παῖς clearly mean "son" (Jn 4:51). For the rest it seems to mean "servant" (cf. Mt 14:2; 12:18) or "youngster" (cf. 17:18).' Using the translation 'boy' keeps the ambiguity.

In Luke, Jesus does not speak the command and does not meet the centurion; his friends discover the slave well when they return to the house (Lk. 7.10).

This healing appears in Matthew and Luke as the healing of a Gentile, but in Jn 4.46-54, in altered form, it appears as the healing of a Jewish official's son, a fundamental ethnic (and probably familial) difference which changes its entire meaning.[35] There has been scholarly debate on the relationship between the Synoptic and Johannine versions since Irenaeus (*Adv. Haer.* 2.22.3). Shared elements of the stories are the locus of Capernaum, the appeal to Jesus, the sick boy/slave/son, and the distance from which healing is effected. However, as well as these similarities there are also significant differences, such as the location of Jesus (in Cana in John; in Capernaum in Matthew and Luke) and the Johannine designation of the man as βασιλικὸς, 'royal officer', instead of centurion. The most convincing explanation is not one of inter-textual dependence,[36] but one that suggests both stories evolved out of the same oral tradition.[37]

In both Matthew and Luke[38] the account follows teaching blocks (the Sermon on the Mount and the Sermon on the Plain respectively). In Matthew additionally the healing of the leper's body (8.1-4) interpolates, thus creating a juxtaposition of the healing of a Jewish outcast, via bodily contact, and the healing of a Gentile's son, via an effective exhortation from a distance, 'let it be for you' (ὡς ἐπίστευσας γενηθήτω σοι). In Luke it commences a section (7.1–8.3) which sees Jesus encountering a variety of people—a Gentile, the widow at Nain, John the Baptist's disciples, a sinful woman, and some female supporters—which pivots on the allusion to Jesus as a prophet helping people, in 7.16. Thus, in both Matthew and Luke the placement of this healing works towards the didactic purpose of each Gospel-writer.

The setting of this healing is Capernaum, a town near the border of lower Galilee and close to a major trade route to Damascus, and the

35. Bird, *Mission*, p. 119: 'The Gentile ethnicity of the individual seems slightly more probable'.

36. E.g. Ulrich Luz, *Matthew: A Commentary* (trans. James E. Crouch; 3 vols.; Minneapolis: Fortress Press, 2007), p. 9; Bird, *Mission*, p. 119.

37. E.g. Davies and Allison, *Matthew*, p. 18; Ernst Haenchen and Ulrich Busse, *A Commentary on the Gospel of John* (trans. Robert W. Funk; Philadelphia: Fortress Press, 1984), p. 236; François Bovon, *A Commentary on the Gospel of Luke* (trans. Christine M. Thomas; Minneapolis: Fortress Press, 2002), p. 259; Joseph A. Fitzmyer, *The Gospel According to Luke* (2 vols.; New York: Doubleday, 1985), p. 648.

38. This is the only healing in Matthew which is not in Mark.

appearance of a centurion, indisputably Gentile and evocative of unpopular pagan Roman authority,[39] is unsurprising. The import of this passage in Matthew lies in its interpolation at vv. 11-12, a section which appears in Luke in a totally different context (13.28-29, in a teaching segment) and arranged in reverse order.[40] This is a clear reference to the eschatological inclusion of the Gentiles who would be drawn towards Israel in the end-times,[41] and is described by Bird as the 'quintessential passage for expounding the historical Jesus' supposed view of the fate and future of the Gentiles'.[42] The image of the patriarchs sitting down with Gentiles is surprising given concerns about bodily ritual defilement from such associations (Jn 18.28; Acts 10.28-29; *m. Ohol.* 18.7),[43] and the references to 'east and west' echo the Old Testament 'gathering texts',[44] which refer originally not to the ingathering of Gentiles, but of *Israel* returning from exile.[45] This is a carefully measured Matthaean arrangement, the severity of which creates a warning to Israel that 'has no equal in rabbinic and apocalyptic literature'.[46]

---

39. Keener, *Matthew*, p. 265: 'When Matthew is writing (especially if somewhere in the decade following 70), his Jewish readers in the vicinity of Syria or Palestine would be tempted to hate Romans passionately, especially Roman soldiers, and perhaps especially their basic soldiers. (Centurions were the officers ordinary citizens of other lands most frequently had to confront). Also Bird, *Mission*, p. 121, describes it as 'startling' that 'Jesus performs a healing for someone who was potentially an enemy'.

40. Luz, *Matthew*, p. 9: 'In my judgement the Matthaean form, with its neat parallelism that contrasts with Luke 13.28-29 where the logion has been adapted to its context, is primary'.

41. See n. 21 above.

42. Bird, *Mission*, p. 83.

43. Cf. Christine E. Hayes, *Gentile Impurities and Jewish Identities: Intermarriage and Conversion from the Bible to the Talmud* (New York: Oxford University Press, 2002), pp. 19-67.

44. John Nolland, *The Gospel of Matthew: A Commentary on the Greek Text* (Grand Rapids: Eerdmans, 2005), p. 357.

45. Hagner, *Matthew*, p. 205: 'Until this point, such a banquet was thought to be a strictly Jewish affair... The Gentiles would indeed make their pilgrimage to Jerusalem at the end (cf. Isa. 2:2-3), but mainly as witnesses of God's blessing of Israel, not as direct participants in it.' Ps. 107.3; Isa. 43.5-6; 49.12; Zech. 8.7; Bar. 4.37.

46. Robert H. Gundry, *Matthew: A Commentary on His Handbook for a Mixed Church Under Persecution* (Grand Rapids: Eerdmans, 1994), p. 146. He continues: 'The more disjointed arrangement in Luke has the appearance of spoken words; the careful parallelism in Matthew the appearance of literary artistry with theological purpose' (p. 147).

This caution is emphasized yet further in these verses with the threat that the υἱοὶ τῆς βασιλείας, 'sons/children of the kingdom', will be cast out in to the outer darkness[47] (8.12), a Matthaean particularity which introduces the idea that inclusion in the eschatological banquet of the Kingdom of Heaven will not be on the basis of nationhood, and Gentiles who show faith will take the place of Jews who do not.[48] In this account, the criteria for entrance into the community of God are being redrawn. Matthew's much harsher version than Luke's is demonstrative of his strong polemic against Judaean legal hegemonies with their authority base in Jerusalem, evidenced also, for example, at 21.42, ch. 23 and 27.25, and he casts this healing story with an eschatological hue which is missing from Luke's narrative.

Faith is the driving force in both Synoptic versions of this healing story, and each author has characteristic ways to emphasize the import of the declaration of Mt. 8.10/Lk. 7.9.[49] In Matthew it appears in a section focused on faith,[50] and the positioning of vv. 11-12, discussed above, links the centurion's faith with the suggestion of an eschatology inclusive of Gentiles. Before this though is Jesus' declaration at Mt. 8.7 that he would come and heal the boy, something that divides commentators on whether Jesus is acquiescing or instead asking a question intended to ascertain if the centurion has faith.[51] Whether implicit or otherwise, the centurion passes this test with his response that he is not worthy to have Jesus come under his roof (Mt. 8.8/Lk. 7.6), which not only demonstrates faith, but also heightens it by demonstrating awareness of the prohibitions against association with Gentiles. The later,

47. Hagner, *Matthew*, p. 206: 'The expression τὸ σκότος τὸ ἐξώτερον, "the outer darkness", here refers to the greatest possible contrast with the brilliantly illuminated banquet hall (cf. 22:13; 25:30)'.

48. Richard T. France, *The Gospel According to Matthew: An Introduction and Commentary* (Leicester: InterVarsity Press, 1985), p. 160. Gundry, *Matthew*, p. 146. 'The very ambivalence of "the sons of the kingdom", which may refer either to Israel or to the church, helps make the present statement precursive of the warnings to the church—and even itself an indirect warning to the church'.

49. France, *Matthew*, p. 159, re. ἐθαύμασεν: '[This is] a strong word used of Jesus only here and in Mark 6:6 where it was caused by *lack* of faith among his own people!' Hagner, *Matthew*, p. 205: 'The effect of this statement is…a criticism of the slowness of Israel to believe, a motif that will have increasing prominence as the Gospel [of Mt.] proceeds'.

50. Nolland, *Matthew*, p. 356: 'Half of Matthew's uses of "faith" will be in chaps. 8–9'.

51. E.g. Luke Timothy Johnson, *The Gospel of Luke* (Collegeville: Liturgical Press, 1991), p. 113; France, *Matthew*, p. 158; Davies and Allison, *Matthew*, p. 22; cf. Hagner, *Matthew*, p. 204.

closing command by Jesus in Mt. 8.13 ('Go, as you have had faith, let it be for you', Ὕπαγε, ὡς ἐπίστευσας γενηθήτω σοι) directs attention back to the centurion's faith as the power initiating the miracle, in contrast with its omission in Luke.

In the Lucan version faith is emphasized in different ways, such as the poorer physical state which the slave is in (Mt. 8.6; cf. Lk. 7.2). Luke builds on the faith motif with the insertion of vv. 3-5, when the Jewish elders praise the centurion as αξιός, 'worthy', and a synagogue-builder, thereby a so-called 'God-fearer',[52] which is characteristic of his theme of salvation for all (e.g. Lk. 2.14, 32; 3.38; 4.25-27; 10.30-37; 17.15-19; 24.46-47). However, the effect of this is complicated when the centurion again sends friends in Lk. 7.6-8 to tell Jesus what the Matthaean centurion says himself (8.8-9);[53] most scholars agree, though, that the content of this request emphasizes that the indirectness of the appeal is due to a profusion of faith, not a deficiency.

In short, what we see in this story is an emphasis on the faith of Gentiles as providing their access to both bodily healing and the Kingdom, but Jesus remains bodily removed from the Gentile who is being healed.

IV. *The Syrophoenician Woman's Daughter: Mark 7.24-30 (parr. Matthew 15.21-28)*[54]

[24]He went up from there and came out to the borders of Tyre. And he went into a house but did not want anyone to know, but he was unable to escape being noticed.[55] [25]Now a woman whose little daughter was possessed by an unclean spirit, on hearing about him, immediately came to him and fell down at his feet. [26]The woman was a Greek (Ἑλληνίς), of the Syrophoenician people (Συροφοινίκισσα τῷ γένει), and she asked him to cast the

52. Marshall, *Luke*, p. 280: 'The giving of contributions by Gentiles towards the upkeep of synagogues is well attested... That a Gentile should have built the synagogue itself, however, is unusual. Possibly he was simply a large, or the main, benefactor.'

53. Johnson, *Luke*, p. 115: 'Whether the Q form contained these intermediaries is unclear. Luke may have added them in keeping with his conviction that Jews and their synagogues served as intermediaries in the Gentile mission of the early Church. Or Matthew may have deleted them in light of his editorial policy of omitting unnecessary details and his antipathy toward "their synagogues".'

54. Guelich, *Mark*, p. 383: 'Most...view Matthew's story to be the evangelist's redactional product that included combining Mark with other traditional material drawn from Q and M'.

55. This may reflect Mark's secrecy motif, as opposed to deliberate hiding from Gentiles, and is omitted in Matthew; so Bird, *Mission*, p. 113.

demon out of her daughter. [27]And he said to her, 'Let the children first be filled with food (Ἄφες πρῶτον χορτασθῆναι τὰ τέκνα), for it is not right to take the children's food and throw it to the small dogs (τοῖς κυναρίοις βαλεῖν)'. [28]But she answered, 'Lord, even the dogs under the table eat the children's crumbs'. [29]And he said to her, 'because of this statement, go (Διὰ τοῦτον τὸν λόγον ὕπαγε)—the demon has gone out from your daughter'. [30]And she went to her house and found her child lying on the bed, with the demon gone.

It is helpful to consider this story in terms of the issue of bodily ritual purity. The placement of this narrative in both Mark and Matthew is highly significant, following immediately from the disciples' inability to understand Jesus' teaching on defilement (Mt. 15.1-20; Mk 7.1-20). By contrast, here, the Gentile mother is one who demonstrates understanding through her faith and humility, willing to pick up the crumbs left over from the table where Israel's 'children' eat. Not only is she Gentile, and thereby intrinsically not capable of being purified in accordance with the laws of ritual purity for Israel,[56] but the spirit possessing her daughter is unclean (ἀκάθαρτος, Mk. 7.25 against Mt. 15.22.), though is classified as such only in Judaism. Jesus announces that her statement to him substantively functions as an action of faith creating an exorcism of the unclean demon from her daughter, though he does not declare her daughter 'clean'. The positioning of the story after the discussion of the necessity for inner purity and the contaminating impurity of evil thoughts (Mt. 15.18-20; Mk 7.21-23) is then followed by an example to reflect upon: a Gentile woman who exhibits 'pure' thoughts and thereby enables the 'impure' demon to be expelled. Mark's editorial declaration at 7.19 that Jesus declared all foods clean, omitted in Matthew, is reflective of debates contemporary to its composition of the role of Gentiles in the earliest Christian communities. Clearly, Jesus did not himself announce the purity of all foods, or else there would not have been the debates we find evidenced in Pauline literature (especially in Gal. 1–2). However, the commencement of a 'breaking down of the religious barrier separating Jew from Gentile'[57] is suggested by the juxtaposition of the narrative with the Syrophoenician woman and the scene which precedes it.

In terms of the location of this incident, some ancient manuscripts add καὶ Σιδῶνος after Τύρου in Mk 7.24, but this was probably a deliberate

56. Hayes, *Gentile Impurities*, pp. 19-67 has argued that Gentiles were not technically 'impure', but see Joan E. Taylor, *The Immerser: John the Baptist within Second Temple Judaism* (Grand Rapids: Eerdmans, 1997), pp. 66-68; as Taylor notes, even if they were not always viewed as technically 'impure', they were outside the system by which they could become pure.

57. Meier, *Marginal Jew*, p. 660.

echo of Mt. 15.21 and Mk 7.31.[58] The Gentile nature of the location in Matthew is more ambiguous than Mark, with Jesus moving *towards* the Gentile area, and no indication of an arrival. The ethnicity of the woman is clearer and also pertinent though. She is described in Mark as a Greek of the Syrophoenician people (and in Mt 15.22 as a Χαναναία, Canaanite), likely an ethnic Syrophoenician who had attained 'Greek' city citizenship in Tyre, and by deduction probably from the educated upper classes.[59] The term *Syro*phoenician distinguishes the woman from the *Liby*phoenicians of North Africa, around Carthage, in common nomenclature, but more than this, it marks her out as being a local Gentile of unpopular heritage,[60] with whom Jews could spar. Thus, for first-century Jews, her Syrophoenician ethnicity and 'Greek' (Tyrian) identity would have added to the negative status which her Gentile status already conferred on her. Likewise in the Matthaean version, Χαναναία rings of the neighbours who are the juxtaposed, pagan antitheses of the Jews in the scriptures.[61]

The hostile connotations of the woman's ethnicity are evident in Jesus' first response to her, in which he classifies her among the 'dogs' (Mk 7.27), a designation which could only be taken as pejorative (Exod. 22.31; 1 Sam. 17.43; 2 Sam. 16.9; Ps. 22.16; Isa. 56.10-11; Mt. 7.6; Phil. 3.2; 2 Pet. 2.22; Rev. 22.15),[62] and a common term for Gentiles in literature of Second Temple Judaism.[63] She is then defined as a scavenger, and not a member of the family of Israel.

However, despite this insult, the interchange creates an image of the eschatological banquet, on several counts. First, *Midr. Ps.* 4.11 similarly compares righteous Gentiles to dogs at the eschatological banquet; the dogs eat, but not as well as the human guests.[64] Secondly, the word χορτασθῆναι, literally meaning 'to feed until full up', is echoed in Mk

58. Marcus, *Mark*, p. 462; France, *Matthew*, p. 295.

59. Gerd Theissen, *The Gospels in Context: Social and Political Tradition in the Synoptic Tradition* (Edinburgh: T. & T. Clark, 1992), p. 69.

60. *Apion* 1.70; *Ant.* 14.313-21; *War* 2.478. Marcus, *Mark*, p. 461: 'There was bad blood between the Tyrians and Galileans, partly because much of the agricultural produce of Jewish Galilee ended up in Gentile Tyre, the main urban area near Galilee, while the Jewish peasants often went hungry'. See also Theissen, *Gospels in Context*, pp. 72-80.

61. So Hagner, *Matthew*, p. 441.

62. Hugh Anderson, *The Gospel of Mark* (Grand Rapids: Eerdmans, 1996), p. 190: 'By reason of its apparent harshness, Jesus' reply has perplexed the commentators'.

63. See Bird, *Mission*, pp. 48-50.

64. Marcus, *Mark*, p. 464; Bird, *Mission*, p. 48.

6.42 and 8.8 in the miraculous feedings, the first being understood as a
feeding of Jews, and the second as a feeding of Gentiles. The Marcan
narrative of the Syrophoenician woman acts as a pinnacle on which the
writer's view of salvation history rests;[65] having *first* (πρῶτον) ensured
that the Jews, God's children, had been satisfied, food remains to feed
the Gentile 'dogs', reminiscent of the twelve baskets of bread and fish
remaining in 6.43, following the feeding of the five thousand (Jews).[66]
The key verse, Mk. 7.27a, does not appear in Matthew (cf. Mt. 15.26),
meaning that both the notion of Israel πρῶτον, 'first', and the concept of
Israel eating until full up, are absent.[67] Again, the idea of Jewish priority
and Gentile inclusion have strong Pauline overtones,[68] and are suggestive
of the inclusion of Gentiles in the end-times.[69]

Jesus' initial refusal to heal is frequently understood as a test for the
woman to demonstrate her faith, and thus her child's worthiness for
healing,[70] reminiscent of Jesus' words to both the father of the epileptic
boy in Mk 9.23 and to the centurion at Mt. 8.7; all can be seen as tests
of faith prior to bodily healing, which the petitioners 'pass'. Similarly
in Matthew's version of the healing of the Syrophoenician woman's

65. Schweizer, *Matthew*, p. 151: 'This section is a single story organised entirely
around the saying in vss.27f... the story must have been directed from the very
beginning to the problem of the relation of the Gentiles to the Jews'.

66. Bird, *Mission*, p. 111: 'Though speculative, it remains plausible that the
twelve baskets in Mark 6 represent the twelve tribes of Israel, while the seven
baskets in Mark 8 represent the nations. If the shape of the narrative is to function as
a symbolic anticipation of the messianic banquet, it could be inferred that Jews and
Gentiles are said to participate and Jesus' miraculous action is a foretaste of that
inclusion'.

67. Marcus, *Mark*, p. 463, citing Mk 3.27; 7.27; 9.11-12; 13.10, asserts that
πρῶτον is often attributed to Mark's redaction, in part because it is always used by
him in the neuter singular form 'for events on the eschatological time line'. So
Guelich, *Mark*, p. 383; Schweizer, *Matthew*, p. 152.

68. Marcus, *Mark*, p. 463: 'It was uncertain whether Mark's Pauline-sounding
formulation meant that he knew Paul or whether it just meant that he moved in the
same circles that Paul did...so here it is uncertain whether Mark is in contact with
Paul or merely with the sort of tradition that Paul picked up'.

69. Cf. Bird, *Mission*, p. 116: 'Whereas the salvation of the Gentiles was ordinarily programmed to occur at the eschaton, here the in-breaking of the kingdom and
the gradual restoring of Israel was already bringing immediate results for Gentiles...
In this sense, interpreting the pericope in terms of "Jew first and then Gentile" fails
to grapple with the significance that a partially realized restoration has for Gentiles.'

70. Lane, *Mark*, p. 262; Keener, *Matthew*, p. 417; France, *Mark*, p. 298; Marcus,
Mark, pp. 468-69; Morna D. Hooker, *The Gospel According to St Mark* (London:
Continuum, 2009), p. 183. Cf. Gundry, *Matthew*, p. 375.

daughter (Mt. 15.21-28), the woman's unquestioning acceptance of the Jewish view of salvation, and her perseverance, impress Jesus enough that he heals her daughter; her faith is presented as even greater for her determination, especially following the disciples' request to send her on her way (Mt. 15.23) and Jesus' declaration that he was sent only for Israel (Mt. 15.24). The motif of faith is much clearer in Matthew than in Mark,[71] since not only is there this emphasis on the Israel-centric purpose of Jesus' mission (Mt. 15.24),[72] but also the Matthaean Jesus makes explicit that the bodily healing has only been effected in consequence of her faith (Mt. 15.28; cf. Mk 7.29). Furthermore, the woman in the Matthaean version *twice* requests healing from Jesus (vv. 22, 25), and is thus presented with twice the faith of the Marcan woman. Finally, the *children*'s crumbs of Mk 7.28b have now become the *masters*' crumbs in Mt. 15.27b, and thus 'the faith of the woman is heightened by this admission that the Jews are masters over the Gentiles'.[73] The interchange is perhaps reflective of discussions in Matthew's community of how Jewish Christians could live alongside their Gentile counterparts.[74]

V. *The Absence of Physical Contact and the Requirement of Faith*

Significantly, both healings of Gentile bodies are carried out from a distance, and the disciples' request at Mt. 15.23 that Jesus send the Syro-phoenician woman away suggests an additional desire not only to avoid contact, but to be held physically apart, though in Mark she has actually come very close to his body, to his feet (Mk 7.25).[75] In the healing of the centurion's boy/servant, though, Jesus does intend to set off towards the sick boy in order to heal him (Mt. 8.7; Lk. 7.6), but never gets there.

The physical distance is highly significant, given that we do not have a single account of Jesus healing a *Jewish body* from afar.[76] Furthermore,

71. Cf. Lane, *Mark*, p. 263, re. Mk 7.29a: 'The command to return home is important, for in Mark Jesus speaks in this manner each time he perceives the profound confidence of those who request healing (Chs. 2.11; 5.34; 7.29; 10.52)'.

72. Jesus as shepherd of Israel is a common motif in Matthew (9.36; 10.6; 18.12).

73. John C. Fenton, *The Gospel of St Matthew* (Harmondsworth: Penguin, 1963), p. 256.

74. Johnson, *Luke*, p. 238.

75. Cf. Bird, *Mission*, p. 123: 'Jesus begins accepting Gentiles as Gentiles'.

76. Johnson, *Luke*, p. 116, discusses the rabbinic account of Hanina ben Dosa's healing from a distance of Gamaliel's son in *b. Ber.* 34b as 'a parallel' in its 'strange motif of healing at a distance'. However, while Hanina prays to God for healing, Jesus is presented as much more autonomous in his healing.

in the synoptic accounts Jesus uses touch as a healing mode with great frequency,[77] and thus it is conspicuous here by its absence. Some have suggested that Jesus avoided bodily contact with Gentiles for purity reasons,[78] but given the evidence of his healing *Jews* made impure by illness or death by using bodily contact, this cannot be upheld. Indeed, the sick *were* to be kept apart from the divine precincts of the Temple: Lev. 21.16-23 explicitly forbids anyone with a physical defect from approaching the altar to offer food to God, while, similarly, Deut. 15.21 states that if an *animal* is defected or flawed, it must not be sacrificed to God.[79] Jesus is clearly presented across the Synoptic Gospels as being unconcerned by the risk of defilement or impurity through bodily contact with those in need of physical restoration, and there is thus no reason to believe that avoidance of contracting ritual impurity would have been a reason for his not touching the Gentiles he healed. More explicitly, his choice to touch a corpse in the revivification of Jairus's daughter (Mt. 9.25; Mk 5.41; Lk. 8.54) and the funeral bier of the boy at Nain (Lk. 7.14) would have normatively rendered Jesus defiled,[80] as would the healing of the leper, which overcomes the community exclusion specifically prescribed in Num. 5.2.

There are of course narrative-specific explanations for the lack of bodily contact. The Syrophoenician woman's daughter, is, technically speaking, an exorcism, and Jesus is always reported as carrying these out with words, as opposed to touch, in comparison with some of his contemporaries, such as Eleazar who used a ring, roots and water.[81] However, more pertinent was the faith factor. Faith is not attributed the same emphasis in accounts of other healings, either across the ancient world[82] or in the Synoptic Gospels. Indeed, faith plays an important part in Jesus'

77. See n. 2 above.
78. E.g. Guelich, *Mark*, pp. 382-83.
79. This is reinforced at Mal. 1.8, 13b. Donald J. Wiseman, 'Medicine in the Old Testament World', in Bernard Palmer (ed.), *Medicine and the Bible* (Exeter: Paternoster Press, 1986), pp. 15-42 (22): 'The principle was that such defective persons, like any defective offerings (Deut. 15:21) would detract from the wholeness (holiness) of God'.
80. Num. 5.1-3; 19.11-13, 16; 31.19-20. For discussion on the different kinds of defilement, see Jonathan Klawans, *Impurity and Sin in Ancient Judaism* (New York: Oxford University Press, 2000); and Hayes, *Gentile Impurities*.
81. *Ant.* 8.46-47.
82. Gerd Theissen and Annette Merz, *The Historical Jesus: A Comprehensive Guide* (London: SCM Press, 1998), p. 293, re. the epileptic boy: 'The promise "Your faith has saved you" is without parallel in connection with miracles in antiquity…only in the case of Jesus does faith become a miracle-working power which precedes the miracle'.

healings of the haemorrhaging woman,[83] the epileptic boy,[84] the para-lytic,[85] and the sight-healings of the blind man/men of Jericho,[86] the two blind men in Capernaum,[87] and the man born blind;[88] but half of these are sight restorations, emphasizing the strong theological connections between faith, spiritual sight, and bodily sight.

Gentiles were required to demonstrate similar spiritual insight, namely faith, in order to receive healing, the nature of which was not a 'vague, unfocused wishful thinking, but a seriously practical and purposeful resolve'.[89] The effect of faith's absence is presented in Matthew and Luke's rejection of Jesus at Nazareth (Mt. 13.53-58; Lk. 6.1-6), and his consequent inability or unwillingness to perform any substantial miracle in the face of this. A similar theme is found in the Matthaean account of the exorcism of the (Jewish) epileptic boy in which the disciples are unable to heal, again—according to Jesus—because of their inadequate faith (17.19-20).[90] Both of these examples suggest that although Jesus asserted little or no control over a sick person's faith in his curative abilities, his healings (or lack thereof) depended to a degree on the presence of such faith, and it is presented as a dominant external influence on his readiness and ability to heal.

The power of faith for healing is also demonstrated in the healing of the haemorrhaging (Jewish) woman (Mt. 9.18-29; Mk 5.21-43; Lk. 8.40-56), which presents faith having an almost uncontrollable effect on Jesus, when physical contact is made not even with him, but with his garment.[91] The Marcan and Lucan versions show faith in its rawest

83. Mt. 9.18-29; Mk 5.21-43; Lk. 8.40-56.

84. Mk 9.24 (against Matthew and Luke). The Matthaean version emphasizes the necessity of *Jesus'* faith in the healing (17.19-21, against Mark and Luke).

85. Mt. 9.2; Mk 2.5; Lk. 5.20. John Wilkinson, *The Bible and Healing: A Medical and Theological Commentary* (Edinburgh: Handsel Press, 1998), p. 101: 'Modern commentators usually understand this to refer to the faith of the sick man and his friends, rather than to that of the friends alone, which was the view of the older commentators'.

86. Mk 10.52; Lk. 18.42, against Matthew.

87. Mt. 9.28-29.

88. Retrospectively, at Jn 9.38. N.B. *all* of these sight restorations involve physical contact in healing, compared with only the haemorrhaging woman in the healings of other bodily afflictions.

89. Colin Sedgwick, 'Healed, Restored, Forgiven', *ET* 118 (2007), pp. 261-66 (263).

90. It is also implied in the Lucan account at 9.41 but technique is instead blamed in the Marcan parallel (9.29).

91. Hooker, *Mark*, p. 148: 'It was common at the time to think of clothing as an extension of personality, and the woman's desire to touch his clothes was natural'.

form[92] as a force almost at the boundaries of Jesus' control, which connects with him through touch to achieve bodily healing. Jesus felt the healing power come out from him, accomplished by physical contact and compelled by faith; he was not simply a conductor of healing who emanated curative power to all who touched him, for the woman was but one of many people in the crowd who made physical contact with him (Mk 5.24, 31; Lk. 8.42, 45 against Matthew), and yet seemingly the only one who was healed, because she had reached out to him in *faith*.

This is where the answer to our question lies. Jesus' mission was *not* directed towards Gentiles, evident in his apparently deliberate avoidance of bodily contact with them, yet those who appealed with faith were, according to the Gospels, restored to a state of health, wholeness and well-being. In addition, not only were those discussed Gentile, but the Gospel-writers have presented Gentiles of 'types' that would have attracted especially sharp Jewish hostilities: the centurion represented the Roman authorities, while the Tyrian Syrophoenician woman was also part of a distrusted group. The faith required of them was thus exaggerated due not only to their Gentile status, but also to the connotations of their social and ethnic groups, to the extent that it was of such potency that it effected healing across great distances. This was both the test and fulfilment; the power of the faith required in the Gentile healings is evidenced in the absence of bodily contact in effecting restoration to health.

Conclusions

In the Synoptic accounts of both the centurion's boy and the Syrophoenician woman's daughter, although each bears the hallmark of the Gospel in which it is situated, there are some common elements. Faith is put forward as a test which needs to be passed, in order for Gentiles to ignite Jesus' engagement and 'qualify' for bodily healing, and it must be of such potency that it can effect Jesus' healing across distance. His reticence to heal Gentiles is self-evident in the absence of bodily contact and the emphasized requirement of faith in these accounts.

The healings discussed here are presented as a foreshadowing of later Gentile inclusion, but not, as Bird asserts, indicative that the restoration of Israel 'was partially realised [and so] it was becoming possible in the

---

92. Mk 5.29; Lk. 8.44, against Matthew, whose account is much briefer and omits many of the details in Mark and Luke. However, Hagner, *Matthew*, p. 249: 'It was her faith, exemplified in her desire to touch Jesus' garment, that appropriated the healing power of Jesus'.

present time for Gentiles to experience the salvation associated with the arrival of the eschatological age'.[93] The Synoptic Gospels as a whole suggest that the Gentile mission was quite *peripheral* to Jesus' ministry,[94] and, in the words of James Dunn, that Jesus 'did not seek out Gentiles but responded positively to faith and commended unreservedly neighbourly love wherever and by whomsoever it was expressed'.[95] It would have been more convenient, given later Pauline theology, if Jesus *had* shown more enthusiasm for Gentile inclusion, and an invented story of Gentile healings would surely have presented a Jesus immediately willing to welcome righteous Gentiles.

Jesus' marked detachment from Gentile bodies in the Synoptic healing narratives suggests little interest in the restoration and salvation of Gentiles, at least in his lifetime. Jesus' Gentile healings, though briefly deferred by the requirement of faith, were—because of this uncomfortable portrayal—probably historical. They tread a fine line between what is 'unlawful' and what was appropriate for the Kingdom. That the Gospel of John in fact has no Gentile healings, with the 'centurion's son/slave' found as the son of a royal official (Jn 4.46-53), the 'second sign [to the Jews] that Jesus performed when he had come from Judaea into Galilee' (v. 54), would suggest too that this story did not even necessarily circulate in a 'Gentile-friendly' form in all churches, leaving only the story of the Syrophoenician woman's daughter as the definitive Gentile healing, included in the narrative additionally to highlight how much a Gentile woman's faith and right-thinking could critique concepts of purity in Israel. To conclude, for all their Israel-centricism these stories remain key inclusions in the Gospels, given the import and controversy of later Gentile inclusion in the churches.

---

93. Bird, *Mission,* p. 173 (my italics).
94. So Keener, *Matthew*, p. 263.
95. James D. G. Dunn, *Jesus Remembered* (Grand Rapids: Eerdmans, 2003), p. 539.

6

JEWISH BLESSING OR THYESTEAN BANQUET?
THE EUCHARIST AND ITS ORIGINS

Katie Turner

'What Jesus was doing at the Last Supper has not been understood for the better part of 2,000 years', writes Bruce Chilton.[1] While many would counter that they do indeed understand what Jesus was doing, Chilton is correct in so far as there has been a great deal of debate surrounding the Eucharist, and academia certainly has not reached a consensus.[2] In this essay I will be dealing with the more historically based parts of the debate as opposed to the theological—namely, asking what Jesus' words *were* rather than what he meant by them—and thus I will be focusing on the Synoptic gospels and Paul's account, leaving the theology of John aside for now. I will provide an overview of the history of the blessing itself, including its cultural origins. It is this latter aspect that drew myself and others to this topic, as it is very difficult to imagine a first-century Jewish teacher invoking blood imagery in a blessing directed to a Jewish audience (especially as his audience, at least in the Synoptic gospels, displays no adverse reaction). This essay, therefore, will address

---

1. Bruce Chilton, 'The Eucharist—Exploring Its Origins', *Bible Review* (December 1994), pp. 36-43 (36).
2. It is anachronistic to call whatever Jesus did over bread and wine during his last meal the 'Eucharist'. The Eucharist is a ritual practice based on theological developments and the formation of the Church. When someone states that they are looking at the origin of the Eucharist, they could be studying exactly that, the formal-ized, Church-sanctioned ritual. I will, however, for simplicity's sake, be using the term 'Eucharist' to connote the actions of Jesus during the Last Supper as reported by the Synoptic gospels and Paul. To differentiate this from the formal sacrament institutionalized by the Church, I will refer to the latter as communion. Though there is a difference between communion as practiced by the Roman Catholic and Orthodox Churches and Protestant denominations, I will not be addressing later developments and therefore do not feel it is necessary to designate a further term to denote this difference.

some of the common questions found within this aspect of the debate, namely: Did the blessing originate with Jesus himself? How does one explain the blood symbolism within a Jewish context? Does the blood symbolism indicate a different source or cultural influence?

I. *Blood Language*

Before I address the scholarly arguments surrounding the origin of the Eucharist, it is important to discuss why the 'blood language' is so problematic, as it plays into each aspect of the wider debate. When Jesus blessed bread and wine during the Last Supper, he pronounced the bread his 'body' and the wine his 'blood', asking his disciples to partake in each (Mk 14.22-24; Mt. 26.26-28; Lk. 22.17-20; 1 Cor. 11.23-26). However, this consumption of blood, whether taken literally or figuratively, sits in stark violation of Jewish law. According to the Hebrew Bible, Jews are forbidden from consuming blood (Gen. 9.3-4) as 'blood is the life' and thus belongs to God (Deut. 12.23). Even after animals are cooked, the blood is still prohibited (Lev. 3.17; 7.26; 17.10; 19.26; Deut. 12.16; 15.23). The rabbis extended the original biblical prohibitions, for example by forbidding the eating of bread if stained with blood from one's own gums.[3] The importance of keeping this law is even carried through into the New Testament and directed toward Gentiles, when James, leader of the Jerusalem church, asks Gentiles 'turning to God' to 'abstain from…what is strangled and from blood' (Acts 15.20), most likely following the Noahide rules for 'resident aliens' as found in Lev. 17.10-12.[4] Thus, Geza Vermes pointed out the difficulty posed by the Eucharist to historians: 'the imagery of eating a man's body and especially drinking his blood…, even after allowance is made for metaphorical language, strikes a totally foreign note in a Palestinian Jewish cultural setting. With their profoundly rooted blood taboo, Jesus' listeners would have been overcome with nausea at hearing such words.'[5] It is worth noting that even though the prohibitions given in the Hebrew Bible are of a physical nature, and thus Vermes's assertion that even 'metaphorical language' would be appalling might seem exaggerated, Jesus himself warns against a thought process that may lead to breaking the law (Mt. 5.18-19, 22, 28).

3. 'Blood', in R. J. Zwi Werblowsky and Geoffrey Wigoder (eds.), *The Encyclopedia of the Jewish Religion* (New York: Holt, Rinehart & Winston, 1965), p. 73.
4. Alan Segal, *Paul the Convert: The Apostolate and Apostasy and of Saul the Pharisee* (New Haven: Yale University Press, 1990), pp. 198, 219.
5. Geza Vermes, *The Religion of Jesus the Jew* (London: SCM Press, 1993), p. 16.

How is it, then, if Vermes's assessment is to be accepted (and I feel it should be, unless a valid alternative can be provided), that the gospels record no adverse reaction from the disciples? On other occasions when Jesus' teaching proved difficult for the disciples to understand, the gospels record their reactions (cf. Mk. 8.14-21, 31-33; Lk. 2.47-51). John 6.52-58 contains the one exception. This passage describes Jesus instructing his followers that his flesh is 'true food' and his blood is 'true drink',[6] but not in the same way as found in the Synoptics and 1 Corinthians.[7] However, it is only here that the troubling nature of the blessing is recognized: 'When many of his disciples heard it, they said, "This teaching is difficult; who can accept it?"'(Jn 6.60). It was, in fact, so disconcerting that after this discussion all but 'the twelve' abandoned Jesus (6.66). Gillian Feeley-Harnik has offered a possible explanation for this discrepancy, suggesting that the Synoptics also represent the disciples' struggle to understand Jesus' words. After the Last Supper, when Jesus goes out to pray alone, his disciples fall asleep, despite his repeated requests that they stay awake and keep watch. Feeley-Harnick

6. In Jn 6.53 Jesus is said to command his followers to 'eat' his flesh using the word τρώγων, a verb meaning 'bite' or 'chew' (τρώγων μου τὴν σάρκα), so BDAG, p. 1019.

7. Nevertheless, many scholars understand these verses as implying the Eucharist; see A. J. B. Higgins, 'The Origins of the Eucharist', *NTS* 1 (1955), pp. 200-209, as reviewed in Peder Borgen, *Bread from Heaven: An Exegetical Study of the Concept of Manna in the Gospel of John and the Writings of Philo* (Leiden: Brill, 1965), pp. 96-97; Raymond E. Brown, *The Gospel and Epistles of John: A Concise Commentary* (Collegeville: The Order of St. Benedict, Inc., 1988), pp. 45-47. The language used by the evangelist (see n. 6) would have sounded vile, even symbolically, to an audience outside of this context, indicating an awareness that the Eucharistic ritual was problematic within Judaism. The use of the verb τρώγων, therefore, must have been a conscious decision in an attempt to convey deeper meaning (possibly to combat Docetism), and could only be read as such if interpreted as a direct reference to the institution of the Eucharist. The setting of the narrative during Passover; the distribution of bread by Jesus; a sacramental act similar to that performed during the Last Supper; the didactic monologue involving manna from Heaven and Moses, as well as the reference to Judas as the betrayer found at the end of the chapter all point to vv. 51-58 as being the near climax of a fully Eucharistic scene. See: Craig A. Evans (ed.), *The Bible Knowledge Background Commentary: John's Gospel, Hebrews–Revelation* (Colorado Springs: Cook Communications Ministries, 2005), pp. 70-76. Unlike the Synoptic gospels, this is not a scene played out historically, but more a discourse of the real meaning for the reader. It is sacramental in a typical Johannine fashion—it tells the reader of the importance of the Eucharist in salvation theology Because of this, however, I would contend that the passage cannot be used to determine what Jesus *actually* taught.

interprets this, as well as their flight upon his arrest, as the disciples not understanding or accepting Jesus' teaching during the Eucharist.[8] However, I find this analysis to be a stretch too far. In the examples cited above, the gospels are clear that the disciples 'lack understanding'; they respond immediately to the confusion.

If Feeley-Harnick's interpretation is accepted, a delay is introduced between the point of contention (in this case the 'blood' language) and the disciples' display of misunderstanding (their 'sleeping' and 'fleeing'). This is a pattern that does not fit the other instances in the gospels where a misunderstanding is presented. Many studies that have examined the origins of the Eucharist do so without properly exploring the blood prohibition. Michael J. Cahill has addressed the lack of adequate responses to this conundrum. He catalogues extensively the work done in this field, covering various approaches to the study (many of which will be covered in this chapter) and offering criticism. According to Cahill, scholars need to be able to address how such a blessing could arise within a Jewish context, and if they cannot, provide an alternative possibility. As he states, 'It is a key problem; if this can be solved, then much of the problem of the origins and growth of the Christian Eucharist will be resolved'.[9] Unfortunately, in order properly to continue this essay, I will have to repeat much of Cahill's work. As he has done, I will be looking at various responses scholarship has provided, examining Jesus, Paul, and pagan origins theories.

II. *Paul as Originator*

Some scholars have suggested that Paul is actually the originator of the Eucharistic blessing as it is written in the New Testament—whether that be the blessing in its entirety, or simply its recorded form. John Dominic Crossan theorized that Paul received a sacramental tradition already in place within the early Christian communities, and altered it based on how he conceived of its meaning. Crossan argued that although Jesus did have a 'last meal', what was finally recorded in the gospels represents a tradition that went through 'five (six if John is counted) stages of

---

8. Gillian Feeley-Harnik, *The Lord's Table: Eucharist and Passover in Early Christianity* (Symbol and Culture; Philadelphia: University of Pennsylvania Press, 1981), p. 66.

9. Michael J. Cahill, 'Drinking Blood at a Kosher Eucharist? The Sound of Scholarly Silence', *Biblical Theology Bulletin: A Journal of Bible and Theology* 32, no. 168 (2002), pp. 168-81 (175).

development'.[10] Over time, a tradition that began with open commen-sality, following the social egalitarianism of Jesus' community, became, through Paul's involvement, a 'ritual meal with Christian commen-sality'.[11]

It took an understanding of Jesus as a martyr for the body and blood terms to be incorporated into the blessing, as the pairing of these two words together is specific to martyrological texts. The normal combi-nation of terms that one would have used in a Judaic context to refer to the self would have been גוף and נפש (body and soul), whereas בשר and דם (flesh and blood) were the standard pairing used for a physical body. The fact that the Eucharist instead contains the pairing גוף and דם (body and blood) indicates that either Jesus conceived of himself as a martyr and spoke with that language in mind or, after his death, he was seen as a martyr and these terms were applied. Crossan argues the latter.[12]

Already, Rudolph Bultmann argued that Paul received the tradition and re-imagined it as a 'representational right', similar to the 'acted rights' of the mystery cults; in essence, the Eucharist *acts out* the death of Christ. The meaning of the Eucharist and the accompanying liturgical words developed in parallel with theological explanations for Jesus' death; 'in Hellenistic Christianity, the Lord's Supper…is understood *as a sacrament in the sense of the mystery religions*'.[13] Paul's use of the phrase 'the table of the Lord' (1 Cor. 10.21) is, according to Bultmann, a Hellenistic term for cultic banquets, thus likening the Lord's Supper to those cults. It is entirely possible that Paul simply used this language to make it more understandable to the gentile Christians that were his audience, though Bultmann does not offer this as an explanation.

A. N. Wilson went further than Bultmann when he argued that the Eucharist, and even the depiction of the Last Supper, derives singularly from Paul, suggesting that Paul borrowed the term 'Lord's Supper', κυριακὸν δεῖπνον, from the Mithraic cult. According to Wilson, Paul combined elements together (such as a possible last *Passover* meal had by Jesus) into the sacrament of the Eucharist with no indication that he received the tradition from anybody other than 'Christ' (1 Cor. 11.23, which reads 'Lord' in Greek). This is contrary to Bultmann and Crossan, who focus on the 'reception' (παρέλαβον), taking it as an indication of a

10. John Dominic Crossan, *The Historical Jesus: The Life of a Mediterranean Jewish Peasant* (Edinburgh: T. & T. Clark, 1991), p. 360.

11. *Ibid.*, p. 367.

12. *Ibid.*, pp. 364-65.

13. Rudolf Bultmann, *Theology of the New Testament*, I (trans. Kendrick Grobel; 2 vols.; London: SCM Press, 1952), p. 148.

tradition passed through an earlier community with 'Christ' signifying that community. Wilson was correct when he echoed the sentiments of Vermes and others, stating that 'the idea that a pious Jew such as Jesus would have spent his last evening on earth asking his disciples to drink a cup of blood, even symbolically, is unthinkable'.[14]

Unless a sufficient theory can be offered to explain how Jesus would have come to use this language, then Wilson (and Vermes *et al.*) should be supported in his assessment of the troubling nature of the language. However, to attribute the entirety of the blessing to the creative thoughts of Paul alone is, I believe, one step too far. Bultmann's and Crossan's respective theories that a tradition was in existence but developed further in response to the growing Christian community are more plausible.

Cahill provides further criticism of those arguments presented above by Bultmann, Wilson, and Crossan. He claims that those scholars who offer this alternative have just as much responsibility to explain how Paul, also a Jew, would initiate a blessing that incorporates the consumption of blood as they do for Jesus.[15] I disagree: failure to circumcise was punishable by death (Gen. 17.14) and yet Paul argued against the need for circumcision based on his theological understanding of Christ (Rom. 2.29; 1 Cor. 7.19; Gal. 2.11-14; 5). It is likely, based on what one can discern of Paul's character, that he would have found the blood symbolism acceptable if he felt the message behind the ritual (as all rituals are acts intended to convey special meaning) was more important than or superseded the prohibition. This does not mean, however, that Paul developed the tradition himself. As Bultmann states, given Paul's attitude to flesh and blood (1 Cor. 15.50), this is highly unlikely.[16] It is more probable that if Paul affected the Eucharist at all, it was as a recipient of an already established tradition.

III. *Looking to the Text*

In order to examine properly the idea that Paul received and perhaps altered the tradition of the Eucharist, the text requires analysis. There are four variations of the Eucharist in the New Testament—Mk 14.22-25; Mt. 26.26-29; Lk. 22.17-20; 1 Cor. 11.23-26. The Synoptic gospels indicate that the words were said during a Passover meal. The Gospel of John we will leave to one side, since there are no Eucharistic words said in the

14. A. N. Wilson, *Paul: The Mind of the Apostle* (London: W. W. Norton & Co., 1997), pp. 165-67.
15. Cahill, 'Drinking Blood', p. 170.
16. Bultmann, *Theology of the New Testament*, I, p. 150.

Johannine Last Supper, and this is, additionally, not a Passover meal. While most historians of Jesus tend to favour the Synoptic presentation, that Jesus did not eat the Passover meal but rather a meal on the eve of Passover, has been strongly argued by Vermes, and is relevant, as we shall see below.[17] In fact, though Paul has the Eucharistic words (unlike in John), Paul never indicates that the night Jesus was betrayed was Passover, and talks of Jesus instead as the 'Passover lamb' (1 Cor. 5.7); the lambs were slaughtered on the eve of Passover.

The actual words spoken over the bread and the wine differ in each version, although there seem to be two basic formats, with Matthew following Mark and Luke following Paul (see Table 1). As Paul Bradshaw has concluded from detailed linguistic analysis, Mark, and therefore Matthew, is Semitic in construction; this is indicated by the opening clause 'as they were eating', and the fact that they first 'bless' the bread and then 'give thanks' over the cup. Although Matthew repeats Mark's parallel phrases 'this is my body' and 'this is my blood', he adds commands to 'eat' and 'drink', as well as a theological explanation that the blood is 'for the forgiveness of sins'. In Paul and Luke, however, Jesus tells his disciples to repeat his actions 'in remembrance' of him. Paul and Luke are more Hellenistic in their constructions, separating the blessing with the phrase 'after the supper' and 'giving thanks' over both the bread *and* the wine.[18] Bultmann proposes that Paul also contains Semitic elements, as 'of the covenant' and 'poured out' are Jewish in tradition.[19] Luke differs from Paul, as well as from Mark and Matthew, in one very interesting respect: unlike the others, Luke's version of the Eucharist has two cups of wine. While in Paul, Mark, and Matthew Jesus blesses the bread and then the wine, in Luke Jesus blesses the wine, the bread, and then the wine again (see Table 1). Some manuscripts of Luke, however, have only a shorter blessing—the wine and then the bread—with no 'blood' imagery.[20] The longer form of Luke, with the 'blood' imagery, is generally the accepted version; but this then raises the question: Why does the shorter version exist? It is highly unlikely that a redactor would *remove* the element that is central to this important Christian ritual.[21] Bart

---

17. Geza Vermes, *The Passion* (London: Penguin Books, 2005), pp. 96-97, 112, 115-16; Fergus G. B. Millar, 'Reflections on the Trials of Jesus', in Philip R. Davies and Richard T. White (eds.), *A Tribute to Geza Vermes: Essays on Jewish and Christian Literature and History* (Sheffield: Sheffield Academic Press), pp. 355-81.

18. Paul F. Bradshaw, *Eucharistic Origins* (London: SPCK, 2004), pp. 1-23.

19. Bultmann, *Theology of the New Testament*, I, p. 149.

20. Luke 22.19b-20 are omitted in the codex Bezae and some Old Latin versions.

21. Bradshaw, *Eucharistic Origins*, p. 5.

Ehrman has suggested that these verses 'were added to stress that it was Jesus' broken body and shed blood that brought salvation "for you"', as an element of anti-docetic redaction.[22]

Table 1. Comparison of the eucharistic wording as found within the New Testament, trans. K. Turner. Square brackets indicate variant manuscripts; round brackets words that need to be supplied in translation.

Mt. 26.20-29	Mk 14.17-25	Lk. 22.14-20	1 Cor. 11.23-27
[20] When it was evening, he was reclining at the table with the twelve; [21-25] and as they were eating he said, 'Truly I say to you, one of you will betray me'...Judas, who betrayed him, said, 'Surely not I Rabbi?'; He replied, 'You have said so.'	[17] And when it was evening, he came with the twelve. [18-21] And as they reclined and were eating, Jesus said, 'Truly I tell you, one of you will betray me, one who is eating with me...it would have been better for that one not to have been born.'	[14] And when the hour came, he reclined at the table, and the apostles were with him. [15-16] And he said to them, 'With great desire I desired to eat this Passover with you...in the Kingdom of God.' [17] And having taken a cup and given thanks, he said, 'Take this and share it among yourselves; 18 for I say to you, that from now on I will not drink of the fruit of the vine until the Kingdom of God comes.'	[23] For I received from the Lord that which I passed on to you, that the Lord Jesus on the night he was betrayed
[26] While they were eating, Jesus took bread, and having blessed it he broke it and gave it to the disciples, and said, 'Take, eat; this is my body.'	[22] And while they were eating, having taken bread and blessed it. He broke it and gave it to them and said, 'Take, this is my body.'	[19] And having taken bread and given thanks, he broke it and gave it to them saying, 'This is my body [which (is) given for you, do this in my remembrance.'	took bread, [24] and having given thanks, he broke (it) and said, 'This is my body (given) on behalf of you; do this in my remembrance.'

22. Bart Ehrman, *Misquoting Jesus: The Story Behind Who Changed the Bible and Why* (San Francisco: Harper, 2005), pp. 166-67.

²⁷ And having taken the cup and having given thanks, he gave it to them saying, 'Drink from it, all (of you), ²⁸ for this is my blood of the [new] covenant which (is) poured out for many for the forgiveness of sins. ²⁹ And I say to you, from now on I will not drink from the fruit of the wine until that day when I drink it new with you in my Father's kingdom.'	²³ Then, having taken a cup, and having given thanks, he gave it to them, and all of them drank from it. ²⁴ And he said to them, 'This is my blood of the covenant, which is poured out for many. ²⁵ Truly I tell you, I will no longer drink of the fruit of the vine until I drink it new in the kingdom of God.'	²⁰ And he did the same with the cup after (they) ate, saying, 'This cup (is) the new covenant in my blood, poured out for you.']	²⁵ In the same way he took the cup after eating saying, 'This cup is the new covenant in my blood, do this, as often as you drink it, in my remembrance.' ²⁶ For as often as you eat this bread and drink the cup, you proclaim the death of the Lord until he comes. ²⁷ So whoever eats the bread and drinks the cup of the Lord unworthily, will be guilty of the body and blood of the Lord.

According to Bradshaw, the two different verbs found in Mark/ Matthew and Paul/Luke—εὐλογήσας, 'bless', and εὐχαριστήσας, 'give thanks'—represent two different traditions (as they would not have been used interchangeably), developed through varied theologies. However, this does not tell us which, if either, would more accurately represent Jesus' own words. Paul's version is the oldest and therefore closest in dating to the historical Jesus, whereas Mark's version, as stated above, is more in keeping with Semitic language. Yet, both still present the troubling 'blood' language. There is one additional text that could provide a possible alternative—the *Didache*, an early Christian 'handbook' of church practice. Although the author, exact date of composition, and area of composition are unknown, the document describes communal practice in a Christian community sometime in the first century, perhaps not long after the time of the Gospels.²³ The reason the *Didache* is of interest in this particular discussion is because it contains the oldest formation of the Eucharistic blessing, found in two forms, neither of which contain the 'blood' language (see Table 2). In this respect, the blessing is, as Bultmann states, 'quite in keeping with Jewish tradition'.

23. See F. L. Cross and E. A. Livingstone (eds.), 'Didache', in *Oxford Dictionary of the Christian Church* (3rd ed.; Oxford: Oxford University Press, 2005), p. 482.

Table 2. The eucharistic blessings found within
the *Didache* (second century). Trans. K. Turner.

The Didache
Chapter 9. The Eucharist. [1] Concerning the Eucharist, give thanks this way. [2] First, concerning the cup: We give you thanks, our Father, for the holy vine of your servant David which you have made known to us through your servant Jesus. To you, the glory forever. [3] Concerning the broken (bread): We give you thanks, our Father, for the life and knowledge that you have revealed to us through your servant Jesus; To you, the glory forever. [4] Just as this broken (bread) was (grain) once scattered over the hills, and after being gathered together, became one; likewise may your church be gathered together from the ends of the earth into your kingdom. Yours is the glory and the power through Jesus Christ forever. [5] May no one eat or drink from your Eucharist except those baptized in the name of the Lord; for the Lord has said himself concerning this: 'Do not give what is holy to the dogs.'* *Chapter 10. Prayer after Communion.* [1] After being satisfied, give thanks this way: [2] We give you thanks, holy Father, for your holy name which you cause to dwell in our hearts, and for the knowledge and faith and immortality which you have revealed to us through your servant Jesus. To you, the glory forever. [3] You, almighty Lord, created all things for the sake of your name, both food and drink you have given to people to enjoy, in order that they might give you thanks; but to us you have graciously given spiritual food and drink for life eternal through your servant. [4] Above all things, we give you thanks because you are powerful. To you, the glory forever. [5] Remember, Lord, your church, to save it from all evil and to perfect it in your love, sanctify and gather it together from the four winds into your kingdom which you have prepared for it; because yours is the power and the glory forever. [6] Let grace come, and let this world pass away. Hosanna to the God (Son) of David! If anyone is holy, let him come; if anyone is not so, let him repent. Maranatha. Amen. [7] Turn toward the prophets (for them) to give thanks as much as they desire.

* Mt. 7:6

The blessing format found in the *Didache* has the bread *following* the wine, in a similar fashion to the shorter form of Luke's Gospel, which likewise contains no blood imagery. In Rabbinic Judaism this is the standard order that blessings should take—wine, then bread. However, when the Mishnah was being composed, this order was a matter of debate, which implies that in the first century blessings could have been bread then wine, *or* wine then bread (the preferred order of Hillel).[24] Therefore, this difference between Mark, Matthew, and Paul, on the one hand, and the *Didache* and Luke's shorter form, on the other, cannot be used to argue for a preference in terms of historicity. Finally, that the *Didache* contains no reference to a Last Supper, Passover, or the death of Jesus,[25] and does not include the words of institution, might indicate that the earliest form of the Eucharist was not associated with these things and only came to be as theology surrounding Jesus' death developed. Conversely, the absence of these key elements could indicate, as has been a persistent question in the study of the *Didache*, that chapters 9 and 10 are not referencing the sacrament of the Eucharist at all, but some other community blessing entirely.[26]

If the *Didache* truly does represent the oldest and most likely form, then at some point the bread and wine grew to be understood as sacrificial elements—Jesus' body and blood. I have suggested above that this most likely happened before Paul's letter to the Corinthians and was not the invention of Paul alone. Alfred Loisy, however, proposed that the Eucharistic passage in 1 Corinthians was an interpolation added to the text sometime between the apostolic age and the writing of the gospels.[27] He does not think it would be necessary to reiterate things to a community already versed in this practice. One might wonder, then, why the same message is reiterated frequently in modern forms of religion, where the leader is not disconnected from his church community—Paul was addressing a crumbling church from the other side of the Aegean Sea, and if he felt a particular teaching needed reinforcing, there is no specific reason why he would not restate it. Loisy also argues that a generation expecting the imminent return of their Christ would not have employed a redemption ritual.[28] What he does not state is that the Corinthian church was being addressed some twenty years after Jesus' crucifixion—enough time for redemption theology and futurist eschatology to develop. As

24. 'Kiddish', in Werblowsky and Wigoder (eds.), *Encyclopedia of the Jewish Religion*, p. 227.
    25. Crossan has stated, 'I cannot believe that they knew all about those elements [Passover/Last Supper/Passion Narrative] and studiously avoided them'. *The Historical Jesus*, p. 364.
    26. Harold W. Attridge and Kurt Niederwimmer, *The Didache: A Commentary* (trans. Linda M. Maloney; Minneapolis: Fortress Press, 1998), pp. 139-47.
    27. Alfred Loisy, *The Birth of the Christian Religion* (trans. L. P. Jacks; New Hyde Park: University Books, 1962), pp. 244-45.
    28. *Ibid.*

Loisy did not produce any linguistic evidence for the hand of a redactor, he has given us very little reason to investigate his claims of interpolation further.

Thus far it has not been possible to attribute any version of the Eucharist to Jesus with any level of certainty. Although it can be accepted that *a* tradition did exist before Paul's first letter to the Corinthians, it is not clear what form that tradition took, whether it was associated with the Passover, and how Paul altered it, if at all. It is possible that the inclusion of Gentiles into the early Christian community—which shall be discussed further below—fostered this 'blood' imagery. Alternatively, or perhaps in addition, is it possible to discover a Judaic context in which this could happen?

IV. *Cultural Contexts*

As is well known, from the Hellenistic period to the triumph of Constantine so-called 'mystery cults' were flourishing in the Roman world. These cults varied greatly in terms of geographic location, historical development, and 'theological orientation', but they have been considered to be similar enough to be categorized together, with the most prevalent mysteries being that of Mithras and Isis. Marvin Meyer has noted that several of the cults' deities experienced death but ultimately life triumphed, as it does in nature: if human beings could appropriate that which 'made life triumphant...they too might live in a more complete way. Just how the initiates into the mysteries appropriated this power we do now know, but they may have understood themselves to have experienced an immediate or mystical encounter with the divine.'[29]

It is these similarities between the mysteries and Christianity—both ritualistically and in the overarching themes of death and rebirth—that have led many to attribute the origin of the Eucharist directly to these cults. Christianity developed in regions where the mystery religions were active, and many gentile converts would have been former adherents of the mysteries; it is probable that they no longer felt bound to the secrecy element of their former cult and revealed practices.[30] As Helmut Koester put it, Christianity certainly 'appropriated numerous foreign elements'[31] as it grew into a formal religion separate from Judaism. However, exactly

29. Marvin W. Meyer, *The Ancient Mysteries: A Sourcebook of Sacred Texts* (Philadelphia: Harper Collins, 1987), pp. 7-8.

30. *Ibid.*, p. 4

31. Helmut Koester, *History, Culture and Religion of the Hellenistic Age* (Philadelphia: Fortress Press, 1982), p. 167.

what Christianity borrowed from the mysteries in the early stages of its development is very difficult to determine. Some coincidences may be just that, as Judaism, Christianity, and Graeco-Roman cults lived side by side in the same contexts and thus faced similar problems and had comparable worldviews. In addition, as Christianity became ever more popular, it is possible that mysteries borrowed from it as well.

The problem faced when studying the mysteries ultimately comes down to their nature: as secretive cults, the sources are scarce. Some cults, such as that of Mithras, have little-to-no written documentation despite a wealth of archaeological finds.[32] However, scholars who have made links from particular cults to the Eucharist do not always address this polemic. Despite the limitations of evidence it is clear that certain rituals within the mystery cults involved the consumption of food and/or drink to create a 'mystical encounter' in a way that was possibly similar to the Eucharist.[33] Although it has been determined that the mysteries had communal meals that were often sacramental or celebratory in nature, the details, as Meyers notes, 'like so many other features of the mystery religions…remain shrouded in secrecy'.[34] The Mithraic cult was known to have included a bread and water ritual similar to the Eucharist, while the blood of Dionysus was thought to be synonymous with wine (although in a cultic setting this was 'poured out' in a ritual libation).[35] A god's 'blood' is presumably different from human blood, and could be entirely understood as physically manifesting itself as grape juice. The many depictions of Dionysus/Bacchus as having 'hair' of grape clusters would suggest this. However, whether the cults viewed the consumption

32. See the evidence presented in Mary Beard, John North, and Simon Price, *Religions of Rome* (Cambridge: Cambridge University Press, 1998), I, pp. 279-80; II, pp. 305-19 (12.5); 'Mithras', in Simon Price and Emily Kearns (eds.), *Oxford Dictionary of Classical Myth and Religion* (Oxford: Oxford University Press, 2003), pp. 354-56.

33. Barry Powell has argued that cult worshippers believed Dionysus could dwell in them through the consumption of wine; this notion of the intermingling of God and worshipper is also central to Christianity: Barry Powell, *Classical Myth* (2nd ed.; London: Prentice Hall International, 1998), pp. 274-76.

34. Meyer, *The Ancient Mysteries*, p. 12.

35. Justin Martyr (*1 Apol.* 66) angrily wrote that the 'wicked devils' of the Mithraic cult were imitating the Eucharistic rite. In the fourth-century BCE play *The Bacchae* by Euripides the audience is urged to see wine itself as associated with the god's blood: 'Next came Dionysus, the son of the virgin, bringing the counterpart to bread: wine / and the blessings of life's flowing juices. / His blood, the blood of the grape, / lightens the burden of our mortal misery. / Though himself a God, it is his blood we pour out / to offer thanks to the Gods. And through him, we are blessed' (*The Bacchae* lines 340-60).

of fluid as symbolic of blood or not is uncertain. G. W. Bowersock, in fact, states that the 'blood' invocation of the Eucharist was strange in either a pagan or a Jewish context—'partaking of divinity by eating human flesh and drinking blood was not a familiar occurrence to the Greeks and Romans'.[36] That the early Christians were seen to be doing just that—eating flesh and drinking blood—led to erroneous reports that Christian's were partaking in Thyestean banquets (a mythological banquet in which Thyestes is made to eat his own children by his twin brother, used in the ancient world as an overt allusion to cannibalistic behaviour).[37] It is important for scholars to be cautious when comparing Christianity to the mystery cults. This does not mean, however, that the mystery cults are not a good place to look—it would be naive to deny the similarities, the crossing of cultures, and the intermingling of ideas among first-century religions—but the problem is that at the moment there is not enough clarity to draw any conclusions about dependence.

Turning one last time back to Judaism, in his comprehensive multi-volume work *Jewish Symbols in the Greco-Roman Period*, Erwin R. Goodenough discusses the intermingling of blood and wine in the circumcision ritual as an example of a situation in which blood *can* be consumed in the Jewish community, and wine takes a 'higher' level of importance. Goodenough describes a now-controversial procedure known as *metzitzah b'peh*,[38] in which the mohel (a Jewish official trained to provide circumcisions), having removed the foreskin from the infant, takes wine into his mouth before sucking blood from the infant's wound. The mixed wine and blood are then spat into a receptacle specified for the purpose. According to Goodenough, after the naming of the child, the mohel then gives the infant a few drops of the wine/blood mixture to drink. This ritual seems to show that in certain instances, as Goodenough states, 'wine and blood [together] were considered a powerful medium of a covenant'.[39] Perhaps this is a case that can be used to substantiate Jesus' words, as he uses the wine/blood imagery as a symbol of a covenantal promise.[40] However, whilst *metzitzah* is Mishnaic in origin

36. G. W. Bowersock, *Fiction as History* (London: University of California Press, 1994), p. 127.

37. Notions of Christian cannibalism are recorded in Pliny the Younger's letter to Emperor Trajan, *Epistles* 10.96; also, Eusebius's *Historia Ecclesiastica* 5.1.52.

38. This aspect of the ritual is today only practiced within some ultra-orthodox Jewish communities, though without any 'consumption' element.

39. Erwin R. Goodenough, *Jewish Symbols in the Greco-Roman Period*, VI (New York: Pantheon Books, 1956), p. 146.

40. The *Jewish Encyclopedia* explains the procedure as follows: 'The mohel takes some wine in his mouth and applies his lips to the part involved in the operation, and

(*m. Shab.* 19.2, cf. *m. Ned.* 3.11; *b. Shab.* 133b; *b. Ned.* 32a), the tracts do not mention the intermixing with wine, nor is there any mention of the blood being given, in any form, to the infant. It is this later aspect of Goodenough's description that is relevant to the discussion presented in this chapter (the mohel after all does not consume the blood, but spits it out in keeping with Jewish law); as he does not provide any citations or references, further examination is restricted, and Goodenough's theory cannot be used convincingly to support the Jewish acceptance of 'wine as blood' symbolism. In addition, Shaye Cohen has identified the early ninth century as a turning point in Jewish thought regarding circumcision. Until that time, it had been only the act of circumcision, and not the blood drawn, that was regarded as necessary to fulfil the covenantal promise: 'Nowhere in these discussions [Biblical or Rabbinic texts] is any significance or power attributed to the circumcision blood itself... If the Talmudic rabbis subscribed to a theology of circumcision blood, our corpora have failed to record it.' Though from approximately 800 CE onwards the Rabbis do begin to attribute salvific power to the blood drawn during circumcision, this late dating prohibits any association with first-century Jewish thought and practice.[41]

There is one final instance that might suggest why this symbolism is not antithetical to Judaism. Joseph Tabory, in the *JPS Commentary on the Haggadah*, notes that at no point in any Haggadah, the book read during the Passover meal, is the significance of the wine ever explained. It is perhaps this omission that led Isaac ben Moses (d. 1260 CE) to discuss the symbolism of the wine in his seminal halakhic work *Or Zaru'a*. There he states that red wine is meant to signify blood, either of suffering (the blood of the Jewish children shed by the Pharaoh) or redemption (blood of circumcision and/or that shed by the paschal lamb). This example might be able to be used to show that the *symbolism* (not literalism) of wine as blood was perhaps not as abhorred by Jews as some have suggested. However, the late dating of this writing, to the thirteenth century, would make this comparison very difficult. A few possibilities can be suggested: it could be symbolism borrowed from

exerts suction, after which he expels the mixture of wine and blood into a receptacle provided for the purpose'. After the procedure, different remedies are applied. 'Circumcision' in Isidor Singer (ed.), *The Jewish Encyclopedia*, IV (London: Funk & Wagnalls, 1925), p. 99.

41.   Shaye J. D. Cohen, *Why Aren't Jewish Women Circumcised? Gender and Covenant in Judaism* (London: University of California Press, 2005), pp. 28-29; Also, Elizabeth Wyner Mark (ed.), *The Covenant of Circumcision: New Perspectives on an Ancient Jewish Rite* (Lebanon: Brandeis University Press, 2003).

Christianity; it could be a strictly post-Second Temple phenomenon, as the symbolism of the wine as the blood of the lamb would not have been necessary when the Temple was still in use; or lastly, it might have been symbolism that developed earlier among Jews in the Diaspora who were unable to make the pilgrimage to the Temple. Although it is clearly problematic, ben Moses presents us with a potential avenue to explore, one that might allow for the Eucharistic language to have developed in a Jewish context.

VI. *New Approaches*

Thus far I have addressed some of the more controversial polemics in the study of the origin of the Eucharist. From the above analysis it appears unlikely that Paul was the sole originator of the blessing at the Last Supper, although he may have contributed to its development; the *Didache* should be explored further as a potential example of the earliest tradition; and, it is possible that symbolic language involving blood was not entirely antithetical to Judaism. However, each of these 'conclusions' leads to many more questions and requires a great deal more exposition. When the Synoptic texts are examined, the blood prohibition addressed, the historical context of the blessing questioned (i.e. Was the 'Last Supper' a Passover *Seder* in the modern sense, a different type of Passover meal, or something else entirely?), and Jesus' own teachings on the Law brought into the debate, a situation is left that appears barely resolvable. Cahill is right to criticize scholars for their ineffectual or even negligent studies on the blood issue. However, barring the discovery of new texts or archaeological evidence, this question is not answerable from within our understanding of first-century Judaism alone, since our evidence is too thin.[42]

Perhaps the best solution to this quest lies in new approaches to the study of the Eucharist. Cahill notes that the rituals of the mystery cults, even if the specifics are unknown, had much to do with communing with the divine. He therefore suggests that 'the divinization of Jesus [should] be studied in tandem with the emergence of the blood drinking compo-

---

42. Some have used exactly this dilemma—the impossibility of sufficiently answering these questions—to argue for the historicity of the Eucharistic blessing. A. D. Nock, for example, stated that it is 'much harder to imagine someone else inventing the words than Jesus uttering them'. However, this 'Occam's Razor'-type conclusion is unpersuasive as it suffers from the same lack of evidentiary support. See: A. D. Nock, *Early Gentile Christianity and Its Hellenistic Background* (New York: Harper & Row, 1962), p. 125; also Goodenough, *Jewish Symbols*, VI, p. 136.

nent of the Eucharist'.[43] Cahill is not commenting either way on whether
or not Christianity borrowed a ritual from another religion;[44] what he is
theorizing is that perhaps as Jesus grew to be seen *as God* (this development alone being 'more intelligible in a Gentile setting'[45]), methods of
communing with him and remembering his sacrifice changed and developed as well, becoming removed from their Judaic context.

In addition, I would propose a move away from the scholarly certainty
on the historicity of the Last Supper narrative. Regarding the Eucharist
portion of the narrative, E. P. Sanders writes, 'The passage in general has
the strongest possible support [for authenticity], putting it on par with the
saying on divorce in terms of certainty'; in no small part because it
'reached us through two independent channels, the Synoptic tradition
and the letters of Paul'.[46] This assessment of historic reliability may be
our biggest roadblock in affectively dealing with the blood problem. If
we view the Last Supper narrative as *history* and the Eucharistic blessing
as an accurate representation of Jesus' words, we are then forced to find
an historic situation in which a Jew would speak in such seemingly anti-
Judaic terms (which, as the above discussion demonstrated, is quite
difficult). I would like to propose instead that the Last Supper narrative
represents *heritage*, not history.

VII. *Heritage and the Eucharist*

David Lowenthal warns against confusing history with heritage: 'Heritage is not history, even when it mimics history. It uses historical traces
and tells historical tales, but these tales and traces are stitched into fables
that are open neither to critical analysis nor to comparative scrutiny.'
Heritage is 'a declaration of *faith* in [the] past… [It] attests our identity
and affirms our worth.'[47] For nation states, much of what constitutes
nationalism is heritage; a combination of history and myth, collective
memory and identity. 'History tells all who will listen what has happened
and how things came to be as they are. Heritage passes on exclusive

43. Cahill, 'Drinking Blood', p. 177.
44. Cahill argues that 'previous suggestions supporting the non-Jewish source
have been vitiated by vague generalities or by association with inappropriate pagan
rituals'. *Ibid.*, p. 179.
45. *Ibid.*, p. 177.
46. E. P. Sanders, *The Historical Figure of Jesus* (London: Penguin, 1995),
p. 263.
47. David Lowenthal, *The Heritage Crusade and the Spoils of History*
(Cambridge: Cambridge University Press, 2003), p. 121.

myths of origin and endurance, endowing us alone with prestige and purpose.'[48] Although it may seem that the gospels are reporting history, they are actually passing on heritage. Heritage is about creating an impression of belonging, generating a sense of identity for both the individual and the community. It is an emotional construct designed to develop attachment to a group. Unlike history, which aims to be a correct if somewhat cold account of what has come before, heritage does not discover the past but rather encourages an identity. As Lowenthal states, 'historians aim to reduce bias; heritage sanctions and strengthens it'.[49] Although this might seem quite negative, it is important to note that the creation, or formation of heritage from history, myth, and the 'narrativization' of events is usually (though not always) unintentional.

Hayden White introduces narrative, an essential component of heritage, as something that 'translates *knowing* into *telling*'.[50] He suggested that through narrative we can understand a story from another culture much more easily than the 'specific thought patterns' of that culture, however different it is from our own. Narrative is 'translatable', a 'human universal on the basis of which transcultural messages about the nature of a shared reality can be transmitted'.[51] Like much of the gospels, the Last Supper is narrative in form—it is not just a bullet-pointed list of facts about Jesus' final day, but a tale that can be dramatized, shared across cultures. The narrativization of fact (or fiction) aids communication, making oral transmission easier and written text more relatable.

A particularly pertinent form of narrative is that of myth, which can be defined as a 'sacred narrative about past events (frequently at the beginning of time) or about events in the future (usually the end of time)… [I]t may justify past action, or explain action in the present, or generate future action.' It is important to note that the '"truth" of myth is not that same as…empirical truth… The power of myth comes from their ability to make life meaningful for those who accept them. Myths therefore possess an intersubjective truth, rooted in metaphor.'[52] Walter Burkert has argued that to classify something as myth one need not look to the

48. *Ibid.*, p. 128.
49. David Lowenthal, 'Fabricating Memory', *History and Memory* 10 (1998), pp. 5-24 (8).
50. Hayden White, 'The Value of Narrativity in the Representation of Reality', in W. J. T. Mitchell (ed.), *On Narrative* (London: University of Chicago Press, 1981), p. 1.
51. *Ibid.*, p. 2.
52. Emily A. Schultz and Robert H. Lavenda (eds.), *Cultural Anthropology: A Perspective on the Human Condition* (6th ed.; Oxford: Oxford University Press, 2005), pp. 173-74.

structure or content of the narrative but to how the narrative functions
when read, told, or received: 'myth is a traditional tale with secondary,
partial reference to something of collective importance'.[53] Accordingly,
the death and resurrection of Jesus can rightfully be described as myth,
and so too can certain stories of his life, especially that of the Last
Supper; it explains an action, it provides meaning for those who believe
it, and it is 'rooted in metaphor'. In addition, as Richard Wagner (later
supported by C. Levi-Strauss) stated, 'myth [has] the power to convey
messages that ordinary language cannot... [T]hese extra linguistic forms
ultimately functioned to unify and coordinate the worldview and morality of a community'.[54] The 'Passoverization' of the Last Supper narrative
may have functioned in the same way as Wagner's myths; Jesus' death
may not have been comprehensible or communicable to the early Christian community. By associating Jesus with the Passover meal and the
redemption the holiday signifies, the incommunicable *became* comprehensible.

Following this, there is an added relationship when the ritual of the
Eucharist is brought *into* the narrative. Ritual can 'enact the ideas
embodied' in myth,[55] or myth may justify the ritual. William Robertson
Smith pioneered the myth-ritualist theory, arguing that myth and ritual
are dependent on one another, usually with the myth arising after the
ritual.[56] Fiona Bowie, Bronislaw Malinowski, and Mircea Eliade disagree, however, suggesting the 'benefits' one gains from ritual can be
achieved through recitation of the myth.[57] Myths *can* be constructed or
used to 'validate' certain cultural behaviours and principles,[58] but they do
not have to be. In the case of the Eucharist, however, I propose that the
ritual associated with Jesus' last meal (what we now know as the Eucharist) developed *before* the Last Supper narrative. (Bowie, Malinowski,
and Eliade's analyses do allow for this to be the case.) This myth-
narrative grew to 'validate' the ritual, to explain its importance as the

53. Walter Burkert, *Structure and History in Greek Mythology and Ritual*
(Berkeley: University of California Press, 1982), p. 22.
54. 'Myth and Mythology', in Alan Barnard and Jonathan Spencer (eds.), *The
Routledge Encyclopedia of Social and Cultural Anthropology* (2nd ed.; London:
Routledge, 2010), p. 494.
55. *Ibid.*
56. Robert A. Segal, *The Myth and Ritual Theory: An Anthology* (Oxford:
Blackwell, 1998).
57. Bronislaw Malinowski, *Myth in Primitive Psychology* (London: Routledge,
1926).
58. Fiona Bowie, *The Anthropology of Religion* (Oxford: Blackwell, 2000),
pp. 136-37.

theology surrounding Jesus' death and resurrection developed, and to communicate this importance to other cultures and subsequent genera- tions. The ritual of communion is about the association Christians make with the historical reality of Jesus' death (and resurrection)—the origins of their faith. Eliade further explains that both myth and ritual allow people to transport themselves to a sacred plane. 'In imitating the exem- plary acts of a god or of a mythic hero, or simply by recounting their adventures, the man of an archaic society detaches himself from profane time and magically re-enters the Great Time, the sacred time'.[59] Commu- nion re-enacts the final mystical act of Jesus while the Last Supper narrative conveys this association and binds each individual Christian together as a community (like the community that shared in the meal with Jesus). It is about remembering the past in order to locate oneself 'in time and space—in history'.[60]

Conclusions

This does not leave us with an historical Passover meal celebrated by Jesus, in which he gave a proto-Eucharistic statement requiring his disciples to drink wine as his blood in remembrance of him. However, by understanding much of what seems to be 'history' in the New Testament as 'heritage', we might be better equipped to deal with the complexities, ambiguities, and at times downright contradictions that we find in the texts, especially in the Last Supper narratives. In addition, the study of heritage fosters an interdisciplinary approach as it deals not only with history but with memory, identity, cultural contexts, and rituals. I have offered, therefore, a few areas of Heritage Studies, many of which are rooted in anthropology, which can be used to explore the Last Supper and the Eucharist. Lowenthal quotes from a museum worker who explained that the point of heritage is 'not that the public should learn something but that they should *become* something'.[61] This is what we find to be the purpose of much of the New Testament texts. The gospels and epistles were written to build and develop communities, to share in the transformative experience of Christianity. Heritage ultimately, like religion, informs us about ourselves.

---

59. Mircea Eliade, *Myth and Reality* (trans. Willard R. Trask; New York: Harper & Row, 1963), p. 7.

60. Paul Basu, *Highland Homecomings: Genealogy and Heritage Tourism in the Scottish Diaspora* (London: Routledge, 2007), p. 157.

61. Lowenthal, 'Fabricating Heritage', p. 19.

The connection one makes to the 'ancestors' of their faith through sharing in a tradition that spans generations can be powerful and should be explored further. It would be interesting if, instead of searching for the origins of the Eucharist, we asked why we find it necessary to search. Does the average Christian focus on the historical particulars of the Last Supper and the Eucharist, or is the connection they make through the act of the ritual and the sharing in a communal experience more important? By looking at how the narrative is received, we might be able to gain insight into why it was written. This, then, might lead us to explore anew what sort of narrative the Last Supper is and open the door for multiple origins from communities or persons with varying ideas about 'blood'— what it means and how it can be appropriated.

'HOW ARE THE DEAD RAISED?':
THE BODILY NATURE OF RESURRECTION
IN SECOND TEMPLE JEWISH TEXTS

Daniel W. Hayter

Belief in the eschatological resurrection of the dead was one of the core tenets of both early Christianity and Rabbinic Judaism. For Christians, Jesus' own resurrection, of course, took the centre-stage, but many New Testament writings also mention the raising of the faithful at the eschaton.[1] On the Jewish side, the Rabbis eventually made belief in resurrection a requirement for inheriting the world to come.[2] In light of the doctrine's later importance, it is surprising that the Hebrew Bible has very little to say about resurrection: Elijah and Elisha performed miracles in which the dead come back to life (1 Kgs 17.17-24; 2 Kgs 4.18-37), but these are better described as resuscitations than resurrections, since 'resurrection', ἀνάστασις, denotes rising to an everlasting and immortal life in the eschaton.[3] The vision of dry bones coming back to life in Ezekiel 37 and Isaiah's claim that '[Israel's] dead shall live; their corpses shall arise' (26.19) were both central to the development of the Jewish doctrine of resurrection. Originally, though, these passages were probably metaphors for national restoration.[4] A description of future resurrection

1. E.g. Rom. 6.5; 1 Cor. 15; Phil. 3.11; 2 Tim. 2.18; Heb. 6.2; Rev. 20.4-6.
2. E.g. *m. Sanh.* 10.1.
3. See James Charlesworth's helpful definition in 'Where Does the Concept of Resurrection Appear and How Do We Know That?', in James H. Charlesworth (ed.), *Resurrection: The Origin and Future of a Biblical Doctrine* (Faith and Scholarship Colloquies; New York: T&T Clark International, 2006), pp. 1-21 (2): '[Resurrection is] God's raising the body and soul after death (meant literally) to a new and eternal life (not a return to mortal existence)'.
4. That this is so in Ezek. 37 is clear from 37.11-14: Moshe Greenberg, *Ezekiel 21–37: A New Translation with Introduction and Commentary* (AB 22A; New York: Doubleday, 1997), pp. 741-51. Whether Isa. 26.19 is about national restoration or

does appear in Dan. 12.2, which states that 'many of those who sleep in the dust of the earth shall awaken'; yet, even here, details are sparse.

It is only in non-biblical, Jewish writings from the Second Temple period that these earlier hints solidify into more concrete beliefs in resurrection. This phenomenon has benefitted from a significant amount of study over the last few decades, with the publication of a large number of full-length treatments of early Jewish afterlife beliefs.[5] These have helpfully highlighted the immense variety of views which existed, even among Jews who believed in resurrection.[6]

Yet, despite the ample amount of literature on the subject, large areas of disagreement persist. One particular unresolved debate is whether belief in resurrection necessarily entailed belief in a raised *body*. For some, the answer is clearly 'yes', as illustrated by N. T. Wright's insistence that '[resurrection] clearly refers to a newly *embodied* existence; it is never a way of talking about ghosts, phantoms or spirits'.[7] Others are not so convinced. For example, in his excellent introduction to early Judaism, Shaye Cohen confidently writes: 'In some texts the resurrection is bodily, while in others it is only spiritual'.[8]

---

personal resurrection is less certain: see John J. Collins, *Apocalypticism in the Dead Sea Scrolls* (London: Routledge, 1997), p. 111; Joseph Blenkinsopp, *Isaiah 1–39: A New Translation with Introduction and Commentary* (AB 19; New York: Doubleday, 2000), pp. 370-71; Brevard S. Childs, *Isaiah* (OTL; Louisville: Westminster John Knox Press, 2001), pp. 190-91.

5. Particularly noteworthy are George W. E. Nickelsburg, *Resurrection, Immortality, and Eternal Life in Intertestamental Judaism* (HTS 26; Cambridge, MA: Harvard University Press, 1972); and the updated edition *Resurrection, Immortality, and Eternal Life in Intertestamental Judaism* (exp. ed.; HTS 56; Cambridge, MA: Harvard University Press, 2006); Hans C. C. Cavallin, *Life After Death: Paul's Argument for the Resurrection of the Dead in I Cor 15: Part I: An Enquiry into the Jewish Background* (ConBNT 7/1; Lund: Gleerup, 1974); Émile Puech, *La Croyance des Esséniens en la Vie Future: Immortalité, Résurrection, Vie Éternelle? Histoire d'une Croyance dans le Judaïsme Ancien* (2 vols.; EBib; Paris: J. Gabalda, 1993).

6. For details, see the surveys in the studies listed above. Outside of resurrection, views included among others are a complete denial of the afterlife (Mt. 22.23-33; Mk 12.18-27; Lk. 20.27-38; Acts 23.6-8; Josephus, *War* 2.165; *Ant.* 18.16; Sir. 17.27-28; 18.23-24) as well as a very Hellenistic view of disembodied future bliss: Wis. 3.1; Philo, *Migr. Abr.* 9; *Gig.* 14 (compare Plato, *Phaedo* 80a-81a); *Ps.-Phoc.* 105-15 (but cf. 103-4); *T. Ash.* 6.5; *4 Macc.* 7.3; 18.23-24.

7. N. T. Wright, *The Resurrection of the Son of God: Christian Origins and the Question of God* (London: SPCK, 2003), p. 130 (italics mine).

8. Shaye J. D. Cohen, *From the Maccabees to the Mishnah* (Louisville: Westminster John Knox Press, 2006), p. 87. See also Collins, *Apocalypticism*, pp. 112-13.

In this chapter, which surveys some of the clearest non-biblical references to resurrection in Second Temple Jewish texts, I argue that eschatological resurrection was likely always viewed as a bodily phenomenon
by early Jews. It was not a way of referring to disembodied immortality,
nor was it a way of speaking of the raising of a soul or spirit.[9] This seems
to be, as we shall see below, the safest interpretation of the textual data.
Yet the debate cannot be resolved on exegetical grounds alone. Rather, a
few methodological and terminological issues must be taken into account
before turning to the textual evidence.

I. *Describing the Body*

Debates concerning the bodily nature of resurrection are fraught with
terminological challenges. Speaking of the human body may at first seem
like a fairly straightforward exercise, but imprecision is actually a significant danger, particularly when dealing with an ancient and non-
scientific culture. From a modern, materialistic perspective, it can be
tempting to suppose that a body is a well-defined entity, consisting of
particular substances and obeying certain physical laws, and to assume
that if a description of resurrection does not fit this mould then it is not
a body which is raised. However, even today, anthropologists and
sociologists note the difficulty of actually *defining* the human body. For
example, in his historical survey of conceptions of the body in Western
society, Bryan Turner writes that 'we cannot take "the body" for granted
as a natural, fixed and historically universal datum of human societies'.[10]
In the same volume, Sarah Coakley explains that '[the body] is all we
have, but we seemingly cannot grasp it; nor are we sure we can control
the political forces that regiment it'.[11] This modern uncertainty over what

9. For the purpose of this paper, the terms 'soul' (ψυχή) and 'spirit' (πνεῦμα) are
simply meant to refer to the part of a human that is distinct from the body; the words
will be used fairly interchangeably throughout this chapter. Of course, in reality,
many ancient authors differentiated between the two. For a recent and extensive
discussion on ancient *tripartite* views of anthropology (humans as spirit/mind, soul
and body), see Geurt H. van Kooten, *Paul's Anthropology in Context: The Image
of God, Assimilation to God, and Tripartite Man in Ancient Judaism, Ancient
Philosophy and Early Christianity* (WUNT 232; Tübingen: Mohr Siebeck, 2008)
(esp. pp. 269-312).
10. Bryan S. Turner, 'The Body in Western Society: Social Theory and Its
Perspectives', in Sarah Coakley (ed.), *Religion and the Body* (CSRT; Cambridge:
Cambridge University Press, 1997), p. 17 (see also pp. 17-20).
11. Sarah Coakley, 'Introduction: Religion and the Body', in Coakley (ed.),
Religion and the Body, p. 3.

the human body actually is should make us cautious of prematurely adhering to a particular definition and imposing that onto an ancient writing. Rather, we must allow the texts to speak fully within their own cultural context.

If any significant progress is to be made in debates over the nature of resurrection, more terminological care must be taken in order to avoid the charge of anachronistically imposing *a priori* views of what a body is on ancient writings. For one, care must be taken to avoid pitting terms such as 'spiritual' and 'bodily' against each other, as if the two were dichotomous. Scholars have often been guilty of doing this, as the previous quote from Cohen shows. Yet this oversimplification obfuscates more than it clarifies: one scholar may use 'spiritual' to mean 'non-bodily', whereas another may mean something else. Additionally, this dichotomy cannot bear the weight of historical textual evidence. The apostle Paul, himself a Second Temple Jew, had no qualms, in 1 Cor. 15.44, about using the term 'spiritual' (πνευματικός) to qualify, rather than oppose, the word 'body' (σῶμα). Therefore, for the sake of clarity in this discussion, I resist using terms such as 'spiritual', in case it is assumed to mean 'non-bodily'. Furthermore, the ancient text itself must be allowed to define what counts as a 'body' or as 'bodily'. As shall become clear, in some descriptions of resurrection (particularly *2 Bar.* 49–51), the body that is raised is changed, with regard to both its appearance and physical limitations, to such a degree that it would not fit into most modern definitions of what the human body is. This body could legitimately be described using terms such as 'astral' or 'angelic', terms that do not usually signify bodily existence in a modern sense. However, unless the author makes it clear, we should resist the temptation of claiming this no longer counts as bodily resurrection. The text itself must be allowed to define what can be thought of as a body.

A final methodological point must be made before proceeding. Some writings that refer to resurrection do not mention a body, or in fact anything about the nature of resurrection. Some have proceeded with caution and pointed out that in such cases we cannot be certain whether resurrection is bodily or not.[12] Caution is obviously required in any historical study, but, in my view, once all references to resurrection have been dealt with, explicit descriptions should be used to interpret the non-explicit passages. Clearly, there is a sampling of ambiguous texts, such as *Jub.* 23.30-31 and *1 En.* 103.4 (both dealt with below), but the majority

12. See, outside the relevant texts below, Cavallin's caution on *1 En.* 92.2-5 in *Life After Death*, pp. 42-43 and his view that in *1 Enoch*, 'the resurrection of the body is explicitly proclaimed only by Sim' (p. 48).

of passages, we shall see, either clearly describe a bodily phenomenon, or else use the terminology of resurrection without mentioning the presence or lack of a body. Absence of evidence does not amount to evidence of absence. To take a somewhat trivial example, the phrase, 'I left my house in a hurry' does not explicitly mention the use of the door. However, unless there are reasons to believe otherwise (such as a widespread cultural practice of avoiding leaving houses by the door), it would be odd to suppose that exiting by the window is just as likely. If the most explicit references to resurrection describe a bodily phenomenon, it is safer to suppose that non-explicit texts assume the presence of a body, unless there is actually clear evidence to the contrary.

II. *Resurrection of the Body in Ancient Judaism*

With these cautions in mind, I will now survey, in broadly chronological order, the most salient references to resurrection in non-biblical Second Temple Jewish texts. I am interested, here, in writings from the pre-rabbinic period. Unfortunately, lack of space has meant omitting the evidence of the Targumim and the LXX as well as the *Apocalypse of Moses*.[13] Despite these regretful, but necessary, omissions, the writings surveyed come from a broad range of Jewish backgrounds.

a. 1 Enoch
Some of the earliest references to eschatological resurrection appear in the 'Book of Watchers' (*1 En.* 1–36),[14] usually dated to the late third/ early second century BCE.[15] In 22.13, while visiting the abode of the souls of the dead, Enoch is told that the wicked 'will not rise from there'—a

13. For the Rabbis, LXX and Targumim, see the surveys in Wright, *Resurrection*, pp. 147-50, 190-200; Puech, *Croyance*, pp. 201-42. The omission of the *Apocalypse of Moses* is not particularly problematic since the work clearly refers to a bodily, physical resurrection: *Apoc. Mos.* 13.2-6 (despite Cavallin's caution in *Life After Death*, p. 73).

14. The translation of *1 Enoch* used is Ephraim Isaac's translation of the Ethiopic text, from *OTP*. The original work was almost certainly in Aramaic or Hebrew: cf. *OTP*, I, p. 6. Significantly, a number of Aramaic fragments of the book have been found in Qumran: see Józef T. Milik, *The Books of Enoch: Aramaic Fragments of Qumrân Cave 4* (Oxford: Clarendon Press, 1976). Sections of the work have also been found in Greek (cf. Matthew Black [ed.], *Apocalypsis Henochi Graece* [PVTG 3; Leiden: Brill, 1970]), and a Latin fragment of 106.1-18 was also discovered by M. R. James (see *OTP*, I, p. 6 n. 8 for details).

15. Puech, *Croyance*, p. 106; George W. E. Nickelsburg, *1 Enoch 1: A Commentary on the Book of 1 Enoch, Chapters 1–36; 81–108* (Hermeneia; Minneapolis: Fortress Press, 2001), p. 293.

possible denial of resurrection to sinners and *ipso facto* a confirmation of resurrection for the just.[16] A later reference to the inheritance of the righteous after the day of judgment strongly intimates that future life will be bodily:

> [The tree of life] is for the righteous and the pious. And the elect will be presented with its fruit for life…its fragrance shall (penetrate) their bones, long life will they live on earth, such as your fathers lived in their days. (25.5-6)

This description is, as Elledge notes, 'remarkably physical and this-worldly'.[17] It is not completely clear whether 'long life' is a euphemism for eternal life or not, though imagery of the tree of life suggests that it is. Whatever the case, the passage envisages an earthly, embodied future life (most likely resurrection) for the righteous.

No fragments from the 'Similitudes of Enoch' (*1 En.* 37–71) have been found at Qumran. Therefore, a pre-Christian date cannot be absolutely certain.[18] Still, the work clearly refers to resurrection and it is worth citing the relevant evidence.

Short allusions to resurrection appear in 46.6 and 48.10, but the most extant description is in ch. 51. Here, unlike elsewhere in the Similitudes, the author envisages a general resurrection:[19]

> In those days, the earth[20] will bring together all her deposits and Sheol will bring together all her deposits which she has received. And he shall choose the righteous and the holy ones from among (the risen dead)… And the faces of all the angels in heaven shall glow with joy, because on that day the Elect One has arisen. And the earth shall rejoice; and the righteous ones shall dwell upon her and the elect ones shall walk upon her. (51.1-5)

16.   The verse is badly preserved in the Aramaic fragments from Qumran; thus the Aramaic behind 'rise up' is uncertain. The Greek, in the sixth-century Gizeh manuscript (cf. text in Black, *Apocalypsis Henochi Graece*), is μετεγερθῶσιν, not included in LSJ, but clearly having to do with the idea of awakening. Matthew Black wonders whether the author had Dan. 12.2 in mind: Matthew Black, *The Book of Enoch, or I Enoch: A New English Edition* (SVTP 7; Leiden: Brill, 1985), p. 168. If so, a reference to resurrection of some kind is plausible. Puech thinks that this is possible: *Croyance*, p. 110.

17.   Casey D. Elledge, *Life After Death in Early Judaism: The Evidence of Josephus* (WUNT 208; Tübingen: Mohr Siebeck, 2006), p. 8.

18.   On dating, cf. Isaac in *OTP*, I, p. 7; Puech, *Croyance*, p. 199; Elledge, *Life After Death*, p. 10 and the discussion in n. 33.

19.   *Contra*, notably, Puech, *Croyance*, p. 119.

20.   For this rendering, cf. Cavallin, *Life After Death*, pp. 44-45; Wright, *Resurrection*, p. 155; Elledge, *Life After Death*, p. 11.

Clearly, bodily resurrection is in view: the earth gives back its deposits and the righteous dwell and walk upon it.[21] An alternative translation, by Knibb, suggests that the righteous themselves *become* angels.[22] If this is correct, angelic imagery is closely associated with bodily resurrection. This should warn against driving a wedge between astral and angelic immortality, and bodily resurrection. Additionally, transformation or glorification of the resurrection body may be hinted at in 62.15-16, which states that the risen saints will wear 'the garments of glory'.[23] So then, pre-Christian or not, the 'Similitudes' holds together both this-worldly descriptions of resurrection and references to transformed, almost angelic existence. The language of astral or angelic immortality cannot *de facto* necessitate the absence of a body. Rather, a less restrictive view of the nature of the body is required.

The final section of *1 Enoch*, the so-called 'Epistle of Enoch' (chs. 91–105), which was probably in fairly extant form by the beginning of the first century BCE,[24] seems to give mixed signals about the afterlife. On the one hand, the work ostensibly contains allusions to resurrection: for instance, 91.10 explains that the 'righteous one' (probably a collective singular)[25] 'shall arise from his sleep', and in 92.3-5 the resurrected saints walk in eternal light.[26] On the other hand, as Elledge states, '[t]here is no explicit concern for the bodies of the dead' in this epistle.[27] There is also a puzzling reference in 103.4:

> The spirits of those who died in righteousness shall live and rejoice; their spirits shall not perish, nor their memorial from before the face of the Great One unto all generations of the world. Therefore, do not worry about their humiliation.

On the face of it, this is at odds with the teaching of the rest of the epistle, and also seems to hint at the possibility of a non-bodily resurrection.[28]

---

21. So Cavallin, *Life After Death*, p. 45; Elledge, *Life After Death*, p. 11.

22. Knibb in Wright, *Resurrection*, p. 155.

23. Black notes that, since Dillman, commentators have been reluctant to see resurrection here: *1 Enoch*, p. 237. Yet I think he is right to claim that this is resurrection, since the righteous rise from the earth.

24. Cf. Nickelsburg, *1 Enoch 1*, p. 8; Loren T. Stuckenbruck, *1 Enoch 91–108* (CEJL; Berlin: W. de Gruyter, 2007), pp. 5-14.

25. Cf. Cavallin, *Life After Death*, p. 42; Black, *1 Enoch*, p. 282.

26. So Stuckenbruck, *1 Enoch 91–108*, pp. 228-29. *Contra* Nickelsburg who thinks this is a reference to the awakening of the community to knowledge: *1 Enoch 1*, p. 432.

27. Elledge, *Life After Death*, p. 10. Cf. also Puech, *Croyance*, p. 116.

28. Wright, somewhat confusingly, claims that this is probably bodily resurrection: Wright, *Resurrection*, p. 156 n. 105.

However, it is not clear that this passage is meant to refer to resurrection at all. It may refer to an intermediate disembodied state prior to resurrection, something which had already been hinted at in 100.4-9.[29] In fact, since the author tells the reader not to worry about the humiliation (i.e. death) of the righteous, 103.4 likely refers to a reality immediately subsequent to death; it is not necessarily a description of resurrection at all. Whatever the case, nothing explicit is said about the nature of resurrection in the 'Epistle of Enoch', and we should not press the text further than is appropriate; this work cannot be adduced as evidence for or against a non-bodily form of resurrection.

b. *2 Maccabees*

2 Maccabees contains some of the clearest descriptions of resurrection from the Second Temple period. Although a small minority of scholars, most notably Kellermann,[30] claim that the work describes a heavenly, transcendent resurrection upon death, the book unambiguously refers to a very physical, material resurrection.

Chapter 7 contains the bulk of the evidence. It is a rather morbid description of the martyrdom, under Antiochus IV, of seven Jewish brothers and their mother. Rather than turn away from 'the laws of [their] fathers' (7.2), the brothers endure torture and death because of the promise of resurrection. For example, one of the brothers claims: 'the King of the cosmos will raise us to an everlasting renewal of life (εἰς αἰώνιον ἀναβίωσιν ζωῆς ἡμᾶς ἀναστήσει) because we died for his laws' (7.9). Another sibling sticks his hands and tongue out, ready to lose them to the torturers, claiming, 'from heaven I got these and because of its/his own laws I despise them, and from it/him I hope again to get them back' (7.11).[31] The mother's encouragement to the youngest son is also very revealing: 'receive death, so that in mercy I might get you back with your brothers' (7.29). The chapter paints a highly physical, almost crude picture of resurrection as a reward for faithfulness to Torah.

The writer subsequently alludes to resurrection a couple of times, building on the picture painted in ch. 7. The description of Razi's suicide in ch. 14 ('holding out his entrails and taking them in each of his hands

29. Cf. also *4 Ezra* 7.88-99.
30. Ulrich Kellermann, *Auferstanden in Den Himmel: 2 Makkabäer 7 und die Auferstehung der Märtyrer* (Stuttgarter Bibelstudien 95; Stuttgart: Verlag Katholisches Bibelwerk, 1979).
31. The expression ἐξ οὐρανοῦ is a reference to God: Jonathan A. Goldstein, *II Maccabees: A New Translation with Introduction and Commentary* (AB 41A; Garden City: Doubleday, 1983), p. 306; Daniel R. Schwartz, *2 Maccabees* (CEJL; Berlin: W. de Gruyter, 2008), p. 305.

he hurled them at the crowds, and calling on the master of life and spirit to give them back, he died in this way' [14.46]) supports the physical, graphic view of resurrection explored above. In 12.42-44, additional information is given about the timing of the resurrection. Judas Maccabeus prays for dead Judaean soldiers and the author justifies his actions by claiming that, 'if he were not expecting those who have fallen to rise, it would have been remarkable and foolish to pray for the dead' (12.44). This shows that resurrection, for our author, does not happen *upon* death, but *after* death.[32]

2 Maccabees is clear: death for the sake of Torah can be embraced because of the reality of resurrection. The expression εἰς...ἀναβίωσιν ζωῆς in 7.9 may hint at a change of bodily appearance; nonetheless, resurrection is clearly very literal and physical, and this betrays a very high view of the physical body. This is all the more significant when one considers that this is most likely a work from outside Palestine and therefore more likely to be influenced by Hellenistic views of disembodied immortality.[33]

c. *The Exception of* Jubilees?

In my view, a short passage from the second-century Palestinian book of *Jubilees* is the most problematic text for the view that resurrection was always thought of as a bodily phenomenon:[34]

> And the LORD will heal his servants, and they will rise up and see great peace. And they will drive out their enemies, and the righteous ones will see and give praise, and rejoice forever with joy; and they will see all of their judgments and all of their curses among their enemies. And their bones will rest on the earth, and their spirits will increase joy. (23.30-31)

This could well be our only reference to resurrection of the spirit from the Second Temple period.[35] However, I am not convinced that the

32. Possibly at the final judgment (as in *2 Bar.* 50; *4 Ezra* 7.33-44; *Sib. Or.* 2.214-20; 4.179-92; *Ps.-Philo* 3.10).

33. Cf. John R. Bartlett, *The First and Second Books of the Maccabees* (CBC; London: Cambridge University Press, 1973), p. 215; Elledge, *Life After Death*, p. 111; Schwartz, *2 Maccabees*, p. 38; Casey D. Elledge, 'Resurrection and Immortality in Hellenistic Judaism: Navigating the Conceptual Boundaries', in Stanley E. Porter and Andrew W. Pitts (eds.), *Christian Origins and Hellenistic Judaism: Social and Literary Contexts for the New Testament* (Early Christianity in Its Hellenistic Context; Leiden: Brill, 2013), pp. 101-33.

34. On dating and provenance, as well as translation from the Ethiopic, cf. Orval S. Wintermute in *OTP*, II, pp. 43-45.

35. Even Wright, who is adamant that resurrection is always physical, admits this possibility: Wright, *Resurrection*, p. 144. Puech and Collins certainly think this

terminology is clear enough to be absolutely certain. For one, the expression 'rise up' in v. 30 is not explicitly connected with the later 'their spirits'. Furthermore, as the text stands, it is unclear whether the 'servants', who rise up, are the same as the 'righteous ones' whose spirits increase joy. It is possible that those who rise up are actually alive at the time described in 23.28-31 and that they rise up, not from the dead, but in order to defeat their enemies; the righteous, who are dead, observe this from their post-mortem state and rejoice. This does not remove the difficulty of this passage, but it may not be as clear as it seems.

d. *Dead Sea Scrolls*

Did the writers of the Dead Sea Scrolls believe in resurrection? Scholarship is at an impasse on answering this question.[36] Whatever those responsible for the Scrolls believed, though, the documents themselves do contain three works which at least *allude* to resurrection of the dead: 4Q521, 4Q385 and 1QH.[37] In all three, resurrection, whether metaphorical or literal, is thought of in bodily terms.

Prior to the publication of 4Q521 and 4Q385, debates concerning resurrection in the Dead Sea Scrolls usually revolved around 1QH (*Hodayot*). Some think that these hymns refer to a literal resurrection,[38] but others argue that they use the language of resurrection metaphorically in order to refer to an awakening to knowledge.[39] Nothing in this work excludes literal resurrection *a priori*.

is resurrection of the spirit: Puech, *Croyance*, pp. 104-5; Collins, *Apocalypticism*, p. 113. However, Gene L. Davenport (*The Eschatology of the Book of Jubilees* [Studia Post Biblica 20; Leiden: Brill, 1972], p. 40 n. 2) claims that '*bones* and *spirits* does not mean a resurrection of the spirit... Man is a unity, even in death.'

  36. For helpful summaries of views, cf. Wright, *Resurrection*, pp. 181-89; John J. Collins, 'The Essenes and the Afterlife', in Florentino García Martínez, Annette Steudel and Eibert J. C. Tigchelaar (eds.), *From 4QMMT to Resurrection: Mélanges Qumraniens en hommage à Émile Puech* (STDJ 61; Leiden: Brill, 2006), pp. 35-53.

  37. 4Q521 and 4Q385 are usually categorized as 'non-sectarian' (i.e. not written by the supposed Qumran community itself); 1QH is grouped with 'sectarian' works. On this classification, cf. Devorah Dimant, 'The Qumran Manuscripts: Contents and Significance', in Devorah Dimant and Lawrence H. Schiffman (eds.), *Time to Prepare the Way in the Wilderness: Papers on the Qumran Scrolls by Fellows of the Institute for Advanced Studies of the Hebrew University, Jerusalem 1989–1990* (STDJ 16; Leiden: Brill, 1995), pp. 23-58.

  38. So E. P. Sanders, *Judaism: Practice and Belief, 63BCE–66CE* (London: SCM Press, 1992), p. 302. See also Elledge, *Life After Death*, p. 22 n. 86.

  39. E.g. Nickelsburg, *Resurrection*, pp. 146-56; Collins, *Apocalypticism*, pp. 121-22.

The two most significant passages are 1QH 14.29-34 and 19.12-14:

> the sword of God will hasten at the time of judgment and all the sons of his tr[u]th will awaken to destroy [the sons of] wickedness, and all the sons of wrong-doing will be no more… The dwellers of the dust hoist a banner and the worms of the dead lift an ensign. (1QH 14.29-30, 34)[40]

> in order to raise the worms of the dead from the dust to the eve[rlasting] council and from a twisted spirit to [your] understanding and so that he might stand in service before you with a continual host, and the spirits of […] to renew himself with all that will be and with those who know, in unity of joy. (1QH 19.12-14)

Scholars might be less reticent to see resurrection here had Josephus not claimed that the Essenes believed in disembodied immortality.[41] It is of course *possible* that these passages describe what Cavallin calls 'a present realized resurrection',[42] but I am not sure that this does justice to the eschatological context (particularly of 1QH 14) or to the biblical imagery of dwelling in the dust as a metaphor for death (Dan. 12.2; Isa. 26.19).[43] More cautiously, we might agree with Brooke, who suggests that this kind of language probably indicates that belief in resurrection at least *underlies* some sections of the *Hodayot*.[44] It is clear, though, that whatever the description of resurrection is supposed to *denote* (a literal reality or an awakening to knowledge), the language itself describes something very physical and bodily, which apparently takes place on earth;[45] this is not terminology of the raising of a soul or spirit.

The most explicit description of resurrection in the whole corpus of the Dead Sea Scrolls is in 4Q385, one of the fragments that make up *Pseudo-Ezekiel*. This composition, most likely from the second century BCE,[46] contains a reinterpretation of Ezekiel's vision of the valley of dry

---

40. Translations are based on the Hebrew text in Eibert J. C. Tigchelaar and Florentino García Martínez (eds.), *The Dead Sea Scrolls Study Edition* (2 vols.; Leiden: Brill, 1997–98).

41. Cf. *War* 2.154-58.

42. Cavallin, *Life After Death*, p. 64.

43. Cf. Nickelsburg, *Resurrection*, p. 17.

44. George J. Brooke, 'The Structure of 1QH XII 5-XIII 4 and the Meaning of Resurrection', in Martínez, Steudel and Tigchelaar (eds.), *From 4QMMT to Resurrection*, p. 33 on 1QH 12.5–13.4.

45. The earthly locus is clear from the context of the eschatological battle in 1QH 14.

46. The earliest manuscript from the work is 4Q391 and most likely dates to the second half of the second century BCE, marking the *terminus ad quem*: cf. Albert L. A. Hogeterp, 'Belief in Resurrection and Its Religious Settings in Qumran and the

bones (Ezek. 37.1-14). In 4Q385, however, Ezekiel, rather than Yahweh (as in Ezek. 37.3), asks the leading question: '[Yahweh,] I saw many from Israel who loved your name and walked in the ways of [righteousness; and th]ese things, when will they be? And how will their piety be rewarded?' (4Q385 fr. 2 2-3). What ensues is a very crude description of the resurrection of the bones that parallels the account of Ezekiel 37. But, as Ezekiel's question in 4Q385 shows, the narrative is no longer simply a metaphor for national restoration. Rather, a literal reward for righteous dead individuals is envisaged.[47] Furthermore, the language of bones and flesh highlights the continuity between the present body and the resurrection.[48] This implies that the writer, like that of 2 Maccabees, held a very high view of human physicality: no particular bodily change seems to be required; restoration is an appropriate reward.

Finally, two of the fragments contained in 4Q521 (*Messianic Apocalypse*) clearly mention resurrection. According to fr. 2, after the coming of the Messiah, 'the Lord will do glorious things as have not (yet) been, according to what he s[aid, for] he will heal the wounded and the dead he will make live, to the poor he will proclaim good news...' (4Q521 fr. 2 ii.11-12). The context is clearly eschatological, as shown by the phrase 'glorious things as have not (yet) been',[49] and resurrection is associated with the coming of the Messiah.[50] However, God, and not the Messiah, is the subject of יחיה ('he will make to live'): he is the one who raises the dead.[51] The strong similarity between the language in this passage and

New Testament', in Florentino García Martínez (ed.), *Echoes from the Caves: Qumran and the New Testament* (STDJ 85; Leiden: Brill, 2009), p. 273.

47. So most commentators: Puech, *Croyance*, p. 614; Émile Puech, 'Messianisme, Eschatologie et Résurrection dans les Manuscrits de la Mer Morte', *RQ* 18, no. 2 (1997), pp. 255-98 (290); Wright, *Resurrection*, p. 188; Brooke, 'Structure', pp. 17-18; Mladen Popović, 'Bones, Bodies and Resurrection in the Dead Sea Scrolls', in Tobias Nicklas, Friedrich V. Reiterer and Joseph Verheyden (eds.), *The Human Body in Death and Resurrection: Deuterocanonical and Cognate Literature Yearbook 2009* (Berlin: W. de Gruyter, 2009), pp. 221-42; *contra* Johannes Tromp, 'Can These Bones Live? Ezekiel 37:1-14 and Eschatological Resurrection', in Henk Jan de Jonge and Johannes Tromp (eds.), *The Book of Ezekiel and Its Influence* (Aldershot: Ashgate, 2007), pp. 61-78, who argues that Ezek. 37 was never used as a basis for belief in resurrection prior to the Christian Era.

48. Puech, *Croyance*, p. 613.

49. So Hogeterp, 'Belief in Resurrection', p. 280. Cf. Mt. 24.3; Mk 13.4; Lk. 21.7.

50. As *4 Ezra* 7.26-32; *2 Bar.* 30.1-5.

51. So Johannes Zimmermann, *Messianische Texte aus Qumran: Königliche, Priesterliche und Prophetische Messiasvorstellungen in den Schriftfunden von Qumran* (WUNT 104; Tübingen: Mohr Siebeck, 1998), pp. 363-64.

the ministries of Elijah and Elisha (especially 1 Kgs 17.8-24; 2 Kgs 4.1-37; 5.1-14) makes it unlikely that resurrection is not bodily. If disembodied bliss were envisaged here, what need would there be to heal the wounded?

In the second relevant fragment (fr. 7), which describes eschatological judgment and separation between the wicked and the righteous, God is called 'the one who raises the dead of his people (המחיה את מתי עמו)' (4Q521 fr. 7 + 5 ii.6). The similarities between this expression and later Jewish prayers such as the *Shemoneh Ezrei*, as well as early Christian formulations of God as the one who raised Jesus from the dead, have not gone unnoticed.[52] Nothing explicit is said, though, in either of the fragments, about the precise nature of the resurrection body.

e. Testaments of the Twelve Patriarchs

The *Testaments of the Twelve Patriarchs*[53] offer some more insight on the question of resurrection. However, they bear the marks of later Christian editing, and scholars are uncertain to what extent the early Jewish source can be restored (if it ever existed).[54] Therefore, any conclusions must be, at best, tentative.

Beyond the odd exception of *T. Ash.* 6.5, 'the concept of resurrection with its terminology dominates the impressions which Te[s]tXIIPatr give about life after death'.[55] Four passages in the various Testaments attest to this belief. First, in *T. Sim.* 6.7, Simeon exclaims: 'then I will rise up (ἀναστήσομαι) with happiness and I will bless the Highest One for his wonders'. Resurrection apparently happens 'upon the earth (ἐπὶ γῆς)' (6.5),[56] and therefore is probably bodily. A second reference appears in *T. Jud.* 25.1-5:

---

52. On the former cf. Wright, *Resurrection*, p. 187. On the latter, cf. Zimmermann, *Messianische Texte*, p. 373; Acts 4.10; Rom. 10.9; Gal. 1.1.

53. Translations based on the Greek text in Marinus de Jonge, *The Testaments of the Twelve Patriarchs: A Critical Edition of the Greek Text* (PVTG 1; Leiden: Brill, 1978). Manuscripts and fragments of the Testaments have also been found in Armenian, Slavonic, Hebrew and Aramaic (for a summary of manuscripts, see Harm W. Hollander, *The Testaments of the Twelve Patriarchs: A Commentary* [SVTP 8; Leiden: Brill, 1985], pp. 10-12). For a brief overview on provenance, dating and original language, cf. Kee in *OTP*, I, pp. 775-78.

54. For a negative assessment cf. Hollander, *Twelve Patriarchs*, p. 85. Kee is more positive in *OTP*, I, p. 778.

55. Cavallin, *Life After Death*, p. 55.

56. The possibility of this expression being part of a Christian interpolation, though, should not be forgotten.

> And after these things Abraham and Isaac and Jacob will be raised to life,
> and I and my brothers shall become leaders of our tribes (σκήπτρων–
> 'staffs/sceptres') in Israel…and those who died in sadness will be raised
> in Joy, and those (who died) in poverty because of the Lord shall become
> rich, …and those who died because of Lord shall be awakened from sleep
> into life. (25.1, 4)

Here, there are no obvious Christian interpolations.[57] The ingathering of
the twelve tribes and the patriarchs' reign over Israel suggest an earthly
locus, and therefore some kind of embodied resurrection.[58] The theme of
the risen patriarchs reign is repeated in *T. Zeb.* 10.2 where Zebulun
asserts: 'I shall rise up (ἀναστήσομαι) again in your midst as a leader in
the midst of his sons, and I shall rejoice in the midst of my tribe'. The
context of the *Testament of Zebulun* indicates that the hearers' sons are
alive at the time of his resurrection. This, again, makes an earthly locus,
and therefore a bodily resurrection, most likely.

A final mention of resurrection, the most extant in the whole of the
Testaments, appears in the *Testament of Benjamin*. It is also, unfortunately, the most Christianized of the four. The text contains a sequence
of three resurrections:

> Then you shall see Enoch, Noah and Shem and Abraham and Isaac and
> Jacob raised up at the right hand with rejoicing. Then we also shall be
> raised, each over our tribe (σκῆπτρον)…then all shall also be raised up,
> some to glory, others to dishonour. (10.6-8)

This order is without parallel in all Jewish literature:[59] first the ancestors
of Israel, then the twelve patriarchs, then everyone else. In 10.8, the
author has clearly drawn on Dan. 12.2 by claiming that some are raised
to glory (δόξα) and others to dishonour (ἀτιμία).

These four references share much in common. Resurrection is apparently a bodily phenomenon. The idea of being raised to glory in *T. Ben.*
10.8 might indicate that bodily transformation occurs. Furthermore,
resurrection is linked with the ingathering of the twelve tribes. This
implies that, for this author, what matters most is restoration of what was
lost, not escape from the present world.

57.   So Casey D. Elledge, 'The Resurrection Passages in the Testaments of the
Twelve Patriarchs: Hope for Israel in Early Judaism and Christianity', in James H.
Charlesworth (ed.), *Resurrection: The Origin and Future of a Biblical Doctrine*
(Faith and Scholarship Colloquies; London: T&T Clark International, 2006), pp. 88-
89; Anders Hultgård, *L'Eschatologie des Testaments des Douze Patriarches* (AUU
6; Uppsala: Uppsala Universitet, 1977), p. 246.
58.   On the ingathering theme, see Hultgård, *Eschatologie*, p. 236.
59.   *Ibid.*, p. 261.

f. Sibylline Oracles

In the Jewish-Hellenistic *Sibylline Oracles*,[60] a work dating from the second century BCE to (possibly) the seventh century CE,[61] eschatology is not a prominent feature. This makes two clear references to resurrection, both probably dating to the first century CE,[62] all the more significant:

> then to those underground (the dead) the heavenly one will give souls and spirit and speech, and bones joined together by all kinds of fastenings, flesh and sinews […] and veins and skins around the body and former hairs, put together immortally, breathing and set in motion: bodies of earthly ones shall be raised in one day. (2.221-26)

> God himself will give shape to the bones and ashes of men again and will raise mortals again, as they were beforehand. And then there will be a judgment, over which God will be judge himself, judging the world over again. (4.181-84)

Although the first passage is often left out of treatments of Jewish afterlife beliefs because book 2 was heavily redacted by Christians, nothing in the passage sounds un-Jewish, nor does it differ much from 4.179-84; in fact, Collins claims that it is 'quite possibly Jewish'.[63] I have therefore included it here. Both passages envisage a universal and highly physical resurrection. The authors of both oracles emphasize the strong continuity of the raised body with the present, physical body. Whoever penned these lines felt that restoration and recreation, but not necessarily visible transformation, were necessary. Nothing here hints at anything other than a very high view of human physicality.

g. Pseudo-Philo

Pseudo-Philo,[64] most likely a Palestinian work from the second half of the first century CE,[65] is important in this discussion. Although the work

60.   Translations in this chapter are based on the Greek text in Johannes Geffcken (ed.), *Die Oracula Sibyllina* (GCS; Leipzig: J. C. Hinrichs, 1902).

61.   On dating, cf. Collins in *OTP*, I, p. 317.

62.   See *ibid.*, pp. 331, 381-82.

63.   *Ibid.*, p. 333.

64.   The translation is Daniel J. Harrington's from the Latin in *OTP*, II, pp. 298-99, who argues that the original language was Hebrew. For an extensive discussion, see Howard Jacobson, *Commentary on Pseudo-Philo's 'Liber Antiquitatum Biblicarum'* (2 vols.; AJU 31; Leiden: Brill, 1996), pp. 215-24.

65.   On dating, see *ibid.*, pp. 199-210; Daniel J. Harrington, 'Afterlife Expectations in Pseudo-Philo, 4 Ezra, and 2 Baruch, and Their Implications for the New Testament', in Reimund Bieringer, Veronica Koperski and Bianca Lataire (eds.), *Resurrection in the New Testament* (Festschrift J. Lambrecht; BETL 165; Leuven: Leuven University Press, 2002), p. 22. On provenance, in addition to the above, cf.

presents challenges, Jacobson's assertion that finding a 'coherent and consistent view of the afterlife and eschatology in *Pseudo-Philo* is doomed to failure',[66] is somewhat of an overstatement. There are issues to iron out, but such an extreme claim is warranted only if one concludes *a priori* that resurrection, sleep, chambers of souls, and post-mortem punishments and rewards are incompatible. There are difficulties and discrepancies, but the book's eschatology is at least partially consistent.

Death, according to *Pseudo-Philo*, is the separation of soul and body (44.10). While bodies sleep in the earth (3.10), the souls of the righteous are stored in chambers (23.13; 32.13).[67] This, however, is reversed by resurrection:

> when the years appointed for the world have been fulfilled, then the light will cease and darkness will fade away. And I will bring the dead to life and raise up those who are sleeping from the earth. And hell will pay back its debt, and the place of perdition will return its deposit so that I may render to each according to his works... (3.10)

A bodily resurrection is clearly in view. Indeed, it apparently involves the reuniting of soul and body, since those sleeping in the earth (i.e. corpses) are raised, and hell and the place of perdition give back their deposits—surely the souls of the dead.[68] Since later in 3.10, heaven and earth are recreated, Jacobson is presumably right to claim that the locus of the resurrected saints is probably like this world, but perfect and everlasting.[69]

It is more difficult to ascertain whether the resurrection body is changed, as in *2 Bar.* 49–51 (see below), or not. Heaven and earth are recreated and renewed in 3.10, but this phenomenon is not explicitly applied to the raised bodies. Some have adduced 28.9 (in Harrington's translation, 'they will be transformed') as evidence for bodily transformation.[70] In my view, though, Jacobson has persuasively argued that the Latin *mutabuntur* ('they will be transformed') is based on a possible mistranslation of the Hebrew יחלפו. The Piel or Hiphil can mean 'change' or 'transform',[71] but the Qal ('pass on' or 'pass away') suits the

Daniel J. Harrington, Charles Perrot and Pierre Bogaert, *Les Antiquités Bibliques* (2 vols.; SC 229-230; Paris: Editions du Cerf, 1976), pp. 28-39.

66. Jacobson, *Liber Antiquitatum Biblicarum*, pp. 249-50.

67. As *1 En.* 22; *4 Ezra* 4.41; *2 Bar.* 30.2; Josephus, *War* 3.374.

68. Cf. *4 Ezra* 7.32.

69. Jacobson, *Liber Antiquitatum Biblicarum*, p. 328.

70. Cf. Harrington, Perrot and Bogaert, *Antiquités*, p. 164.

71. Gen. 31.7, 41; 35.2; 41.14; Lev. 27.10; 2 Sam. 12.20; Isa. 9.9; 40.31; 41.1; Ps. 102.27; Job 14.7.

context much better.[72] Although it would make sense for a renewed and transformed creation to be inhabited by renewed and transformed bodies, the author does not express a particular interest in this.

Pseudo-Philo contains a high view of bodily life. Death, in which soul and body are separated, will be reversed at resurrection, when the two are reunited. Some form of embodied existence is preferable for this author.

h. 4 Ezra *and* 2 Baruch

The late first-century CE Jewish apocalypses *4 Ezra* and *2 Baruch* have much in common with *Pseudo-Philo* when it comes to afterlife beliefs.[73] In the wake of the crisis of 70 CE, these two works ask searching questions about justice, evil, death and theodicy.[74]

In *4 Ezra*,[75] as in *Pseudo-Philo*, death is the separation of soul and body.[76] After a brief period (described in 7.75-101), the souls of the dead are stored in 'chambers' (e.g. 4.41; 7.32) awaiting the eschaton. A 400-year messianic reign (7.26-29) and a turning back of the world to 'primeval silence for seven days' (7.30) are followed by the general resurrection of the dead, which involves the reuniting of body and soul:

> After seven days the world that is not yet awake shall be roused, and that which is corruptible shall perish. The earth shall give up those who are asleep in it, and the dust those who rest there in silence; and the chambers shall give up the souls that have been committed to them. (7.31-32)

In this passage, as Stone rightly points out, nothing hints at a loss of physicality.[77] Indeed, the language of the earth and dust giving up those who sleep in it shows that bodies are in view. At the same time, the

72. Jacobson, *Liber Antiquitatum Biblicarum*, p. 821.

73. Harrington, 'Afterlife Expectations'. On dating and provenance, cf. Jacob M. Myers, *I and II Esdras: Introduction, Translation and Commentary* (AB 42; Garden City: Doubleday, 1974), p. 129; Michael E. Stone, *Fourth Ezra: A Commentary on the Book of Fourth Ezra* (Hermeneia; Minneapolis: Fortress Press, 1990), pp. 9-11; Cavallin, *Life After Death*, p. 86; Klijn in *OTP*, II, p. 617.

74. Cf. for example Tom W. Willett, *Eschatology in the Theodicies of 2 Baruch and 4 Ezra* (JSPSup 4; Sheffield: Sheffield Academic Press, 1989).

75. Translations are from the NRSV of 2 Esd. 3–14. The original language is almost universally thought to be Semitic: see Myers, *I and II Esdras*, pp. 115-19; Michael A. Knibb and Richard J. Coggins, *The First and Second Books of Esdras* (CBC; Cambridge: Cambridge University Press, 1979), p. 110. The work is extant in Latin, Syriac, Ethiopic, Arabic and Armenian (*OTP*, I, pp. 518-19).

76. Cf. *4 Ezra* 7.78, 88, 100. On the soul in *4 Ezra*, cf. Michael E. Stone, *Features of the Eschatology of IV Ezra* (HSS; Atlanta: Scholars Press, 1989), pp. 144-45.

77. Stone, *Fourth Ezra*, p. 220.

writer envisages that the future existence of the righteous will supersede their pre-death existence: he later writes that the faces of the risen righteous will 'shine like the sun' and that they will be like 'the light of the stars' (7.97). So for *4 Ezra*, resurrection is bodily, but clearly of a somewhat different nature to pre-resurrection life.

The same is true in *2 Baruch*,[78] which explicitly describes resurrection on three occasions.[79] In the first instance, 30.1-5, bodies are not mentioned, but the text refers to those sleeping in hope of the Messiah rising and to treasuries giving back souls. In the second passage, however, resurrection is unambiguously bodily: 'corruption will take away those who belong to it and life those who belong to it. And dust will be called, and told, "Give back that which does not belong to you and raise up all that you have kept until its own time"' (42.7-8). As in *4 Ezra* 7.31-32, the language of dust suggests that bodies are raised.[80]

The third passage (chs. 49–51) is, to my knowledge, the most extensive description of resurrection in all Jewish Second Temple literature. In 49.2, Baruch asks God, 'in what shape will the living live in your days? Or how will remain their splendour which will be after that?' In response, God explains that, first, all the dead will be raised, 'not changing anything in their form' (50.2) in order 'to show those who live that the dead are living again' (50.3). Subsequently, though, both the righteous and the wicked will be transformed: the righteous' 'splendor will then be glorified by transformations, and the shape of their face will be changed into the light of their beauty' (51.3); they will be 'like the angels and equal to the stars. And they will be changed into any shape which they wished' (51.10). This is not a description of disembodied spirits, but it is clear that the body is quite free from the constraints of the present earthly one and that physical laws can be suspended at will. The author, then, envisages the future body as a dramatic development and improvement over the present one. However, at no point does the author suggest that this existence is disembodied.

78.   The translation used is Albertus F. J. Klijn's from the Syriac contained in *OTP*, I. Klijn argues (p. 616) that the work was originally in Hebrew. An extant Arabic version of the work has also been discovered and published (with translation) in Fred Leemhuis, Albertus F. J. Klijn and Geert J. H. van Gelder (eds.), *The Arabic Text of the Apocalypse of Baruch: Edited and Translated with a Parallel Translation of the Syriac Text* (Leiden: Brill, 1986).

79.   Willett, *Theodicies*, p. 119, cites the additional, but ambiguous, 23.4-5.

80.   Cavallin, *Life After Death*, p. 91; Puech, *Croyance*, p. 139; Harrington, 'Afterlife Expectations', p. 30.

i. *Josephus*

Here, we look at Josephus's descriptions of the afterlife beliefs of the Pharisees and his own, since they are very similar. We would probably be forgiven for assuming that Josephus would describe the Pharisees' views by using the language of resurrection, but we are faced with the puzzling conundrum that 'within the entire corpus of [Josephus's] works, one looks in vain for a single definitive reference to resurrection from the dead'.[81] Instead Josephus's most explicit descriptions of Pharisaic afterlife views, and of his own, are as follows:[82]

> [the Pharisees say that] every soul is incorruptible, but that only the soul of the good passes into another body; the souls of the wicked, instead, are punished with everlasting retribution. (*War* 2.163)[83]

> The souls [of those who die in accordance with the law of nature] remain clean and obedient, having obtained a most holy heavenly land, from where, at the turning of the ages (ἐκ περιτροπῆς αἰώνων), they are given a new home in pure bodies (ἁγνοῖς...σώμασιν) again. (*War* 3.374)

At first sight, these descriptions seem to have more in common with the Pythagorean doctrine of transmigration than with Jewish belief in resurrection. Yet there are compelling reasons to see resurrection lurking beneath these texts, whether or not Josephus expected his Graeco-Roman readers to realize this.[84] Indeed, Steve Mason has identified some key differences between these descriptions and the traditional idea of transmigration (e.g. reincarnation as reward rather than punishment; the description of *pure* bodies rather than just another body).[85] These differences suggest that belief in resurrection lies beneath Josephus's descriptions. Also, bearing in mind the overwhelming evidence elsewhere that

81. Elledge, *Life After Death*, p. 45.

82. See also *Ant.* 18.14; *Apion* 2.218, but these are not as detailed as the passages cited here.

83. The translation is based on the Greek text in Benedict Niese (ed.), *Flavii Iosephi Opera* (6 vols.; Berlin: Weidmann, Editio minor, 1888–95).

84. On Josephus's purpose and Roman audience in *War*, see the brief summaries and bibliographies provided in Steve Mason, 'Josephus: Value for New Testament Study', in Craig A. Evans and Stanley E. Porter (eds.), *Dictionary of the New Testament Background* (Downers Grove: IVP, 2000), pp. 596-97; Steve Mason, James S. McLaren and John M. G. Barclay, 'Josephus', in John J. Collins and Daniel C. Harlow (eds.), *Early Judaism: A Comprehensive Overview* (Grand Rapids: Eerdmans, 2012), pp. 297-98. On the 'apologetic' purpose of his afterlife passages in a Graeco-Roman context, see Wright, *Resurrection*, pp. 177-79; Elledge, *Life After Death*.

85. Steve Mason, *Flavius Josephus on the Pharisees: A Composition-Critical Study* (SPB; Leiden: Brill, 1991), pp. 166-70.

the Pharisees believed in resurrection,[86] it is likely that Josephus had this belief in mind when he wrote these accounts.

By reading between the lines, therefore, a few suggestions can be made about this Pharisaic belief, at least as Josephus understood it. Resurrection comes after a disembodied intermediate state[87] and is quite explicitly a bodily phenomenon. This could not be any clearer from Josephus's mention of 'another body'. However, this new bodily life apparently surpasses pre-resurrection existence since Josephus describes these new bodies as 'pure' (ἀγνοῖς). Just how different he envisaged them being remains unclear.[88] Whatever the case, though, Josephus has embodied eschatological life in view.

Conclusions

This chapter has argued that in Jewish writings from the Second Temple period, eschatological resurrection was understood to be a bodily phenomenon. There were, as the above survey shows, differing views on the exact nature of this body, but there is no indisputable evidence from this period attesting to a belief in a non-bodily resurrection. (*Jubilees* 23.30-31 and *1 En.* 103.4 are problematic, but not clear enough to be conclusive.) Some texts do not detail what is raised, but these passages should not be taken as evidence *against* bodily resurrection. Other writings highlight the strong continuity between the body which dies and the one which is raised. Yet other texts describe a transformation of the body after resurrection. *2 Baruch* 49–51 in particular describes a resurrected body which does not sit comfortably within a materialistic, scientific worldview of today. However, the writer himself gives no indication that it has ceased to be a body. The most extensive descriptions of resurrection that we surveyed are clear: a body of some kind is raised. Therefore, in the absence of certain evidence to the contrary, it is most reasonable to assume that belief in resurrection implied a belief in a resurrected body.

86.   Cf. the helpful survey in Puech, *Croyance*, pp. 213-42.

87.   As *1 En.* 22; 100.4-9; 103.4 (?); 2 Macc. 7.36; 12.39-45; *Ps.-Philo* 23.13; 32.13; *4 Ezra* 4.41-42; *2 Bar.* 30.2; *Apoc. Mos.* 13.6.

88.   Drane's suggestion may not be far from the truth: '[m]aking due allowance for [Josephus's] desire to explain Jewish religion in terms of Greek philosophy, it would be possible to fit his description of Pharisaic belief into something like that of 2 Baruch': John W. Drane, 'Some Ideas of Resurrection in the New Testament Period', *TynBul* 24 (1973), pp. 99-110 (103).

To believe in resurrection, then, was to hold a high view of the human body.[89] To say that God would raise the dead was to affirm that the body, however much it needed to be restored, and changed, was something good. Against those who claimed that the body (and the created order) was something to escape from, communities that believed in resurrection argued that it was something to be redeemed, sometimes quite dramatically, but not thrown away. In the face of Greek scoffing and ridicule, many ancient Jews could envisage God looking at the prospect of a resurrected people living in new bodies in a new creation and saying, as he had done in Genesis 1, 'it is very good'.

89. The language in this final paragraph is very much indebted to N. T. Wright's popular work on the Christian view of resurrection in *Surprised by Hope* (London: SPCK, 2007).

8

FLESH FOR FRANKEN-WHORE:
READING BABYLON'S BODY IN REVELATION 17*

Michelle Fletcher

You, my creator, would tear me to pieces, and triumph.
—Mary Shelley[1]

I too want to make sense of the Apocalypse—to examine every seam and stitch, and to trace the way the book is held together.
—Tina Pippin[2]

'There's nothing to fear. Look. No blood, no decay, just a few stitches', declares Henry Frankenstein, in James Whale's film *Frankenstein* (1931), upon first glimpsing his creation. This is what seems to be needed to calm revulsion when faced with fleshy horror: a safe and sterile gore-free description. Current scholarship on the whore of Babylon strives to make the same 'nothing to fear' claims regarding the portrayal of her textual body. What could be read as a 'text of terror', describing the destruction of a female body, is now sanitized by the majority of both feminist and non-feminist readings.[3] The whore is viewed as only figurative, symbolic of a city, and stripped of fleshly connotations. Though labelled 'Babylon', she is most widely read as representing the threatening powers of

---

* All translations are my own, unless otherwise stated. Greek Texts are from Michael W. Holmes and Society of Biblical Literature, *Greek New Testament: SBL Edition* (Atlanta: Society of Biblical Literature, 2010).

1. Mary Wollstonecraft Shelley, *Frankenstein or The Modern Prometheus* (ed. Maurice Hindle; rev. ed.; London: Penguin Books, 2003), p. 147.

2. Tina Pippin, *Death and Desire: The Rhetoric of Gender in the Apocalypse of John* (Louisville: Westminster John Knox Press, 1992), p. 88.

3. Notable exceptions include Marla J. Selvidge, 'Powerful and Powerless Women in the Apocalypse', *Neotestamentica* 26 (1992), pp. 157-67; Pippin, *Death and Desire*; Tina Pippin, *Apocalyptic Bodies: The Biblical End of the World in Text and Image* (London: Routledge, 1999). For an overview of feminist readings, see Alison Jack, 'Out of the Wilderness', in Stephen Moyise (ed.), *Studies in the Book of Revelation* (Edinburgh: T. & T. Clark, 2001), pp. 149-62.

the city of Rome and its ability to seduce people into economic relationships and/or idol worship,[4] though some have suggested Jerusalem.[5] Such
symbolic readings are rich in their results and have provided invaluable
insights into the text and the world in which it was created, by not
focusing on the flesh but on the wider textual fabric. They have also
introduced reading practices designed to look beyond gendered violence,
aiming to resist systems of power.[6] However, sanitized descriptions of
fleshly horror do not mean that gory threats do not continue to lurk in the
dark. Whale's Frankenstein soon finds he has created something far more
than 'just a few stitches': he has produced a flesh and blood monster that
elicits fear he had not imagined.

In this chapter I will explore how the whore of Babylon, like Frankenstein's monster, also presents unseen fleshly threats which still lurk in
scholarly darkness. I will argue that her body itself offers a threatening
flesh and blood presence in the text of the book of Revelation which has
been overlooked by safe, symbolic readings. In essence, in this exploration I will attempt to 'flesh out' the whore of Babylon by focusing on her
body. To do this I use an innovative approach: a comparative analysis
using Frankenstein's monsters.

I. *Monsters*

The portrayal of a creature with visible stiches and infamous neck bolt is
instantly recognizable as Frankenstein's monster (Figure 1). Yet this
iconic image bears little resemblance to the creature presented in the

4. For examples of arguments that she is Rome, the new Babylon, see M. Eugene
Boring, *Revelation* (Louisville: John Knox Press, 1989), p. 179: 'Revelation deploys
it [the whore] as a figure of speech in order to characterize the idolatrous imperial
power of Rome'. Elisabeth Schüssler Fiorenza, *The Book of Revelation: Justice and
Judgement* (Minneapolis: Fortress Press, 1998), p. 218: 'Babylon is the city of
Rome...the critique in chapters 17–18 primarily economic'. Richard Bauckham, *The
Theology of the Book of Revelation* (Cambridge: Cambridge University Press, 1993),
p. 36.

5. A minority of scholars argue for this identification: Alan James Beagley, *The
Sitz im Leben of the Apocalypse with Particular Reference to the Role of the
Church's Enemies* (Berlin: W. de Gruyter, 1987); Josephine Massyngberde Ford,
Revelation (AB 38; Garden City: Doubleday, 1975); and Kenneth L. Gentry, *Before
Jerusalem Fell: Dating the Book of Revelation* (Fountain Inn: Victorious Hope
Publishing, 2010).

6. Elisabeth Schüssler Fiorenza argues that feminist readings should resist the
kyriarchical gendered system in the book of Revelation by looking past feminine
images to what they represent. Elisabeth Schüssler Fiorenza, *The Book of Revelation: Justice and Judgement* (Minneapolis: Fortress Press, 1998).

original text. In fact, Mary Shelley was notoriously vague about the monster's appearance and even about how it was made.[7] It has been left to film-makers to give a body to the monster, to inscribe flesh to the text of *Frankenstein*.[8] In my task of fleshing out the body of Babylon these bodily incarnations of a textual monster prove most useful, and will be used as points of discussion throughout this chapter.[9] I will use them to give us fresh perspectives on traditional readings, enabling us to look away from figurative Rome/cities and back onto the literal body as presented in Revelation 17.[10] I will also use them to explore how scholars have envisioned the whore of Babylon's textual body, what has been inscribed upon her and also what has been overlooked in her destruction. By the end of this exploration I will argue that Babylon is not only a city-symbol; she can also be read as a fleshly Franken-whore.

7. For a discussion on portrayals and the lack of textual details see John Sutherland, 'How Does Victor Make His Monsters?', in *idem, Is Heathcliff a Murderer? Great Puzzles in Nineteenth-Century Fiction* (Oxford: Oxford University Press, 1998), pp. 24-34.

8. This chapter will focus on well-known Frankenstein films, with instantly recognizable portrayals of the monster. For an exhaustive list of what could be classed as a version of Frankenstein's monsters see Timothy Morton, *A Routledge Literary Sourcebook on Mary Shelley's Frankenstein* (London: Routledge, 2002), pp. 64-77, and also Caroline Joan S. Picart, Frank Smoot and Jayne Boldgett, *The Frankenstein Film Sourcebook* (Westport: Greenwood Publishing, 2001).

9. The two share many scholarly themes: the concept of the monstrous, the depiction of horror, the need for destruction, the responsibility of the creator for evil. However, meetings are rare; both Babylon and Frankenstein's monsters feature in Laura Lunger Knoppers and Joan B. Landes, *Monstrous Bodies/Political Monstrosities: In Early Modern Europe* (Ithaca: Cornell University Press, 2004). Pippin notes Frankenstein's monsters in relation to female monsters in the book of Revelation. Pippin, *Apocalyptic Bodies*, p. 135 n. 12. *Frankenhooker* (1990) features a man reading Rev. 17 outside the bar where the female monster is. Finally our title term 'Frankenwhore' is defined by the urban dictionary as 'an extremely ugly woman that still seems to be able to sleep with men'. Online: http://www.urbandictionary.com/define.php? term=frankenwhore (accessed 17 May 2013). This neatly (albeit rather tastelessly) unites the monstrous and the promiscuous.

10. Revelation 17 is most often read in light of Rev. 18, the latter read back into the former, in order to discover who the whore is. Here I concentrate on Rev. 17 only, presenting an audience response reading of the text. This allows us to focus on how the whore is first presented in the text and resist inscribing her with later textual declarations. In the same way readings of ch. 17 often focus on the beast first in order to understand who the whore is, with an aim to decipher the symbolism. As our aim here is to re-animate the discussion surrounding *her body* as an independent entity and threat, the beast will not be our focus unless directly relating to the description of the whore.

Figure 1. James Whale's *Bride of Frankenstein* (1935). Boris Karloff as the Monster with his infamous bolt. Source: Universal/The Kobal Collection.

II. *Nothing to Fear… Just a Few Stitches*

Our search for Babylon's body begins by looking at current scholarly perceptions. The general consensus it that Revelation 17's presentation of the whore of Babylon is constructed from Hebrew Bible source texts. Different textual 'allusions' are brought together to create the powerful image of the whore, who is essentially a multi-sourced textual body.[11] The original contexts of her 'textual parts' are then identified in order to indicate how she should be understood and what is so threatening about her. The object is to find the key source texts so that the whore can be understood.[12] This envisioning of her textual body is remarkably similar to the fleshly body most often given to Frankenstein's monster in filmic portrayals. The image we have come to expect on screen is of a monster whose body is constructed from variously sourced body parts sewn together with the connecting seams still visible, taken to the extreme in

11. 'The figure of the prostitute brings to mind numerous prophetic texts of the OT': Pierre Prigent, *Commentary on the Apocalypse of St. John* (Tübingen: Mohr Siebeck, 2004), p. 485. David Aune notes 'the artificial composite literary character of this vision': David E. Aune, *Revelation 17–22* (WBC 52C; Nashville: Thomas Nelson, 1998), p. 925. Texts that have been identified include Ezek. 16 and 23, portraying Jerusalem; Jer. 4 and 51 (27 LXX), portraying Babylon; Isa. 23, portraying Tyre; Nah. 3, portraying Nineveh; Prov. 1–9, portraying a wicked life path; and Dan. 2 and 4, portraying Babylon and pagan kingdoms.

12. 'Many commentators are concerned to isolate the biblical antecedents to John's vision of the Great Harlot'. Ian Boxall, 'The Many Faces of Babylon the Great: Wirkungsgeschichte and the Interpretation of Revelation 17', in Moyise (ed.), *Studies in the Book of Revelation*, p. 53.

Kenneth Branagh's *Mary Shelley's Frankenstein* (1994) where the monster resembles a baseball (Figure 2). A key element in Frankenstein film plots is the origin of these body parts; the body they first belonged to influences the creature's behaviour and its threat. For example, when the monster has a brain taken from a criminal, as in Whale's 1931 rendition, it turns to murderous ways. In Frank Henenlotter's *Frankenhooker* (1990) the head of Frankenstein's girlfriend is attached to parts sourced from prostitutes, creating a monster looking for punters. In Paul Morrissey's *Flesh for Frankenstein* (1973) the head of the 'stud' monster comes from an ascetic, so preventing the sexual mating Frankenstein hoped for. Thus, the viewers are beckoned to guess how the monster will develop ways to threaten as the film progresses, based on where the body parts have been collected from. Will it be good or bad, sex-mad or sterile?

Figure 2. Kenneth Branagh's *Mary Shelley's Frankenstein* (1994).
Robert De Niro with very visible seams.
Source: Tri-Star/American Zoetrope/The Kobal Collection.

Scholars reading Revelation 17 obviously do not want to 'guess' about the threat posed by the whore of Babylon. The aim is to discover exactly what her origins are so that she can be accurately read and understood. However, this is not an easy task, for her 'source texts' seem to have undergone textual blending; Gregory Beale comments that in the book of Revelation it is not unusual to find that: 'four, five or more different OT references are merged into one picture', leading him to ask 'how are such combined allusions to be studied?'.[13] The textual body is evidently not very easy to dissect. However, Beale does believe that the seams holding the texts together are visible. Therefore, he proposes that we separate images out into 'layers' and then relocate each back into its primary location.[14] This is done by finding 'clear allusions' to Hebrew Bible texts.[15] The reader can then observe from which text the most important/most number of 'clear allusions' have been taken and therefore which 'textual parts' govern how the image should be interpreted.[16] Beale's reading of ch. 17 is long and highly complex, but it still essentially follows the above pattern, concluding that the whore of Babylon's key textual parts are from Daniel 4 and 7 and Isaiah 23.[17] These texts govern his interpretation of her, so he concludes that she represents the threat of a seductive pagan economic power, whose fornication involves seducing other nations into economic alliances, like Tyre in Isaiah and Babylon in Daniel.[18] The other texts which he observes are there because they are thematically compatible with these key textual parts.[19]

Yet other scholars aiming to 'un-sew' the whore find themselves staring at different textual fragments. Pierre Prigent argues that she is primarily created from material originating in Jeremiah 51, indicating that she represents Babylon reborn in the form of Rome.[20] For Barbara Rossing her most predominant features derive from the errant woman

---

13. Gregory K. Beale, *The Book of Revelation: A Commentary on the Greek Text* (Grand Rapids: Eerdmans, 1999), p. 79.

14. 'Often a greater understanding is gained and emotive effect felt when the various allusive parts of these visionary amalgamations are studied separately in their various OT contexts'. *Ibid.*

15. See *ibid.*, pp. 77-86, particularly p. 78. Also Gregory K. Beale, *The Use of Daniel in Jewish Apocalyptic Literature and in the Revelation of St. John* (Lanham: University Press of America, 1984), pp. 43-44 n. 62, and see Jon Paulien, 'Criteria and the Assessment of Allusions to the Old Testament in the Book of Revelation', in Moyise (ed.), *Studies in the Book of Revelation*, pp. 113-30.

16. Beale's belief in being able to see the seams and guiding parts is grounded in the idea that the original meaning of the text intended by the author can be recovered. For a full discussion see Gregory K. Beale, *John's Use of the Old Testament in Revelation* (Sheffield: Sheffield Academic Press, 1998), pp. 51-59.

17. Beale, *The Book of Revelation*, pp. 850, 890. This is primarily due to what he deems a 'clear allusion' in 17.2 to Isa. 23, and μυστήριον in Rev. 17.6, which he equates with Dan. 4.

18. Beale, *The Book of Revelation*, p. 850.

19. Tensions between texts should be understood in light of 'supplementary aspects of an author's one meaning'. Beale, *John's Use of the Old Testament in Revelation*, p. 52.

20. Prigent, *Commentary on the Apocalypse of St. John*, p. 498.

trope, particularly Proverbs 1–9, representing the seductive path of a wicked city.[21] For Jean-Pierre Ruiz she is primarily constructed from Ezekiel 16 and 23, giving her the appearance of Jerusalem chasing after foreign gods.[22]

Each of these scholars' readings are complex and nuanced but all believe in searching for the seams which join past texts together in order to make accurate incisions, with an aim to separate them to see how the component parts functioned prior to combination. However, the results of such textual unpicking have to be questioned simply on the basis of the diversity of sources identified. There is no one 'clear allusion'. Scholars do not see the same primary parts as governing the text, which indicates that her 'seams' are not as evident as hoped for. What is more, envisioning of the whore's textual body and the threat she poses in this way leads to a complete overlooking of her fleshly nature as a whole. She is not viewed as a literal woman but rather as a figurative one.[23] The focus is on viewing the description of the whore not as depicting an actual female body, no matter how symbolic, but rather a city. Therefore, finding her textual origins has been important in order to unearth which city is symbolized. With Babylon being only figurative it is not the bodily aspect of her textual parts which is the focus for scholars. Instead, they look to cities such as Nineveh, Tyre, Jerusalem as well as Babylon. Therefore, this woman's threat is declared to be that she is a powerful city/economic system enticing people into idolatry/alliances.[24]

However, if we look at her body, we see a very fleshly description of 'Babylon'. Revelation 17 focuses on bodily functions by describing who she has been penetrated by (v. 2), what she wears (v. 4), what she adorns herself with (v. 4), what has been inscribed upon her (v. 5),[25] whom she

21. Barbara R. Rossing, *The Choice Between Two Cities: Whore, Bride, and Empire in the Apocalypse* (Harrisburg: Trinity Press International, 1999), pp. 76-77.

22. Jean-Pierre Ruiz, *Ezekiel in the Apocalypse: The Transformation of Prophetic Language in Revelation 16, 17–19, 10* (Frankfurt am Main: Peter Lang, 1989), pp. 292-378; see also Albert Vanhoye, 'L'utilisation du livre d'Ezechiel dans l'Apocalypse', *Biblica* 43 (1962), pp. 436-70.

23. 'We are told in the book's introduction that the majority of the material in it [the book of Revelation] is revelatory symbolism… Hence, the predominant manner by which to approach the material will be according to a nonliteral interpretative method.' Beale, *The Book of Revelation*, p. 52.

24. As stated earlier, the general consensus is that for the audience of the book of Revelation this would have been taken to mean Rome and its economic and/or idol temptations. Fiorenza, *Revelation*, p. 218; Bauckham, *The Theology of The Book of Revelation*, p. 36.

25. That this means she is a tattooed slave is suggested by C. P. Jones, 'Stigma: Tattooing and Branding in Graeco-Roman Antiquity', *JRS* 77 (1987), pp. 139-55

has given birth to (v. 5) and what she consumes (v. 6).[26] While the reasons for reading her as primarily symbolic have a firm grounding, her fleshly nature is abandoned by such practices. If she is simplified, with only the figurative interpretation focused upon and her body turned into sanitized sections, we lose her flesh and important layers of her textual fabric.[27] Therefore, although these readings are insightful, they are also ignoring the very thing they are staring at: a fleshly body.

This brings us back to Frankenstein films, for the same can be said of Henry Frankenstein in Whale's film. By declaring 'no blood, no decay, just a few stitches' he overlooks the fleshly and focuses on the sanitized. However, it is the fleshly nature of the body which he comes to fear as the film progresses. We have seen how the reading practices above have also focused on stitches rather than flesh, making the whore's textual body safe by focusing on symbolic threats and the origins of parts, rather than the sum of them. We now turn to the text of Revelation 17, with our focus on the fleshly rather than the figurative.

III. *I'm All Woman*

The importance of reading the whore as figurative rather than fleshly is strongly supported by Rossing, who believes that 'only in a brief section Rev. 17.3-4, is Babylon primarily personified as a woman'.[28] After this 'the author constructs Babylon predominately as a city, in the tradition of biblical city personifications'.[29] However, the text actually urges its readers to resist rendering her *only* symbolic. Revelation 17 opens with the announcement of the whore's judgment and a description of the

(151), and furthered in Jennifer A. Glancy and Stephen D. Moore, 'How Typical a Roman Prostitute is Revelation's "Great Whore"?', *JBL* 130 (2011), pp. 551-69 (559-60).

26. These descriptions echo current themes in studies on 'the body'. For an excellent survey of how consumption, childbirth, attire and penetration have become focal points for body theory, see Julia Twigg, *The Body in Health and Social Care* (Basingstoke: Palgrave Macmillan, 2006), pp. 13-39. For how these descriptions impact male readers, see Greg Carey, 'A Man's Choice: Wealth Imagery and the Two Cities of the Book of Revelation', in Amy-Jill Levine (ed.), *A Feminist Companion to the Apocalypse of John* (London: T&T Clark International, 2009), pp. 147-58.

27. As Eugene Boring states: 'His [John's] images are not one-to-one allegories that may be neatly "decoded"—they overlap and fade into each other with more than one meaning at a time'. Boring, *Revelation*, p. 179.

28. Rossing, *The Choice Between Two Cities*, p. 61. She argues that the female is only used to indicate the two-path topos of evil/good woman known throughout classical literature, before quickly becoming a city.

29. *Ibid.*, p. 62.

kings' fornication with her (v. 2). It then introduces her body to the audience, detailing how it is seated on a beast (v. 3), dressed in scarlet and purple and adorned with gold and precious stones (v. 4), holding a cup (v. 4), having words on her forehead describe her as 'Babylon the Great, mother of the whores and abominations of the earth' (v. 5)[30] and drunk on the blood of the saints (v. 6). The beast she rides is then described in more detail and its interpretation offered (vv. 7-13). The whore is then returned to and her future destruction described in great and gory detail (vv. 15-16), destroyed by the ten horns and the beast, who have also waged war on the Lamb. Only then, after she has been annihilated, are the readers told: 'The woman (ἡ γυνὴ) whom you saw is the great city (ἡ πόλις ἡ μεγάλη) that has a sovereignty over the kings of the earth' (v. 18).

Therefore, it appears narratively logical, however disturbing it might be, to argue that she is presented to the audience as a fleshly body, not just at the start as Rossing claims, but right through until the end of her destruction. The fleshly is not entirely turned to symbol for, as David Aune points out: 'the interpretation of the woman is not made explicit until v. 18'.[31] Elisabeth Schüssler Fiorenza makes a similar concession: 'in chapter 17 Babylon is seen primarily as a feminine figure (17.1-7, 9, 15-16) and secondarily as a city (17.5, 18)'.[32] While ch. 18 focuses on the whore as a city, ch. 17 does not abandon the feminine, despite tell-tale cyphers and female city images being brought into the picture.[33] Therefore, it is logical to argue that the body of the whore, its threatening nature, and its destruction have an important fleshly aspect which ought to be acknowledged in readings.

We have seen above how current readings generally overlook her female body as presented by the text, cutting her up and focusing on her as a city. However, have these readings actually ignored all things feminine, or have some elements of the female body remained in the symbolic interpretations? We now turn to portrayals of female monsters in Frankenstein movies to help us imagine the fleshly whore, and to assist our understanding of how a female body has effected scholarly perceptions even though the flesh has not been the focus.

30. It is interesting to note that prostitutes were required to register under Roman law and during this process they chose the name they wished to trade under, and so Babylon would be her trade name, not her own.

31. Aune, *Revelation 17–22*, p. 934.

32. Fiorenza, *The Book of Revelation*, p. 219.

33. For a supporting 'all woman' reading of ch. 17 see Caroline Vander Stichele, 'Re-membering the Whore: The Fate of Babylon According to Revelation 17.16', in Levine (ed.), *A Feminist Companion*, pp. 107-8.

IV. *She's Alive, Alive!*

Frankenstein films have produced many female monsters. They range from the ugly and traumatized, such as James Whale's *Bride of Franken-stein* (1935) and Helen Bonham Carter's portrayal in Branagh's *Mary Shelley's Frankenstein* (1994), to the seductive killer in Terence Fisher's *Frankenstein Created Woman* (1967), and the sexually stimulating in Paul Morrissey's *Flesh for Frankenstein* (1973) (Figure 3). Their bodies are brought to life by film makers in the same way as their male counterparts, generally by being sewn together from the parts of others.[34] However, the purpose of their bodies is somewhat different. When the female monsters are introduced onto the scene then the agenda turns to sex. The creation of a female body creates sexual urges in men, including Frankenstein, the male monster and various others who happen to encounter her. These sexual urges lead to destruction; sometimes the destruction of her body, and often also of the men who desire her.[35]

Figure 3. Paul Morrissey's *Flesh for Frankenstein* (1973).
Frankenstein creates a male sexual fantasy.
Source: C.C.C./The Kobal Collection.

34. Christina in *Frankenstein Created Woman* (1967) is an exception, a reani-mated and improved version of her former self infused with the soul of her dead lover.
35. See below for more discussion.

Likewise, the introduction of the whore of Babylon in Revelation 17 seems to have the same effect. The scene opens with John hearing that he is going to see a prostitute and that the kings of the earth have fornicated (ἐπόρνευσαν) with her (v. 2). What is this fornication? The verb πορνεύω—usually translated as 'fornicate'—had a broad usage within the Graeco-Roman world, but is directly associated with the word for 'whore', πόρνη.[36] It could be used figuratively, often occurring in the LXX to describe idol worship. However, its most literal meaning is 'to engage in sexual immorality, engage in illicit sex, to fornicate', and is generally used to refer to acts separate from adultery (μοιχεία).[37] So, from a literal perspective, when the whore arrives this term clearly indicates that sex is on offer.[38] Figurative readings of the text obviously argue that the passage is not about sex but that the term is being used to symbolize her seducing people to go astray through idolatry/economic relationships.[39] As Rossing states 'the author constructs Babylon…drawing on prostitution imagery to warn of Rome's seductive economic power'.[40] While we have seen that her fleshly body is generally overlooked in symbolic readings, the desires it provokes are not.[41] Her seductive aspects are still noticed, with her ability to lead people astray one of her key threats: 'The two verbs in Rev. 17.2, "commit prostitution" (πορνεύω) and "become drunk" (μεθύω), make clear the great prostitute's danger in seduction and intoxicating the world', states Rossing.[42] Beale comments on 'the outward attractiveness by which whores try to seduce others'[43] and Ian Boxall notes that essentially 'the scene functions on the association of the female, with the alluring seductive whore'.[44] Even Adela Yarbro Collins, who sees no sexual desire, still describes the

---

36. For the complex usage of the substantive term porneia from Classical Greek through to the fourth century CE, see Kyle Harper, 'Porneia: The Making of a Christian Sexual Norm', *JBL* 131 (2012), pp. 363-83.

37. BDAG, p. 854.

38. For the convincing argument that she is a whore, rather than a beautiful courtesan, see Glancy and Moore, 'Revelation's "Great Whore"?'.

39. 'The meaning is figurative rather than literal'. Aune, *Revelation 17–22*, p. 907. BDAG, p. 854.

40. Rossing, *The Choice Between Two Cities*, p. 62.

41. The most in-depth reading of the whore in relation to desire, particularly male sexual desire, is carried out in Pippin, *Death and Desire*, and furthered in Pippin, *Apocalyptic Bodies*.

42. Rossing, *The Choice Between Two Cities*, p. 69.

43. Beale, *The Book of Revelation*, p. 854.

44. Ian Boxall, *The Revelation of Saint John* (BNTC; London: Continuum, 2006), p. 249.

whore as 'seductive'.[45] This reveals that no matter how much her symbolic city identity is focused upon, the ability of a fleshly female to 'seduce' and to 'cause desire' is still retained.[46]

Yet ironically, this reading of the whore as an active seductress inscribes onto her fleshly body something it is not specifically accused of. The only person charged with such actions is Jezebel in Rev. 2.20: 'she leads my servants astray into sexual immorality' πλανᾷ τοὺς ἐμοὺς δούλους πορνεῦσαι (v. 20). References to Babylon as she is portrayed in chs. 18 and 19 are more active; directly accused with a second person singular address: 'because all the nations were led astray by your magic/potion', ὅτι ἐν τῇ φαρμακείᾳ σου ἐπλανήθησαν πάντα τὰ ἔθνη (18.23). Her active sin was to corrupt: 'she corrupted the earth by her fornication', ἔφθειρεν τὴν γῆν ἐν τῇ πορνείᾳ αὐτῆς (19.2).[47] But these references are later in the text. The initial description of the whore does not mention leading astray or actively seducing into fornication, despite the number of scholars who read it this way. Such readings involve inscribing these other parts of the text onto ch. 17.[48] Revelation 17.2 actually indicates that it is those who have committed sex acts with the whore who have been active, instead of innocents seduced by a rampant evil woman:

45. Adela Yarbro Collins, 'Feminine Symbolism in the Book of Revelation', in Levine (ed.), *A Feminist Companion*, p. 128.

46. It also reveals an inherent androcentric bias in readings, with scholars referring to the whore as seductive to 'people' when in reality this means seductive to 'hetero-normative men' for that is the clientele of a female Graeco-Roman prostitute. There is a clear replication of the 'stimulated male gaze' in the language used in describing what the whore represents and the effect she has on readers. For the argument that the book of Revelation is written specifically for the male gaze in order to stimulate sexual desires, see Pippin, *Death and Desire*. For a refreshing queer reading, see Lynn R. Huber, 'Gazing at the Whore: Reading Revelation Queerly', in Teresa J. Hornsby and Ken Stone (eds.), *Bible Trouble: Queer Reading at the Boundaries of Biblical Scholarship* (Atlanta: SBL, 2011), pp. 301-20, who wants to show that 'Revelation's apparent attempt at capturing the attention or the gaze of the male audience member has worked to capture the gaze of the lesbian-identified interpreter'. *Ibid.*, pp. 307-8.

47. Rev. 14.8 announces that Babylon has fallen, and states how she has 'given the nations to/made the nations drink (πεπότικεν) the wine of the wrath of her fornication'.

48. Those who argue she should be read alongside Jezebel include Paul B. Duff, *Who Rides the Beast? Prophetic Rivalry and the Rhetoric of Crisis in the Churches of the Apocalypse* (Oxford: Oxford University Press, 2001) and David L. Barr, 'Women in Myth and History: Deconstructing John's Characterizations', in Levine (ed.), *A Feminist Companion*, pp. 55-68.

μεθ' ἧς ἐπόρνευσαν⁴⁹ οἱ βασιλεῖς τῆς γῆς καὶ ἐμεθύσθησαν οἱ κατοικοῦντες τὴν γῆν ἐκ τοῦ οἴνου τῆς πορνείας αὐτῆς.

[the prostitute] with whom the kings of the earth have committed fornication and those who inhabit the earth have been made/become drunk from the wine of her prostitution/fornication. (Rev. 17.2)

The whore is not the subject of ἐπόρνευσαν, accused of seducing unsuspecting punters, but rather the object: 'they have fornicated/had sex with her. There is no mention of leading astray, in contrast to the accusations bought against Jezebel. It appears the punters have been happy to engage with her in the first place. Like the female in *Flesh for Frankenstein* (1973), men approach her for sex rather than her actively seducing them into it.⁵⁰ The whore of Babylon is not so much the evil seductress as the prostitute whom many men chose to visit. Therefore, we can see that the key charge brought against the whore in Rev. 17.2 is not that she has seduced the king's into fornication, but rather that the kings have *carried out* fornication with her: a subtle difference. Her ability to be penetrated is ignored when she is rendered symbolic of idol worship, and her ability to seduce brought to the fore and inscribed upon her.

This reveals two important points. First, it shows that it is difficult not to read seduction onto woman's body, even when reading practices actively try to ignore the flesh. Secondly, it shows that the literal sex acts which have been carried out are overlooked in ch. 17 when symbolic practices are focused upon. These two factors have led to the whore of Babylon being understood as an evil seductress, rather than a multiply penetrated prostitute.

---

49.   The variant ἐποίησαν πορνείαν in ℵ (Codex Sinaiticus) and the fourth-century commentary on the book of Revelation by Andreas of Caesarea still retain the active sense of their participation; see Aune, *Revelation 17–22*, p. 907.

50.   To read the kings as being innocent is somewhat naïve, particularly given that Jezebel's leading astray and deceiving is made clear and Babylon's is not. Babylon is a prostitute and those who visit a prostitute generally know what they are getting. Indeed, in the Graeco-Roman world brothels were commonplace, and areas where prostitutes frequented were well known: taverns, ports etc. It was a taxable trade and they were to register under their trade name. For an in-depth discussion see Thomas A. J. McGinn, *Prostitution, Sexuality, and the Law in Ancient Rome* (New York: Oxford University Press, 1998). For a wider cultural discussion, see Marylyn B. Skinner, *Sexuality in Greek and Roman Culture* (Oxford: Blackwell, 2005). For a discussion on the lack of choice many women had in the matter of their trade see Rebecca Flemming, 'Quae Corpore Quaestum Facit: The Sexual Economy of Female Prostitution in the Roman Empire', *JRS* 89 (1999), pp. 38-61, and Glancy and Moore, 'Revelation's "Great Whore"?'.

V. *Flesh and Blood Destruction*

We have seen how the whore of Babylon, like Frankenstein's females in their various guises, presents a body which brings sex into the picture. We have also seen how her body can be read as fleshly, as well as symbolically. We now turn our focus to how she has a fleshly body which is destroyed by the males who had sex with her. To re-imagine her destruction we turn again to Frankenstein's females and their gory ends, for as already mentioned above, the female monsters in Frankenstein movies are also often destroyed. For example, in *Bride of Frankenstein* (1935), when the female rejects the advances of the monster, he destroys them both. In *Mary Shelley's Frankenstein* (1994) Elizabeth realizes she is hideous and burns herself to death. In *Flesh for Frankenstein* (1973) Frankenstein's assistant Otto wants to penetrate the body of the female, but he is too brutal, ripping her open and very visibly disembowelling her. This final example with its gory detail is most similar to the destruction of the whore of Babylon, who is stripped, eaten and burnt (v. 16). However, this similarity is easy to miss if only reading scholarly interpretations of Babylon's end. Indeed, the general consensus is that we should actively resist such gory readings because, by the time of her destruction, she is only a city/system being attacked.[51] This 'nothing to fear, no blood' approach is perhaps epitomized by Beale's section title: 'At the End of History God Will Inspire the State and Its Allies to Turn Against the Economic-Religious System in Order to Remove Its Security and Destroy It'.[52] No blood, no gore and certainly no flesh.

To demonstrate the validity of such sanitized readings Rossing carries out a detailed study of the terms used to depict the whore's destruction in v. 16. She concludes that Babylon is 'all city', because in the Hebrew Bible these terms are most frequently used against cities.[53] However, as we have already established, the text urges the audience to refrain from leaving the image of a woman's body behind until after her destruction. In light of this we now ask whether the terms used in v. 16 can be seen as fitting the destruction of a woman's body, rather than a city.

---

51. There are exceptions, for example Selvidge, 'Powerful and Powerless Women in the Apocalypse', pp. 157-67; Pippin, *Death and Desire*; and Vander Stichele, 'Re-membering the Whore', who read Babylon's destruction as highly sexualized, involving rape and cannibalism.

52. Beale, *The Book of Revelation*, p. 882.

53. Rossing, *The Choice Between Two Cities*, pp. 87-97.

Verse 16 describes in detail the stages of the whore's destruction carried out by the kings/horns who had previously had sex with her: she will be 'made desolate', or rather 'made barren' (ἠρημωμένην)⁵⁴ and naked (γυμνήν); she will then have her flesh eaten (φάγονται) and finally she will be burnt (κατακαύσουσιν).

καὶ τὰ δέκα κέρατα ἃ εἶδες καὶ τὸ θηρίον, οὗτοι μισήσουσι τὴν πόρνην, καὶ ἠρημωμένην ποιήσουσιν αὐτὴν καὶ γυμνήν, καὶ τὰς σάρκας αὐτῆς φάγονται, καὶ αὐτὴν κατακαύσουσιν ἐν πυρί·⁵⁵

And the ten horns which you saw and the beast, these will hate the whore, and they will make her barren/depopulated and naked and they will eat her flesh and they will burn her with fire. (Rev. 17.16)

Let us begin with the most 'fleshly' of descriptions: 'they will eat her flesh' τὰς σάρκας αὐτῆς φάγονται. There is nothing which points away from the body in this term. The object of the action is flesh (σάρκας) and the phrase itself generally refers to consuming something which has been alive.⁵⁶ Even Beale points out that 'she is devoured like a victim of a wild animal'.⁵⁷ This element of her punishment can clearly be aimed at the physical body, and is more appropriate when directed at flesh, rather than figuratively at a city. Indeed, this term is tellingly overlooked in Rossing's analysis.

Burning with fire can be aimed at a city, but it can also be done to the physical body. It is precisely what was ordered in Lev. 21.9 for the daughter of a priest accused of harlotry.⁵⁸ Beale sees a similarity to the burning of houses in Ezek. 16.41 and 23.47, but Aune reminds us that this image is used regarding the burning of the *survivors* in Ezek. 23.25.⁵⁹ Therefore, this action can be seen as a punishment being inflicted upon someone 'in the flesh' just as much as upon a city.

Making γυμνήν (naked) can be used figuratively to mean 'uncovered', but is obviously primarily an action done to a body, making it 'naked' or

54. For an explanation of this translation, see below.

55. καὶ γυμνήν is omitted from 046 and the fourth-century commentary on the book of Revelation by Andreas of Caesarea but is attested in other manuscripts. There are also attestations of a repetition of ποιήσουσιν αὐτὴν in some later manuscripts. These variations have little impact on our focus. For further discussion see Aune, *Revelation 17–22*, p. 911.

56. BDAG, p. 396.

57. Beale, *The Book of Revelation*, p. 883.

58. 'When the daughter of a priest profanes herself through prostitution, she profanes her father; she shall be burned to death' (Lev. 21.9, NRSV).

59. Beale, *The Book of Revelation*, p. 883; Aune, *Revelation 17–22*, p. 957.

'bare'.[60] Beale points out that Babylon is 'stripped like a whore',[61] indicating that this punishment has overriding bodily connotations. Rossing lists many places where γυμνήν is used figuratively, but has to admit that it is primarily a physical action.[62] Therefore, three of the four actions can, and most often do, target the physical body.

So it is the first verb of the scene, ἐρημόω, which becomes the battle-ground for city readings, and appears to be Rossing's stronghold. I have translated it as both 'depopulated' and 'barren' to counter this emphatically. It occurs as a perfect passive participle accusative feminine: ἠρημωμένην. The preferred translation of the verb is 'desolate', and, as Rossing convincingly shows, ἐρημόω as a verb is 'almost exclusively' used in the Hebrew Bible to represent a city or landscape being destroyed.[63] Is there any flesh to be found? Even when the subject is a city, the verb itself does actually have a wider meaning, not only of being desolate, but also of being depopulated. As Aune points out in relation to the whore: 'since the whore is a city, the phrase ἠρημωμένην ποιήσουσιν αὐτήν, "they will make her desolate", i.e., depopulate her, is appropriate'.[64] However, the verb does not presume that the subject is a city alone: it is used also of persons, to mean also 'isolated', 'bereft' or 'stripped bare'.[65]

Likewise, the cognate adjective ἔρημος can apply to landscapes, cities *and* people. When referring to people it can mean: 'Desolate, deserted …a childless woman',[66] Gal. 4.27 being an example of the latter, which speaks of how those women who are 'desolate' will be greater than those with children.[67] This is a direct quotation of Isa. 54.1 (LXX), in which the word relates to both σπεῖρα, 'barren woman' and—implicitly—χήρα, 'widow', 'bereft one'. Philo of Alexandria uses the term alongside 'sterile and childless' (*Vit. Cont.* 62).[68] Thus, this term has a fleshly quality about it involving both being isolated, as a body, and being childless. In Rev. 17.16 ἠρημωμένην is a passive participle, and so this is not something intrinsic to the whore, but rather something that will be

60. BDAG, p. 208.
61. Beale, *The Book of Revelation*, p. 883.
62. Rossing, *The Choice Between Two Cities*, pp. 92-97.
63. *Ibid.*, p. 89.
64. Aune, *Revelation 17–22*, p. 957.
65. See LSJ, p. 687 for examples.
66. BDAG, p. 391.
67. Which is in turn quoting Isa. 54.1; *ibid.*
68. In this passage the term is used in reference to cities, but in regard to what shall happen if same sex couples inhabit them (no children will be produced).

done to her. As a participle it carries an adjectival sense alongside γυμνήν as objects of 'they will make her' (ποιήσουσιν).

Thus, if we look for a fleshly resonance, we can see there are indications that her body is being made childless/barren. Or, to put it even more graphically, as Aune does unwittingly, she is being 'depopulated'. She is isolated, desolate and she cannot now bear children. This term, when read with a woman's body as the target, can have the sense of damaging the body so that no child dwells in it anymore nor ever will again.

Therefore, in its totality, the punishment can be seen as her being made barren, stripped naked, eaten and burnt. This can be read as the most embodied of punishments, which is overlooked when the body is cut up and made safe as symbol of a city. We can see that there is a clear fleshly reading of not only the body of the whore, but also her bodily destruction, in a similar gory way to that of Frankenstein's females: lots of blood, lots of decay. Therefore, we now ask if there is also a fleshly threat to fear from the whore lurking in the narrative of the book of Revelation which has been overlooked by 'nothing to fear' symbolic readings. We have explored the original text of Revelation 17 to uncover the body of the whore. We now turn to the original text of *Frankenstein* and its portrayal of the female monster to assist us in understanding the very real threatening nature of the female body.

VI. *Revelation's Franken-whore*

Despite the creation of filmic female monsters, Mary Shelley's original text actually has no animated female. In the novel the monster persuades Frankenstein to create a mate and so Victor resumes his work to create a female. However, late one night, while toiling over the female body, Victor sees the male monster smiling down above him and realizes the terrifying threat of the female. Upon this realization, rather than carry on with his work, 'trembling with passion, [I] tore to pieces the thing on which I was engaged'.[69] 'The thing' is of course the female.[70] Why does he feel the need to tear her body to pieces? He presents several reasons, all revolving around her future autonomy: she might 'delight, for its own sake, in murder and wretchedness',[71] or 'might turn with disgust from

69. Shelley, *Frankenstein or The Modern Prometheus*, p. 171.
70. It is interesting that here Frankenstein turns the female body into a 'thing' in order to allow himself to destroy flesh and face up to gore, as scholars do with Babylon in order to understand her destruction.
71. Shelley, *Frankenstein or The Modern Prometheus*, pp. 170-71.

him [the monster] to the superior beauty of man',[72] or worst of all she may propagate terror: 'one of the first results of those sympathies for which the daemon thirsted would be children, and a race of Devils would be propagated upon the earth, who might make the very existence of the species of man's condition precarious and full of terror'.[73] Frankenstein has uttered the terror he fears most from the bodily form of a female: her ability to make children.[74] Although females are introduced into Frankenstein films to bring sex into the picture by provoking male desires, in the original text it is not desire which is the root of the threat, but rather it is one of the outcomes of sex: offspring. The introduction of the female is a very real threat as it would take the creative power from Frankenstein and he fears she might be penetrated by the monster or 'men'. Therefore, he realizes his only option is to tear her to pieces before life is given to her and she can give life to others.

Turning to the whore of Babylon again, we have seen that the original text of Revelation 17 presents us with a woman who is not primarily seductive, but rather penetrated. She is a fleshly woman with whom many men have committed sex acts. What are the results of these sex acts? They are inscribed upon her forehead:

Βαβυλὼν ἡ μεγάλη, ἡ μήτηρ τῶν πορνῶν[75] καὶ τῶν βδελυγμάτων τῆς γῆς.

Babylon the great, the mother of whores/fornicators and of abominations of the earth. (Rev. 17.5)

The whore of Babylon, unlike Frankenstein's female, has procreated, and she has procreated many times. As a prostitute, her children would naturally also take on her trade, or other disapproved of professions such as acting or pimping.[76] Therefore, 'whores/fornicators and abominations'

---

72. *Ibid.*, p. 170.

73. *Ibid.*, p. 171.

74. See Anne Kostelanetz Mellor, *Mary Shelley: Her Life, Her Fiction, Her Monsters* (London: Routledge, 1988), pp. 115-26, particularly pp. 119-20, which details her threat as a reproductive female and her ability to mate with many men.

75. Although πορνῶν, the plural of the feminine noun ἡ πόρνη, is nearly unanimously preferred, there is also MS attestation for πόρνων, from the masculine noun ὁ πόρνος. Early manuscripts reading ΠΟΡΝΩΝ would have been ambiguous. See Aune, *Revelation 17–22*, p. 909.

76. In the Graeco-Roman world the children of prostitutes were not given any legal status, and they too would take on prostitution as their trade. These are illegitimate children, with no paterfamilias to come under and no legal rights. Aline Rousselle and Felicia Pheasant, *Porneia: On Desire and the Body in Antiquity* (Oxford: Blackwell, 1988), p. 94. McGinn, *Prostitution, Sexuality, and the Law in Ancient Rome*, p. 98.

can be read on a literal level as her offspring.[77] The fact that she is procreating and, what is more, that this is threatening, is demonstrated through her destruction involving being 'depopulated' and destroyed in the flesh which makes it clear she will never procreate again. Like Frankenstein's female monster, this baby-making is part of what is so threatening about her, and so her destruction is designed to prevent its occurrence.

But why is her baby-making so threatening? The original text of *Frankenstein* presents us with a possible answer: pro-creation is taken away from the hands of the creator. The creator in the book of Revelation, just like Victor Frankenstein, makes it clear that at the end he alone must hold the keys to creation, with no rivals.[78] Therefore, the final act of creation in the text comes from the one seated on the throne who declares, 'Behold *I* am making all things new' Ἰδοὺ καινὰ ποιῶ πάντα (Rev. 21.5). The whore has the power of creation and the demand for her services. She has procreated and created children like herself, who will in turn take on her trade and further breed with anyone and everyone. Therefore, Baby(maker)lon must be removed so the male creator God can create on his own, with no baby-making rival. For this sole creative act to be able to occur the whore is destroyed and her womb depopulated forever. The path for children is shut.

Indeed, at the end of the book of Revelation we are presented with a totally sterile landscape. The 140,000 male virgins (παρθένοι) who follow the lamb around have never penetrated anything (Rev. 14.1-8).[79] No women are mentioned as entering into the female Holy City,[80] and the text culminates in the marriage of the New Jerusalem and the Lamb. This means that there will be no more baby-making, for the only female left in the text is Jerusalem who is quickly rendered a city, and she will never

77. Indeed, those who are classed as 'whores/fornicators and abominations' will also be destroyed at the end of the book of Revelation (Rev. 21.8).

78. As Judith Lee observes, 'In Revelation John bears witness directly to the power of the Divine Word to *uncreate* the world… God's presence is revealed in two ways: in the destruction of the body/text of the earth, and in the grotesque forms of human usurpation of a generative power that belongs only to the creator.' Judith Lee, 'Sacred Horror: Faith and Fantasy in the Revelation of John', in George Aichele and Tina Pippin (eds.), *The Monstrous and The Unspeakable: The Bible as Fantastic Literature* (Sheffield: Sheffield Academic Press, 1997), pp. 220-39 (225).

79. Lynn R. Huber, 'Sexually Explicit? Re-Reading Revelation's 144,000 Virgins as a Response to Roman Discourses', *Journal of Men, Masculinities and Spirituality* 2, no. 1 (2008), pp. 3-28.

80. Indeed, the book of Revelation is a female-free text, bar Jezebel, the Earth, the woman clothed like the sun, the New Jerusalem and Babylon.

be a mother for she is marrying a Lamb, which is sterile as an undeveloped child, not able to impregnate *anything*. Creation lies only in the hands of the one seated on the throne, with life-giving water flowing from it.[81] Therefore, the whore's body presents a very real threat in the literal narrative of the book of Revelation; unbridled procreation with a woman who is penetrated by everyone, rather than controlled creation from the divine.[82] This literal threat is rooted in the fleshly body presented in ch. 17. Our reading has therefore presented her as functioning not only as symbolic of a city, but also as a character in her own right, with her own threatening nature in the unfolding story of the text.

Conclusions

In filmic portrayals Frankenstein's female monsters are presented as sewn together sex-symbols, provoking desires in men and often being destroyed as result. The whore of Babylon is presented by scholars as being sewn together from textual fragments, a city-symbol, alluring people into illicit economic/idolatrous relationships and being destroyed as a result. Therefore, these terrifying females have much in common. Yet I have argued that both these presentations overlook their original textual portrayals. Most importantly, we have seen how the whore of Babylon's seams are not easy to trace; that she can be read as fleshly as well as symbolic, and also that Revelation 17 focuses on the act of sex, rather than seduction. Symbolic readings have overlooked her being penetrated by many men, and have therefore also overlooked the results of such penetration: fleshly children which Babylon is rendered unable to continue to have by the end of the passage. This means that the fleshly threat she presents in the narrative—that of taking power away from the one who is seated on the throne, the sterile Lamb and its sterile followers—is overlooked. The 'no blood' readings have literally sterilized her bodily threat; overlooking her body as a living reproductive entity, and ignoring her 'sterilization' during her destruction.

81. This ends in the 'annihilation of human creativity': Yarbro Collins, 'Feminine Symbolism in the Book of Revelation', p. 129.

82. The whore has been seen as the archetypal 'Great Mother Goddess' but only in relation to her as a metaphorical mother rather than as a fleshly woman making fleshly children. See *ibid.*, pp. 127-30; Duff, *Who Rides the Beast?*, p. 86. For mythical readings of this image, see Adela Yarbro Collins, *Crisis and Catharsis: The Power of the Apocalypse* (Philadelphia: Westminster Press, 1984).

Re-reading the whore of Babylon alongside Frankenstein's monsters has allowed us to explore her from a fleshly angle, to re-examine how her body has been viewed and what has been inscribed upon her. In doing so we have not seen her as a seductive woman leading people astray into idolatry, but as the Franken-whore of Baby(maker)lon. Therefore, through this exploration of Babylon's body, we have revealed further unimagined threats hiding in the dark. They will be dealt with textually in Rev. 21.8, when the 'fornicators' and 'abominations' will be burnt in a lake of fire. Nevertheless, perhaps Babylon still has the last sardonic laugh, as she continues to evade sterilizing readings, with flesh and blood threats ready to be unleashed upon unsuspecting readers.

CAN A BODY CHANGE?
JOSEPHUS'S ATTITUDE
TO CIRCUMCISION AND CONVERSION*

Davina Grojnowski

The male body, by virtue of being circumcised, becomes a religious, ethnic and cultural entity by which the man himself proclaims his Jewishness, and is recognized as such by others.[1] Suetonius, for example, graphically describes for us how Roman officials examine a man in their efforts to collect the Jewish tax under the Emperor Domitian (*Domitian* 12).[2] Within that framework, circumcision also functioned as the bodily

---

*   I would like to thank Professor Martin Goodman for his invaluable help and advice when I first embarked on this topic at the Oxford Centre for Hebrew and Jewish Studies. I would also like to thank Professor Steve Mason for his helpful and supportive feedback on an earlier version of this article which was presented at the 2012 SBL Josephus seminar.

1.   Although circumcision was not exclusive to Jews in antiquity (cf. Herodotus 2.104), in Roman literature it was frequently associated with Judaism; see the various references to circumcision in Menahem Stern, *Greek and Latin Authors on Jews and Judaism* (3 vols.; Publications of the Israel Academy of Sciences and Humanities, Section of Humanities; Jerusalem: Israel Academy of Sciences and Humanities, 1974–80). The terminology of, and difference between, Jew, Jewish and Judaean has benefitted from a long academic debate, see, e.g., Shaye J. D. Cohen, *The Beginnings of Jewishness: Boundaries, Varieties, Uncertainties* (Hellenistic Culture and Society 31; Berkeley: University of California Press, 1999), Chapter 3, *passim*; Steve Mason, 'Jews, Judaeans, Judaizing, Judaism: Problems of Categorization in Ancient History', *JSJ* 28 (2007), pp. 457-512; Daniel Schwartz, 'Doing Like Jews or Becoming a Jew? Josephus on Women Converts to Judaism', in Jörg Frey, Daniel Schwartz and Stephanie Gripentrog (eds.), *Jewish Identity in the Greco-Roman World* (Ancient Judaism and Early Christianity 71; Leiden: Brill, 2007), pp. 93-110. As this chapter discusses the literary presentation of the circumcised body and conversion rather than their historicity, the terms Jews/Jewish will be used; the only exceptions will be made regarding reference to the actual Judaean state.

2.   The literature concerned with the question 'who was a Jew?' is vast. For general discussions and overviews, see Mason, 'Jews, Judaeans'; Martin Goodman,

commitment of a male convert to Judaism; the convert could use his body as a religious and cultural symbol of his dedication towards his adopted religion. The ancient debate concerning the importance of male circumcision within the conversion process has consequently been a lively one, participants including Jewish authors such as Philo (e.g. *Spec. Leg.* 1.1-11), Paul (e.g. Rom. 2.25-29) and the authors of *Jubilees* (e.g. *Jub.* 15.25-26) and the Adiabene narrative (*Ant.* 20.17-96).[3]

We also find several instances of male circumcision and conversion to Judaism (both male and female) in the writings of Josephus. While individual narratives have benefitted from much interest, there have been very few studies on Josephus's personal attitude towards, and depiction of, circumcision as part of the conversion process and its effect on the human body, and even fewer studies that attempt to analyse all such narratives in Josephus together as part of the contemporaneous discourse.[4] Of these, Shaye Cohen and Steve Mason have admirably attempted to extract and analyse the individual conversion narratives to gauge Josephus's opinion towards conversion, circumcision and proselytes and his methodology of employing conversion narratives, with both scholars, despite analysing the same passages, reaching contradicting conclusions regarding Josephus's position (see below). Honora Chapman, meanwhile, focuses only on Josephus's depiction of forced circumcision.[5]

'Identity and Authority in Ancient Judaism', *Judaism* 39 (1990), pp. 192-201. For arguments that the concept of conversion was contested by some Jews in antiquity, see esp. Matthew Thiessen, *Contesting Conversion: Genealogy, Circumcision, and Identity in Ancient Judaism and Christianity* (Oxford scholarship online; New York: Oxford University Press, 2011).

3. For a collection and discussion of the relevant passages, see most recently Nina E. Livesey, *Circumcision as a Malleable Symbol* (WUNT 2/295; Tübingen: Mohr Siebeck, 2010).

4. Various authors have used individual passages for their research; see the relevant discussions below, *ad locum.*

5. Shaye Cohen, 'Respect for Judaism by Gentiles According to Josephus', *HTR* 80 (1987), pp. 409-30; Steve Mason, '*Contra Apionem* in Social and Literary Context: An Invitation to Judean Philosophy', in Louis Feldman and John R. Levison (eds.), *Josephus' Contra Apionem: Studies in Its Character and Context with a Latin Concordance to the Portion Missing in Greek* (Arbeiten zur Geschichte des antiken Judentums und des Urchristentums 34; Leiden: E. J. Brill, 1996), pp. 187-228; *idem*, 'Should Any Wish to Enquire Further (*Ant.* 1.25): The Aim and Audience of Josephus's Judaean Antiquities/Life', in Steve Mason (ed.), *Understanding Josephus: Seven Perspectives* (JSPSup 32; Sheffield: Sheffield Academic Press, 1998), pp. 64-103; Honora Howell Chapman, 'Paul, Josephus, and the Judean Nationalistic and Imperialistic Policy of Forced Circumcision', *Ilu, Revista de Ciencias de las Religiones* 11 (2006), pp. 131-55. Schwartz, 'Doing Like Jews',

Under these circumstances, a re-evaluation of the evidence seems relevant, with a focus on those Josephan circumcision/conversion episodes which have already been the subject of Cohen's and Mason's analyses: the embezzlement of Fulvia (*Ant.* 18.81-84); conversions for the sake of marriage (*Ant.* 20.139-45; 16.225, cf. *War* 1.347); the Idumaean and Ituraean conversions (*Ant.* 13.257, 318-19); conversion in the Esther narrative (*Ant.* 11.285); the conversion of Metilius (*War* 2.454); the Adiabene narrative (*Ant.* 20.18-96); and unspecified groups in *Apion* 2.123, 209-10.[6]

The focus of this analysis is on Josephus's literary presentation of these conversions and their literary functions, as opposed to the historicity of events narrated and the factual complexity of the issue who was and who was not a Jew. A prominent aspect, therefore, is the conception of circumcision as an action done to a male body, its perceived consequences within the conversion process and how Josephus depicts the relationship between the physical, bodily, alteration and the religious change attributed to the physical alteration. The analysis will be supplemented by a terminological overview, in which I shall look at which words and phrases Josephus employs to denote conversion, in order to see whether we can establish Josephus's own thoughts beneath the literary level of the narrative. It will become evident that for the benefit of his audience and his narrative goals, Josephus clearly distinguishes between who he wants to present as a convert using what language, and who not.[7] It will also be revealed that Josephus shows himself to be

looks at female conversion, and Livesey limits herself to a discussion of the Adiabene narrative in Livesey, *Circumcision.*

6. Cohen, 'Respect', Mason, 'Should Any Wish to Enquire'. The passages represent the totality of definitive conversion narratives in Josephus and stand in contrast to some of Josephus's more obscure references to Gentiles who join 'in some manner' (e.g. *War* 7.45; *Apion* 2.261). The Samaritans will not be discussed, despite a reported conversion story of 'Chouthians' at their foundation (*Ant.* 9.288-90) and their self-perception as part of Israel. On the surface this narrative demonstrates few irregularities compared to the other conversion narratives, yet Josephus accuses the Samaritans of duplicity (*Ant.* 9.291; 11.340; 12.257) and various offences against the Judaeans, Jerusalem and the Temple (*Ant.* 12.10; 13.74-79; 18.30). Josephus presents the Samaritans as not being acceptable in terms of the true Israel. For a full discussion of the Samaritans in Josephus, see Reinhard Pummer, *The Samaritans in Flavius Josephus* (Tübingen: Mohr Siebeck, 2009).

7. Multiple valuable suggestions for various audience constellations have been put forward and cannot be reviewed here, although all agree on an educated audience. See the exemplary Mason, 'Should Any Wish to Enquire', arguing for a Roman audience, and suggesting a Jewish audience, most recently John Curran, 'Flavius Josephus in Rome', in Jack Pastor, Pnina Stern and Menahem Mor (eds.),

conscious of when and how, from a narratological perspective, he inserts or omits conversion narratives and references to circumcision, effectively playing them as literary tools and devices.

I. *Previous Contributions*

Cohen discusses what forms of respect Gentiles adopted towards Judaism according to Josephus; he states that, for Josephus, conversion entails a full social commitment, but concludes that out of deference towards his Roman audience, Josephus neglects to mention this point explicitly. Cohen also alleges that Josephus portrays conversion negatively, as all instances of conversion carry with them negative consequences.[8] Thus, according to Cohen's readings of Josephus's conversion narratives, the author did not believe Judaism to be a missionary religion and disapproves of any attempts at conversion; in contrast to the respect for Judaism expressed by Gentiles, which Josephus praises and readily accepts, Josephus's conversion narratives clearly do not present a 'favourable model' for future converts.[9] This conclusion forces Cohen to bracket the Adiabene narrative, attributing the positive attitude towards conversion to Josephus's 'sloppiness' in transcribing his source material.[10]

Mason offers an alternative view of Josephus's conversion narratives, reading the *Antiquities* as a handbook for interested Gentiles.[11] With the exception of the Adiabene narrative, Mason asserts that the majority of the conversion narratives are merely 'incidental references' or 'scenery'.[12]

Flavius Josephus, Interpretation and History (JSJSup 146; Leiden: Brill, 2011). For the sake of the argument, this chapter assumes an educated audience in Rome with an express interest in Josephus and his writings, without attempting to limit the audience based on religious affiliation.

    8. Cohen, 'Respect', p. 422.

    9. *Ibid.*, pp. 424, 428.

    10. *Ibid.*, p. 424. However, Cohen does not provide an alternative or conclusive answer for Josephus's potential thought process. Following on from his hypothesis that Josephus disapproved of proselytes and was advocating deterrence from conversion, Cohen is forced to reject the *Contra Apionem*, which boasts of the fact that many Jewish customs had spread throughout non-Jewish communities, and ascribes the main tone of the text to a Judaeo-Alexandrian source probably contemporary with Philo: *ibid.*, p. 425. Cohen here is not consistent—if he discredits the ideas of *Contra Apionem* by stating that Josephus simply transcribed his source material, he cannot use the text as evidence in his discussion of Gentile officials and their respect for Judaism as described by Josephus: *ibid.*, p. 413.

    11. Mason, 'Should Any Wish to Enquire', p. 79.

    12. *Ibid.*, p. 92; *idem*, '*Contra Apionem*', pp. 202, 204. Due to his focus on the *Antiquities* only, Mason omits the Metilius passage in *War* 2.454.

In contrast to Cohen, Mason claims that the *Antiquities* culminate in the Adiabene narrative, exemplifying Josephus's attempts to compel his interested Gentile audience to convert, thus understanding the passage as a deliberate inclusion by Josephus to end his corpus on a high note for potential proselytes.[13] Overall, Mason understands the *Antiquities* and the *Contra Apionem* even more so, as a 'primer' for interested Gentiles and a 'recommendation of conversion', although not on the basis of the individual conversion narratives inserted by Josephus.[14]

More recently, Chapman has concentrated on the aspect of forced circumcision itself, rather than conversion as a whole, asking why Paul and Josephus represent themselves in their writings as choosing not to support forced circumcision.[15] Chapman posits that both authors write in reaction to the memory of Hasmonaean expansionist history and thus reject the policy of forced circumcision of Gentiles. However, while Chapman's discussion of Paul is substantial, she bases her theory on only two passages in Josephus, and one passage by omission (namely Josephus's retelling of the Rape of Dinah, *Ant.* 1.337-41).[16] Chapman refers to the circumcision of the Roman general Metilius and the importance of the passage's context, which has Josephus lament the beginning of the end for Jerusalem.[17] However, the passage featuring the men from Trachonitis who move to Galilee during Josephus's time as general, and whom Josephus rescues from forced circumcision (*Vita* 112–13), must be read considering the tendentious character of the *Vita's* genre and should not be accepted at face value.[18] To date, to my knowledge, no

13. Mason, 'Should Any Wish to Enquire', p. 94.

14. Mason, '*Contra Apionem*', pp. 188, 208; cf. *idem*, 'Should Any Wish to Enquire', p. 94. Mason's assumption that Josephus wished to make a positive case for conversion raises the question why Josephus should wait twenty books before offering his audience a single case study, which had very little practical relation to his local Roman audience.

15. Chapman, 'Paul, Josephus'.

16. *Ibid.*, pp. 151-54.

17. See also below the discussion of Metilius and the issue of his circumcision for a different interpretation.

18. Josephus's autobiography, the *Vita*, has until very recently been considered to have been written as a self-defence; see, e.g., Tessa Rajak, 'Justus of Tiberias', *ClQ* New Series 23, no. 2 (1973), pp. 345-68. Recent trends have tended to move away from this theory, reading the *Vita* as Josephus's attempt to present his ideal character, most prominently Steve Mason, 'An Essay in Character: The Aim and Audience of Josephus' *Vita*', in Folker Siegert and Jürgen U. Kalms (eds.), *Internationales Josephus-Kolloquium Münster 1997. Vorträge aus dem Institutum Judaicum Delitzschianum* (Münsteraner Judaisitische Studien; Münster: LIT Verlag,

other scholar has focused exclusively on the collection of Josephan conversion narratives. Terence Donaldson has collected a vast number of
texts dealing with the religious relationships between Jews and Gentiles,
but comments on them all individually and does not focus on the small
number of Josephan conversion narratives in detail, and Daniel Schwartz
has focused on female converts in Josephus.[19] Nina Livesey had set out
to demonstrate the diversity in Second Temple Judaism's understandings
of circumcision and while she discusses authors such as Philo and Paul at
length, arguing that all ancient authors treated the issue differently in
different passages, she concentrates only on what she perceives to be the
fullest treatment of circumcision in Josephus, namely the Adiabene
narrative.[20]

II. The Circumcision/Conversion Narratives

a. *Fulvia,* Ant. *18.81-84*

Fulvia is introduced into the narrative as a noble woman (τῶν ἐν ἀξιώματι
γυναικῶν) who had converted during the reign of Tiberius in 19 CE
(νομίμοις προσεληλυθυῖαν τοῖς Ἰουδαϊκοῖς, *Ant.* 18.82).[21] When four
devious Jews embezzle the monetary gifts she intended for the Temple,
Fulvia complains to her husband Saturnius, a close friend of the emperor
who in turn reports the events to Tiberius himself (*Ant.* 18.83). Subsequently, Josephus tells us that Tiberius ordered the expulsion of the

1998), pp. 31-77. This still means that Josephus may have misrepresented his actions
and events, and his representation of his own actions must be taken with a pinch of
salt. See also below for advised caution when dealing with this *Vita* passage.

    19.   Chapman, 'Paul, Josephus'; Terence L. Donaldson, *Judaism and the Gentiles:
Jewish Patterns of Universalism* (Waco: Baylor University Press, 2007); Schwartz,
'Doing Like Jews'. See also Andreas Blaschke, *Beschneidung. Zeugnisse der Bibel
und verwandter Texte* (Tübingen: Francke Verlag, 1998).

    20.   Livesey, *Circumcision.* Livesey thus contradicts herself as she had previously
criticized scholarship for only concentrating on 'certain treatments' by ancient
authors in order to extrapolate their opinions, rather than considering the 'full range'
of passages: *Ibid.*, pp. 3-6.

    21.   The issue of female conversion to Judaism is a protracted one; for informed
discussions of the issue, see Shelly Matthews, *First Converts: Rich Pagan Women
and the Rhetoric of Mission in Early Judaism and Christianity* (Contraversions:
Jews and other Differences; Stanford: Stanford University Press, 2001), Judith Lieu,
'Circumcision, Women and Salvation', *NTS* 40 (1994), pp. 358-70, and Shaye
Cohen, *Why Aren't Jewish Women Circumcised? Gender and Covenant in Judaism*
(Berkeley: London: University of California Press, 2005). Schwartz, 'Doing Like
Jews', suggests that in the eyes of Josephus—and others—female conversion did not
exist; women could act like Jewish women, but not become them.

entire (πᾶν) Jewish community living in Rome.[22] This passage has been read and discussed from a variety of angles, although most scholars focus either on the historicity of the events—did Tiberius really expel the Jews because of active missionizing behaviour?[23]—or on the question whether or not Fulvia had actually converted, considering the complexity of women converting.[24]

Turning to the text, several scholars have noted the fact that Josephus in this passage is intent on placing the blame for the expulsion onto four men only (*Ant.* 18.81-82).[25] However, they have not connected this observation with the fact that this was one of Josephus's ongoing themes: only a handful of misguided Jews were responsible for any and every calamity or misfortune that the Jews as a whole had to suffer. Hence it is possible to postulate a reading of the passage that sees Josephus inserting this conversion narrative consciously, without worrying about offending his Roman audience, in order to continue and adapt a theme that was already familiar to him and to an attentive audience. Such a theory agrees with both Cohen and Mason that Josephus inserted the passage in an authoritative manner to offer his explanation of the expulsion, but one

22.   The expulsion is also reported by Tacitus (*Annales* 2.85), Suetonius (*Tiberius* 36) and Cassius Dio (57.18.5). Opinion is divided whether the expulsion was ordered based on active proselytizing and missionary behaviour; see, e.g., Louis Feldman, *Jew and Gentile in the Ancient World: Attitudes and Interactions from Alexander to Justinian* (Princeton: Princeton University Press, 1993), pp. 302-3, and Martin Goodman, *Mission and Conversion: Proselytizing in the Religious History of the Roman Empire* (new ed.; Oxford: Oxford University Press, 1995), p. 83.

23.   Both Cohen, 'Respect', p. 424 and Mason, '*Contra Apionem*', pp. 203-4, agree that Josephus used the Fulvia story to cover up the historical background for the expulsion; cf. also Donaldson, *Patterns*, p. 330, arguing that Josephus suppresses the truth. Goodman, *Mission*, p. 83, suggests that it would be implausible for Josephus to hide active missioning behaviour, and that he would instead have tried to explain and justify rather than hide it. Matthews, *First Converts*, pp. 10-23, sets the whole passage including the neighbouring Isis scandal (*Ant.* 18.65-80) into the historical context of Domitian's hostility towards Jews and his support for the Isis cult. She suggests that Josephus was attacking Domitian's support for Isis by high-lighting the religious misconduct of Isis officials and followers, in contrast to the actions of some Jews; Matthews thus also implies a literary function of the passage in the narrative.

24.   Cohen, *Beginnings*, pp. 170-71, suggests that Josephus did not mean full conversion, and proposes that alongside other women, Fulvia had expressed some interest in Judaism. Schwartz, 'Doing Like Jews', p. 96, suggests that Josephus merely describes 'what Fulvia had done'. See above for female conversion.

25.   Cf. Mason, '*Contra Apionem*', p. 204, who points out that Josephus wants to isolate the scoundrels as 'aberrant specimens'; Donaldson, *Patterns*, p. 330.

must ask: Why mention the fact that Fulvia converted at all? Why focus on the conversion of a high-ranking Roman figure?

As a good historian, surely Josephus had to mention the expulsion of Jews under Tiberius, but clearly did not—or could not—state the historical reason behind this expulsion. Josephus thus forges a relationship between Tiberius and the Jews via a high-ranking convert with direct access to the emperor because he wants and needs to create a direct link. He can then explain the expulsion without making the Jews as a whole look bad or weak in the eyes of his audience, presenting them as victims. Furthermore, because Tiberius would not intervene on behalf of anyone, Josephus introduces Fulvia. Ironically, Tiberius is now acting to protect his friend's wife, presented as a convert by Josephus, regardless of her religious beliefs. Evidently, Josephus does not hesitate to use the conversion of Fulvia as a literary tool, nor is he troubled by the issue of the possibility of women converting, who cannot demonstrate the same level of bodily commitment. No bodily commitment or physical change was required to present Fulvia as a convert and to make the story work for Josephus within the narrative framework.

b. *Metilius,* War *2.450-56*

At the beginning of the Jewish war against Rome, the Roman garrison in Jerusalem capitulated and agreed on safe passage with the rebels. Leaving their weapons behind, they were made to leave Jerusalem but were attacked and brutally murdered by the same rebels. The only survivor was their Roman commander Metilius, who promised (ὑποσχόμενον) to judaize (ἰουδαΐσειν) up to the point of circumcision (μέχρι περιτομῆς) in order to save his life (*War* 2.454). The main scholarly debate has centred on the translation and meaning of ἰουδαΐσειν and μέχρι, asking whether Metilius converted, whether he pretended to convert, whether he was forced to convert, whether he altered his physical appearance through circumcision or whether he stopped just short of circumcision: Cohen emphasizes the ambiguity of Metilius's situation, and suggests that he defected on a political level.[26] The thought is mirrored by Mason, who understands ἰουδαΐσειν in this case as a cultural movement.[27] Mason,

---

26. Quote in Cohen, *Beginnings*, p. 183. On Metilius's defection, see *ibid.*, p. 155. For Cohen's analysis of the term ἰουδαΐσειν, see *ibid.*, Chapter 6, *passim.* He suggests three basic translations and understandings: to give political support, to adopt any of the distinctive customs and manners and to speak the language.

27. Mason, 'Jews, Judaeans', p. 464. Cf. also Feldman, *Jew and Gentile*, pp. 349-50, who translates the term as 'turning Jew', and Goodman, *Mission*, p. 82, who translates as 'to behave as a Jew'.

furthermore, suggests that this episode demonstrates that the adoption of Jewish laws and culture under duress was 'repugnant' to Josephus, quoting *Vita* 112-13, where Josephus as governor of Galilee defends non-Jewish fugitives from Trachonitis from forcible circumcision.[28] However, using the *Vita* passage as a basis for judging Josephus's attitude towards forced circumcision is something to be done with caution, largely because of the *Vita*'s contentious nature, and because Josephus continues the same story with a very different emphasis and ending in *Vita* 149-55, when Josephus and his opposition take on very different character roles.[29] Not only does Josephus add new details, but the entire passage is narrated in a more negative tone during which Josephus admits failure—he has to send the fugitives away because he cannot win his argument against the Galileans.[30]

Instead, it is important to consider Josephus's narrative goal in employing this conversion story. Reading the passage from this perspective there is some literary evidence that suggests that Josephus actively and consciously uses Metilius to offset, and emphasize, the death of the garrison, and to demonstrate that what had happened was—again—the responsibility of only a handful of rebels: οἱ περὶ τὸν Ἐλεάζαρον—'those around Eleazar' (*War* 2.453). The double effect of ἰουδαΐσειν and circumcision offsets the reference to a group of ambiguous Judaizers in Syria a few passages later (τοὺς ἰουδαΐζοντας, *War* 2.463). Josephus contrasts the rebels with the masses in a οἱ μὲν/οἱ δὲ structure (*War* 2.449-50), stating that the people only collaborated in the betrayal and murder of the garrison because they had been tricked. He explicitly dates the events to a sabbath (*War* 2.456). This makes not only the attack offensive, but also the (possible) conversion of Metilius illegal, and emphasizes the impiety

28. Steve Mason (ed.), *Flavius Josephus: Translation and Commentary*. IX, *Life of Josephus* (Leiden: Brill, 2001), p. 333 n. 2794. He also refers to the praise that Josephus extends to Prince Izates from Adiabene and King Azizus of Emesa, who both convert, although Mason's argument that Josephus praises Azizus remains unsubstantiated.

29. Josephus also uses a different terminology in the *Vita* passage, cf. n. 50, below.

30. The different versions of the same story and its relevance seem to have escaped many scholars who base their theories of Josephus's attitude towards forced conversion in any context on this passage, e.g. Mason, *Commentary*, p. 74 n. 544; S. Cohen, 'Respect', p. 423; Chapman, 'Paul, Josephus'; Donaldson, *Patterns*, p. 322. In fact, this second version of the men from Trachonitis appears as part of a longer narrative in which Josephus faces constant opposition in his position as governor of Galilee—the story of the men from Trachonitis therefore has little to do with forced conversion or circumcision, and everything to do with Josephus's self-portrayal.

of the rebels.[31] Lastly, Josephus evokes covenantal language by having the Roman soldiers cry out and remind their attackers of the covenant and oaths (τὰς συνθήκας καὶ τοὺς ὅρκους), rather than having them fight back (*War* 2.453). Josephus appears intent on emphasizing the brutality and lawlessness of the situation, and presents the rebels as acting in contrast to the Jews as a whole. It is likely, therefore, that Josephus consciously included the reference to circumcision in order to make the scene more dramatic, using a conversion narrative and reference to circumcision as a literary tool in order to achieve his narrative goal.[32]

c. *Marriage*

Josephus clearly states that in order to marry a Jewish woman, conversion and circumcision was a mandatory requirement for non-Jewish men.[33] Josephus reports several instances of the Herodian family demanding the conversion of possible husbands for their female relatives.[34] Herod asks the Arab Sylleus to 'inscribe himself into the customs

31. Mason, *Commentary*, p. 336 n. 2812, demonstrates that there are only four occurrences of the sabbath terminology in *War*, and suggests that Josephus uses the visual term to stress that the holy day had been violated.

32. *Contra* Honora Chapman, 'Spectacle in Josephus' *Jewish War*', in Jonathan Edmonson, Steve Mason and James Rives (eds.), *Flavius Josephus and Flavian Rome* (Oxford: Oxford University Press, 2005), pp. 289-313, who states that Josephus narrates the surrender of Metilius as a non-spectacle in contrast to the surrender of Josephus at Jotapata. Also *contra* Donaldson, *Patterns*, p. 294, who states that Josephus did not attach any rhetorical significance to the passage. Mason, *Commentary*, p. 334 n. 2795, does refer to the Josephan theme of guilt and lawlessness, but does not see Metilius as a further way of introducing the theme, similar to the Fulvia passage, above.

33. In cases of intermarriage where the potential bride is not Jewish, Josephus is less consistent. At times he points out the negative consequences and prohibitions (*Ant.* 11.71, 139-53; 18.345-47), and at times he mentions Gentile women marrying Jewish men without any complications (*Ant.* 2.91; 5.319; 8.21; 17.19). Furthermore, in his collection of marriage laws (*Apion* 2.199-203), Josephus does not make any reference to the prohibition of intermarriage. *Contra* Louis Feldman, 'Philo, Pseudo-Philo, Josephus, and Theodotus on the Rape of Dinah', *JQR* 94 (2004), pp. 253-77 (263), who states that Josephus was sensitive about the topic and thus omitted the demands of circumcision directed at the Shechemites.

34. The Jewishness of the Herodian family has frequently been debated. Within the limits of this chapter, it suffices to note that Josephus presents the Herodians as Jewish enough to demand conversion from non-Jews prior to marriage, and that the potential husbands accept their authority. For detailed discussions, see most recently: Juila Wilker, *Für Rom und Jerusalem: die herodianische Dynastie im 1. Jahrhundert n.Chr.* (Studien zur alten Geschichte 5; Frankfurt am Main: Verlag Antike, 2007); Benedikt Eckhardt, '"An Idumean, That Is, a Half-Jew": Hasmoneans and Herodians

of the Jews' (ἐγγραφῆναι τοῖς τῶν Ἰουδαίων ἔθεσι, *Ant.* 16.225) in order to marry Salome, Herod's sister. Drusilla, sister of King Agrippa II, agrees to marry Azizus, King of Emesa, who had consented to be circumcised (περιτέμνεσθαι) after Epiphanes, son of King Antiochus, had refused to take on Jewish customs (τὰ Ἰοθδαίων ἔθη, 20.139). Berenice, sister to Drusilla and Agrippa II, herself convinces Polemo (πείθει Πολέμωνα) to be circumcised (περιτεμόμενον) and subsequently to marry her (20.146). Reviewing these stories, Cohen does not foresee married bliss for the couples, but only negative consequences; the marriages of Azizus and Polemo with the Herodian princesses Drusilla and Berenice respectively break down.[35] However, Josephus in fact does not state that the marriages broke down because the men had converted, and thus does not qualify their actions: Azizus's failed marriage to Drusilla is the consequence of a quarrel between Drusilla and her sister Berenice (20.143), and Polemo's divorce is merely one of several failed marriages for Berenice, who had previously been married to Marcus Julius Alexander (Philo's nephew, 19.276-77), and her uncle Herod, King of Chalcis (19.277)—both Jews.[36]

It is also possible that Josephus purposefully included these conversion narratives and marital anecdotes at this specific place within the structure of the *Antiquities*. Within the framework of the larger narrative, the passage is set into an account of the Emperor Claudius's reign (41–54 CE) and contemporary events in Judaea. Immediately preceding the passage under discussion is Josephus's remark that Claudius had granted Agrippa II several territories to rule (*Ant.* 20.138). Although Agrippa is praised by Josephus for defending the Jews in Rome (20.136-38), Josephus does not continue the laudation of Agrippa as a ruler. He distracts the audience with Herodian marital history (20.137-47) and then refocuses on events in Rome (20.148) and the death of Claudius.

Between Ancestry and Merit', in *idem* (ed.), *Jewish Identity and Politics Between the Maccabees and Bar Kokhba: Groups, Normativity and Rituals* (JSJSup 155; Leiden: Brill, 2012), pp. 91-115.

35. Cohen, 'Respect', p. 424.

36. The historical Jewishness of both Herod of Chalcis and Marcus Julius Alexander is contested; see n. 34, and Josephus's comments about Philo's extended family's renunciation of their Jewish heritage in favour of political advancement (*Ant.* 20.100). It seems Berenice's marriages were unlucky throughout. Also relevant is the political dimension of elite marriages; these marriages could be—and were—broken regularly, and so the individual experiences of Azizus and Polemo cannot be attributed to negative consequences of their circumcision. Cf. Seth Schwartz, 'Conversion to Judaism in the Second Temple Period—a Functional Approach', in Shaye Cohen and Joshua Schwartz (eds.), *Studies in Josephus and the Varieties of Ancient Judaism: Louis H. Feldman Jubilee Volume* (Ancient Judaism and Early Christianity 67; Leiden: Brill, 2007), pp. 223-36.

Sporadic references such as *Ant.* 17.28, concerning taxation, indicate that Agrippa was in fact a controversial ruler, and we also know that Claudius took Chalcis away from him (20.138).[37] It may therefore be possible to read the passage as entertainment, in that Josephus here consciously used these anecdotes involving mandatory circumcision in order to entertain his audience, as a distraction technique and literary tool, being unwilling to discuss Agrippa's rule.[38]

d. *Idumaea*, Ant. *13.257-58*[39]

Josephus describes how the Hasmonaean ruler John Hyrcanus forcibly converted the Idumaeans in *Ant.* 13, a book that overall is concerned with Ptolemaic and Seleucid power struggles and the consequences for the Hasmonaean territories. Having captured the Idumaean cities of Adora and Marisa and having subdued 'all the Idumaeans' (ἅπαντας τοὺς Ἰδουμαίους), Hyrcanus allowed them to continue living on their land under the condition that 'the genitals be circumcised' (εἰ περιτέμνοιντο τὰ αἰδοῖα) and 'they agree to adopt the laws of the Jews' (τοῖς Ἰουδαίων νόμοις χρήσασθαι, *Ant.* 13.257).

In the passage immediately following on from Hyrcanus's subjugation of the Idumaeans and the conversion narrative, the Hasmonaeans agree to renew a treaty with the Roman Republic (*Ant.* 13.259-66). The treaty itself is important for Josephus, who inserts transcripts of what purports to be the original communication between the Senate and Hyrcanus (13.260-64), as it highlights the success of the Hasmonaean Empire and the official acknowledgment it had received; the scene acts as a reminder

37. The same diversion technique is evident when Josephus briefly mentions that Claudius appoints Agrippa as successor to his uncle, Herod of Chalcis, and then goes straight on to report the Passover uprising in Jerusalem (*Ant.* 20.104). Other examples of Agrippa offending his subjects, making him look like a bad ruler, are mentioned in *Ant.* 20.189-96; 211-12; 217.

38. Mason, '*Contra Apionem*', p. 204, suggests an alternative reading of the passage, namely that Josephus was scandalised by Berenice's and Drusilla's behaviour, using them as examples of Jews diverging from their laws. Such actions were to bring about God's punishment and the destruction of the Temple.

39. Other accounts of the events have survived in Ptolemy (*Historia Herodis*, frag. *apud*: Ammonius, *De Adfinium Vocabulorum Differentia* 243, in *GLAJJ*, #146, p. 356) and Strabo (*Geography* 16.2.34, *apud* Josephus, *Ant.* 13.319). According to Cohen, 'Respect', p. 423, Josephus consciously rewrote history and portrayed the Judaean takeover as forceful, rather than following Strabo and presenting it as voluntary, because he did not want to endorse Roman fears and suspicions about the dangers of conversion. Discussions on whether or not Maccabaean policy involved forced conversion abound; for a recent overview and bibliography, see Eckhardt, 'An Idumean', p. 101 n. 32.

that the relationship between Rome and Jerusalem had once been mutually beneficial and not always dominated by aggression. Josephus now
wants to present Hyrcanus and Judaea as a strong force worthy of
Rome's partnership and achieves his aim by focusing on Hyrcanus's
military abilities—an important feature in ancient society—which culminate in his subjugation of an entire nation, a concept more alien to us
today than to an ancient audience. Again, it is possible to read the
passage with the understanding that Josephus purposefully employs a
conversion narrative as a literary device to achieve his respective
narratological aims.[40]

e. *The Royal Family of Adiabene,* Ant. *20.17-96*
Josephus narrates how the royal family of Adiabene converted to
Judaism in the early first century CE; the first part of the narrative is
primarily concerned with Izates's conflict on whether circumcision was
necessary for Izates to consider himself, and to be considered, Jewish.[41]
The remainder of the narrative is concerned with the good deeds of
Dowager Queen Helena benefitting Jerusalem, and Izates's political and
military achievements, which eventually convince his entire family to
convert. It is clear that Josephus here uses an external source, although
most scholars agree that Josephus made the narrative his own rather than
blindly copy his source material.[42]

---

40. Mason, '*Contra Apionem*', p. 203, suggests that Josephus presents the
Hyrcanus passage as a 'glowing tale of his virtuous reign'.

41. For further studies concerning this episode, see Gary Gilbert, 'The Making
of a Jew: "God-Fearer" or Convert in the Story of Izates', *USQR* 44 (1991), pp. 299-
313, and Jacob Neusner, 'The Conversion of Adiabene to Judaism: A New
Perspective', *JBL* 83 (1964), pp. 60-66.

42. *Contra* Lawrence Schiffman, 'The Conversion of the Royal House of
Adiabene in Josephus and Rabbinic Sources', in Louis Feldman (ed.), *Josephus,
Judaism and Christianity* (Detroit: Wayne State University Press, 1987), pp. 293-
312 (294). He argues that as Josephus did not see fit to delete several cross-
references appropriate only for the original text, he did 'little, if anything, to modify
this passage'. See Ingo Broer, 'Die Konversion des Köngishauses von Adiabene
nach Josephus (Ant. XX)', in Cornelius Petrus Mayer *et al.* (eds.), *Nach den
Anfängen fragen: Herrn Prof. Dr. Theol. Gerhard Dautzenberg zum 60. Geburtstag
am 30. Januar 1994* (Giessen: Selbstverlag des Fachsbereichs Evangelische Theologie und Katholische Theologie und deren Didaktik, 1994), pp. 133-62, for a recent
overview of the evidence. Mason, '*Contra Apionem*', p. 205, defends his position
that Josephus actively included the narrative to highlight conversion by insisting that
Josephus made the narrative his own with the inclusion of typical Josephan language
and motives. In contrast, Lawrence Wills, *The Jewish Novel in the Ancient World*
(Ithaca: Cornell University Press, 1995) notes that many of the motives Mason

In this respect, the narrative must be distinguished from the other conversion narratives discussed so far, which were all comparably short and more integral to the flow of the narrative. Thus, rather than considering the literary aims of only the conversion narratives, the analysis must expand to include the whole Adiabene story. Mason understands the Adiabene narrative as a deliberate inclusion by Josephus to end his corpus on a high note for potential proselytes.[43] He also suggests that it forms the counterpart to Abraham's circumcision (*Ant.* 1.191-93) in the concentric structure of the *Antiquities.*[44] Seth Schwartz has suggested that Josephus included the narrative to memorialize benefactors. Ingo Broer takes Josephus literally and accepts that Josephus included the passage because he wanted to explain the circumstances of Izates's conversion (cf. *Ant.* 20.17).[45] Other suggestions are also possible: the narrative presents a part of the contemporary Judaeo-Christian circumcision debate also reflected by Paul, Philo and others; it is part of Josephus's brief to narrate the history of Jews; it reminds the Romans of Jewish strength and it reminds Josephus's Jewish audience, some of whom might be distant Adiabene royalty, of their strength. Given this wide variety of reasons put forward, the Adiabene narrative was an obvious choice for Josephus to include. In regards to the question posed in this context, Josephus's immediate purpose for including the narrative remains elusive, but it is evident that circumcision and conversion feature prominently within it and that, despite or because of that reason, Josephus actively included the story.

f. *The* Contra Apionem *Passages*

There are two explicit references to non-Jews converting to Judaism in *Contra Apionem.* Both are general remarks uttered within the framework of defending Judaism against perceived slanders, and both are related to rebutting attacks against the Jews' alleged misanthropy. The first

regards as being inherent to Josephus and the Adiabene narrative are in fact inherent to various contemporary novels, so asserts that we cannot ascribe them to Josephus's adaptation, but would instead suggest that Josephus included the narrative because its main tenets agreed with his view. Cf. Donaldson, *Patterns*, p. 337: '…the Izates story must be seen as carrying Josephus's full endorsement'; note endorsement rather than involvement. For Cohen's position, see p. 168, above.

43. Mason, '*Contra Apionem*', pp. 205-7.

44. Mason, *Commentary*, pp. xxiii-xxiv, for concentric structure.

45. Seth Schwartz, 'Euergetism in Josephus and the Epigraphic Culture of First-Century Jerusalem', in Hannah Cotton *et al.* (eds.), *From Hellenism to Islam: Cultural and Linguistic Change in the Roman Near East* (Cambridge: Cambridge University Press, 2009), pp. 75-92; Broer, 'Konversion', p. 156.

passage concerns an oath which the Egyptian Apion attributes to the Jews, in which they swear to show no goodwill to any foreigners (*Apion* 2.121). Josephus launches his counterattack, insisting that, of the many Greeks ('many among them', πολλοὶ παρ' αὐτῶν) who had chosen to adopt Jewish laws ('our laws', τοὺς ἡμετέρους νόμους), none (οὐδεὶς) had reported such an oath (*Apion* 2.123-24). He concludes by ridiculing Apion, stating that he must have been the only one to hear such an oath, being its inventor.

Similarly, the second passage reacts to an (unverbalized) attack on Jewish misanthropy: Josephus praises Moses for focusing his laws on the welcoming treatment of foreigners, in that he protected Judaism from foreign influences while simultaneously welcoming everyone who wished to share and live under Jewish laws ('who living with us by those laws', ὑπὸ τοὺς αὐτοὺς ἡμῖν νόμους ζῆν). Josephus implies that a multitude of Greeks had been welcomed warmly (*Apion* 2.209-10).

Misanthropy was a frequent accusation levelled against the Jews, and Josephus rejects Apion's accusations by going on the attack, contradicting the Egyptian and other accusers by the most logical defence: Judaism was so welcoming that many people converted. It appears that Josephus deemed such an argument appropriate, reasonable and comprehensible, and furthermore, he utilized the subject of conversion emphatically as a literary tool if it so suited his narrative, and in this case rhetorical, goals.

g. *The Esther Narrative*
In contrast to the other passages discussed here, this conversion narrative is part of Josephus's retelling of the Bible, specifically the story of Esther (*Ant.* 11.186-296). Josephus has a prominent authoritative source for his material and its location within his larger narrative; thus it is problematic to determine any ulterior literary purpose to this conversion narrative as was possible for the previous examples. Specifically, Josephus narrates how following the success of Esther and her uncle Mordechai over their opponent Haman, 'many from other nations' (πολλὰ τῶν ἄλλων ἐθνῶν) 'circumcised the member' (περιτεμνόμενα τὴν αἰδῶ) from 'fear' (φόβον, *Ant.* 11.285).

It is, of course, noteworthy that Josephus does not omit to mention that non-Jewish men were circumcised out of fear, but the passage is part of the climactic success story of Esther and her uncle Mordechai, so any knowledgeable Jewish audience might have noted the omission—in stark contrast to Josephus's promise not to add, omit or amend anything to his biblical narrative (*Ant.* 1.17).

However, Josephus does amend the passage. A comparison of the possible sources—namely the Hebrew Bible or the Septuagint—shows that while the Hebrew reads 'judaized' (מִתְיַהֲדִים, Est. 8.17), the Septuagint states that the masses 'circumcised and judaized' (περιετέμνοντο καὶ ἰουδάιζον, LXX Est. 8.17). Josephus reports merely 'circumcising the member' (περιτεμνόμενα τὴν αἰδῶ, *Ant.* 11.285).[46] Josephus actively omits the term 'to judaize' regardless of what source he was using, and limits his comments to a reference to circumcision. Nevertheless, Mason understands the passage as conversion, and Donaldson similarly ascribes the passage to his 'conversion' category.[47]

III. *Terminology*

Having reviewed the conversion and circumcision narratives in Josephus to determine how he employs them as literary devices, it has become evident that he actively engages with the issue, giving the narratives a positive value within the literary framework. He does not appear to be concerned with a potentially adverse reaction of his audience to the act of circumcision or conversion, but instead hopes to focus their attention directly onto the narratives, using circumcision or conversion as auxiliary focal points. In light of this review the next step must include a consideration of Josephus's terminology within the narratives to see whether it is possible to distinguish whether Josephus viewed these cases positively or negatively.

Here the concern will be to analyse the actual terms Josephus uses to denote conversion, and several observations can be made.

First, Sylleus (*Ant.* 16.225) and Epiphanes (20.139) act as contrasts to Azizus (20.139) and Polemo (20.145-46) in the marriage narratives. The former reject adoption of Jewish customs (ἔθεσι/ἔθη), which implicitly include circumcision. In contrast, where the marriage takes place, Josephus uses circumcision terminology (περιτέμνεσθαι/περιτεμνόμενον), which arguably allows a measure of insight into his choice of language and perception of the relative place of circumcision and bodily change with the framework of conversion: while Azizus and Polemo agree to be

---

46. There exists a general consensus that Josephus used the LXX as a source for his Esther narrative: Elias Bickerman, 'Notes on the Greek Book of Esther', *Proceedings of the American Academy for Jewish Research* 20 (1951), pp. 101-33; Louis Feldman, *Studies in Josephus' Rewritten Bible* (JSJSup 58; Atlanta: Society of Biblical Literature, 2005), p. 525 n. 22; Cohen, *Beginnings*; and Donaldson, *Patterns*, p. 316.

47. Mason, '*Contra Apionem*', p. 203; Donaldson, *Patterns*, pp. 315-16.

circumcised, they are not reported to adopt a deeper Jewish behaviour or follow Jewish customs, and mere circumcision, despite the physical commitment of the body, becomes a token gesture that does not equal conversion in itself.

Secondly, the wives in the harem at Charax Spasini and Izates's brother Monobazus within the Adiabene narrative act as a contrast to Helena and Izates themselves, who are the perfect converts. They frame the Adiabene narrative and, having adopted Jewish customs only ('to use the customs of the Judaeans', ἔθεσι χρῆσθαι τοῖς Ἰουδαίων, *Ant.* 20.72)— quickly disappear from the narrative again. As Daniel Schwartz has pointed out, Helena and Izates are contrasted by adopting Jewish νόμοι, laws, and demonstrating Jewish behaviour: Helena travelled to Jerusalem, helped the city during a famine and was buried there (20.51-53, 95), while Izates insists on circumcision, holds his faith in God and is generally described as 'pious' (εὐσεβής, 20.46-47, 48). Consequently, when Josephus mentions the adoption of Jewish 'laws' (νόμοι or νόμιμα), he wishes to present the characters in question as converts who have transformed themselves, not just their bodies.

This is borne out by his terminology in the case of Fulvia (*Ant.* 18.82), who also demonstrates Jewish behaviour by wishing to donate to the Temple, and who needs to be presented as a convert for the story to work. Additionally, there is Josephus's reminder about the Idumaean conversion in *Ant.* 15.254, where he refers to 'customs and laws' (ἔθη καὶ νόμιμα). Finally, Josephus also presents the other side of the coin, referring to Drusilla, sister of Agrippa II, who transgresses the 'laws' (νόμιμα) in order to marry the Roman procurator Felix (*Ant.* 20.143);[48] Drusilla leaves her Jewish heritage behind to marry an uncircumcised Gentile and therefore becomes an apostate to her religion in the eyes of Josephus.[49]

48.   Josephus makes no remarks about Felix himself in this passage—he places the shame on Drusilla for marrying out, rather than demanding circumcision from Felix. *Contra* Donaldson, *Patterns*, p. 339, who interprets *transgressing the ancestral laws* as Josephus being critical of Felix because he did not convert, and also *contra* Mason, *Commentary*, p. 75 n. 544.

49.   Cf. John Barclay, 'Who Was Considered an Apostate in the Jewish Diaspora?', in Guy Stroumsa and Graham N. Stanton (eds.), *Tolerance and Intolerance in Early Judaism and Christianity* (Cambridge: Cambridge University Press, 1998), pp. 80-98. Barclay offers many examples of apostasy taken from Josephus, and the terminology is largely consistent with the Drusilla episode, although Barclay does not use this reference in his discussion. We must also consider the conclusions recently reached by Daniel Schwartz, 'Yannai and Pella, Josephus and Circumcision', *Dead Sea Discoveries* 18 (2011), pp. 339-59 (348). Analyzing at the use of

In stark contrast, thirdly, there are the narratives that use circumcision terminology only (Esther, Azizus, Metilius, Polemo). There is a lack of explicit reference to Jewish behaviour or customs, but instead an emphasis on a base motive for the bodily change in the form of circumcision—political advantage or fear.[50] Thus, Josephus appears to devalue the physical commitment and bodily alteration and does not consider circumcision a binding sign of conversion, although he acknowledges the value of circumcision as a Jewish custom. This comes through in his treatment of his source material. Josephus amends his source for the Esther narrative to state only that the men were circumcised. This may seem surprising in light of the Metilius passage mentioned earlier. However, it is highly likely that Josephus wanted the Metilius passage to be more intriguing to a Roman audience, and more shocking; so his literary aims came to the fore. In contrast, in the Esther passage, it was always clear that the circumcision of the masses was a spontaneous reaction possibly exaggerated for literary effect, which, for Josephus, had nothing to do with conversion. Consequently, it is also possible to explain Josephus's amendments of his source material regarding the conversion of the Ituraeans under Hasmonaean rule (*Ant.* 13.318). Josephus uses circumcision and νόμος, 'law', terminology when he narrates how Aristobulus I (reigned 104–3 BCE) subjugated a large part of Ituraean territory ('much of their country', πολλὴν αὐτῶν τῆς χώρας) and forced the inhabitants 'to be circumcised and live according to the laws of the Judaeans' (περιτέμνεσθαι καὶ κατὰ τοὺς Ἰουδαίων νόμους ζῆν, *Ant.* 13.318). In contrast, his source material taken from Strabo, which he cites subsequently, mentions only circumcision ('the circumcision of the private parts', τῇ τῶν αἰδοίων περιτομῇ, *Ant.* 13.319).[51]

Overall, the evidence does not indicate Josephus's rejection of forced circumcision, but rather that he simply does not accept men who have been forcibly circumcised or who chose to do so for base reasons as automatically Jewish. The reading of the relevant passages advanced in this analysis demonstrates that Josephus accepts conversions but expects

ἔθος vs. νόμος in *Ant.* 13, he concludes that looking from the inside out, 'there are distinctions between laws and customs'. When Josephus speaks of νόμοι, 'laws', he is speaking as a Jew about law-abiding Jews—and within the framework of this chapter, this transfers to his terminology on those whom he presents as converts.

50.   We see the same limited terminology in *Vita* 113, where Josephus refers only to the physical requirement of circumcision (περιτέμνεσθαι) as a condition for the fugitives from Trachonitis staying in Galilee.

51.   Cf. also Schwartz, 'Yannai', p. 351 n. 37, where he refers to *Ant.* 15.254-55; Josephus reiterates the Idumaean conversion with reference to Jewish customs and laws, as opposed to circumcision.

a convert to adhere to the entire corpus of Jewish laws: while customs are transferable and adaptable, laws remain consistent and mandatory and circumcision alone does not change a person. Josephus does not automatically correlate bodily change with conversion—in his perception, while a body can change, the change need not impact on his perception of the person.

Conclusions

Summing up, it is now possible to state the following conclusions concerning Josephus's use of conversion narratives, his attitude to circumcision and the concept of the religious change of the body itself, all of which allow a more nuanced reading of the narratives. Josephus can be read as placing his conversion narratives strategically for literary effect, and thereby does not demonstrate any overreaching concerns that they, or their implications, might upset his audience; rather, attention is drawn onto the narratives, giving them a positive function in their larger framework. Simultaneously, adding a further layer that emerges only after consideration of the narratological function of the passages, Josephus constructs his terminology according to a pattern that adds value to the conversion narratives over and beyond their use as literary devices. In his perception, the act of male circumcision does not imply, nor does it achieve, conversion. This implies the accepted possibility of female conversion, which could not, and in Josephus's presentation need not, offer the same level of bodily commitment, as is demonstrated by the cases of Fulvia and Helena, whom Josephus presents as main actors in his conversion narratives. With the background of previous scholarship in mind, the present approach, reading the passages from a narratological point of view rather than an historical one, allows a more nuanced understanding that demonstrates the quality of Josephus's literary craftsmanship. It also allows us to access to his own views.

THE ACTS OF PAUL AND THECLA:
VIOLATING THE INVIOLATE BODY—THECLA UNCUT

Rosie Ratcliffe

The Acts of Paul and Thecla (*APTh*) is found within the apocryphal *Acts of Paul*, normally dated to the second century. The story concerns a young betrothed virgin in Roman Iconium who, upon hearing Paul preach, decides to pursue a chaste Christian life. Spurning her fiancé, and thus rebelling against societal norms, she finds that family, society and city administration contrive to put an end to her life. She is thrown naked into the arena on two occasions, once to be burned and again to face the wild beasts. However, through miraculous interventions, Thecla triumphantly overcomes the many ordeals that are sent to challenge her. The climax of the story sees Thecla don male apparel and receive Paul's blessing to

Ὕπαγε καὶ δίδασκε τὸν λόγον τοῦ Θεοῦ

Go and teach the Word of God.[1]

It is not surprising that this Christian text, which has as its focus a female protagonist who is authorized to teach by Paul, has been seized upon by scholars keen to highlight exemplary women and their important roles in early Christianity, most recently by Kate Cooper, in her book *Band of Angels*.[2] Cooper describes Thecla as an independently minded young woman who is subversive and dangerous in deciding to jilt her fiancé and follow Paul.[3] Her rebellious behaviour results in a 'face-off' with her mother after which she runs away from home eventually to preach and

1. *APTh* 41. All translations are my own, apart from where otherwise indicated.
2. Kate Cooper, *Band of Angels: The Forgotten World of Early Christian Women* (London: Atlantic Books, 2013).
3. *Ibid.*, p. 77, 79.

baptise with Paul's blessing.[4] Thecla, closely associated with Paul, was the subject of a number of writings, artistic representations and a cult clearly evidenced in sources from the fourth century onwards.[5] However, while the *APTh* is the earliest extant writing about her, I will explore here how *APTh* is highly androcentric and marginalizing in its treatment of Thecla. I will provide a fresh analysis of the distinctive Christian message conveyed by her presentation.

My reasons for exploring this come from a deep suspicion that a text that presents a woman's body in what is essentially a voyeuristic and, indeed, pornographic, way assumes a male gaze at variance with a female view of a woman who is seen to be empowered and liberated. It is also at variance with the evidence of the Thecla cult and its literature, which could otherwise suggest an oral tradition of Thecla largely preserved by women. That the text of the *APTh* is embedded within a work designed to emphasize Paul's status, the *Acts of Paul*, should naturally make one suspicious.

This is a new angle, because even with a shift in the hermeneutical climate to an appreciation of the androcentric ideology and rhetorical strategies that shaped representations of women in ancient texts, specifically the strategies of the 'hermeneutics of suspicion' advocated by Elisabeth Schüssler Fiorenza, the *APTh* continues to be discussed as a positive representation of a female figure.[6] The text of Thecla is unique in its focus upon an indestructible female protagonist, but, since ancient male writers used women 'to think with', as Peter Brown has highlighted, women functioned as tropes in masculine Christian discourse.[7] Even with some positive elements for women's agency, this text does not emphasize the teaching of Thecla or her role as a leader,[8] but rather

4. *Ibid.*, p. 77, 79, see also p. 94.

5. See Stephen J. Davis, *The Cult of Saint Thecla: A Tradition of Women's Piety in Late Antiquity* (Oxford: Oxford University Press, 2001).

6. See, for example, Kate Cooper at http://phys.org/news/2013-08-christians-airbrushed-women-history.html#jCp, 'Thecla...should be an inspiration...for the people campaigning for women bishops and priests'.

7. Peter Brown, *The Body and Society: Man, Women and Sexual Renunciation in Early Christianity* (London: Faber, 1990), p. 153; see also Kate Cooper, *The Virgin and the Bride: Idealized Womanhood in Late Antiquity* (Cambridge, MA: Harvard University Press, 1996), pp. 3-4, 13-14, 55.

8. There is just a hint at this only at the end, though there are different versions in the manuscript tradition. In the shortest version she 'slept with a noble sleep' and 'enlightened many'; in another she is attacked by certain men of the city, who are threatened by her effective healings, and is swallowed up by a rock which conveys her to Rome and in a third version she is the leader of a group of women ascetics

the story strongly presents a female *body* as an entity that cannot be annihilated.

I will suggest, therefore, that the ideological function of Thecla here is as a constructed body that transcends 'natural' feminine weakness by divine intervention. Furthermore, Thecla's inviolate body is linked to the self-identity of male Christians and communicates conceptions of inviolability of the Church against an invasive and phallic concept of Rome. Thecla is thus re-embodied as an image of Christian resistance that speaks back to the Roman Empire. Within this process there is no escaping the very violent and hostile treatment that Thecla's body is subjected to. Anyone who reads the text participates in gazing upon a tortured, naked, sexualized woman.

I. *Looking Back at Thecla*

The *APTh* is part of a corpus of traditions about Thecla, the exemplary virgin martyr, which culminated in the popular cult of Saint Thecla close by Seleucia of Isauria, near Ephesus in western Asia Minor, which spread to Egypt and Syria, and elsewhere.[9] Thecla apparently lived in a cave, and was buried (or disappeared alive into the earth) here; the ruins of fourth- and fifth-century churches have been uncovered by archaeologists.[10] Late in the fourth century the pilgrim Egeria (*Itin.* 23.1-6) visited the site, where both men and women lived as cave anchorites, and read a work she calls the *Acts of Holy Thecla*.[11] Thecla is defined as an apostle in the hagiographical writing entitled *The Acts of the Holy Apostle and Witness of Christ Thekla*, also called *The Life and Miracles of Saint Thecla*, dated to the fifth century.[12] The first volume of this is a different

---

who learn the 'oracles of God' from her; see 'Acts of Paul and Thecla', in Alexander Roberts and James Donaldson (eds.), *The Ante-Nicene Fathers*, VIII (Edinburgh: T. & T. Clark, 1885–87; repr. Peabody: Hendrickson, 1994), pp. 491-92. Both the second and third endings indicate healing and teaching, respectively.

    9. See Davis, *The Cult of Saint Thecla*.

    10. The site is called Meriemlik or Ayatekla, and is just south of Silifke (Seleucia). See Dennis R. Macdonald, *The Legend and the Apostle: The Battle for Paul in Story and Canon* (Philadelphia: Westminster Press, 1983), pp. 92-93; Kate Cooper, 'A Saint in Exile: The Early Medieval Thecla at Rome and Meriamlik', *Hagiographica* 2 (1995), pp. 1-23.

    11. John Wilkinson, *Egeria's Travels* (rev. ed.; Warminster: Aris & Philips, 1981), pp. 121-22, 288-92.

    12. Manuscript copyists originally attribute this text to the fifth-century bishop Basil of Seleucia. However, Gilbert Dagron has contested this ascription on the basis of internal evidence within the text. In *Miracle* 12 the anonymous author actually

version—often considered a paraphrase—of the *APTh*, and the second is a collection of 46 healing miracles of Thecla, otherwise not extant in earlier texts.[13] In the fourth century she is extolled as a brilliant teacher by both Methodius and Gregory of Nyssa.[14]

The *APTh*, however, despite being the earliest text presenting the Thecla tradition, is not about Thecla herself but is part of the larger apocryphal *Acts of Paul*, expanding on Paul's travels and preaching throughout Asia Minor. It is contained in Books 3 and 4 of this larger work. The Greek text of the *APTh* was published in the critical edition of the *Acts of Paul* by Lipsius-Bonnet in 1852, but, while this edition was based on eleven Greek manuscripts, there are now more than 80 extant manuscripts, papyrus fragments and ancient translations of the *APTh*,[15] and a new critical edition, edited by Willy Rordorf, is now in preparation in the *Corpus Christianorum Series Apocryphorum*.[16] Important is the critical discussion and translation done previously by Willy Rordorf,[17]

attacks Basil, making it unlikely that Basil himself authored the text; see Gilbert Dagron and Marie Dupré de la Tour, *Vie et Miracles de Saint Thècle. Texte Grec. Traduction et Commentaire* (SHG 62; Brussels: Société des Bollandistes, 1978), pp. 13-15. For the dating of the text see Dagron and Dupré de la Tour, *Vie et Miracles de Saint Thècle*, pp. 17-18.

13. Macdonald, *Legend and Apostle*, pp. 92-93; Gail P. C. Streete, *Redeemed Bodies: Women Martyrs in Early Christianity* (Philadelphia: Westminster John Knox Press, 2009), pp. 93-94. For the text, see Dagron and Dupré de la Tour, *Vie et Miracles de Saint Thècle*.

14. Methodius, the fourth-century bishop of Olympus and Patara in Lyria, Asia Minor, wrote a *Symposium*, in which Thecla provides the most impressive philosophical speech; see Macdonald, *Legend and Apostle*, p. 91. Likewise, Gregory of Nyssa, in his *Life of Saint Macrina*, emphasizes Thecla's intellectual example as a teacher; see Patricia Wilson-Kastner, 'Macrina: Virgin and Teacher', *Andrews University Seminary Studies* 17 (1979), pp. 105-17 (108).

15. Richard Adelbert Lipsius and Maximillian Bonnet, *Acta apostolorum apocrypha* (Leipzig: Hermann Mendelssohn, 1891–1903; repr. Hildenscheim: G. Olms Verlagsbuchhandlung, 1959). Hans-Josef Klauck, *The Apocryphal Acts of the Apostles* (Waco: Baylor University Press, 2008), p. 49; Jeremy M. Barrier, *The Acts of Paul and Thecla: A Critical Introduction and Commentary* (Tübingen: Mohr Siebeck, 2009), pp. xiii-xvi.

16. However, it is unlikely that this edition will be available for some time; see Ross Shepard Kraemer, *Unreliable Witnesses: Religion, Gender and History in the Greco-Roman Mediterranean* (New York: Oxford University Press, 2011), p. 121 n. 15.

17. Willy Rordorf in collaboration with Pierre Cherix and Rudolphe Kasser, trans., *Actes de Paul* (ed. François Bovon and Pierre Geoltrain; Écrits apocryphes chrétiens; Bibliothèque de la Pléiade; Saint Herblain: Gallimard, 1997), pp. 1127-77.

and the critical commentary, with discussion of manuscript variants and reconstruction, produced by Jeremy Barrier.[18]

The majority of scholars subscribe to a late second-century date for the *Acts of Paul* (180–90 CE), though it may have been composed earlier.[19] Eugenia of Alexandria, the daughter of the Roman proconsul of Egypt, under Commodus (180–92), is said to have taken Thecla as her model after reading the text.[20] Tertullian, writing in Carthage in North Africa around the year 200 CE, provides a key external reference to it. In the text of the *De Baptismo* Tertullian mentions a work on Paul, which provides the example of Thecla as one who baptizes and teaches (*De Baptismo* 17.5):[21]

18. Barrier, *Acts of Paul and Thecla*.

19. See, for example, Carl Schmidt and Wilhelm Schubart, Πραξεις Παυλου, *Acta Pauli nach dem Papyrus der Hamburger* (Glückstadt: Staats & Universitäts-Bibliothek; Hamburg: J. J. Augustin, 1936), p. 127, where it is dated to 190–200 CE; W. Schneemelcher (ed.), *New Testament Apocrypha* (trans. R. McL. Wilson; 2 vols.; rev. ed.; Cambridge: James Clarke; Louisville: Westminster John Knox Press, 1992), II, pp. 214, 245, dates it to 185–195 CE; see also Peter M. Peterson, *Andrew, Brother of Simon Peter* (Leiden: Brill, 1963), pp. 25-26; Jan N. Bremmer, 'Magic, Martyrdom and Women's Liberation in *The Acts of Paul and Thecla*', in Bremmer (ed.), *The Apocryphal Acts of Paul and Thecla* (Kampen: Kok Pharos, 1996), pp. 36-59 (57); and see Barrier, *Acts of Paul and Thecla*, pp. 23-24, who suggests that in fact the process of it reaching the final form may have spanned one hundred years.

20. Here 'there fell into her hands the *History* of the holy Apostle Paul and of the blessed Virgin Thekla, and as she read it in secret, day after day…' (*Acts of Eugenia* 2); so Frederick C. Conybeare, *The Apology and Acts of Apollonius and other Monuments of Early Christianity* (London: Swan, Sonnenschein, 1894), p. 158. Like Thecla, Eugenia rejected marriage to a man of high standing who was not a Christian. Before she could be betrothed a second time she disguised herself as a man and joined a monastic community of men where, after some years, she was elected Abbott. She was eventually martyred in Rome around 257 CE; see Laura Swan, *The Forgotten Desert Mothers: Sayings, Lives and Stories of Early Christian Women* (Mahwah: Paulist Press, 2001), pp. 81-82. In a similar vein Pelagia, a prostitute from Antioch, in the late fourth century, converts to Christianity and then secretly runs away to Jerusalem, where she disguises herself as a male eunuch and lives in a monastery. Only on her death is her identity eventually discovered; see Sebastian P. Brock and Susan Ashbrook Harvey, *Holy Women of the Syrian Orient* (Berkeley: University of California Press, 1987), pp. 25, 40-62.

21. Up to 1916 *De Baptismo* was only known through the 1545 edition of the (now lost) Mesnartius manuscript, which was reproduced in Oehler's critical edition published in 1853. This text refers to 'writings which wrongly go under Paul's name'. In 1916, however, a twelfth-century manuscript, *Codex Trecensis* 523, came to light and this explicitly refers to the discredited writings as *Acta Pauli*. See A. Hilhorst, 'Tertullian on the Acts of Paul', in Bremmer (ed.), *Apocryphal Acts*, pp. 150-63. At 17.5, this manuscript reads: *Quod si quae Pauli, quae perperam*

> But if wrongly they read the writings on Paul with the example of Thecla
> to defend women's licence to teach and immerse, let them know that the
> presbyter in Asia who constructed that writing, adding enrichments of his
> own to Paul's reputation, was found guilty and confessed that he did it for
> a love of Paul, [so] left the place.

Tertullian then indicates that this was penned by a 'presbyter in Asia' out of 'love of Paul', *not* a love of Thecla. This comment should alert us to ways that the presentation of Thecla here serves to insist on the greater status of Paul. As Hilhorst has noted, despite what Tertullian states, the text of *APTh* that we possess does not show us Thecla as baptizing others or teaching. In *APTh* the 'baptizing' of Thecla is only of herself:

> And when she had completed the prayer she turned around and saw a
> great pit full of water and she said, 'Now is the time to wash myself'.
> And she threw herself in saying 'In the name of Jesus Christ I baptize
> myself on the last day'. (34)

Although we are told that she 'instructs' (κατηχήσασα) Tryphaena (39) and is commanded by Paul to 'teach the word of God' (41), despite 'enlightening many' with God's word (43), there is no specific teaching indicated, and so Hilhorst suggests there was an earlier version that did so.[22] The *exemplum Theclae* that Tertullian mentions is not one that is presented in the text, but rather is found in a wider Thecla tradition, one that the *APTh* alludes to, but does not wholly represent. This has been noted by Sheila McGinn, who has suggested that the *APTh* is redaction rather than simple preservation: 'a well-placed male member of the mainline Christian church in Asia Minor…took a woman's folktale about Thecla and "domesticated" it, giving Paul more prominence in the story, and transforming it from the Acts of Thecla to the Acts of Paul and Thecla'.[23]

Nevertheless, with a chaste female protagonist as the focus of its narrative, the instruction for Thecla to teach, along with her heroic endurance of violence and the prominence of female characters in the second half of the story, the *APTh* has become an important text for scholars interested in women in early Christianity. Studies have concluded that the text of

---

scripta sunt, exemplum Theclae ad licentiam mulierum docendi tinguendique defendunt, sciant in Asia presbyterum qui eam scripturam construxit quasi titulo Pauli de suo cumulans, convictum atque confessum id se amore Pauli fecisse, loco decessisse. I am grateful to Joan Taylor for the Latin translation of this passage.

22. Hilhorst, 'Tertullian', pp. 157-58.

23. Sheila E. McGinn, 'The Acts of Thecla', in Elisabeth Schüssler Fiorenza (ed.), *Searching the Scriptures*. II, *A Feminist Commentary* (New York: Crossroad, 1994), pp. 800-828 (805).

Thecla is an example of early female liberation that provides evidence of women who were rebelling against the social and sexual constraints of conventional roles. It has been able to affirm a certain 'proto-feminism' in early Christianity where women transcended their otherwise limited and inferior status by embracing a life of asceticism, raising important questions about the social roles of women in early Christianity.[24]

There have also been questions about the composition of the narrative itself. Three seminal works, by Stevan Davies, Dennis MacDonald and Virginia Burrus, have each argued that certain stories within the *Apocryphal Acts of the Apostles*, including the *APTh*, have female-focused antecedents and originate from communities of independently minded celibate women.[25] Although more recent studies of the *APTh* demonstrate a more muted approach in the claims that are made about women in antiquity,[26] scholars continue to read the story of Thecla as a woman-affirming text. Most recently Kate Cooper, for example, notes that Thecla strikes out on her own 'as an apostle, rather than playing sidekick to the great man' (i.e. Paul).[27]

However, there is in the *APTh* a very ambivalent treatment of the proto-martyr Thecla.[28] As a physically beautiful virgin, attractive to men,

---

24. See, for example, Virginia Burrus, *Chastity as Autonomy: Women in the Stories of the Apocryphal Acts* (Lewiston: Edwin Mellen, 1987); McGinn, 'The Acts of Thecla'; Luise Schottroff, 'Non Violence and Women's Resistance in Early Christianity', in Harvey L. Dyck (ed.), *The Pacifist Impulse in Historical Perspective* (Toronto: University of Toronto Press, 1996), pp. 79-89.

25. Stevan L. Davies, *The Revolt of the Widows: The Social World of the Apocryphal Acts* (Carbondale: Southern Illinois University Press, 1980); Burrus, *Chastity as Autonomy*; MacDonald, *Legend and Apostle.*

26. See, for example, Melissa Aubin, 'Reversing Romance? The Acts of Thecla and the Ancient Novel', in Ronald F. Hock, J. Bradley Chance and Judith Perkins (eds.), *Ancient Fiction and Early Christian Narrative* (Atlanta: Scholars Press, 2003), pp. 257-72; Elisabeth Esch, 'Thekla und die Tiere. Oder: Die Zähmung der Widerspenstigen', in Martin Ebner (ed.), *Aus Liebe zu Paulus? Die Akte Thekla neu aufgerollt* (Stuttgart: Katholisches Biblewerk, 2005), pp. 159-79; Elisabeth Esch-Wermeling, *Thekla—Paulusschülerin wider Willen? Strategien der Leserlenkung in den Theklaakten* (Münster: Aschendorff, 2008); see also the more recent compendium on the *Apocryphal Acts of the Apostles*, Amy-Jill Levine, with Maria Mayo Robbins (eds.), *A Feminist Companion to the New Testament Apocrypha* (London: T&T Clark International, 2006). Here, rather than reading the text of Thecla as a reflection of women's historical reality, these scholars explore the possible 'liberating models' the text may have provided for women in antiquity.

27. Cooper, *Band of Angels*, p. 92; see also n. 6 above.

28. In its original meaning the Greek word 'martyr' (μάρτυς) simply meant 'witness' and was used in the secular sphere as well as in the New Testament. In this

in a culture of honour and shame Thecla bears the ultimate humiliation through the continued exposure of her body.[29] At one point she is tied naked by the legs between two bulls in an arena of fully clothed men and women (*APTh* 35). No aspect of Thecla's body is veiled from sight. Nothing (other than rape) could have been more humiliating for an elite virgin in antiquity.

Moreover, although many scholars, most recently Cooper, have consistently argued that Thecla becomes male by cutting her hair and by donning a male *chiton*, χιτών, a short tunic, at the close of the narrative (*APTh* 40), her masculine transformation in the *APTh* is not quite so apparent.[30]

With regard to Thecla's supposed haircut, the narrative reads:

> …And Thecla said to Paul, 'I will cut my hair and follow you wherever you may go'. But he said, 'The time is inappropriate (shameful/ugly, αἰσχρος), and you are beautiful (εὔμορφος). Beware lest any other temptation, worse than the first, overtake you and you cannot endure but play the coward'. And Thecla said, 'only give me the seal in Christ and temptation will not touch me.' And Paul said, 'Thecla, be patient and you will receive the water'. (25)

Thus despite Thecla's offer to cut her hair, this text quite explicitly shows Paul prohibiting Thecla from doing so, because she is 'beautiful' (εὔμορφος) and the time is inappropriate (shameful/ugly, αἰσχρος). The adjective εὔμορφος, 'well formed', 'attractive', both masculine and neuter,

respect Thecla is always understood to be a martyr, in that she testified/witnessed to her Christian faith. However, over time the connotation of the term changed so that 'martyr' came to mean an individual who chose to die rather than renounce their Christian faith or devotion to Christ. See Candida R. Moss, *Ancient Christian Martyrdom: Diverse Practices, Theologies and Traditions* (New Haven: Yale University Press, 2012), pp. 2-3.

29.   For a discussion on notions of honour and shame, public and private, see Margaret Y. MacDonald, *Early Christian Women and Pagan Opinion: The Power of the Hysterical Woman* (Cambridge: Cambridge University Press, 1996), pp. 30-34.

30.   Cooper, *Band of Angels*, p. 230. See also, for example, Willi Braun, 'Physiotherapy of Femininity in the Acts of Thecla', in Stephen G. Wilson and Michel Desjardins (eds.), *Text and Artifact in the Religions of Mediterranean Antiquity: Essays in Honour of Peter Richardson* (Waterloo: Wilfrid Laurier University Press, 2000), pp. 209-29; John C. B. Petropoulos, 'Transvestite Virgin with a Cause: The Acta Pauli et Thecla and Late Antique Proto-"Feminism"', in Brit Berggreen and Nanno Marinators (eds.), *Greece and Gender* (Oslo: The Norwegian Institute at Athens, 1995), pp. 125-39; Aubin, 'Reversing Romance', pp. 257-72; Margaret P. Aymer, 'Hailstorms and Fireball: Redaction, World Creation and Resistance in the Acts of Paul and Thecla', *Semeia* 79 (1997), pp. 45-61.

was amended by later scribes to read γυνὴ εὔμορφος, 'an attractive woman', in order to emphasize Thecla's womanhood.[31] This prohibition against Thecla's hair-cutting correlates with Canon 17 of the Synod of Gangra (340 CE): 'When, under the pretext of asceticism, a woman cuts off the hair that God gave her in order to remind her of her subjection, thus abolishing, as it were the commandment of obedience, let her be anathema'.

The equivocal nature of Thecla's manly transformation is also reflected in the manuscript tradition.[32] One of the longer endings describes how 'lawless men' approaching her cave attempt to tear off Thecla's (womanly) veil: here she is not assumed to be wearing men's clothing.[33]

This is also in line with the iconography that was informed by the *APTh*. Later portraits overwhelmingly preserve an image of Thecla as a bound and sexualized female prisoner wearing female clothing. An excellent example of this may be seen in a fifth- to eighth-century medallion which pictures Thecla in a flowing skirt with her upper torso naked and her hands tied behind her back (Figure 1).[34] Her breasts, hips and pelvic area are accentuated and her uncut hair is braided in a womanly way.[35] Nauerth and Warns note that out of 35 surviving representations of Thecla, seven represent Thecla as nude or partially nude, with her breasts always distinct.[36] There is one notable exception of a relief that represents Thecla with short hair, looking very 'boyish'.[37]

31. This variant is evident in the Greek manuscripts F and G, dated to the eleventh and twelfth century respectively; see Lipsius and Bonnet (eds.), *Acta Apostolorum Apocrypha*, p. 253 and see also the variants they outline.

32. On the manuscript history, see Barrier, *Acts of Paul and Thecla*, pp. 26-30.

33. The longer ending manuscript is dated around the fourth century. See Ross Shepard Kraemer (ed.), *Women's Religions in the Greco-Roman World: A Sourcebook* (Oxford: Oxford University Press, 2004), pp. 298, 306-8.

34. See also the description and discussion in Claudia Nauerth and Rüdiger Warns, *Thekla. Ihre Bilder in der frühchristlichen Kunst: Göttinger Orientforschungen, Studien zur spätantiken und frühchristlichen Kunst*; Bd. 3 (Wiesbaden: Harrassowitz, 1981), pp. 31-34, Figure 14.

35. This 'Eastern style' representation of Thecla is typical of a number of pilgrims' souvenirs in the form of flasks and oil lamps. See, for example, David R. Cartlidge and J. Keith Elliott, *Art and the Christian Apocrypha* (London: Routledge, 2001), p. 155.

36. Nauerth and Warns, *Thekla*, pp. 93-99, Tables I–XVI; see also Dagron and Dupré de la Tour, *Vie et miracles*, p. 37.

37. Nauerth and Warns, *Thekla*, Panel II (4) Relief in Etschmiadzin (zu S.11).

Figure 1. Saint Thecla with wild beasts and angels, Egyptian,
fifth century CE. Limestone, 3 ¾ × 25 ½ inches (9.5 × 64.8 cm).
Image courtesy of the Nelson-Atkins Museum of Art, Kansas City, Missouri
(purchase: William Rockhill Nelson Trust, 48-10; photo: Jamison Miller).

Therefore, the *APTh* appears to be reacting against a notion that Thecla cut her hair and instead insists that Paul advised her against it, in order to ensure her femininity and beauty; artists representing this text understood this. Clearly, then, two quite distinct traditions informed the Thecla legend in antiquity: one of a hair-cutting, more masculinized Thecla, and another that insisted on her femininity. The masculinized Thecla is actually attested in the *Life and Miracles of Saint Thecla*, not in the *APTh*. Within the *Life and Miracles*, although Paul initially rejects Thecla's offer to cut her hair, reasoning that she is too beautiful and too weak to endure like a man, she argues back and insists that she is strong enough to withstand any trials. Paul, therefore, responds: '...since you are resolved on this matter, so be it! From now you will participate in my travels and, after a while, you will also receive holy baptism...'[38] Even if this text is to be dated as late as the fifth century, the traditions that inform it must be more ancient, as evidenced by the prohibitions of the Synod of Gangra, which not only proscribe against women cutting

38. *The Life and Miracles of Saint Thecla* (14), Dagron and Dupré de la Tour, *Vie et miracles*, pp. 226-27 (my translation).

their hair but also rule against them dressing as men: 'If any woman, under pretence of asceticism, shall change her apparel and, instead of a woman's accustomed clothing, shall put on that of a man, let her be anathema' (Canon 13).[39]

However, it was the safer, feminine, Thecla that was most endorsed by the Church, which also celebrated the *APTh*. Later Romanesque carvings and images preserve much of this iconography of Thecla, representing her as a beautiful woman with a full figure and with her upper body naked.[40] This artistic tradition of the feminine and naked Thecla parallels the enduring popularity of the *APTh*. If anything, *APTh* 40 leaves her with a shorter manly tunic that would have revealed her legs as an object of sexual desire to the male gaze. Indeed, prostitutes were known to adorn themselves in masculine tunics in order to captivate the attention of clients.[41] In this respect the text plays tantalizingly with Thecla's body, effecting a transformation that is sexy and alluring to men. This 'prurient gaze', and the violence and objectification that often accompany it, has been explored by David Frankfurter, who writes that, 'The nude, partially-nude, or otherwise sexually-provocative-yet-resistant bodies of young women provide the clearest victims for the violent delectation of the prurient gaze'.[42]

In addition, despite her rebellion against family and marriage (*APTh* 7–10; 18), eventually achieving some level of autonomy and freedom, Thecla in reality never disrupts the pattern of male power and dominance in speech, action or characterization. In her studies of martyrdom literature, Gail Streete has highlighted the importance of oppositional speech, and notes that in the *APTh* Thecla is a 'complicated exception' who says little or nothing.[43] Unlike Thecla, however, Paul is endowed with the power of speech and gives an eloquent sermon in the form of μακάριοι, 'blessing statements' (*APTh* 5–6). This power of rhetoric is

39. Jerome (*Epistle* 22.27) is also known to have strongly attacked the practice of female ascetics cross-dressing and cutting their hair.

40. Cartlidge and Elliott, *Art and the Christian Apocrypha*, p. 158.

41. Hans Herter, 'The Sociology of Prostitution in Antiquity in the Context of Pagan and Christian Writings', in Mark Golden and Peter Toohey (eds.), *Sex and Difference in Ancient Greece and Rome* (trans. Linwood DeLong; Edinburgh: Edinburgh University Press, 2003), pp. 57-113 (88-89). See also Kelly Olson, *Dress and the Roman Woman: Self-Presentation and Society* (New York: Routledge, 2008), pp. 47-49, 127-28.

42. David Frankfurter, 'Martyrology and the Prurient Gaze', *JECS* 17 (2009), pp. 215-45 (227).

43. Gail P. C. Streete, *Redeemed Bodies: Women Martyrs in Early Christianity* (Louisville: Westminster John Knox Press, 2009), pp. 26, 44.

underscored when Paul is brought before the Governor for questioning. He impresses the Governor to the point that he has him led back to prison so that 'he could find leisure to give him a more attentive hearing' (*APTh* 17). This representation of Paul is in stark contrast with Thecla, who is initially presented as a body that is silent and immovable (*APTh* 7; 8), 'bound' (δεδεμένη) and held captive by the power of Paul's words, as if in a spider's web (κρατεῖται, ἑάλωται, *APTh* 9).[44] She barely speaks at all in the *APTh*, and provides no foundation for the tradition exploited by Gregory of Nyssa in extolling the renowned teacher Macrina the Younger as a 'second Thecla' who was also a 'Christian Socrates'.[45] While Paul instructs Thecla to teach at the end of this story, there is no portrayal of her teaching or baptism of others and her verbal witness in the text is substantially lacking.

However, despite this unfavourable representation it is at the same time undeniable that the text also alludes to Thecla as an exceptional woman. Thus, when Thecla faces death by fire 'the governor wept and marvelled at the power (δύναμιν) that was in her' (*APTh* 22). Thecla also gains the upper hand in a skirmish with the 'powerful' (δυνάμενος) Alexander (*APTh* 26), thus demonstrating *andreia*, 'courage', or 'manly virtue'. In addition, a lioness protects her and defers to her by licking her feet (*APTh* 28.33). The lion, as monarch of animals, incorporates power, leadership and courage and thus represents the power of the highest Greek deities.[46] Thecla is delivered from both the fire and the wild beasts (*APTh* 22; 35).

However, if the author really considered Thecla to be such a remarkable and inspirational woman, why is she silenced, degraded and objectified? How is it possible to make sense of a text that continually emphasizes an eroticized female body subjected to exposure and violence? In her book *The Body in Pain*, Elaine Scarry argues that physical pain not only resists language but actively destroys it. In pain people revert to wailing, screaming, whimpering, the sounds and cries people make before language is learned. In this way, being reduced to a pre-linguistic state,

---

44. For the translation ἀράχνη (*APTh* 9) as 'spider's web', see Janet E. Spittler, *Animals in the Apocryphal Acts of the Apostles* (Tübingen: Mohr Siebeck, 2008), p. 164.

45. Ute E. Eisen, *Women Officeholders in Early Christianity: Epigraphical and Literary Studies* (trans. Linda Maloney; Collegeville: Liturgical Press, 1996), p. 99, also Ruth Albrecht, *Das Leben der heiligen Makrina auf dem Hintergrund der Thekla-Traditionen* (Studien zu den Ursprüngen des weiblichen Mönchtums im 4 Jahrhundert in Kleinasien; Göttingen:Vandenhoeck & Ruprecht, 1986). See above, n. 14.

46. See Esch, 'Thekla und die Tiere', p. 169.

torture contributes to a loss of subjectivity.[47] Thecla is subjected to unspeakable terror and yet she never murmurs a sound during her worst ordeals. While it may be argued that this may reflect the suffering servant of Isa. 53.7 (and allude to Christ, Acts 8.32-33), does Thecla's refusal to wail and scream when exposed to terror and pain speak well for female subjectivity, or actuality?

The *APTh* is not intent on challenging antique notions of gender hierarchy. Nowhere within the story can we find traces of the female protagonist's strategy to challenge dominant gender norms. Thecla remains a desirable, beautiful woman who pleasures the male gaze and her body is repeatedly flaunted for all to see. This erotically charged text, therefore, contains the inherent violence and misogyny of a patriarchal cultural system. Both sexualized violence and humiliation of women are juxtaposed with reverence for the chaste or virgin female body. However, unlike other martyr stories, which graphically emphasize the pain and precious blood of martyrs spilt in the arena to heighten sympathy and encourage resilience, Thecla remains completely immune to any physical assaults upon her body.[48]

Martyr's bodies—venerated in cults throughout the Mediterranean world—were torn, dismembered and burned, but, despite her ordeals, Thecla's body is undamaged and retains its integrity. As far as the ancient construction of masculinity is concerned, it is in this way, more than any other, that Thecla 'becomes male'.[49] Even two bulls, symbols of the phallus[50] designed to rip her apart, can do no damage. In surviving extreme torture and danger unscathed, Thecla's body receives the highest accolade possible from a masculine perspective: it is inviolable. A virgin who is never free from male control has a body that behaves in the way a man's body *should* and *ought* to behave: it is impenetrable.

47. Elaine Scarry, *The Body in Pain: The Making and Unmaking of the World* (New York: Oxford University Press, 1985), pp. 4-6.

48. See, for example, Gillian Clark, 'Bodies and Blood: Late Antique Debate on Martyrdom, Virginity and Resurrection', in Dominic Montserrat (ed.), *Changing Bodies, Changing Meanings: Studies on the Human Body in Antiquity* (London: Routledge, 1998), pp. 99-115 (108).

49. For notions of Roman masculinity and male inviolability, see Jonathan Walters, 'Invading the Roman Body: Manliness and Impenetrability in Roman Thought', in Judith P. Hallett and Marilyn B. Skinner (eds.), *Roman Sexualities* (Princeton: Princeton University Press, 1997), p. 30.

50. 'The ταῦρος bull…is the phallus'; Jeffrey Henderson, *The Maculate Muse, Obscene Language in Attic Comedy* (New Haven: Yale University Press, 1975), p. 127.

Clearly, then, bodily inviolability is axiomatic within the text. We are encouraged to gaze upon the symbolically naked Thecla even though she is never described. All of this takes place in the Roman arena, a space that Donald Kyle describes as 'a marginal liminal site where Romans confronted the limits of the human versus the natural world'.[51] Why, when most martyr stories inevitably end in the martyr's death, is there such a focus on this woman's invincible body?

II. *Picturing Male and Female Representation*

Until now the *APTh* story has been read variously as a struggle about gender and authority within the Church, with Thecla representing Christian women leaders,[52] or as means of subverting the social order of society which promotes a restrictive concept of marriage and maternity.[53] However, I want to suggest an alternative way in which this story may have been received in antiquity by men and women alike.

Thecla in the *APTh* is a constructed, symbolic, body: by transcending the 'natural' weakness and sub-ordination of her gender, by surviving the physical torments unharmed, Thecla is re-embodied as an image of the Church itself. Her story defines a Christian resistance and resilience that speaks back to the Roman Empire. In speaking about the ideological function of 'virgins' in early Jewish and Christian martyrologies, both Daniel Boyarin and Virginia Burrus have argued that both Rabbis and Church Fathers 'identified' with female virgins as a way of 'dis-identification' with Rome. This is especially because Rome's power was stereotyped as a highly sexualized penetrative male.[54] The female virgins

51. Donald G. Kyle, *Spectacles of Death in Ancient Rome* (New York: Routledge, 1998), p. 10.

52. See, for example, Burrus, *Chastity as Autonomy*; Davies, *The Revolt of the Widows*; MacDonald, *Legend and Apostle.* More recently see Cooper, *Band of Angels*, pp. 92-94.

53. See Cooper, *The Virgin and the Bride*; Judith Perkins, *The Suffering Self: Pain and Narrative Representation in the Early Christian Era* (London: Routledge, 1995); Aubin, 'Reversing Romance', pp. 257-72. While it is certainly the case that the texts of the *Apocryphal Acts of the Apostles* in general demonstrate the destabilizing nature of the Christian chaste ascetic message upon society, and while this motif is also present within the *APTh*, this particular text is unique in its focus upon one indestructible female protagonist and, therefore, warrants individual attention in this regard.

54. Daniel Boyarin, *Dying for God: Martyrdom and the Making of Christianity and Judaism* (Stanford: Stanford University Press, 1999), pp. 67-92, 79; Virginia Burrus, 'Reading Agnes: The Rhetoric of Gender in Ambrose and Prudentius', *JECS* 3 (1995), pp. 25-48.

reflected an ego identification, on the part of male writers, with vulnerable but chaste female bodies over against the invasive violence of Rome.[55] The virgin thereby serves as a trope for early Christian (and Jewish) writers to locate themselves and their communities in opposition to Rome's power and violence, imagined in terms of sexualized masculinity and aggression. This approach would help to explain the significant focus upon female virginity within the text of the *APTh*. Such a reading would see Thecla embody and dramatize issues and concerns that deeply affected male Christian authors and readers as much as women.[56] Thus, as virgin, Thecla represents vulnerable male Christians, while the highly sexualized civic males of the *APTh* (Alexander, Thamyris, the Governor) represent the invasive might of Rome who stand over and against the virgin (Church). The female virgin's body communicates conceptions of the Church's inviolability against invasive, phallic Rome.

This is, then, a contest between the aggressive threatening masculinity of imperial Rome and the vulnerable body of the Church. In identifying with the vulnerable virgin Christians reconfigure their world in gendered terms that stand in contrast to the dominant hierarchical paradigm of the period. The contest between the Christians and Rome takes place in the Roman arena where the might of Rome is met with resistance and resilience—it is here that the Christian 'Virgin Body' challenges and rejects Rome's imperial power.

In early Christian iconography, the Church is often represented as a chaste woman, the 'Bride of Christ' (Rev. 19.7). For example, the fourth-century mosaic of Santa Pudenziana in Rome shows the 'Church of the Gentiles' and the 'Church of the Circumcision' as two nun-like figures. However, Rome could also make use of the female figure, either as triumphant Roma, or Victory, or as a means of indicating captive nations. Davina Lopez has examined three specific representations of how the Roman Empire communicated an ideology of world rule through the use of gendered imagery in personification of different ἔθνη, 'nations': the Judaea Capta coin; the cuirassed statue of Augustus at Prima Porta and reliefs from the Sebasteion, the Roman Imperial cult complex, at Aphrodisias.[57] These examples demonstrate not only how Roman imperial

55. Boyarin, *Dying for God*, pp. 67-92; Burrus, 'Reading Agnes', pp. 46-48.

56. See Cooper's book, *The Virgin and the Bride*, which provides an extended exploration of the ways in which male authors in antiquity utilize female representation in rhetorical struggles for prestige and power.

57. Davina C. Lopez, 'Before Your Very Eyes: Roman Imperial Ideology, Gender Constructs and Paul's Inter-Nationalism', in Todd Penner and Caroline Vander Stichele (eds.), *Mapping Gender in Ancient Religious Discourses* (Leiden: Brill, 2007), pp. 115-62.

ideology is depicted as thoroughly patriarchal but also how Romans are 'rendered as victorious "super-men" and defeated nations are consolidated into dejected, racially specific, women's bodies'.[58] Likewise, Natalie Boymel Kampen argues that the ideological task of representation is to 'reconfigure the world' and, in the process, to 'challenge or to reproduce social arrangements in such way as to make institutions and practices seem completely natural, so inevitable and universal'.[59] The images or 'visual narratives' noted above convey sexual status and deliver a gendered imperial Roman message. They establish the 'proper' Roman power relationship, defining and maintaining the norms of Roman masculinity, state and power. The use of such visual images would thus naturalize ideas about Roman hegemony and domination among both elites and the wider population. As Lopez highlights, all who could see and walk past a victory monument would be able to 'read' it. In this way public art formed a 'symbolic system' or 'grammar' that articulated and naturalized power relationships.[60]

Figure 2. 'Judaea Capta' coin issued following the destruction of Jerusalem.
Image courtesy of www.romancoins.info, copyright Andreas Pangerl.

The Judaea Capta coin type noted by Lopez (Figure 2) provides a prime example of the gendered visual propaganda imagery employed by Rome. This commemorative coin series was issued to celebrate the capture and destruction of Jerusalem in 70 CE and was much re-issued. The coin shows a veiled female figure sitting under a palm tree, mourning

58. *Ibid.*, p. 118.
59. Natalie Boymel Kampen, 'Epilogue, Gender and Desire', in Ann Olga Koloski-Ostrow and Claire L. Lyons (eds.), *Naked Truths: Women, Sexuality and Gender in Classical Art and Archaeology* (London: Routledge, 1997), pp. 267-77 (267).
60. Lopez, 'Before Your Very Eyes', p. 118.

and looking dejected. Standing next to her is a victorious Roman soldier who has a very large body in comparison to the woman. He holds a staff upright in his right hand and a *parazonium* scabbard in his left. The representation highlights the difference between conquered and conqueror. The woman looks crestfallen while the Roman soldier in contrast looks powerful. The imagery on the coin is clearly meant to convey the idea that Roman forces have defeated and feminized (that is, placed into a subordinate role) the people of Judaea.[61] There is little doubt that the positioning of the *parazonium* scabbard in the Roman soldier's groin is meant to allude to notions of phallic penetration, domination and submission. Antique notions of gender relations and hierarchy are utilized to represent territorial conquest.

Figure 3. Emperor Augustus in military dress:
marble figure from the Prima Porta.
Image courtesy of the Vatican Museums, Vatican State.

61. *Ibid.*, p. 123.

The statue of a cuirassed Augustus from Prima Porta similarly reveals this same use of gendered imagery to communicate the conquering of lands (Figure 3). The statue depicts the emperor dressed in full military parade costume. Such statues were erected throughout the Roman world in honour of reigning and deceased emperors and functioned as an important form of honorific dedication, while simultaneously providing a rich visual medium for celebrating the military victories of Rome. They also documented the course of Roman territorial expansion throughout the Mediterranean world.[62] This particular statue depicts the emperor Augustus as a powerfully built 'Herculean' type figure who is well proportioned with tame hair and muscular legs. These features all work together to depict an ideal Roman masculinity and impenetrable stability.

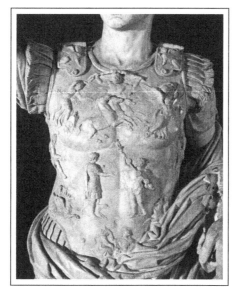

Figure 4. Cuirass of Augustus from Prima Porta, Hispania and Gaul.
Image courtesy of the Vatican Museums, Vatican State.

The manliness of Augustus is underscored by the figures of two women, almost under his nipples (see Figure 4).[63] The figures represent conquered ἔθνη situated at the borderlands of the Roman Empire. Each woman is depicted in traditional dress with attributes of the ethnic group

62. See Richard A. Gergel, 'Costume as Geographic Indicator: Barbarians and Prisoners on Cuirassed Statue Breastplates', in J. Sebesta and L. Bonfante (eds.), *The World of Roman Costume* (Wisconsin: University of Wisconsin Press, 2001), pp. 191-208.
63. Lopez, 'Before Your Very Eyes', p. 132.

that she personifies. Under Augustus's left armpit is Gaul. She is fully clothed and wears tight-fitting trousers typical of northern barbarians, while her empty sheath indicates disarmament. The female figure under the right armpit is Hispania, referring to Augustus's conquests of Spanish territory. By contrast her sheath has a sword in it, meant to indicate the fact that the area is an assimilated or client nation. Her crouching stance under the trophy decorated with the weapons and armour of her people designates her as a nation 'brought to the ground' by Roman forces.[64] These female characters at the margins function to indicate that the borders of the Roman Empire are under control. The images of domination and subordination reflect the 'naturalized' power relations between male and female bodies. Such images serve to enhance the domineering masculinity and submissive femininity at the core of Roman imperial consciousness. As noted with the Judaea Capta coin, sexual overtones are clearly evident in depicting Rome's victory over conquered nations; military men are shown dominating 'native' women.

Figure 5. Relief of Emperor Claudius triumphing over Britannia
from the Sebasteion at Aphrodisias.
Image courtesy of the Aphrodisias Excavations, New York University.

64. *Ibid.*, p. 133.

The third image, displaying even more overtly violent imagery, comes from a relief from the Sebasteion at Aphrodisias (Figure 5) and shows the Emperor Claudius conquering Britannia. Apart from his helmet, cloak billowing behind, sword belt and scabbard, the warrior Claudius is heroically naked: the male body is not humiliated by the nudity common in athletic contests and military training. He is depicted as victoriously beating down the defeated figure of Britannia, who is being pulled back by her flowing hair. Claudius pins Britannia down by her legs and, although his right arm is missing, he looks poised to deliver the death blow to the slumped figure of Britannia. Britannia is dressed in an appropriate (for the country) *peplos* style tube dress that has lost its brooch at her right shoulder, so that her right breast is exposed, and the dress has been pulled up to expose her legs.[65] A bare breast is a popular motif in depictions of women as violently defeated, and also characteristic of depictions of Amazon warriors.[66] The north portico of the relief is decorated with a number of scenes of Rome conquering various peoples of the world and each nation is represented as a life-size image of a captured woman alongside a victorious Roman emperor;[67] one of the images includes the 'rape' of Armenia by the emperor Nero.

The language and iconography of empire is thus full of violent sexual imagery. Gender is overtly and conspicuously correlated with ethnicity and utilized to portray hierarchy and power relationships. The women are shown as captured and subdued while male Roman bodies, by contrast, are shown to be powerful, domineering and in control.

If we read the *APTh* with such images in mind, it is possible to see the Virgin Body as a public display of power and resistance. Thus when Thecla is tied naked between two bulls, she survives, despite scorching irons being applied to their genitals to enrage them. The symbolism of the bulls, owned by the male Alexander, with their red-hot genitals is, as Streete highlights, 'not difficult to read'.[68] The scene is overtly in line with the lustful and penetrative masculinity of imperial Rome. The Virgin Body becomes a visual and textual device that is put to use in the

65. This shows the normal clothing for women in Britain and northern Europe in Roman and Anglo-Saxon times; see Gale Owen-Crocker, *Dress in Anglo-Saxon England* (Woodbridge: Boydell & Brewer, 2004), pp. 42-54.
66. Beth Cohen, 'Divesting the Female Breast of Clothes in Classical Sculpture', in Ann Olga Koloski-Ostrow and Claire L. Lyons (eds.), *Naked Truths: Women, Sexuality and Gender in Classical Art and Archaeology* (London: Routledge, 1997), pp. 66-92 (72, 74, 77); see also Lopez, 'Before Your Very Eyes', p. 137.
67. Lopez, 'Before Your Very Eyes', pp. 140-41.
68. Streete, *Redeemed Bodies*, p. 88.

service of the writer's rhetoric;[69] it becomes a written witness. The Virgin Body as spectacle becomes a symbol of God's power. Thus Thecla's inviolate body becomes a metaphor and a means of conveying status and control.

To return to what Peter Brown has noted, women provided a literary tool for storytellers 'to think with'.[70] Therefore, it is vital that all early Christian texts be examined with a view to establishing their rhetorical strategy and their tendency to tailor both fact and fiction to rhetorical ends.[71]

The *APTh* stands out in contrast to the other stories of the *Apocryphal Acts* in its single-minded focus upon a young virgin protagonist. It also stands out in contrast to most other martyrdom stories since the heroine has a body that is immune to Roman power and brutality. The execution of Christians in the arena as criminals by the Roman imperial government was an attempt, in a literal and immediate way, to exercise power over the bodies of Christians as a counter-cultural group. However, as Virginia Burrus and Rebecca Lyman note, this persecution simultaneously also created the context for the emergence of practices and ideologies of martyrdom that placed Christianity in a public stance of political resistance to notions of Empire.[72] Within the *APTh* the Thecla story speaks its own particular form of political resistance; there is ultimately no contest in the battle between the Kingdom of God and the evil earthly empire of Rome. Any attempt by Rome to triumph over the Christian 'nation' symbolized by Thecla's body is rendered futile. Indeed, Richard Valantasis has cogently argued that Christians identified themselves as a separate race.[73] It is particularly significant that the story of the *APTh* is then embedded in the *Acts of Paul*, the apostle to the 'nations' (Rom. 11.13).

In short, Roman imperial representation employed gendered bodies and sexual difference to communicate, both visually and symbolically,

69. *Ibid.*, p. 15.

70. See n. 7, above.

71. See Kate Cooper, 'Apostles, Ascetic Women and Questions of Audience: New Reflections on the Rhetoric of Gender in the Apocryphal Acts', in Eugene H. Lovering (ed.), *SBL Seminar Papers* (SBLSP 31; Atlanta: Scholars Press, 1992), pp. 147-53 (149).

72. Virginia Burrus and Rebecca Lyman, 'Introduction', in Virginia Burrus (ed.), *Late Ancient Christianity: A People's History of Christianity*, II (Minneapolis: Fortress Press, 2005), pp. 1-26 (7).

73. Richard Valantasis, 'The Question of Early Christian Identity: Three Strategies Exploring a Third Genos', in Levine, with Robbins (eds.), *A Feminist Companion*, pp. 60-76.

that Romans are the dominant masters. Sexual conquest was employed as a metaphor for expansionism in the history of imperial politics because it effectively communicated dominant power relationships.[74] Those who do the penetrating are 'male' and the land is 'female' and vulnerable to penetration. This construction ensures that inhabitants are effeminized by the masculine conquerors. There is little doubt that, as inhabitants of the Empire, Christians will have been exposed to Roman imperial representation. Such imagery would provide a strong impulse and impetus to reconfigure that representation in ways that helped them contest Roman domination. The depiction of Thecla relies on the existing stereotype of woman as weak and vulnerable, much like the early Christians who are victimized and embattled within the Roman Empire. The text seeks to redress this balance of power. Through chastity and the miraculous the Virgin Body demonstrates that the Church as Virgin is an impenetrable 'superman'; they are not without power against the imperial might of Rome. The Roman Empire has no power over this new Christian ἔθνος. The female body is used to speak for Christianity against the Roman subjection of the Church; however, it does not speak against kyriarchy.[75]

Furthermore, that Christians of the first centuries understood this rhetorical purpose is evidenced in extant literature. Monika Peshty notes the unpublished *Cathedral Homily* 97 of Severus of Antioch, the Syrian Orthodox patriarch from 512–18, which was dedicated to Saint Thecla. Here she is explicitly defined as being representative of the Church, the bride of Christ: 'Examine in the case of Thecla what I have said and you will understand at once that through the person of the Church and through what I have said, the martyr has been depicted and represented in advance',[76] states Severus, and, as Catherine Burris and Lucas van Rompay note: '[f]or Severus…Thecla is above all an image of the church'.[77]

---

74. See Richard Trexler, *Sex and Conquest: Gendered Violence, Political Order and the European Conquest of the Americas* (Ithaca: Cornell University Press, 1995).

75. I use the term 'kyriarchal' over 'patriarchal' since it more accurately emphasizes how power and oppression functions beyond gender. Based on the Greek word κύριος, meaning 'lord' or 'master', this term was invented by Elisabeth Schüssler Fiorenza; see her *Bread Not Stone: The Challenge of Feminist Biblical Interpretation* (Boston: Beacon Press, 2002), p. 211 n. 6; *eadem, But She Said: Feminist Practices of Biblical Interpretation* (Boston: Beacon, 1992), pp. 8, 117.

76. Monika Peshty, 'Thecla Among the Fathers of the Church', in Bremmer (ed.), *Apocryphal Acts*, pp. 164-78 (174).

77. Catherine Burris and Lucas van Rompay, 'Thecla in Syriac Christianity: Preliminary Observations', in *Hugoye: Journal of Syriac Studies* 5, no. 2 (July 2002). Online: htto://syrcom.cua.edu/Hugoye/Vol5No2/HV5N2BurrisVanRompay. html, p. 20.

III. *Christian Female Embodiment*

The pummelling Thecla receives and yet endures without harm 'makes a man of her', not her 'supposed' haircut neither her masculine χιτών. Thecla's inviolability turns her into a 'super gladiator' who, on surviving the arena, is rewarded with independence; and so she is commissioned by Paul to teach the Word of God. She is depicted as the Church that is teaching this Word despite the violence that meets 'her'. Making Thecla 'male', through bodily inviolability, and able to teach the Gospel, draws on ingrained Roman concepts of masculinity and femininity.[78]

The representation of Thecla in the *APTh* is a startling instance of the use of woman's body as a signifier for Christian self-definition and a critique of Roman imperial hegemony. Yet, taken as a real woman, the Thecla of the *APTh* is hardly a holistic portrayal: we have the voyeuristic exposure of a young, stunningly beautiful woman, as an object of male lust but no leader, teacher or healer, or even a real companion and co-apostle to Paul. Whether Thecla existed in reality or not, she is presented as an impenetrable, inviolable virgin, surrounded by a kind of magic, guarded and censored. Despite the wider tradition of Thecla, here the focus is only on her body. That it is exposed and tortured should serve as a warning sign to any who might use this text as a positive example of women's subjectivity in antiquity. Always in the grip of some power, Thecla-as-female-body is constrained and acted upon by external forces. She is exposed and tortured by one set of males (Romans) and appropriated by a Christian author for his own ends: to present her as the Church for the nations in the story he tells out of love for Paul.

Thecla's strength and survival is, in fact, a denial of real female corporeality because real women scream when subjected to pain and torment, and eventually their bodies bleed and die. In this respect it is an oppressive discourse for women. To read this text in a positive light is to collude with the negation of female subjectivity.

Furthermore, feminist writers have long noted the correlation between violent pornographic representation and the violence done to women in

---

78. *Gospel of Thomas* (Log. 114), where Christ says he will make Mary male, probably does likewise, as explored by Antti Marjanen, 'What Does It Mean When a Woman Is Called or Portrayed as a Man? The Idea of Gender Transformation in Early Christian Texts and in Modern Times', in Willy Østreng (ed.), *Complexity: Interdisciplinary Communications 2006/2007* (Oslo: Centre for Advanced Study, 2008), pp. 133-38; Marvin W. Meyer, 'Making Mary Male: The Categories "Male" and "Female" in the Gospel of Thomas', *NTS* 31 (1985), pp. 554-70.

reality.[79] The images on the Judaea Capta coin and the image of Claudius striking Britannia signify the very real and frequent violent abuse that women have endured, and continue to endure, from men who rape and torture in times of war. The *APTh* does present a woman who rebels against societal norms and eventually finds a level of independence. But can we find a positive reading in a text which voyeuristically objectifies, abuses and tortures the body of a woman, even if she does survive to teach the Word of God? How can this be a positive text for actual Christian women's embodiment?

Elizabeth Grosz has explored how the body is a signifying system, a vehicle of expression, a mode of rendering public and communicable what is essentially private (ideas, thoughts, beliefs, feelings), and as such it is a two-way conduit. On the one hand it transmits information from outside the organism through sensory apparatus, on the other it is vehicle for the expression of an otherwise sealed and self-contained incommunicable psyche. It is through the body that the subject can express his or her interiority.[80] However, unlike the martyr Perpetua, Thecla in the *APTh* appears to have no interiority to communicate.[81] Created by a male author for male purposes, both power and resistance are mapped onto Thecla's body; as 'Virgin Body/Church' she becomes a 'type' of Roman male, but she is neither real nor human. Thecla is an imaginary body created for mass fantasy, more like Lara Croft of *Tomb Raider* or the cyborg Terminatrix from Terminator 3. She is beautiful, has the perfect bodily statistics and remains inviolable: a fiction created by men for men.

Conclusions

Thecla has long been seen as a model of female rebellion in antiquity, and scholars writing on Thecla today still regard her as an example of a strong Christian woman, important in terms of understanding women's roles in the early Church. In addition scholars have also consistently

79. See, for example, Catherine Itzin, 'Entertainment for Men: What It Is and What It means', in *eadem* (ed.), *Pornography, Women, Violence and Civil Liberties* (Oxford: Oxford University Press, 1992), pp. 27-53; and in the same volume, Susanne Kappeler, 'Pornography: The Representation of Power', pp. 88-101; Diana E. H. Russell (ed.), *Making Violence Sexy: Feminist Views on Pornography* (Buckingham: Open University Press, 1993), esp. p. 8.

80. Elizabeth Grosz, *Volatile Bodies: Towards a Corporeal Feminism* (London: Routledge, 1994), pp. 9-10.

81. *The Martyrdom of Saints Perpetua and Felicitas*, text and translation in Herbert Musurillo, *The Acts of the Christian Martyrs: Introduction Texts and Translation* (Oxford: Clarendon Press, 1972), pp. 106-31.

argued that Thecla's haircut and masculine χιτών make her male, thus providing us with an early example of a woman renouncing her sexuality in order to overcome the limitations of her inferior feminine gender. However, within this chapter I have argued that there is a need to reject interpretations of the text which see within it a strong, liberated woman. First, there is a need seriously to question any 'empowered' reading of Thecla, given that she is a young inexperienced virgin woman who is sexualized, eroticized, exposed and violently abused. Secondly, as I have demonstrated, Thecla's masculine transformation is quite uncertain. Within this text there is a resistance to Thecla cutting her hair, as Paul advises her against it in order to ensure her femininity and beauty. Later artistic representations of Thecla also understood her to be feminine with long hair, and she is not depicted as wearing masculine clothes. I have, therefore, argued that there is a need to reject interpretations of the text which see within it a sanctioning of female autonomy and action.

The narrative carries an ascetic message, and yet within the text there is no attempt to suppress or forsake the female form. Rather, the text relishes Thecla's sexualized body which is voyeuristically displayed and abused. Thecla's female body thus forms the nexus around her para-doxical representation, a curious mix of sexual objectification, female victimization and masculine inviolability: a melding of Roman imperial male and female representation. In this way the author stresses an inviolable, naked, exposed female body.

I have, therefore, suggested that it is more appropriate to read Thecla the Virgin in line with male/female Roman representation, as symbolic of the Church, and that her inviolable body in the arena should be seen as a male Christian response to Roman imperial power. In this way we can make sense of the paradoxical representation of a chaste female virgin body that is subjected to sadistic, humiliating torture.

In the second century, the period in which the *APTh* is dated, Christians were still seen as enemies of Rome.[82] By utilizing Roman imperial representation Thecla's body becomes the site by which Christian men establish and reconfigure their personal and corporate identity over and against Rome. Thecla remains female in form and the ever-increasing sado-erotic violence and abuse which she endures, without complaint, serves a purpose in proving the masculinized perfection of Thecla's body.

82. Cooper, *Band of Angels*, p. 79.

It thus becomes clear that the text, as it stands, packages things in a male-dominant way, indicating both male redactions and ambivalent attitudes to women. Furthermore, the dangers of reading this text without the 'hermeneutic of suspicion' become evident. It is possible that the Thecla tradition goes back to an original female oral tradition. However, the representation of Thecla within this text would strongly suggest that this oral tradition has been moulded and shaped by men. It is, therefore, profoundly apparent that before we can argue that *APTh* is a female affirming text which depicts empowerment, it is important to pay close attention to the kyriarchal dimensions of the text and the features of the story which objectify and speak against women.

11

THE FIRE AND THE FLESH:
SELF-DESTRUCTION OF THE MALE RABBINIC BODY*

Laliv Clenman

The conclusion of Tractate Kiddushin of the Babylonian Talmud includes a series of narratives (known as *aggadah* or *aggadot* in the plural) related to a mishnah, which is concerned with the physical separation of men from women in order to control embodied behaviour and hence avoid sexual impropriety.[1] The potential threat posed by the location of gendered sexual bodies in relation to each other, and the temptation of prohibited sexual relations at times of physical proximity, loom large. These *aggadot* dealing with this cultural anxiety read as a series of fairly straightforward cautionary tales warning that even the greatest, most self-confident and most pious sages with the very best of intentions can and will commit sexual transgressions.[2] In each narrative the powers of the divine, externalized forces of desire, the male will and the male body are pitted against each other again and again.

In the last tale in this sequence, we come upon a sage named Chiya bar Ashi who appears to be particularly concerned about what he calls the 'evil inclination', so much so that he undertakes a regular, special penitential prayer for divine rescue from it.[3] R. Chiya bar Ashi is described in the Babylonian Talmud as a personal servant of the great

*   Grateful thanks are extended to Joan Taylor, Sandra Jacobs, Hannah and Daniel Eilon, Lucetta Johnson, Keren Hammerschlag and Gary Naseby. As always I am indebted to Tirzah Meacham and Harry Fox for encouraging me to appreciate and explore *aggadah*.
    1. *M. Kid.* 4.12. All translations are my own unless otherwise noted. R. Chiya indicates R. Chiya bar Ashi throughout.
    2. *b. Kid.* 81a-81b.
    3. On the evil inclination, see the groundbreaking recent study by Ishay Rosen-Zvi, *Demonic Desires: Yetzer Hara and the Problem of Evil in Late Antiquity* (Philadelphia: University of Pennsylvania Press, 2011).

sage Rav, a humble and dedicated man.[4] As the story reaches its climax in *b. Kid.* 81b, however, it becomes clear that something has gone terribly, horribly wrong.

> Rav Chiya bar Ashi was in the habit of, every time he would fall on his face, saying 'May the Merciful One save me[5] from the evil inclination! (יצר הרע)'. One day his wife heard him. She said, 'Behold,[6] how many years has he separated from me? What is the reason he is saying this?' One day, he was studying in his garden and she adorned herself[7] and passed and [passed] again before him. He said to her, 'Who are you?' She said, 'I am Charuta[8], who has returned yesterday'. He desired her. She said to him, he should bring that pomegranate that is at the top of the branch. He jumped, went and brought it to her. When he came to his house, his wife was heating up the oven. He went up and sat inside it. She

4. See, for example, *b. Zeva.* 94a.
5. Later editions read: us.
6. Later editions read: Now, behold.
7. This term indicates either personal adornment or setting a table, both of which have sexual connotations; see *DJBA*, p. 1048, and Michael Satlow, *Tasting the Dish: Rabbinic Rhetorics of Sexuality* (Atlanta: Scholars Press, 1995), p. 240. It was likely not a disguise; see Gail Labovitz, 'Heruta's Ruse: What We Mean When We Talk About Desire', in Danya Ruttenberg (ed.), *The Passionate Torah: Sex and Judaism* (New York: New York University Press, 2009), pp. 229-44, and Rashi, *b. Kid.* 81b *s.v.* קשטה נפשה. For similar use of this term in a case where a male sage pretends to prepare himself for sexual relations with a Matrona, see *b. Kid.* 40a. If no disguise was intended, the husband's failure to recognize his wife becomes all the more poignant.
8. Or: Cheruta and in manuscript Vatican 111 Charita. Jastrow prefers another version of the name: Chedveta, which he translates as 'reveler, dancer' but this is a problematic variant; see Yonah Frankel, 'Remarkable Phenomena in the Text-History of the Aggadic Stories', in *Proceedings of the 7th World Congress of Jewish Studies: Research in Talmud, Halacha and Midrash* (Jerusalem: World Union of Jewish Studies, 1981), p. 60 n. 7, and Marcus Jastrow, *Dictionary of Targumim, Talmud Babli and Midrashic Literature* (New York: Pardes House, 1950), p. 426. The meaning of her name is uncertain. In his commentary, Rashi notes that Charuta was a well-known prostitute in the area (*b. Kid.* 81b, Rashi *s.v.* אנא חרותא). The name may refer to the palm branch; see *DJBA*, p. 482. Yonah Frankel proposes meanings related to sexual freedom (i.e. promiscuity or harlotry) and freed slaves; see Frankel, 'Remarkable Phenomena', p. 60 n. 73. Shlomo Naeh makes perhaps the most interesting and compelling argument for Cheruta as a term signifying both extremes of celibacy and sexual hedonism in Syriac Christian culture, supporting my argument that this narrative enacts cultural tensions upon the rabbinic body; see his 'Freedom and Celibacy: A Talmudic Variation of Tales of Temptation and Fall in Genesis and Its Syrian Background', in Judith Frishman and Lucas Van Rompay (eds.), *The Book of Genesis in Jewish and Christian Oriental Interpretation: A Collection of Essays* (Louvain: Peeters, 1997), pp. 73-89.

said to him, 'What is this!? (מאי האי?)' He said to her, 'such and such has happened'. She said, 'It was me!' [He did not pay attention to her, until she gave him the signs.][9] He said to her, 'I had intended to do something forbidden'. [All the days of that righteous man, he afflicted himself,[10] until he died of that very death.][11]

This chapter will engage in an exploration of a range of answers to R. Chiya bar Ashi's wife's question, 'What is this?!' (מאי האי?) and aim to render R. Chiya bar Ashi's embodied cultural world interpretable. When contextualized within a literary legal and narrative context, I propose that R. Chiya bar Ashi's destruction of his own body begins to make various kinds of cultural sense as his action is revealed as a rich, meaningful and multivalent physical performance. This tale will lead us into consideration of the myriad tensions with which the rabbinic body must contend in antique rabbinic literary culture.[12]

I. *The Celibate Rabbinic Body*

If indeed something has gone awry for R. Chiya bar Ashi in his negotiation of these cultural tensions, we must consider how and why he may have gone astray from the rabbinic *desideratum*. I propose that our narrative be read as a parodic critique of a rabbi who has veered away from the ideal middle-road and succumbed to a range of temptations and inappropriate practices, which ultimately lead to his unfortunate fate.[13]

9. This phrase is a late addition paralleling the signs left with Tamar by her father-in-law Judah in Gen. 38; see Frankel, 'Remarkable Phenomena', p. 60 n. 71. In both narratives, the signs obtained from the man and presented by the woman serve to support her cultural reading of their physical experience (his: sexual relations with a harlot; hers: sexual relations with her rightful spouse or replacement thereof).

10. Early editions read: מצטער, later editions read מתענה; see Frankel, 'Remarkable Phenomena', p. 60 n. 69. These terms have similar semantic ranges related to affliction or deprivation, but the latter suggests fasting while the former suggests causing oneself grief or trouble.

11. This concluding sentence is in Hebrew (unlike the remainder of the narrative, which is in Aramaic) and appears to be a post-talmudic addition not found in any of the manuscripts, including manuscript Munich 95 and manuscript Vatican 111. The significance of this epilogue will be discussed further below; see *ibid.*, pp. 59-61.

12. At this stage I am relating to the narrative in what is presumably its antique form (as far as can be ascertained in view of extant versions). The later additions, especially the epilogue, will be dealt with as part of a discussion of reception history, below.

13. Holger Zellentin in his book, *Rabbinic Parodies of Jewish and Christian Literature* (Tübingen: Mohr Siebeck, 2011), has demonstrated that parodic sources

The most obvious embodied problem for our sage is his celibacy. R. Chiya's own wife is incredulous at his obsessive-compulsive worry about the evil inclination as she has physically experienced his long-term physical separation from her. The term used for his sexual separation from his wife (פריש) is also used to refer to the practice of celibacy.[14] Eliezer Diamond argues that this terminology refers to the 'voluntary withdrawal from the permitted' and that R. Chiya bar Ashi may be an example of a celibate rabbi.[15] It is reasonable to conclude that ours is a case of the observance of celibacy within marriage. Celibacy was an unusual ascetic practice in rabbinic Judaism and becomes particularly problematic given the commandment for a male to marry, procreate and, additionally, to please his wife.[16] When seen as a positive physical state, celibacy is generally constructed as caused by a devotion to Torah, which often leads the married sage to study in a distant location.[17] R. Chiya bar

may in some cases argue for the middle road between extremes of asceticism and hedonism, as part of an anti-sectarian argument that promotes normative rabbinic culture; see especially his chapter on wine and sectarian asceticism, pp. 51-94. The entire series of stories amongst which our narrative about R. Chiya is included may be read as parodic in nature; see Tal Ilan, *Mine and Yours Are Hers: Retrieving Women's History from Rabbinic Literature* (Leiden: Brill, 1997), p. 71.

14. As in reference to the celibate sage, Ben Azzai, whom the Babylonian Talmud prefers to understand as having married and separated (נסיב ופריש הוה) in *b. Sot.* 4b. This suggests Babylonian rabbinic discomfort with Levantine rabbinic celibacy. Henry A. Fischel in his *Rabbinic Literature and Greco-Roman Philosophy: A Study of Epicurea and Rhetorica in Early Midrashic Writings* (Leiden: Brill, 1973), notes a tradition of apologetics regarding his celibacy, beginning with the Babylonian Talmud and continuing through to the medieval commentators (p. 6 n. 59), which parallels the apologetic approach I have noted with regards to R. Chiya bar Ashi's celibacy.

15. Eliezer Diamond, *Holy Men and Hunger Artists: Fasting and Asceticism in Rabbinic Culture* (Oxford: Oxford University Press, 2004), pp. 85-91 and on R. Chiya p. 38. He notes that Rashi understands R. Chiya as celibate only due to his advanced age, as, incidentally, does Frankel, for whom this premise becomes central to the plot; Rashi, *b. Kid.* 81b *s.v.* דפריש מינאי; and Frankel, 'Remarkable Phenomena', pp. 59-61. I will shortly argue against this interpretation.

16. As opposed to fasting, which appears to have been much more common; see Eliezer Diamond, *Holy Men and Hunger Artists*, pp. 35-54. Note, however, that Adam is described as having fasted and separated (פריש) from his wife Eve for 130 years. Reception of this tradition is varied, but at least one early Palestinian view deemed Adam's ascetic practice to be pious; see Michael Satlow, '"Wasted Seed" The History of a Rabbinic Idea', *HUCA* 65 (1994) pp. 160-61, as well as *b. Eruv.* 18b and *Gen. R.* 20.11 and 24.6.

17. On the seemingly irresolvable contradictory demands of Torah study and marital sexuality and rabbinic approaches to sexuality more generally; see Daniel

Ashi may then be a unique portrayal of a case of a married sage who remains celibate even when living with his wife.[18]

II. *Rabbinic Body as Cultural Metaphor*

It is probably impossible to determine which influences this critique of R. Chiya's celibacy may be targeting, and it is therefore more instructive simply to note the wide range of potential cultural tensions. R. Chiya may represent a rabbinic sage who has come under sectarian influence, perhaps Christian or Palestinian Rabbinic.[19] His apparent celibacy may also represent internal rabbinic cultural tensions regarding the desirability of marriage and sexuality, especially when constructed as at odds with or detracting from the sage's ability to wholly dedicate himself to Torah study and the divine. Michael Satlow has demonstrated that Babylonian rabbinic culture valued early marriage as a means for men to obtain a legitimate sexual outlet, thereby preventing transgressive sexual activity.[20] By marrying but denying himself this outlet, R. Chiya may have rendered himself vulnerable to the very transgression he sought to prevent.[21] R. Chiya's personal failure thus underlines the effectiveness of

Boyarin, *Carnal Israel: Reading Sex in Talmudic Culture* (Berkeley: University of California Press, 1993), Michael Satlow, *Jewish Marriage in Antiquity* (Princeton: Princeton University Press, 2001) and Jeffrey Rubenstein, *The Culture of the Babylonian Talmud* (Baltimore: The Johns Hopkins University Press), p. 102. More generally, see the excellent chapter on the weight upon the body of cultural tensions regarding sexuality, celibacy and freedom in late antiquity, by Peter Brown, 'Bodies and Minds: Sexuality and Renunciation in Early Christianity', in David Halperin, John Winkler and Froma Zeitlin (eds.), *Before Sexuality* (Princeton: Princeton University Press, 1990), pp. 479-94.

18. While he may be unique, his approach is not remarkably deviant and therefore may remain a tempting approach within the culture, for as Diamond notes, 'Even when scholars were living with their wives, their devotion to Torah study led them to attenuate their sexual activity significantly' (*Hunger Artists*, p. 44).

19. See Shlomo Naeh, 'Freedom and Celibacy' and Naomi Koltun-Fromm, 'A Jewish-Christian Conversation in Fourth-Century Mesopotamia', *JJS* 47, no. 1 (1996), pp. 45-63. Koltun-Fromm argues in favour of the existence of active polemic debates between Jews and Christians, during at least part of the talmudic period.

20. Satlow, *Jewish Marriage in Antiquity*, p. 27. This approach is reminiscent of 1 Cor. 7.9: 'For if they are not practicing self-control, they should marry, since it is better to marry than to be burnt up' (NJB translation).

21. I should note that it is not entirely clear that R. Chiya bar Ashi was concerned about sexual transgression *per se*. Indeed, the narrative seems to suggest that he was entirely celibate and may have understood any and all sexual activity as the 'evil inclination' from which he sought rescue.

this Babylonian system for managing the rabbinic male body. Further-more, we may read this tale as a parody of rabbinic concern about the evil inclination itself, for our sage in the oven states not that some externalized disembodied entity made him do it; there is no fire here.[22] Rather, he accepts full responsibility for his desire to transgress.

III. *The Epicurean Garden*

R. Chiya's study in his garden may suggest the famous epicurean Garden, where the philosophers gathered. His isolated location in his garden, apart from his wife and community, and his ultimate sexual hedonism, are all practices commonly associated with Epicureanism (and in the case of the latter, of which Epicureans were commonly accused).[23] This association also extends to the famous tale of the four sages who entered the *pardes* (פרדס), including Elisha ben Abuyah who became a proto-typical heretic.[24] In one tale he actively seeks out a prostitute as a symbol of his alienation from the rabbinic *nomos* and a physical means through which to mark his departure from it.[25] Daniel Boyarin has suggested that '[s]ectarian heresy, prostitution, and collaboration with Roman power had become associated in the cultural "unconscious" of rabbinic Judaism, no doubt at least in part simply because all three are seductive and dangerous'.[26] R. Chiya may then be connected to sages who undertook heretical, unorthodox, dangerous and futile philosophical enquiries and his self-destruction may symbolize the futility of non-normative ideology.

While reading our narrative as a warning against popular notions of epicurean digression and the rabbinic heretic is tempting, Henry Fischel

22. Rav Amram, for example, is able to expel sexual desire in the form of a pillar of fire; see *b. Kid.* 81a and discussion below, p. 217.

23. On the epicurean influences in rabbinic literature see Henry A. Fischel, *Rabbinic Literature and Greco-Roman Philosophy: A Study of Epicurea and Rhetorica in Early Midrashic Writings* (Leiden: Brill, 1973). On false popular accusations of hedonism, see p. 2; on Ben Azzai who may have never consummated his marriage and is called a פריש and whose teachings have an epicurean tone, p. 6 with n. 59; on notions of the sage as insane or a fool, p. 17; of the sage contradicting his own word with his deed, pp. 79-80; and on the sage in the Garden, p. 22 and see there n. 178.

24. 'Enclosure, Pleasure Garden or Park'; so Jastrow, *Dictionary*, p. 1216, and in Aramaic, meaning 'garden' or 'park'; see, for example, *DJBA*, p. 444a.

25. See *b. Ḥag.* 15a and Fischel, *Rabbinic Literature and Greco-Roman Philosophy*, p. 12.

26. Daniel Boyarin, *Dying for God: Martyrdom and the Making of Christianity and Judaism* (Stanford: Stanford University Press, 1999), p. 68.

argues that the term גן (garden), which is used in our tale, can never mean the epicurean Garden, because it exclusively signifies the Garden of Eden (the epicurean Garden should properly be called a *pardes*).[27] Indeed, as well as being suggestive of Epicureanism, the dangers of the *pardes* and the rejection of rabbinic culture by the heretic, our tale may also be an allusion to the Garden of Eden. Several elements of our narrative recall the primordial scene, including the woman's request that he pick a fruit from the tree, the male's transition from asexual to sexually humiliated, the woman's transition from asexual to sexual, all loosely suggesting the themes of female betrayal, testing, temptation, fruit and fertility.[28] Peter Brown has argued that Encratite exegesis understood that the fall from the Garden of Eden into death rendered sexual relations a necessary condition for human survival, much as R. Chiya falls from his own Garden of Eden, wherein his celibate body once studied, into his sexual body and fiery death.[29]

IV. *The Rabbinic Body in the Oven*

R. Chiya bar Ashi's celibacy, his study alone in his garden, his regular prostrate[30] appeal for divine rescue from the evil inclination and his failure to heed his wife in the final analysis all position him as physically and culturally at the fringes of both his marriage and rabbinic society. R. Chiya bar Ashi stands out, however, not only for his celibacy and other quirks; he is remarkable for the very fact that he commits suicide in an oven. The death of the sage was a popular literary motif in antiquity,

27. Fischel, *Rabbinic Literature and Greco-Roman Philosophy*, p. 23 n. 82.

28. The fruit in question here is a pomegranate (though Rashi calls it a palm tree, as read some manuscripts, a symbol of uprightness and righteousness), symbolic of beauty, fertility, the priesthood and of the notion that all, even the emptiest, are full of commandments just as a seed is full of pomegranates (see, for example, *b. Sanh.* 37a). By following his wife's request to pick the pomegranate, and the sexual connection that follows, he momentarily accesses this universe of sexuality, connection to the divine and to human worth in the absence of perfection. The pomegranate may also suggest the heretical sage. See *b. Ḥag.* 15b where R. Meir's willingness to learn from the heretical Acher (also known as Elisha ben Abuyah) is compared to the consumption of the edible inner fruit of the pomegranate, while the peel (i.e. the heresy) is cast aside.

29. Brown, 'Bodies and Minds', p. 484.

30. Some talmudic discussion demonstrates ambivalence regarding the prostrate body. A man of stature is discouraged from falling on his face, unless he may expect an immediate divine response, a response that R. Chiya bar Ashi most certainly did not receive. Rav, whom Rav Chiya bar Ashi may have served as a personal servant, is described as one who did not fall on his face; see *b. Meg.* 22a-b and *b. Taan.* 14b.

and suicide was not an uncommon theme in the honour-driven cultures of the ancient Near East.[31] Drastic methods of suicide were relatively common, but self-burning was most unusual in Greco-Roman culture and appears to have been a practice associated with sages of the Indian subcontinent rather than the Near and Middle East. R. Chiya's choice of method for his self-destruction is likely significant, as Van Hoof notes: 'The selection of the right means had a greater impact on the evaluation of self-killing than it does in our world; especially in the last moments it was of vital importance not to lose face'.[32]

Moreover, the prevalence of shame–honour culture in the rabbinic *nomos* is crucial for the understanding of the role of suicide as a method of engaging with intolerable social and cultural problems.[33] Here we are speaking of a situation where suicide is a remedy for the individual within his *nomos*.[34] R. Chiya seeks precisely such a remedy for the unsustainable horror he senses at his own transgressive intention, which has the potential to shame himself and his fellow sages. The power of this shame in sexual situations is demonstrated in the following narrative, where Rav Amram Chasida (the Pious) manages to stop himself from having sexual relations with redeemed captive women who are being sheltered in his attic by calling for assistance:

> He raised his voice, 'Fire in the House of Amram! Fire in the House of Amram!' The rabbis came and said to him, 'You have shamed us!' [lit: caused us to become silver]. He said to them, better you should be ashamed because of me in this world and not be ashamed because of me in the world to come. He made it swear [that it should leave him]. It left him as a pillar of fire. He said to it, 'See that you are fire and I am flesh and I am better than you'.[35]

---

31. Anton J. L. Van Hoof, *From Autothanasia to Suicide: Self Killing in Classical Antiquity* (London: Routledge, 1990), pp. 40, 58.

32. *Ibid.*, p. 41. While suicide is commonly understood as prohibited under Jewish law, the legal basis for such a ban is not particularly strong. The sage's suicide, whose goal is to avoid committing a transgression, is not uncommon as a form of martyrdom, though suicide following a transgression that has already been committed (or in R. Chiya's case, was intended and physically experienced with that intent) is unusual. On these issues see the excellent article by Yechezkel Lichtenshtein, 'Suicide as an Act of Atonement in Jewish Law', *Jewish Law Annual* 16 (2006), pp. 51-91.

33. On the honour of the suicidal sage, see Diamond, *Hunger Artists*, pp. 55-59.

34. Here I am indebted to Robert Cover's notions of the interrelationships between law and narrative; see his 'The Supreme Court, 1982 Term—Foreword: *Nomos* and Narrative', *Harvard Law Review* 97, no. 1 (1983), pp. 1-68.

35. *b. Kid.* 81a. My translation here is based on manuscript Vatican 111.

This sage avoids the sexual transgression he is about to commit by summoning his inner strength and calling for the help of his friends. Finally, it is Rav Amram's own will that forces the pillar of fire to depart from him. His physical flesh is superior to the fire and exercises control over it. His exposure of his transgressive intention and transgressive body half-way up the ladder in view of his rabbinic colleagues nevertheless results in communal shame. The rabbis accuse Rav Amram of rendering them silver, or pale with shame. Rav Amram justifies himself by privileging the next world over this world, so that shame in this world becomes a reasonable price to pay for honour in the next (and certainly preferable to eternal shame in the next world). The severity of the wrongdoing of shaming one's fellow should not be underestimated, as we see in the following tradition: 'It is preferable (or: comfortable) for a person that he should cast himself into the furnace of fire rather than whiten the face of his fellow in public. Whence do we know this? From Tamar, as it is written, "She was taken out" (Genesis 38:25).'[36] We may thus understand R. Chiya as a rabbi who avoids shaming his fellow sages by throwing himself into the burning hot oven; comparatively his action is preferable, perhaps even comfortable. Jeffrey Rubenstein has written that '[t]he sin [of shame and verbal wrongdoing is]...punished directly by God with eternal perdition, and it should be avoided even at the cost of death'.[37] More specifically, Alyssa Gray writes that, '[f]or a Jew, life lived after the commission of these acts [including sexual immorality] is not a life worth living because those acts, by reducing him to the level of an idolater, have killed his "Israeliteness". The only reasonable alternative is to choose death and the maintenance of the Jewish identity.'[38] Understood in this context, his method of bodily self-destruction is a perfectly sensible response to a cultural intolerance of shame, as it becomes an act of self-rescue from a far worse fate.[39]

---

36. *b. Ber.* 43b. Tamar is brought out to be burned and rather than accusing Judah directly presents the signs and states that she is pregnant by the man to whom they belong. Judah may then have denied his ownership of the signs and that he was the father of her unborn child, and this tradition understands that Tamar would then have gone willingly into the fire rather than shame her father-in-law.

37. Rubenstein, *The Culture of the Babylonian Talmud*, p. 72. He notes further that suffering punishment for shaming another in this world avoids the necessity of punishment in the world to come (p. 77).

38. Alyssa M. Gray, 'A Contribution to the Study of Martyrdom and Identity in the Palestinian Talmud', *JJS* 54 (2003), pp. 242-72 (262).

39. This act of shame avoidance will be met in turn with embarrassment by some later commentators. On this process of engaging with embarrassing religious texts,

Sitting in a fiery oven can also be a method for a sage to rescue himself from sexual transgression. In this sense, R. Chiya bar Ashi is non-
normative in two respects: he seeks not to rescue himself but for the
divine to rescue him, and he sits in the oven *after* having indulged in the
sexual act. The following narrative demonstrates how the sage in the
oven may be constructed as salvific rather than destructive:

> A certain Matrona desired R. Tsadoq. He said to her, 'My heart is faint
> upon me[40] and I am not able. Is there something to eat?' She said to him,
> 'There is something impure'. He said to her, 'What may be derived from
> this?[41] The one who does this, eats that.' She heated the oven and was
> laying out for him. He went up and sat inside it. She said, 'What is this!?'
> He said, 'The one who does this, falls into that'. She said to him, 'If I had
> known all this I would not have distressed you'.[42]

This narrative regarding R. Tsadoq (Rabbi Righteous) appears amongst a
series of stories that emphasize the importance of saving one's self from
sexual predation.[43] It is the sage who rescues *himself* from the advances
of a Matrona who merits having a miracle performed for him.[44] It is in

see Tzemah Yoreh, Aubrey Glazer and Justin Lewis (eds.), *Vixens Disturbing
Vineyards: Embarrassment and Embracement of Scriptures: Festschrift in Honor of
Harry Fox* (Boston: Academic Studies Press, 2010).

40. Or more colloquially, 'I do not feel well'; see Michael Sokoloff, *DJBA*,
p. 466, or 'I feel weak'; see Jay Rovner, 'A Certain *Matronita* Solicited R. Tsadoq:
Eros of Power, Eros of Resistance in a Babylonian Talmudic Narrative', in David
Golinkin *et al.* (eds.), *Torah Lishma: Essays in Jewish Studies in Honor of Professor
Shamma Friedman* (Jerusalem: Bar-Ilan University Press, 2007), p. xlix. The heart
should be understood also as the seat of human thought, whereby we may understand that his heart, that is, his mind, his intention, is not in it. This is in stark contrast to the clear intention of R. Chiya and his immersion in his act and both his body
and that of his wife.

41. This is a talmudic legal technical expression (מאי נפקה מינה). R. Tsadoq's
immersion in his culture of legal argumentation maintains his body as distinct and
detached from that of the Gentile woman.

42. *b. Kid.* 40a.

43. *b. Kid.* 39b. A similar story involving R. Tsadoq is found in two versions in
Avot d'Rabbi Nathan A (ed. Solomon Schechter; New York: Jewish Theological
Seminary, 1997), pp. 63, 160. In this tale, a Roman woman offers a slave woman to
R. Tsadoq and he distracts himself through the night by staring at a wall and
repeating (שונה) rabbinic teachings. Unlike R. Chiya's studying (גורס), which does
not protect him against the distraction presented by his wife in disguise, R. Tsadoq
successfully ignores the sexual offering; Rovner, 'A Certain *Matronita* Solicited R.
Tsadoq', pp. xlvii-lxvi.

44. This may explain, in part, why R. Chiya bar Ashi is neither rescued from nor
protected against the flames.

this manner that several stories in this same *sugya* in *b. Kid.* 39b-41a unfold, as sages endanger their lives (even jumping off a roof) in order to escape the ever-desirous Matrona. These apparent suicides represent an overwhelming determination to avoid the sexual act rather than a desire to die, and are consistently averted by miraculous circumstances (Elijah travels great distances to catch the sage who leaps off the roof).[45] R. Tsadoq's sitting in the oven is likewise driven by a determination to escape. While the Matrona initially responds with disbelief, using language identical to that of R. Chiya's wife, R. Tsadoq's location in the oven effectively communicates his cultural body to her, a culture which she finally comprehends. In contrast, R. Chiya pleaded regularly for divine rescue, and when the time came rather than fleeing from the available woman, he propositioned her; making no effort to rescue himself, he instead acted with transgressive intention and remains alienated from his wife. Our sage has indeed gone awry; he should have sought to rescue himself at all costs instead of relying on divine intervention. Within this intertextual context, it becomes inevitable that he die his fiery death as he has forfeited any other hope of immediate salvation.

If we return to our central *sugya* (*b. Kid.* 81), however, it is possible to make an alternative argument, namely that R. Chiya bar Ashi was in fact saved by the divine and need not have entered the oven at all. Some of the stories presented along with our story about R. Chiya bar Ashi obviously critique regular, individualized, spoken utterances designed to ward off the evil inclination or Satan on specific grounds, such as phrasing that suggests that a person (rather than the divine) may ward off such entities.[46] In relation to this critique of the type of phrasing, R. Chiya's appeal, 'May the Merciful One save me from the evil inclination', appears to be a correction, even a demonstration of the proper thing to say to ward off sexual desire.[47] How then may have the divine saved him? It was in fact his wife with whom he had sexual connection, turning

45. *b. Kid.* 39b. This may also be connected to the set of commandments for which one should rather die than publically transgress, in order to avoid profaning the divine (חילול השם). These laws include idolatry, sexual transgressions (גלוי עריות), traditionally the laws of Lev. 18 and 20, and murder. There was debate regarding which specific sexual prohibitions fall under the scope of this principle, as well as regarding whether or not the principle applies to private as well as public transgressions. For a detailed discussion, see Gray, 'A Contribution to the Study of Martyrdom and Identity'.

46. On the role of the *satan* and demonology in rabbinic notions of the evil inclination, see Rosen-Zvi, *Demonic Desires*, pp. 42-43 and n. 56 there.

47. It bears some similarity to a prayer for deliverance from the evil inclination amongst other negative people and characteristics; see, for example, *b. Ber.* 16b.

his inclination towards transgression into the good inclination towards marital and reproductive relations.[48] From this perspective, our protagonist's final failure is his inability to accept his rescue and his wife's affirmation: 'It was me'.

We have seen how sitting in an oven can be an act of self-preservation. I will now explore how it can also consist of a test of the male body's ability to resist sexual desire, as in this talmudic narrative:

> When R. Zeira went up to the Land of Israel [from Babylon], he sat one hundred fasts, that the Babylonian *gemara* (i.e. learning or tradition) might be forgotten [by him], so that it would not trouble him. He sat one hundred other fasts so that R. Eleazar would not die during his years [i.e. in his lifetime], [for if he R. Eleazar had died] matters of the community would have fallen upon him [i.e. upon R. Zeira]. He sat one hundred other fasts, so that the fire of Gehinnom would not have power over him. Every thirty days he would check himself. He heated the oven, went up into it and the fire did not have any power over him. One day the rabbis gave him the eye and his legs[49] were burned, and [thereafter] they called him Skinny-Burnt-Legs.[50]

In this parodic narrative, denial of the body through extended periods of fasting allows R. Zeira to achieve certain personal and rather self-serving goals (with the ultimate aim of allowing himself to focus exclusively on his Torah study). It is this last individual personalized practice, the cultivation of physical invulnerability to the flames of Gehinnom, which sheds further light on the meaning of the location of our central protagonist, R. Chiya bar Ashi, in his wife's hot oven.

The flames of Gehinnom exist not so much in R. Zeira's oven as in his religious-cultural universe. Gehinnom is the Valley of Hinnom, which biblical sources describe as the site near Jerusalem where the *molekh* ritual was practiced by the Israelites,[51] a ritual related in rabbinic tradition to both child sacrifice and to sexual relations between Jewish men and Gentile women.[52] Gehinnom also developed into a byword for a place of

---

48. On the good inclination and Babylonian and Palestinian constructions of the good vs. the evil inclinations, see, for example, Satlow, *Jewish Marriage in Antiquity*, pp. 3-42.

49. More specifically: his thighs. This suggests a burning of a sexualized portion of the body, namely the loins and possibly the male sexual organs, which might result from sitting in a fiery oven.

50. *b. B. Met.* 85a. Some manuscripts read: 'Burnt One of the Skinny Legs' (see also *b. Sanh.* 37a).

51. As in 2 Kgs 23.10.

52. For a discussion of rabbinic interpretive traditions on the *molekh* ritual, see Laliv Clenman, 'The Faceless Idol and Images of Terror in Rabbinic Tradition on

horror, suffering and punishment; a kind of hell.[53] The rabbinic body in the oven hence becomes a cultural performance related to the *molekh* ritual, representing the actual act (sexual and/or sacrificial) as well as its punishment. The rabbinic body in the oven furthermore experiences the state of Gehinnom, bringing the punishment of the next world into this world—an attempt to mete out such damage onto the body of this world and thereby preserve the goodness of the next.

R. Zeira's rabbinic colleagues noticed R. Zeira's flaunting of his unique physical invulnerability, which was brought about through his unorthodox ascetic praxis. His fellow rabbis follow the normative embodied middle-road rather than R. Zeira's ascetic extreme, and under their envious, critical gaze he suddenly feels the burn of the flames. This respected sage is reduced to a mockery of a nickname: 'skinny-burnt-legs'. In normative rabbinic culture, the male sexual body does and should burn in the flames of the hot oven and in the flames of Gehinnom, to which it remains forever vulnerable. In view of this intertextual reading, R. Chiya's death in the flames may be a test of his physical invulnerability to desire and punishment. His failure is proof of his inescapable normativity; despite his best efforts he is no miraculous ascetic. His normal male body burns in the flames, as it should. His burning body is a symbol of and a punishment for his sexual flesh while also representing a powerful critique of his celibate ascetic practice.

V. *The Body of the Rabbi and the Body of the Text*

The ensuing talmudic discussion, which follows our tale, frames R. Chiya as a sensitive and pious soul. Especially in view of the post-talmudic epilogue to our story, it is ultimately unclear whether R. Chiya is criticized or celebrated for his life-long self-denial (be it sexual and/or through fasting). This dual approach of critique and praise that results from the contextualization of the *aggadah* within the broader talmudic discussion as well as from the later additions may reflect an ambivalence regarding the attraction of the ascetic life and the denial of the body along with the cultural control that this promises.

the *molekh*', in Sarah Pearce (ed.),*The Image and the Prohibition of the Image in Ancient Judaism* (JJSSup 2; Oxford: Oxford University Press, 2013), pp. 143-69.

53.   On the *molekh*, see Geza Vermes, 'Leviticus 18.21 in Ancient Jewish Bible Exegesis', in J. J. Petuchowski and E. Fleischer (eds.), *Studies in Aggadah, Targum and Jewish Liturgy in Memory of Joseph Heinemann* (Jerusalem: Magnes Press, 1981), pp. 108-24.

The reception history of our tale is complex, so I will focus here on two important elements pertaining to the construction and interpretation of R. Chiya bar Ashi's body. I will begin with a discussion of the inner-talmudic interpretation of the *aggadah* in the ensuing *sugya* and then turn to issues of post-talmudic redaction and interpretation. Our tale is followed by a series of *baraitot*,[54] which contextualize R. Chiya's self-destruction within a legal framework wherein the intention to sin, even in the absence of actual transgression, requires both forgiveness and atonement.[55] This redactorial context offers some legal justification for R. Chiya's self-punishment in the oven; he is indeed in need of atonement for having intended to have sexual relations with Charuta even though he actually had permitted relations with his wife.[56] This talmudic reception of this tale thus shifts our tale from the parodic to the serious,[57] and emphasizes the heavy burden of transgression upon the body of the sage.[58] Viewed through these interpretive traditions, R. Chiya bar Ashi becomes an emotional, grieving sage who is unable to sustain the burden of the frailty of his human condition under the relentless stringency of divine law. He finds his sole relief in his (self-) elimination.

If the talmudic contextualization of this narrative transforms R. Chiya's physical act through its interpretive lens, the post-talmudic reception of our tale has been written onto the body of the text, mutilating the

---

54. Early tannaitic rabbinic statements.

55. *b. Kid.* 81b. On the conflation of thought and action, and the sinfulness of thought even in the absence of action in the Babylonian Talmud, see Yishai Kiel, 'Cognizance of Sin and Penalty in the Babylonian Talmud and Pahlavi Literature: A Comparative Analysis', *Oqimta* 1 (2013), pp. 319-67 (322). This seems to be in contradiction to *b. Kid.* 39b which includes the following tradition, 'The Holy One Blessed be He does not connect an evil thought to a deed'. It is worth noting, how-ever, that R. Chiya bar Ashi thinks that he is acting according to his transgressive intention (as does the Nazirite woman in the case that our *gemara* uses as a parallel) thereby connecting his transgressive thought to the action of his transgressive body (despite the fact that no transgression is actually being committed). *b. Kid.* 81b connects R. Chiya's case to that of a woman who has made the Nazirite vow, a vow which her husband has subsequently annulled (see Num. 30.13).

56. Some early Palestinian sages, including R. Akiva, held that death atones; see, for example, *y. Sanh.* 10.1 27d.

57. A critique of the ascetic is simultaneously maintained as the serious vow of the Nazirite is followed by a description of her deliberate consumption and exposure to everything she has denied herself, just as R. Chiya's celibacy is followed by an illicit sexual encounter.

58. Even one who sins unwittingly is considered guilty and requires atonement and forgiveness. See here *b. Kid.* 81b and Lev. 15.17.

very narrative itself.[59] The added epilogue to the story revisions this sage gone astray as a righteous man who subjected his body to a lifetime of affliction. In this process, the cause of his death is rendered ambiguous or even erased, as some commentators claim that he died later on of his extended self-deprivation and others assert that he never entered the oven in the first instance.[60] To similar effect, many commentaries elide the significance of his celibacy by casting R. Chiya as very elderly, so that his sexual separation from his wife is merely a result of his body's inability to perform.[61] Such alteration of his celibate body and fiery death renders his abnormal practice normative, as he transitions from an unorthodox rabbinic monk to a more mainstream fasting sage.[62] I would suggest that such apologetic approaches explain away his celibacy and his self-destruction in a manner that eviscerates the narrative and R. Chiya's body of their cultural power.

Conclusions

These changes to the body of the text and its interpretation are not merely apologetic in nature. They carry ideological and historical significance in relation to medieval rabbinic debates regarding the permissibility of suicide as a form of atonement for transgression, arising in a context of historical martyrdoms as a reaction to the weight of transgression felt after forced conversions. Indeed, Lichtenshtein has demonstrated how our narrative played a role in the deliberation over the relative accept-ability of suicide as a means for atonement under Jewish law.[63] One particular narrative of such a martyrdom bears some resemblance to our tale, as a man who was forced to convert later finds that he cannot sustain the sensation of his transgression and seeks atonement through the

---

59. Note that Frankel locates this reinterpretation as beginning in the post-talmudic period as part of a process of adulterating the genre of talmudic *aggadah*, turning rich, complex and challenging narratives into 'thin gruel' ('Remarkable Phenomena', p. 60). My analysis locates the beginning of this trend within the later layer of the talmudic *sugya* itself.

60. Frankel, 'Remarkable Phenomena', p. 60 n. 68. In contrast to such erasure, Rashi comments that he entered the oven in order 'to kill himself', *b. Kid.* 81b *s.v.* קא יתיב בגוויה.

61. See, for example, Rashi, *b. Kid.* 81b *s.v.* דפריש מינאי, and Frankel, 'Remark-able Phenomena', pp. 59-61, who understands this narrative as an attempt to recover lost youth on the part of R. Chiya's wife.

62. This combination of the elderly fasting man is a particularly normative and popular motif; see Van Hoof, *From Autothanasia to Suicide*, p. 33.

63. Lichtenshtein, 'Suicide as an Act of Atonement'.

horrible sacrifice of his children and the burning alive of both himself and his mother.[64] The alteration of the body of our sage and our text thus plays a key role in the medieval construction of the pious Jewish male body under the terrible pressures of persecution and forced conversion.

This chapter has demonstrated the manner in which a seemingly nonsensical act of rabbinic self-destruction is in fact highly interpretable, open to multivalent meanings. The rabbinic body is subject to contradictory demands and cultural tensions which may easily lead the sage astray from the delicate middle-road. The attempt to exert complete control over these tensions upon the body ends in physical transgression and damage to the body. The act of sitting in an oven is particularly complex and serves numerous purposes: punishing, preserving, rescuing, testing and atoning for the body. Talmudic and post-talmudic apologetic approaches protect R. Chiya's body against himself, at times erasing his suicide in the oven as well as his celibacy, transforming this unique and powerful character into a pious non-entity. Alternatively, where his suicide was acknowledged, he came to be characterized as a self-afflicting, suicidal, righteous sage, no longer a fool or even a sensitive sage, but a righteous martyr. R. Chiya's body is thus inscribed with myriad cultural problems in several layers, which at times utterly destroy him and at others revive him. In all interpretive versions, these cultural tensions and the broader legal and narrative structures are maintained.

In the final analysis, there is something amiss or unusual about the sage, rather than with the rabbinic worlds in which he perishes. If we view the destruction of the problematic antique sage as a hermeneutic technique, the suggestion appears to be that it is a careful balance on the part of the sage that is required, rather than a reconfiguration of these fatal demands. The rabbinic world, along with its cultural and legal pressures, is preserved and perpetuated, while the sage who could not properly negotiate his *nomos* conveniently eliminates himself.

---

64. This narrative shares several common literary motifs with our narrative, further suggesting a common tradition. On this medieval historical tale, see A. M. Haberman, *Book of Persecutions of Ashkenaz and Tsarfat* (Jerusalem: Tarshish and Mosad Harav Kook, c. 1946 [Hebrew]), pp. 36-38; Lichtenshtein, 'Suicide as an Act of Atonement' and Robert Chazan, *God Humanity and History: The Hebrew First Crusade Narratives* (Berkeley: University of California Press, 2000), esp. pp. 80, 122. Chazan notes that this work connects the martyrdom through burning in the synagogue to the burning of the Temples (p. 80). The conclusion of our *sugya* likewise connects R. Chiya bar Ashi to those who mourn and grieve over the destruction of the Temples (*b. Kid.* 81b).

BIBLIOGRAPHY

Abraham, Kathleen, 'West Semitic and Judean Brides in Cuneiform Sources from the Sixth Century BCE: New Evidence from a Marriage Contract from Al-Yahudu', *Archiv für Orientfurschung* 51 (2005/2006), pp. 198-219.

Albrecht, Ruth, *Das Leben der heiligen Makrina auf dem Hintergrund der Thekla-Traditionen* (Studien zu den Ursprüngen des weiblichen Mönchtums im 4 Jahrhundert in Kleinasien; Göttingen: Vandenhoeck & Ruprecht, 1986).

Allen, Leslie C., *Ezekiel 20–48* (WBC 29; Dallas: Word Books, 1990).

Allo, Ernst B., *Saint Paul: Épitres aux Corinthiens* (Paris: Lecoffre, 1956).

Alter, Robert, *The Five Books of Moses: A Translation with Commentary* (New York: W. W. Norton, 2004).

Amnesty International, *Love, Hate and the Law: Decriminalizing Homosexuality* (London: Amnesty International Publications, 2008).

Anderson, Hugh, *The Gospel of Mark* (Grand Rapids: Eerdmans, 1996).

Attridge, Harold W., and Kurt Niederwimmer, *The Didache: A Commentary* (trans. Linda M. Maloney; Minneapolis: Fortress Press, 1998).

Aubin, Melissa, 'Reversing Romance? The Acts of Thecla and the Ancient Novel', in Ronald F. Hock, J. Bradley Chance and Judith Perkins (eds.), *Ancient Fiction and Early Christian Narrative* (Atlanta: Scholars Press, 2003), pp. 257-72.

Aune, David E., *Revelation 17–22* (WBC 52C; Nashville: Thomas Nelson, 1998).

Avi-Yonah, Michael, *Gazetteer of Roman Palestine* (Qedem; Jerusalem: Institute of Archaeology, Hebrew University of Jerusalem, 1976).

Aymer, Margaret P., 'Hailstorms and Fireball, Redaction, World Creation and Resistance in the Acts of Paul and Thecla', *Semeia* 79 (1997), pp. 45-61.

Bahr, Gordon J., 'The Seder of Passover and the Eucharistic Words', *Novum Testamentum* 12.2 (1970), pp. 181-202.

Barclay, John, 'Who was Considered an Apostate in the Jewish Diaspora?', in Guy Stroumsa and Graham N. Stanton (eds.), *Tolerance and Intolerance in Early Judaism and Christianity* (Cambridge: Cambridge University Press, 1998), pp. 80-98.

Bar-Ilan, Meir, 'Jewish Magical Body-Inscription in the First and Second Centuries', *Tarbiz* 57 (1988), pp. 37-50 (Hebrew), trans. Menachem Sheinberger. Online: http://faculty.biu.ac.il/~testsm/tatoos.html, accessed 15 February 2008, pp. 1-22.

———. 'So Shall They Put My Name Upon The People of Israel (Numbers 6:27)', *HUCA* 60 (1989), pp. 19-31 (Hebrew).

Barkay, Gabriel, 'The Priestly Benediction on Silver from Keteph Hinnom in Jerusalem', *Cathedra* 52 (1989), pp. 37-76 (Hebrew).

Barkay, Gabriel, Andrew Vaughn, Marilyn J. Lundberg and Bruce Zuckerman, 'The Amulets from Ketef Hinnom: A New Edition and Evaluation', *BASOR* 334 (2004), pp. 41-71.

Barnard, Alan, and Jonathan Spencer (eds.), *The Routledge Encyclopedia of Social and Cultural Anthropology* (2nd ed.; London: Routledge, 2010).

Barr, David L., 'Women in Myth and History: Deconstructing John's Characterizations' in Levine (ed.), *Apocalypse of John*, pp. 55-68.

Barrier, Jeremy M., *The Acts of Paul and Thecla: A Critical Introduction and Commentary* (Tübingen: Mohr Siebeck, 2009).

Bartlett, John R., *The First and Second Books of the Maccabees* (CBC; London: Cambridge University Press, 1973).

Bauckham, Richard, *The Theology of The Book of Revelation* (Cambridge: Cambridge University Press, 1993).

Beagley, Alan James, *The 'Sitz im Leben' of the Apocalypse with Particular Reference to the Role of the Church's Enemies* (Berlin: W. de Gruyter, 1987).

Beal, Timothy K., 'Cracking the Binding', in Timothy K. Beal and David Gunn (eds.), *Reading Bibles, Writing Bodies: Identity and The Book* (London: Routledge, 2002), pp. 1-12.

Beale, Gregory K., *The Book of Revelation: A Commentary on the Greek Text* (Grand Rapids: Eerdmans, 1999).

———. *John's Use of the Old Testament in Revelation* (Sheffield: Sheffield Academic Press, 1998).

———. *The Use of Daniel in Jewish Apocalyptic Literature and in the Revelation of St. John* (Lanham: University Press of America, 1984).

Beard, Mary, John North and Simon Price, *Religions of Rome* (Cambridge: Cambridge University Press, 1998).

Bell, Catherine, *Ritual Theory, Ritual Practice* (Oxford: Oxford University Press).

Bell, Richard, *Deliver Us From Evil: Interpreting the Redemption from the Power of Satan in New Testament Theology* (Tübingen: Mohr Siebeck, 2007).

Ben-Barak, Zafrira, *Inheritance by Daughters in Israel and the Ancient Near East: A Social, Legal and Ideological Revolution* (trans. B. Sigler Rozen; Jaffa: Tel Aviv Archaeological Center Publications, 2006).

Berlejung, Angelika, 'Washing the Mouth: The Consecration of Divine Images in Mesopotamia', in Karel van der Toorn (ed.), *The Image and the Book: Iconic Cults, Aniconism, and the Rise of Book Religion in Israel and the Ancient Near East* (CBET 21; Leuven: Peeters, 1997), pp. 45-72.

Bernstein, Jeanne W., 'Love, Desire, Jouissance: Two out of Three Ain't Bad', *Psycho-analytical Dialogues* 16 (2007), pp. 711-24.

Berquist, Jon L., *Controlling Corporeality: The Body and the Household in Ancient Israel* (New Brunswick: Rutgers University Press, 2002).

Bersani, Leo, *Homos* (Cambridge, MA: Harvard University Press, 1996).

———. *Is the Rectum a Grave? And Other Essays* (Chicago: University of Chicago Press, 2009).

Best, Ernest, *Mark: The Gospel as Story* (Edinburgh: T. & T. Clark, 1983).

Bickerman, Elias, 'Notes on the Greek Book of Esther', *Proceedings of the American Academy for Jewish Research* 20 (1951), pp. 101-33.

Bird, Michael F., *Jesus and the Origins of the Gentile Mission* (London: Continuum, 2007).

Black, Matthew, *The Book of Enoch, or 1 Enoch: A New English Edition* (SVTP 7; Leiden: Brill, 1985).

Black, Matthew (ed.), *Apocalypsis Henochi Graece* (PVTG 3; Leiden: Brill, 1970).

Blackburn, Barry L., 'The Miracles of Jesus', Bruce Chilton and Craig Evans (eds.), *Studying the Historical Jesus: Evaluations of the State of Current Research* (Leiden: Brill, 1994).

Blaschke, Andreas, *Beschneidung. Zeugnisse der Bibel und verwandter Texte* (Tübingen, Basel: Francke Verlag, 1998).

Blenkinsopp, Joseph, *Isaiah 1–39: a New Translation with Introduction and Commentary* (AB 19; New York: Doubleday, 2000).

Block, Daniel I., *The Book of Ezekiel: Chapters 1–24* (NICOT; Grand Rapids: Eerdmans, 1997).

Boer, Esther de, *The Gospel of Mary: Beyond a Gnostic and a Biblical Mary Magdalene* (London: T&T Clark International, 2004).

Boer, Roland, *The Earthy Nature of the Bible: Fleshly Readings of Sex, Masculinity, and Carnality* (New York: Palgrave Macmillan, 2012).

Borgen, Peder, *Bread from Heaven: An Exegetical Study of the Concept of Manna in the Gospel of John and the Writings of Philo* (Leiden: Brill, 1965).

Boring, M. Eugene, *Mark: A Commentary* (Louisville: Westminster John Knox Press, 2006).

———. *Revelation* (Louisville: John Knox Press, 1989).

Bourdieu, Pierre, *Outline of a Theory of Practice* (Cambridge Studies in Social Anthropology; trans. Richard Nice; Cambridge: Cambridge University Press, 1977).

Bovon, François, *A Commentary on the Gospel of Luke* (trans. Christine M. Thomas; Minneapolis: Fortress, 2002).

Bowersock, G. W., *Fiction as History* (London: University of California Press, 1994).

Bowie, Fiona, *The Anthropology of Religion* (Oxford: Blackwell, 2000).

Boxall, Ian, 'The Many Faces of Babylon the Great: Wirkungsgeschichte and the Interpretation of Revelation 17', in Moyise (ed.), *Revelation*, pp. 51-68.

———. *The Revelation of Saint John* (BNTC; London: Continuum, 2006).

Boyarin, Daniel, 'Are There Any Jews in "The History of Sexuality"?', *Journal of the History of Sexuality* 5 (January 1995), pp. 333-55.

———. *Carnal Israel: Reading Sex in Talmudic Culture* (Berkeley: University of California Press, 1993).

———. *Dying for God: Martyrdom and the Making of Christianity and Judaism* (Stanford: Stanford University Press, 1999).

Bradshaw, Paul F., *Eucharistic Origins* (London: SPCK, 2004).

Braun, Willi, 'Physiotherapy of Femininity in the Acts of Thecla', in Stephen G. Wilson and Michel Desjardins (eds.), *Text and Artifact in the Religions of Mediterranean Antiquity: Essays in Honour of Peter Richardson* (Waterloo: Wilfrid Laurier University Press, 2000), pp. 209-29.

Bremmer, Jan N., 'Magic, Martyrdom and Women's Liberation in *The Acts of Paul and Thecla*', in Bremmer (ed.), *Paul and Thecla*, pp. 36-59.

Bremmer, Jan N. (ed.), *The Apocryphal Acts of Paul and Thecla* (Kampen: Kok Pharos, 1996).

Brenner, Athalya, *The Intercourse of Knowledge: on Gendering Desire and 'Sexuality' in the Hebrew Bible* (Leiden: Brill, 1997).

Brock, Ann Graham, *Mary Magdalene, the First Apostle: The Struggle for Authority* (HTS; Cambridge, MA: Harvard University Press, 2003).

Brock, Sebastian P., and Susan Ashbrook Harvey, *Holy Women of the Syrian Orient* (Berkeley: University of California Press, 1987).

Broer, Ingo, 'Die Konversion des Köngishauses von Adiabene nach Josephus (Ant. XX)', in Cornelius Petrus Mayer *et al.* (eds.), *Nach den Anfängen fragen: Herrn Prof. Dr. Theol. Gerhard Dautzenberg zum 60. Geburtstag am 30. Januar 1994* (Giessen: Selbstverlag des Fachsbereichs Evangelische Theologie und Katholische Theologie und deren Didaktik, 1994), pp. 133-62.

Brooke, George J., 'The Structure of 1QH XII 5-XIII 4 and the Meaning of Resurrection', in García Martínez, Steudel and Tigchelaar (eds.), *From 4QMMT to Resurrection*, pp. 15-33.

Brooks, Beatrice Allard, 'The Babylonian Practice of Marking Slaves', *JAOS* 42 (1922), pp. 80-90.

Brooten, Bernadette, 'Junia… Outstanding among the Apostles', in Swidler and Swidler (eds.), *Women Priests*, pp. 141-44.

Broshi, Magen, and Ada Yardeni, 'On Netinim and False Prophets', *Tarbiz* 62 (1993), pp. 45-54 (Hebrew).

Brown, Peter, 'Bodies and Minds: Sexuality and Renunciation in Early Christianity', in David Halperin, John Winkler, and Froma Zeitlin (eds.), *Before Sexuality* (Princeton: Princeton University Press, 1990), pp. 479-94.

———. *The Body and Society: Man, Women and Sexual Renunciation in Early Christianity* (London: Faber, 1990).

Brown, Raymond E., *The Gospel and Epistles of John: A Concise Commentary* (Collegeville: The Order of St. Benedict, 1988).

Bultmann, Rudolf, *Die Geschichte der synoptischen Tradition* (Göttingen: Vandenhoeck & Ruprecht, 1921).

———. *The History of the Synoptic Tradition* (trans. John Marsh: New York: Harper & Row, 1963).

———. *Theology of the New Testament*, vol. 1 (New York: Scribners, 1951).

———. *Theology of the New Testament*, vol. 1 (trans. Kendrick Grobel; London: SCM Press, 1952).

Burkert, Walter, *Structure and History in Greek Mythology and Ritual* (London: University of California Press, 1982).

Burris, Catherine, and Lucas van Rompay, 'Thecla in Syriac Christianity: Preliminary Observations', *Hugoye: Journal of Syriac Studies* 5.2 (2002). Online: htto://syrcom.cua.edu/Hugoye/Vol5No2/HV5N2BurrisVanRompay.html.

Burrus, Virginia, *Chastity as Autonomy, Women in the Stories of the Apocryphal Acts* (Lewiston: Edwin Mellen Press, 1987).

———. 'The Heretical Woman as Symbol', *HTR* 84 (1991), pp. 229-48.

———. 'Reading Agnes, The Rhetoric of Gender in Ambrose and Prudentius', *JECS* 3 (1995), pp. 25-48.

Burrus, Virginia, and Rebecca Lyman, 'Introduction', in Virginia Burrus (ed.), *Late Ancient Christianity: A People's History of Christianity*, vol. 2 (Minneapolis: Fortress Press, 2005), pp. 1-26.

Butler, Judith, *Bodies That Matter: On the Discursive Limits of Sex* (New York: Routledge, 1993).

———. *Gender Trouble: Feminism and the Subversion of Identity* (Routledge Classics; new ed.; New York: Routledge, 2006).

———. 'Revisiting Bodies and Pleasures', *Theory, Culture and Society* 16.2 (1999), pp. 11-20.

Cahill, Michael J., 'Drinking Blood at a Kosher Eucharist? The Sound of Scholarly Silence', *Biblical Theology Bulletin: A Journal of Bible and Theology* 32.168 (2002), pp. 168-81.

Campbell, William Sanger, *The 'We' Passages in the Acts of the Apostles: The Narrator as Narrative Character* (SBL Studies in Biblical Literature; Atlanta: Society of Biblical Literature; Leiden: Brill, 2007).

Carey, Greg, 'A Man's Choice: Wealth Imagery and the Two Cities of the Book of Revelation', in Levine (ed.), *Apocalypse of John*, pp. 147-58.

Cartlidge, David R., and J. Keith Elliott, *Art and the Christian Apocrypha* (London: Routledge, 2001).

Cavallin, Hans C. C., *Life After Death: Paul's Argument for the Resurrection of the Dead in I Cor 15: Part I: An Enquiry into the Jewish Background* (Coniectanea Biblica 7/1; Lund: Gleerup, 1974).

Chapman, Honora Howell, 'Paul, Josephus, and the Judean Nationalistic and Imperialistic Policy of Forced Circumcision', *Ilu, Revista de Ciencias de las Religiones* 11 (2006), pp. 131-55.

———. 'Spectacle in Josephus' *Jewish War*', in Jonathan Edmonson, Steve Mason and James Rives (eds.), *Flavius Josephus and Flavian Rome* (Oxford: Oxford University Press, 2005), pp. 289-313.

Charlesworth, James H., 'Where Does the Concept of Resurrection Appear and How Do We Know That?', in Charlesworth (ed.), *Resurrection*, pp. 1-21.

Charlesworth, James H. (ed.), *Resurrection: The Origin and Future of a Biblical Doctrine* (Faith and Scholarship Colloquies; New York: T&T Clark International, 2006).

Chazan, Robert, *God Humanity and History: The Hebrew First Crusade Narratives* (Berkeley: University of California Press, 2000).

Childs, Brevard S., *Isaiah* (OTL; Louisville: Westminster John Knox Press, 2001).

Chilton, Bruce, 'The Eucharist: Exploring Its Origins', *Bible Review* (1994), pp. 36-43.

Clark, Gillian, 'Bodies and Blood, Late Antique Debate on Martyrdom, Virginity and Resurrection', in Dominic Montserrat (ed.), *Changing Bodies, Changing Meanings: Studies on the Human Body in Antiquity* (London: Routledge, 1998), pp. 99-115.

Clenman, Laliv, 'The Faceless Idol and Images of Terror in Rabbinic Tradition on the *molekh*', in Sarah Pearce (ed.), *The Image and the Prohibition of the Image in Ancient Judaism* (JJSSup 2; Oxford: Oxford University Press, 2013), pp. 143-69.

Clines, David J. A., *Interested Parties: The Ideology of Writers and Readers of the Hebrew Bible* (JSOTSup 205; Gender, Culture, Theory 1; Sheffield: Sheffield Academic Press, 1995).

———. *What Does Eve Do To Help? And Other Readerly Questions to the Old Testament* (Sheffield: JSOT Press, 1994).

Coakley, Sarah, 'Introduction: Religion and the Body', in Coakley (ed.), *Religion and the Body*, pp. 1-12.

———. *Powers and Submissions: Spirituality, Philosophy and Gender* (Oxford: Blackwell, 2002).

Coakley, Sarah (ed.), *Religion and the Body* (CSRT; Cambridge: Cambridge University Press, 1997).

Cohen, Beth, 'Divesting the Female Breast of Clothes in Classical Sculpture', in Koloski-Ostrow and Lyons (eds.), *Naked Truths*, pp. 66-92.

Cohen, Shaye J. D., *The Beginnings of Jewishness: Boundaries, Varieties, Uncertainties* (Hellenistic Culture and Society 31; Berkeley, University of California Press, 1999).

———. *From the Maccabees to the Mishnah* (Louisville: Westminster John Knox Press, 2006).

———. 'Respect for Judaism by Gentiles According to Josephus', *HTR* 80 (1987), pp. 409-30.

———. *Why Aren't Jewish Women Circumcised? Gender and Covenant In Judaism* (London: University of California Press, 2005).

Collins, John J., *Apocalypticism in the Dead Sea Scrolls* (London: Routledge, 1997).

———. 'The Essenes and the Afterlife', in García Martínez, Steudel and Tigchelaar (eds.), *From 4QMMT to Resurrection*, pp. 35-53.

Conybeare, Frederick C., *The Apology and Acts of Apollonius and other Monuments of Early Christianity* (London: Swan, Sonnenschein, 1894).

Cooper, Kate, 'Apostles, Ascetic Women and Questions of Audience: New Reflections on the Rhetoric of Gender in the Apocryphal Acts', in *SBL Seminar Papers 31* (Atlanta: Scholars Press, 1992), pp. 147-53.

———. *Band of Angels, The Forgotten Work of Early Christian Women* (London: Atlantic Books, 2013).

———. 'A Saint in Exile: The Early Medieval Thecla at Rome and Meriamlik', *Hagiographica* 2 (1995), pp. 1-23.

———. *The Virgin and the Bride: Idealized Womanhood in Late Antiquity* (Cambridge, MA: Harvard University Press, 1996).

Cover, Robert, 'The Supreme Court, 1982 Term—Foreword: *Nomos* and Narrative', *Harvard Law Review* 97.1 (1983), pp. 1-68.

Crisp, Quentin, *The Naked Civil Servant* (rev. ed.; London: Flamingo, 1985).

Cross, F. L., and E. A. Livingstone (eds.), *Oxford Dictionary of the Christian Church* (3rd ed.; Oxford: Oxford University Press, 2005).

Crossan, John Dominic, *The Historical Jesus: The Life of a Mediterranean Jewish Peasant* (Edinburgh: T. & T. Clark, 1991).

Curran, John, 'Flavius Josephus in Rome', in Jack Pastor, Pnina Stern and Menahem Mor (eds.), *Flavius Josephus, Interpretation and History* (JSJSup 146; Leiden: Brill, 2011), pp. 65-86.

Dagron, Gilbert, and Marie Dupré de la Tour, *Vie et Miracles de Saint Thècle. Texte Grec. Traduction et Commentaire* (SHG 62; Brussels: Société des Bollandistes, 1978).

Daly, Robert J., 'Eucharistic Origins: From the New Testament to the Liturgies of the Golden Age', *Theological Studies* 66 (2005), pp. 3-22.

Dandamaev, Muhammad, *Slavery in Babylonia from Nabopolassar to Alexander the Great: 626–331 B.C.* (DeKalb: Northern Illinois University Press, 1984).

Davenport, Gene L., *The Eschatology of the Book of Jubilees* (Studia Post Biblica 20; Leiden: Brill, 1972).

Davidson, Arnold, *The Emergence of Sexuality: Historical Epistemology and the Formation of Concepts* (Cambridge, MA: Harvard University Press, 2001).

Davies, Stevan L., *Jesus the Healer: Possession, Trance, and the Origins of Christianity* (London: SCM Press, 1995).

———. *The Revolt of the Widows: The Social World of the Apocryphal Acts* (Carbondale: Southern Illinois University Press, 1980).

Davies, William D., and Dale C. Allison, *A Critical and Exegetical Commentary on the Gospel According to St Matthew* (3 vols.; London: T&T Clark International, 2004).

Davis, Stephen J., *The Cult of Saint Thecla; A Tradition of Women's Piety in Late Antiquity* (Oxford: Oxford University Press, 2001).

Davis, Wade, 'Foreword', in Rainier (ed.), *Ancient Marks*, pp. 14-19.

De Jonge, Marinus, *The Testaments of the Twelve Patriarchs: A Critical Edition of the Greek Text* (PVTG 1; Leiden: Brill, 1978).

Diamond, Eliezer, *Holy Men and Hunger Artists: Fasting and Asceticism in Rabbinic Culture* (Oxford: Oxford University Press, 2004).

Dimant, Devorah, 'The Qumran Manuscripts: Contents and Significance', in Devorah Dimant and Lawrence H. Schiffman (eds.), *Time to Prepare the Way in the Wilderness: Papers on the Qumran Scrolls by Fellows of the Institute for Advanced Studies of the Hebrew University, Jerusalem 1989–1990* (STDJ 16; Leiden: Brill, 1995), pp. 23-58.

Donahue, John, and Daniel Harrington, *The Gospel of Mark* (Sacra Pagina; Collegeville: Liturgical Press, 2002).

Donaldson, Terence L. *Judaism and the Gentiles: Jewish Patterns of Universalism* (Waco: Baylor University Press, 2007).

Doty, Timothy, 'A Cuneiform Tablet from Tell 'Umar', *Mesopotamia* 13–14 (1978–79), pp. 91-98.

Dougherty, Raymond P., *The Shirkûtu of Babylonian Deities* (New Haven: Yale University Press, 1923).

Douglas, Mary, *Purity and Danger: An Analysis of Concepts of Pollution and Taboo* (London: Routledge & Kegan Paul, 1966; repr., London: Routledge Classics, 2006).

Drane, John W., 'Some Ideas of Resurrection in the New Testament Period', *TynBul* 24 (1973), pp. 99-110.

Duff, Paul B., *Who Rides the Beast? Prophetic Rivalry and the Rhetoric of Crisis in the Churches of the Apocalypse* (Oxford: Oxford University Press, 2001).

Dunn, James D. G., *Jesus Remembered* (Grand Rapids: Eerdmans, 2003).

Dušek, Jan, *Les manuscrits araméens du Wadi Daliyeh et la Samarie vers 450–332 av. j.-c.* (Culture and History of the Ancient Near East 30; Leiden: Brill, 2007).

Eckhardt, Benedikt, '"An Idumean, that is, a half-Jew": Hasmoneans and Herodians between Ancestry and Merit', in Benedikt Eckhardt (ed.), *Jewish Identity and Politics between the Maccabees and Bar Kokhba: Groups, Normativity and Rituals* (JSJSup 155; Leiden: Brill, 2012), pp. 91-115.

Ehrman, Bart, *Misquoting Jesus: The Story Behind Who Changed the Bible and Why* (San Francisco: Harper, 2005).

Eilberg-Schwartz, Howard, 'Problem of the Body for the People of the Book', in Howard Eilberg-Schwartz (ed.), *People of the Body: Jews and Judaism from an Embodied Perspective* (Albany: SUNY Press, 1992), pp. 17-46.

———. *The Savage in Judaism: An Anthropology of Israelite Religion and Ancient Judaism* (Bloomington: Indiana University Press, 1990).

Eisen, Ute, *Women Officeholders in Early Christianity: Epigraphy and Literary Studies* (trans. Linda Maloney; Collegeville: Liturgical Press, 1996).

Eliade, Mircea, *Myth and Reality* (trans. Willard R. Trask; New York: Harper & Row, 1963).

Elledge, Casey D., *Life After Death in Early Judaism: The Evidence of Josephus* (WUNT 208; Tübingen: Mohr Siebeck, 2006).

———. 'Resurrection and Immortality in Hellenistic Judaism: Navigating the Conceptual Boundaries', in Stanley E. Porter and Andrew W. Pitts (eds.), *Christian Origins and Hellenistic Judaism: Social and Literary Contexts for the New Testament* (Early Christianity in Its Hellenistic Context; Leiden: Brill, 2013), pp. 101-33.

———. 'The Resurrection Passages in the Testaments of the Twelve Patriarchs: Hope for Israel in Early Judaism and Christianity', in Charlesworth (ed.), *Resurrection*, pp. 79-103.

Ellens, Deborah L., *Women in the Sex Texts of Leviticus and Deuteronomy: A Comparative Conceptual Analysis* (LHBOTS 458; London: T&T Clark International, 2008).

Esch, Elisabeth, 'Thekla und die Tiere. Oder: Die Zähmung der Widerspenstigen', in Martin Ebner (ed.), *Aus Liebe zu Paulus? Die Akte Thekla neu aufgerollt* (Stuttgart: Katholisches Bibelwerk, 2005), pp. 159-79.

Esch-Wermeling, Elisabeth, *Thekla—Paulusschülerin wider Willen? Strategien der Leserlenkung in den Theklaakten* (Münster: Aschendorff, 2008).

Evans, Craig A. (ed.), *The Bible Knowledge Background Commentary: John's Gospel, Hebrews–Revelation* (Colorado Springs: Cook Communications Ministries, 2005).

Fabry, Heinz-Josef (eds.), *Theological Dictionary of the Old Testament*, vol. 14 (trans. Douglas W. Stott; Grand Rapids: Eerdmans, 2004).

Feeley-Harnik, Gillian, *The Lord's Table: Eucharist and Passover in Early Christianity* (Philadelphia: University of Pennsylvania Press, 1981).

Feldman, Louis, *Jew and Gentile in the Ancient World: Attitudes and Interactions from Alexander to Justinian* (Princeton: Princeton University Press, 1993).

———. 'Philo, Pseudo-Philo, Josephus, and Theodotus on the Rape of Dinah', *JQR* 94 (2004), pp. 253-77.

———. *Studies in Josephus' Rewritten Bible* (JSJSup 58; Atlanta: Society of Biblical Literature, 2005).

Fenton, John C., *The Gospel of St Matthew* (Harmondsworth: Penguin, 1963).

Fischel, Henry A., *Rabbinic Literature and Greco-Roman Philosophy: A Study of Epicurea and Rhetorica in Early Midrashic Writings* (Leiden: Brill, 1973).

Fitzmyer, Joseph A., *The Gospel According to Luke* (2 vols.; New York: Doubleday, 1985).

Flemming, Rebecca, 'Quae Corpore Quaestum Facit: The Sexual Economy of Female Prostitution in the Roman Empire', *JRS* 89 (1999), pp. 38-61.

Ford, Josephine Massyngberde, *Revelation* (AB 38; Garden City: Doubleday, 1975).

Foucault, Michel, *Discipline and Punish: The Birth of the Prison* (trans. A. Sheridan; New York: Random House, 1977).

———. *The History of Sexuality*. Vol. 1, *An Introduction* (trans. Robert Hurley; 5th edn; New York: Vintage, 1990).

———. *Power/Knowledge: Selected Interviews and Other Writings, 1972–1977* (ed. Colin Gordon; New York: Knopf Doubleday, 1980).

Fox, Michael V., 'The Rhetoric of Ezekiel's Vision of the Valley of the Bones', *HUCA* 51 (1980), pp. 1-15.

Fox, Nili S., 'Marked for Servitude: Mesopotamia and the Bible', in Grant Frame *et al.* (eds.), *A Common Cultural Heritage: Studies on Mesopotamia and the Biblical World in Honor of Barry L. Eichler* (Bethesda: CDL Press, 2011), pp. 267-78.

France, Richard T., *The Gospel According to Matthew: An Introduction and Commentary* (Leicester: Inter-Varsity Press, 1985).

———. *The Gospel of Mark* (New International Greek Testament Commentary; Grand Rapids: Eerdmans, 2002).

Frankel, Yonah, 'Remarkable Phenomena in the Text-History of the Aggadic Stories', in *Proceedings of the 7th World Congress of Jewish Studies: Research in Talmud, Halacha and Midrash* (Jerusalem: World Union of Jewish Studies, 1981), pp. 45-69 (Hebrew).

Frankfurter, David, 'Martyrology and the Prurient Gaze', *JECS* 17 (2009), pp. 215-45.

Fuchs, Esther, *Sexual Politics in the Biblical Narrative: Reading the Hebrew Bible as a Woman* (JSOTSup 310; London: Sheffield Academic Press, 2000).

Galambush, Julie, *Jerusalem in the Book of Ezekiel: The City as Yahweh's Wife* (SBLDS 130; Atlanta: SBL, 1992).

Gallop, Jane, 'Beyond the Jouissance Principle', *Representations* 7 (July 1984), pp.110-15.

García Bachmann, Mercedes L., *Women at Work in the Deuteronomistic History* (International Voices in Biblical Studies 4; Atlanta: SBL, 2013).

García Martínez, Florentino, Annette Steudel and Eibert J. C. Tigchelaar (eds.), *From 4QMMT to Resurrection: Mélanges Qumraniens en hommage à Émile Puech* (STDJ 61; Leiden: Brill, 2006).

Garfinkel, Yosef, 'MLS HKRSYM in Phoenician Inscriptions from Cyprus, the QRSY in Arad, HHKRSYM in Egypt and BNY QYRS in the Bible', *JNES* 47.1 (1988), pp. 27-34.

Geffcken, Johannes (ed.), *Die Oracula Sibyllina* (GCS; Leipzig: J. C. Hinrichs, 1902).

Gentry, Kenneth L., *Before Jerusalem Fell: Dating the Book of Revelation* (Fountain Inn: Victorious Hope, 2010).

Gergel, Richard A., 'Costume as Geographic Indicator: Barbarians and Prisoners on Cuirassed Statue Breastplates', in J. Sebesta and L. Bonfante (eds.), *The World of Roman Costume* (Wisconsin: University of Wisconsin Press, 2001), pp. 191-208.

Gilbert, Gary, 'The Making of a Jew: "God-Fearer" or Convert in the Story of Izates', *USQR* 44 (1991), pp. 299-313.

Glancy, Jennifer A., and Steven D. Moore, 'How Typical a Roman Prostitute is Revelation's "Great Whore"?', *JBL* 130 (2011), pp. 551-69.

Goldstein, Jonathan A., *II Maccabees: A New Translation with Introduction and Commentary* (AB 41A; Garden City: Doubleday, 1983).

Goodenough, Erwin R., *Jewish Symbols in the Greco-Roman Period*, vol. 6 (New York: Pantheon Books, 1956).

Goodman, Martin, 'Identity and Authority in Ancient Judaism', *Judaism* 39 (1990), pp. 192-201.

———. *Mission and Conversion: Proselytizing in the Religious History of the Roman Empire* (new ed.; Oxford: Oxford University Press, 1995).

Gray, Alyssa M., 'A Contribution to the Study of Martyrdom and Identity in the Palestinian Talmud', *JJS* 54 (2003), pp. 242-72.

Greenberg, Moshe, *Ezekiel 21–37: A New Translation with Introduction and Commentary* (AB 22A; New York: Doubleday, 1997).

Grimes, Ronald L, *Readings in Ritual Studies* (Upper Saddle River: Prentice–Hall, 1996).

Grisanti, Michael A., 'תועבה', in W. A. Vangemeren (ed.), *New International Dictionary of Old Testament Theology and Exegesis*, vol. 4 (Carlisle: Paternoster Press, 1996), pp. 314-18.

Grosz, Elizabeth, *Volatile Bodies: Toward a Corporeal Feminism* (Theories of Representation and Difference; Bloomington: Indiana University Press, 1994).

Guelich, Robert A., *Mark 1–8:26* (WBC 34A; Dallas: Word Books, 1989).

Gundry, Robert H., *Matthew: A Commentary on his Handbook for a Mixed Church under Persecution* (Grand Rapids: Eerdmans, 1994).

Haberman, A. M., *Book of Persecutions of Ashkenaz and Tsarfat* (Jerusalem: Tarshish and Mosad Harav Kook, c. 1946 [Hebrew]).

Haenchen, Ernst, and Ulrich Busse, *A Commentary on the Gospel of John* (trans. Robert W. Funk; Philadelphia: Fortress Press, 1984).

Hagner, Donald A., *Matthew 1–13* (WBC 33a; Nashville: Nelson, 1993).

Halperin, David M., *One Hundred Years of Homosexuality: And Other Essays on Greek Love* (New York: Routledge, 1990).

Haran, Menaḥem, 'The Gibeonites, The Nethinim and the Sons of Solomon's Servants', *VT* 11 (1961), pp. 159-69.

Harper, Kyle, 'Porneia: The Making of a Christian Sexual Norm', *JBL* 131 (2012), pp. 363-83.

Harrington, Daniel J., 'Afterlife Expectations in Pseudo-Philo, 4 Ezra, and 2 Baruch, and their Implications for the New Testament', in Reimund Bieringer, Veronica Koperski and Bianca Lataire (eds.), *Resurrection in the New Testament* (Festschrift J. Lambrecht; BETL 165; Leuven: Leuven University Press, 2002), pp. 21-34.

Harrington, Daniel J., Charles Perrot and Pierre Bogaert, *Les Antiquités Bibliques* (SC 229–30; 2 vols.; Paris: Éditions du Cerf, 1976).

Hartsock, N., 'Foucault on Power: A Theory for Women?', in Linda Nicholson (ed.), *Feminism/Postmodernism* (New York: Routledge, 1990), pp. 157-75.

Hauptman, Judith, *Re-reading the Rabbis: A Woman's Voice* (Boulder: Westview Press, 1998).

Hayes, Christine E., *Gentile Impurities and Jewish Identities: Intermarriage and Conversion from the Bible to the Talmud* (New York: Oxford University Press, 2002).

Helms, Randall McCraw, *Who Wrote the Gospels* (Altadena: Millennium, 1997).

Henderson, Jeffrey, *The Maculate Muse, Obscene Language in Attic Comedy* (New Haven: Yale University Press, 1975).

Héring, Jean, *The First Epistle of Saint Paul to the Corinthians* (trans. A. W. Heathcote and P. J. Allcock; New York: Wipf & Stock, 2009).

Herter, Hans, 'The Sociology of Prostitution in Antiquity in the Context of Pagan and Christian Writings', in Mark Golden and Peter Toohey (eds.), *Sex and Difference in Ancient Greece and Rome* (trans. Linwood DeLong; Edinburgh: Edinburgh University Press, 2003), pp. 57-113.

Higgins, A. J. B., 'The Origins of the Eucharist', *NTS* 1 (1955), pp. 200-209.

Hilhorst, A., 'Tertullian on the Acts of Paul', in Bremmer (ed.), *Paul and Thecla*, pp. 150-63.

Hoffner, Harry A., 'Symbols for Masculinity and Femininity: Their Use in Ancient Near Eastern Sympathetic Magic Rituals', *JBL* 85 (1966), pp. 326-34.

Hogeterp, Albert L. A., 'Belief in Resurrection and Its Religious Settings in Qumran and the New Testament', in Florentino García Martínez (ed.), *Echoes from the Caves: Qumran and the New Testament* (STDJ 85; Leiden: Brill, 2009), pp. 299-320.

Hollander, Harm W., *The Testaments of the Twelve Patriarchs: A Commentary* (SVTP 8; Leiden: Brill, 1985).

Holmes, Michael W., and Society of Biblical Literature, *Greek New Testament: SBL Edition* (Atlanta: Society of Biblical Literature, 2010).

Hooker, Morna D., *The Gospel According to St Mark* (London: Continuum, 2009).

Huber, Lynn R., 'Gazing at the Whore: Reading Revelation Queerly', in Teresa J. Hornsby and Ken Stone (eds.), *Bible Trouble: Queer Reading at the Boundaries of Biblical Scholarship* (Atlanta: Society of Biblical Literature, 2011), pp. 301-20.

———. 'Sexually Explicit? Re-Reading Revelation's 144,000 Virgins as a Response to Roman Discourses', *Journal of Men, Masculinities and Spirituality* 2.1 (2008), pp. 3-28.

Huehnergard, John, and Harold Liebowitz, 'The Biblical Prohibition Against Tattooing', *VT* 63 (2013), pp. 59-77.

Hultgård, Anders, *L'Eschatologie des Testaments des Douze Patriarches* (AUU 6; Uppsala: Uppsala Universitet, 1977).

Hundley, Michael B., *Keeping Heaven on Earth: Safeguarding the Divine Presence in the Priestly Tabernacle* (Tübingen: Mohr Siebeck, 2011).

Itzin, Catherine, 'Entertainment for Men: What It Is and What It Means', in Itzin (ed.), *Pornography*, pp. 27-53.

Itzin, Catherine (ed.), *Pornography, Women, Violence and Civil Liberties* (Oxford: Oxford University Press, 1992).

Jack, Alison, 'Out of the Wilderness', in Moyise (ed.), *Revelation*, pp. 149-62.

Jacobs, Sandra, *The Body as Object: Physical Disfigurement in Biblical Law* (LHBOTS 582; London: Bloomsbury T&T Clark, 2014).

Jacobson, Howard, *Commentary on Pseudo-Philo's 'Liber Antiquitatum Biblicarum'* (AJU 31; 2 vols.; Leiden: Brill, 1996).

Jastrow, Marcus, *Dictionary of the Targumim, the Talmud Babli, and Yerushalmi, and the Midrashic Literature* (New York: Title, 1943).

Jenkins, Richard, *Pierre Bourdieu* (Key Sociologists; rev. ed.; Abingdon: Routledge, 2002).

Joannès, Francis, and André Lemaire, 'Trois tablettes cunéiformes à onomastique ouest-sémitique (collection S. Moussaieff)',*Transeuphratène* 17 (1999), pp. 17-34.

John, Jeffery, *Permanent, Faithful, Stable: Christian Same-Sex Partnerships* (2nd rev. ed.; London: Darton, Longman & Todd, 2000).

Johnson, Luke Timothy, *The Gospel of Luke* (Minnesota: Liturgical Press, 1991).

Jones, Christopher P., 'Stigma: Tattooing and Branding in Graeco-Roman Antiquity', *JRS* 77 (1987), pp. 139-55.

Kampen, Natalie Boymel, 'Epilogue, Gender and Desire', in Koloski-Ostrow and Lyons (eds.), *Naked Truths*, pp. 267-77.

Kappeler, Susanne, 'Pornography: The Representation of Power', in Itzin (ed.), *Pornography*, pp 88-101.

Keener, Craig S., *And Marries Another: Divorce and Remarriage in the Teaching of the New Testament* (Peabody: Hendrickson, 1991).

———. *The Gospel of Matthew: A Socio-Rhetorical Commentary* (Grand Rapids: Eerdmans, 2009).

Kellermann, Ulrich, *Auferstanden in Den Himmel: 2 Makkabäer 7 und Die Auferstehung Der Märtyrer* (Stuttgarter Bibelstudien 95; Stuttgart: Verlag Katholisches Bibelwerk, 1979).

Kennedy, James M., 'Hebrew *pithôn peh* in the Book of Ezekiel', *VT* 41 (1991), pp. 233-35.

Klauck, Hans-Josef, *The Apocryphal Acts of the Apostles* (Texas: Baylor University Press, 2008).

Klawans, Jonathan, *Impurity and Sin in Ancient Judaism* (New York: Oxford University Press, 2000).

Klein, Anja, *Schriftauslegung im Ezechielbuch: Redaktionsgeschichtliche Unter-suchungen zu Ez 34–39* (BZAW 391; Berlin: W. de Gruyter, 2008).

Klein, Gunter, *Die zwolf Apostel: Ursprung und Gehatt einer Idee* (Göttingen: Vandenhoeck & Ruprecht, 1961).

Knibb, Michael A., and Richard J. Coggins, *The First and Second Books of Esdras* (CBC; Cambridge: Cambridge University Press, 1979).

Knohl, Israel, *The Divine Symphony: The Bible's Many Voices* (Philadelphia: Jewish Publication Society, 2003).

————. *The Sanctuary of Silence: The Priestly Torah and the Holiness School* (Minneapolis: Fortress Press, 1995).

Knoppers, Laura Lunger, and Joan B. Landes, *Monstrous Bodies/Political Monstrosities: In Early Modern Europe* (Ithaca: Cornell University Press, 2004).

Koester, Helmut, *History, Culture and Religion of the Hellenistic Age* (Philadelphia: Fortress Press, 1982).

Koloski-Ostrow, Ann Olga, and Claire L. Lyons (eds.), *Naked Truths: Women, Sexuality and Gender in Classical Art and Archaeology* (London: Routledge, 1997).

Kraemer, Ross Shepard, *Unreliable Witnesses, Religion, Gender and History in the Greco-Roman Mediterranean* (New York: Oxford University Press, 2011).

Kraemer, Ross Shepard (ed.), *Women's Religions in the Greco-Roman World: A Sourcebook* (Oxford: Oxford University Press, 2004).

Kutsko, John F., *Between Heaven and Earth: Divine Presence and Absence in the Book of Ezekiel* (Biblical and Judaic Studies from the University of California, San Diego; Winona Lake: Eisenbrauns, 2000).

Kyle, Donald G., *Spectacles of Death in Ancient Rome* (New York: Routledge, 1998).

Labovitz, Gail, 'Heruta's Ruse: What We Mean When We Talk About Desire', in Danya Ruttenberg (ed.), *The Passionate Torah: Sex and Judaism* (New York: New York University Press, 2009), pp. 229-44.

Landman, Isaac (ed.), *The Universal Jewish Encyclopedia: An Authoritative and Popular Presentation of Jews and Judaism Since the Earliest Times*, vol. 3 (New York: Universal Jewish Encyclopedia, 1948).

Lane, William, *The Gospel According to Mark* (Grand Rapids: Eerdmans, 1974).

Lapsley, Jacqueline, 'Body Piercings: The Priestly Body and the "Body" of the Temple in Ezekiel', *Hebrew Bible and Ancient Israel* 1 (2012), pp. 231-45.

Lee, Judith, 'Sacred Horror: Faith and Fantasy in the Revelation of John', in George Aichele and Tina Pippin (eds.), *The Monstrous and the Unspeakable: The Bible as Fantastic Literature* (Sheffield: Sheffield Academic Press, 1997), pp. 220-39.

Leemhuis, Fred, Albertus F. J. Klijn and Geert J. H. van Gelder (eds.), *The Arabic Text of the Apocalypse of Baruch: Edited and Translated with a Parallel Translation of the Syriac Text* (Leiden: Brill, 1986).

Leonhard, Clemens, 'Blessings Over Wine and Bread in Judaism and Christian Eucharistic Prayers, Two Independent Traditions', in *Jewish & Christian Liturgy and Worship: New Insights into its History and Interpretation* (Leiden: Brill, 2007), pp. 309-26.

Levinas, Emmanuel, *Nine Talmudic Readings* (trans. Anette Aronowicz; Bloomington: Indiana University Press, 1994).

Levine, Amy-Jill (ed.), *A Feminist Companion to The Apocalypse of John* (London: T&T Clark International, 2009).

Levine, Amy-Jill, with Maria Mayo Robbins (eds.), *A Feminist Companion to the New Testament Apocrypha* (London: T&T Clark International, 2006).

Levine, Baruch A., 'The Netînim', *JBL* 82.2 (1963), pp. 207-12.

———. *Numbers 1–20: A New Translation with Commentary* (AB 4; New York: Doubleday, 1993).

Lichtenshtein, Yechezkel, 'Suicide as an Act of Atonement in Jewish Law', *Jewish Law Annual* 16 (2006), pp. 51-91.

Lietzmann, Hans, *Mass and Lord's Supper: A Study in the History of the Liturgy*, vol. 1 (Leiden: Brill, 1979).

Lieu, Judith, 'Circumcision, Women and Salvation', *NTS* 40 (1994), pp. 358-70.

Lim, Timothy, '"The Husband of One Wife", in the Light of the Scrolls', in Jörg Frey and Enno E. Popkes (eds.), *Jesus, Paulus und Qumran: Festschrift Heinz-Wolfgang Kuhn* (WUNT; Tübingen: Mohr Siebeck [forthcoming]).

———. 'A New Solution to the Exegetical Crux (CD IV 20-21)', *RQ* 102.26 (2013), pp. 275-84.

Lipsius, R. Adelbert, and M. Bonnet (eds.), *Acta Apostolorum Apocrypha, Post Constantinum Tischendorf*, Pars prior (Hildesheim: Georg Olms, 1852; repr. 1990).

Livesey, Nina E., *Circumcision as a Malleable Symbol* (WUNT 2; Tübingen: Mohr Siebeck, 2010).

Loisy, Alfred, *The Birth of the Christian Religion* (trans. L. P. Jacks; New Hyde Park: University Books, 1962).

Lopez, Davina C., 'Before Your Very Eyes: Roman Imperial Ideology, Gender Constructs and Paul's Inter-Nationalism', in Todd Penner and Caroline Vander Stichele (eds.), *Mapping Gender in Ancient Religious Discourses* (Leiden: SBL, 2007), pp. 115-62.

Loughlin, Gerard, 'The Body', in John F. A. Sawyer (ed.), *The Blackwell Companion to the Bible and Culture* (London: John Wiley & Sons, 2012), pp. 381-96.

Lowenthal, David, 'Fabricating Memory', *History and Memory* 10 (1998), pp. 5-24.

———. *The Heritage Crusade and the Spoils of History* (Cambridge: Cambridge University Press, 2003).

Luz, Ulrich, *Matthew: A Commentary* (trans. James E. Crouch; 3 vols.; Minneapolis: Fortress Press, 2007).

Macdonald, Dennis R., *The Legend and the Apostle: The Battle for Paul in Story and Canon* (Philadelphia: Westminster Press, 1983).

MacDonald, Margaret Y., *Early Christian Women and Pagan Opinion: The Power of the Hysterical Woman* (Cambridge: Cambridge University Press, 1996).

Magdalene, F. Rachel, and Cornelia Wunsch, 'Slavery Between Judah and Babylon: The Exilic Experience', in Laura Culbertson (ed.) with contributions by Indrani Chatterjee *et al.*, *Slaves and Households in the Near East: Papers from the Oriental Institute Seminar 'Slaves and Households in the Near East'*, Held at the Oriental Institute of the University of Chicago, 5–6 March 2010 (OIS 7; Chicago: The Oriental Institute, 2011), pp. 113-34.

Malinowski, Bronislaw, *Myth in Primitive Psychology* (London: Routledge, 1926).

Marcus, Joel, *Mark 1–8* (AB 27; London: Doubleday, 2005).

Marjanen, Antti, 'What Does It Mean When a Woman Is Called or Portrayed as a Man? The Idea of Gender Transformation in Early Christian Texts and in Modern Times', in Willy Østreng (ed.), *Complexity: Interdisciplinary Communications 2006/2007* (Oslo: Centre for Advanced Study, 2008), pp. 133-38.

———. *The Woman Jesus Loved: Mary Magdalene in the Nag Hammadi Library and Related Documents* (Leiden: Brill, 1996).

Mark, Elizabeth Wyner (ed.), *The Covenant of Circumcision: New Perspectives on an Ancient Jewish Rite* (Lebanon: Brandeis University Press, 2003).

Marshall, Howard, *The Gospel of Luke: A Commentary on the Greek Text* (Exeter: Paternoster, 1978).

Mason, Steve, 'An Essay in Character: The Aim and Audience of Josephus' *Vita*', in Folker Siegert and Jürgen U. Kalms (eds.), *Internationales Josephus-Kolloquium Münster 1997. Vorträge aus dem Institutum Judaicum Delitzschianum* (Münsteraner Judaisitische Studien; Münster: LIT Verlag, 1998), pp. 31-77.

———. '*Contra Apionem* in Social and Literary Context: An Invitation to Judean Philosophy', in Louis Feldman and John R. Levison (eds.), *Josephus' Contra Apionem: Studies in Its Character and Context with a Latin Concordance to the Portion Missing in Greek* (Arbeiten zur Geschichte des antiken Judentums und des Urchristentums 34; Leiden: E. J. Brill, 1996), pp. 187-228.

———. *Flavius Josephus on the Pharisees: A Composition-Critical Study* (SPB; Leiden: Brill, 1991).

———. 'Jews, Judaeans, Judaizing, Judaism: Problems of Categorization in Ancient History', *JSJ* 28 (2007), pp. 457-512.

———. 'Josephus: Value for New Testament Study', in Craig A. Evans and Stanley E. Porter (eds.), *Dictionary of the New Testament Background* (Downers Grove, IL: IVP, 2000), pp. 596-600.

———. 'Should Any Wish to Enquire Further (Ant. 1.25): The Aim and Audience of Josephus's Judaean Antiquities/Life', in Steve Mason (ed.), *Understanding Josephus: Seven Perspectives* (JSPSup 32; Sheffield: Sheffield Academic Press, 1998), pp. 64-103.

Mason, Steve (ed.), *Flavius Josephus: Translation and Commentary*. Vol. 9, *Life of Josephus* (Leiden: Brill, 2001).

Mason, Steve, James S. McLaren and John M. G. Barclay, 'Josephus', in John J. Collins and Daniel C. Harlow (eds.), *Early Judaism: A Comprehensive Overview* (Grand Rapids: Eerdmans, 2012), pp. 290-321.

Matthews, Shelly, *First Converts: Rich Pagan Women and the Rhetoric of Mission in Early Judaism and Christianity* (Contraversions: Jews and Other Differences; Stanford: Stanford University Press, 2001).

McGinn, Sheila E., 'The Acts of Thecla', in Elisabeth Schüssler Fiorenza (ed.), *Searching the Scriptures*. Vol. 2, *A Feminist Commentary* (New York: Crossroad, 1994), pp. 800-828.

McGinn, Thomas A. J., *Prostitution, Sexuality, and the Law in Ancient Rome* (New York: Oxford University Press, 1998).

McKeating, Henry, 'Ezekiel the "Prophet Like Moses"', *JSOT* 61 (1994), pp. 97-109.

McKenzie, John L., *Second Isaiah: Introduction, Translation and Notes* (AB 20; New York: Doubleday, 1968).

McLaren, Margaret A., *Feminism, Foucault, and Embodied Subjectivity* (Albany: SUNY Press, 2002).

McWhorter, L., *Bodies and Pleasures: Foucault and the Politics of Sexual Normalization* (Bloomington: Indiana University Press, 1999).

Meier, John P., 'Jesus, the Twelve and the Restoration of Israel', in James M. Scott (ed.), *Restoration: Old Testament, Jewish and Christian Perspectives* (JSOTSup 27; Leiden: Brill, 2001), pp. 365-404.

———. *A Marginal Jew: Rethinking the Historical Jesus*, vol. 2 (London: Doubleday, 1994).

Melcher, Sarah J., 'Visualizing the Perfect Cult: The Priestly Rationale for Exclusion', in Nancy L. Eiesland and Don E. Saliers (eds.), *Human Disability and the Service of God: Reassessing Religious Practice* (Nashville: Abingdon Press, 1998), pp. 55-71.

Mellor, Anne Kostelanetz, *Mary Shelley: Her Life, Her Fiction, Her Monsters* (London: Routledge, 1988).

Meyer, Marvin W., *The Ancient Mysteries: A Sourcebook of Sacred Texts* (Philadelphia: Harper Collins, 1987).

———. 'Making Mary Male: The Categories "Male" and "Female" in the Gospel of Thomas', *NTS* 31 (1985), pp. 554-70.

Meyers, Carol L., *Exodus: The New Cambridge Bible Commentary* (Cambridge: Cambridge University Press, 2005).

Meyers, Carol L., and Eric Meyers, *Haggai, Zechariah 1–8: A New Translation with Commentary* (AB 25B; New York: Doubleday, 1987).

Mieselman, Moshe, *Jewish Woman in Jewish Law* (New York: Ktav, 1978).

Milgrom, Jacob, *Leviticus 1–16: A New Translation with Introduction and Commentary* (AB 3; New York: Doubleday, 1991).

———. *Leviticus 17–22: A New Translation with Introduction and Commentary* (AB 3A; New York: Doubleday, 2000).

Milik, Józef T., *The Books of Enoch: Aramaic Fragments of Qumrân Cave 4* (Oxford: Clarendon Press, 1976).

Millar, Fergus, 'Reflections of the Trials of Jesus', in *A Tribute to Geza Vermes: Essays on Jewish and Christian Literature and History* (Sheffield: JSOT Press, 1990), pp. 355-81.

Morton, Timothy, *A Routledge Literary Sourcebook on Mary Shelley's Frankenstein* (London: Routledge, 2002).

Moss, Candida R., *Ancient Christian Martyrdom, Diverse Practices, Theologies and Traditions* (New Haven: Yale University Press, 2012).

Moyise, Steven (ed.), *Studies in the Book of Revelation* (Edinburgh: T. & T. Clark, 2001).

Musurillo, Herbert, *The Acts of the Christian Martyrs, Introduction Texts and Translation* (Oxford: Clarendon Press, 1972).

Myers, Jacob M., *I and II Esdras: Introduction, Translation and Commentary* (AB 42; Garden City: Doubleday, 1974).

Naeh, Shlomo, 'Freedom and Celibacy: A Talmudic Variation of Tales of Temptation and Fall in Genesis and its Syrian Background', in Judith Frishman and Lucas Van Rompay (eds.), *The Book of Genesis in Jewish and Christian Oriental Interpretation: A Collection of Essays* (Louvain: Peeters, 1997), pp. 73-89.

Nauerth, Claudia, and Rüdiger Warns, *Thekla. Ihre Bilder in der frühchristlichen Kunst: Göttinger Orientforschungen, Studien zur spätantiken und frühchristlichen Kunst*, Bd. 3 (Wiesbaden: Harrassowitz, 1981).

Neusner, Jacob, 'The Conversion of Adiabene to Judaism: A New Perspective', *JBL* 83 (1964), pp. 60-66.

Newsom, Carol, 'A Maker of Metaphors: Ezekiel's Oracles Against Tyre', *Interpretation* 38 (1984), pp. 151-64.

Nickelsburg, George W. E., *1 Enoch 1: A Commentary on the Book of 1 Enoch, Chapters 1–36; 81–108* (Hermeneia; Minneapolis: Fortress Press, 2001).

———. *Resurrection, Immortality, and Eternal Life in Intertestamental Judaism* (HTS 26; Cambridge, MA: Harvard University Press, 1972).

———. *Resurrection, Immortality, and Eternal Life in Intertestamental Judaism* (HTS 56; exp. ed.; Cambridge, MA: Harvard University Press, 2006).

Niese, Benedict (ed.), *Flavii Iosephi Opera* (6 vols.; Berlin: Weidmann, Editio minor, 1888–95).

Nissinen, Martti, *Homoeroticism in the Biblical World: A Historical Perspective* (trans. Kirsi Stjerna; Minneapolis: Fortress Press, 1998).

Nitzan, Bilha, *Qumran Prayer and Religious Poetry* (STJD 12; Leiden: Brill, 1994).

Nock, A. D., *Early Gentile Christianity and its Hellenistic Background* (New York: Harper & Row, 1962).

Nolland, John, *The Gospel of Matthew: A Commentary on the Greek Text* (Grand Rapids: Eerdmans, 2005).

Odell, Margaret S., *Ezekiel* (Smith & Helwys Bible Commentary; Macon: Smith & Helwys, 2005).

Olson, Kelly, *Dress and the Roman Woman, Self-Presentation and Society* (New York: Routledge, 2008).

Olyan, Saul M., '"And with a Male You Shall Not Lie the Lying down of a Woman": On the Meaning and Significance of Leviticus 18:22 and 20:13', *Journal of the History of Sexuality* 5 (1994), pp. 179-206.

———. *Biblical Mourning: Ritual and Social Dimensions* (Oxford: Oxford University Press, 2004).

Oppenheim, A. Leo, 'Assyriological Gleanings II', *BASOR* 93 (1944), pp. 14-17.

Owen-Crocker, Gale, *Dress in Anglo-Saxon England* (Woodbridge: Boydell & Brewer, 2004).

Paul, Shalom M., 'Heavenly Tablets and the Book of Life', *JANES* 5 (1975), pp. 345-53.

Paulien, Jon, 'Criteria and the Assessment of Allusions to the Old Testament in the Book of Revelation', in Moyise (ed.), *Revelation*, pp. 113-30.

Pearce, Laurie E., 'New Evidence for Judeans in Babylonia', in Oded Lipschits and Manfred Oeming (eds.), *Judah and the Judeans in the Persian Period: Conference Proceedings Held Jointly by the University of Heidelberg, the Hochschule für Jüdische Studien Heidelberg and Tel Aviv University, 15–18 July 2003* (Winona Lake: Eisenbrauns, 2006), pp. 399-411.

Pearce, Laurie F., and Cornelia Wunsch, *Into the Hands of Many Peoples: Judean and West Semitic Exiles in Mesopotamia* (Bethesda: CDL Press, forthcoming).

Perkins, Judith, *The Suffering Self, Pain and Narrative Representation in the Early Christian Era* (London: Routledge, 1995).

Peshty, Monika, 'Thecla Among the Fathers of the Church', in Bremmer (ed.), *Paul and Thecla*, pp. 164-78.

Peterson, Peter M., *Andrew, Brother of Simon Peter* (Leiden: Brill, 1963).

Petropoulos, John C. B., 'Transvestite Virgin with a Cause, The Acta Pauli et Thecla and Late Antique Proto-"Feminism"', in Brit Berggreen and Nanno Marinators (eds.), *Greece and Gender* (Oslo: The Norwegian Institute at Athens, 1995), pp. 125-39.

Phillips, A., *Deuteronomy* (Cambridge: Cambridge University Press, 1973).

Picart, Caroline Joan S., Frank Smoot and Jayne Boldgett, *The Frankenstein Film Sourcebook* (Westport: Greenwood Publishing, 2001).

Pippin, Tina, *Apocalyptic Bodies: The Biblical End of the World in Text and Image* (London: Routledge, 1999).

———. *Death and Desire: The Rhetoric of Gender in the Apocalypse of John* (Louisville: Westminster John Knox Press, 1992).

Popović, Mladen, 'Bones, Bodies and Resurrection in the Dead Sea Scrolls', in Tobias Nicklas, Friedrich V. Reiterer and Joseph Verheyden (eds.), *The Human Body in Death and Resurrection: Deuterocanonical and Cognate Literature Yearbook 2009* (Berlin: W. de Gruyter, 2009), pp. 221-42.

Porten, Bezalel *et al.*, *Elephantine Papyri in English: Three Millennia of Cross-cultural Continuity and Change* (2nd rev. ed.; Documenta et monumenta Orientis antiqui 2; Atlanta: SBL, 2011).

Porter, Stanley, *Paul in Acts: Essays in Literary Criticism, Rhetoric and Theology* (Tübingen: J. C. B. Mohr/Paul Siebeck, 1999).

Postgate, J. Nicholas, *Fifty Neo-Assyrian Legal Documents* (Warminster: Aris & Philips, 1976).

Powell, Barry, *Classical Myth* (2nd ed.; London: Prentice–Hall International, 1998).

Praeder, Susan Marie, 'The Problem of First Person Narration in Acts', *Novum Testamentum* 29 (1987), pp. 193-218.

Pressler, Carolyn, *The View of Women Found in the Deuteronomic Family Laws* (Berlin: W. de Gruyter, 1993).

Price, Simon, and Emily Kearns (eds.), *Oxford Dictionary of Classical Myth and Religion* (Oxford: Oxford University Press, 2003).

Prigent, Pierre, *Commentary on the Apocalypse of St. John* (Tübingen: Mohr Siebeck, 2004).

Propp, William H. C., *Exodus 19–40: A New Translation with Introduction and Commentary* (AB 2A; New York: Doubleday, 2006).

Puech, Émile, *La Croyance des Esséniens en la Vie Future: Immortalité, Résurrection, Vie Éternelle? Histoire d'une Croyance dans le Judaïsme Ancien* (EBib; 2 vols.; Paris: J. Gabalda, 1993).

———. 'Messianisme, Eschatologie et Résurrection dans les Manuscrits de la Mer Morte', *RQ* 18.2 (1997), pp. 255-98.

Pummer, Reinhard, *The Samaritans in Flavius Josephus* (Tübingen: Mohr Siebeck, 2009).

Quesnell, Quentin, 'The Women at Luke's Supper', in Richard J. Cassidy and Philip J. Scharper (eds.), *Political Issues in Luke–Acts* (Maryknoll: Orbis, 1983), pp. 59-79.

Rainier, Chris (ed.), *Ancient Marks: The Sacred Origins of Tattoos and Body Marking* (San Rafael: Earth Aware Editions, 2004).

Rajak, Tessa, 'Justus of Tiberias', *ClQ* New Series 23.2 (1973), pp. 345-68.

Reiner, Erica, 'Runaway: Seize Him', in Jan G. Derckson (ed.), *Assyria and Beyond: Studies Presented to Mogens Trolle Larsen* (Leiden: Nederlands Instituut voor het Nabije Oosten, 2004), pp. 475-82.

Ricci, Carla, *Mary Magdalene and Many Others: Women Who Followed Jesus* (Minneapolis: Fortress Press, 1994).

Richter, Sandra L., *The Deuteronomic History and Name Theology: lᵉšakkēn šᵉmô šām in the Bible and the Ancient Near East* (BZAW 318; Berlin: W. de Gruyter, 2002).

Roberts, Alexander, and James Donaldson (eds.), *The Ante-Nicene Fathers* (Edinburgh: T. & T. Clark, 1885–87; repr. Peabody: Hendrickson, 1994).

Robson, James, *Word and Spirit in Ezekiel* (LHBOTS 447; London: T&T Clark International, 2006).

Rordorf, Willy, in collaboration with Pierre Cherix and Rudolphe Kasser (trans.), *Actes de Paul* (Écrits apocryphes chrétiens; ed. François Bovon and Pierre Geoltrain; Bibliothèque de la Pléiade; Saint Herblain: Gallimard, 1997).

Rosen-Zvi, Ishay. *Demonic Desires: 'Yetzer Hara' and the Problem of Evil in Late Antiquity* (Philadelphia: University of Pennsylvania Press, 2011).

Rossing, Barbara. R., *The Choice Between Two Cities: Whore, Bride, and Empire in the Apocalypse* (Harrisburg: Trinity Press International, 1999).

Roth, Martha T., 'A Case of Contested Status', in Hermann Behrens *et al.* (eds.), *DUMU-E2-DUB-BA-A: Studies in Honor of Åke W. Sjöberg* (Occasional Publications of the Samuel Noah Kramer Fund 11; Philadelphia: University Museum, 1989), pp. 481-89.

Rousselle, Aline, and Felicia Pheasant, *Porneia: On Desire and the Body in Antiquity* (Oxford: Basil Blackwell, 1988).

Routledge, Robin, 'Passover and Last Supper', *TynBul* 53 (2002), pp. 203-21.

Rovner, Jay, 'A Certain *Matronita* Solicited R. Tsadoq: Eros of Power, Eros of Resistance in a Babylonian Talmudic Narrative', in David Golinkin *et al.* (eds.), *Torah Lishma: Essays in Jewish Studies in Honor of Professor Shamma Friedman* (Jerusalem: Bar-Ilan University Press, 2007).

Rubenstein, Jeffrey, *The Culture of the Babylonian Talmud* (Baltimore: The Johns Hopkins University Press).

Ruiz, Jean-Pierre, *Ezekiel in the Apocalypse: The Transformation of Prophetic Language in Revelation 16, 17–19, 10* (Frankfurt am Main: Peter Lang, 1989).

Russell, Diana E. H. (ed.) *Making Violence Sexy: Feminist Views on Pornography* (Buckingham: Open University Press, 1993).

Sacks, Jonathan, *The Yom Kippur Koren Maḥzor* מחזור קורן ליום הכיפורים (Jerusalem: Koren Publishers, 2012).

Sadgrove, Joanna *et al.*, 'Morality Plays and Money Matters: Towards a Situated Understanding of the Politics of Homosexuality in Uganda', *The Journal of Modern African Studies* 50 (2012), pp. 103-29.

Sanders, E. P., *The Historical Figure of Jesus* (London: Penguin, 1995).

———. *Jesus and Judaism* (London: SCM Press, 1985).

———. *Judaism: Practice and Belief, 63BCE–66CE* (London: SCM Press, 1992).

Satlow, Michael, *Jewish Marriage in Antiquity* (Princeton: Princeton University Press, 2001).

———. *Tasting the Dish: Rabbinic Rhetorics of Sexuality* (Atlanta: Scholars Press, 1995.

Sawicki, Jana, 'Foucault, Queer Theory, and the Discourse of Desire', in Timothy O'Leary and Christopher Falzon (eds.), *Foucault and Philosophy* (Oxford: Wiley-Blackwell, 2010).

Sawyer, Deborah, *God, Gender and the Bible* (London: Routledge, 2002).

Scarry, Elaine, *The Body in Pain, The Making and Unmaking of the World* (New York: Oxford University Press, 1985).

Schaberg, Jane, *The Resurrection of Mary Magdalene: Legends, Apocrypha and the Christian Testament* (New York: Continuum, 2004).

Schechter, Solomon (ed.), *Avot d'Rabbi Nathan* (New York: Jewish Theological Seminary, 1997).

Schiffman, Lawrence, 'The Conversion of the Royal House of Adiabene in Josephus and Rabbinic Sources', in Louis Feldman (ed.), *Josephus, Judaism and Christianity* (Detroit: Wayne State University Press, 1987), pp. 293-312.

Schmidt, Brian B., *Israel's Beneficent Dead: Ancestor Cult and Necromancy in Ancient Israelite Religion and Tradition* (Winona Lake: Eisenbrauns, 1996).

Schmidt, Carl, and Wilhelm Schubart, *Πραξεις Παυλου Acta Pauli nach dem Papyrus der Hamburger* (Glückstadt and Hamburg: Staats & Universitäts-Bibliothek, J. J. Augustin, 1936).

Schneemelcher, W. (ed.), *New Testament Apocrypha* (trans. R. McL. Wilson; rev. ed. Cambridge: James Clarke; Louisville: Westminster John Knox Press, 1992).

Schottroff, Luise, 'Non Violence and Women's Resistance in Early Christianity', in Harvey L. Dyck (ed.), *The Pacifist Impulse in Historical Perspective* (Toronto: University of Toronto Press, 1996), pp. 79-89.

Schüle, Andreas, 'Made in the "Image of God": The Concepts of Divine Images in Gen. 1–3', *ZAW* 117 (2005), pp. 1-20.

Schultz, Emily A., and Robert H. Lavenda (eds.), *Cultural Anthropology: A Perspective on the Human Condition* (6th ed.; Oxford: Oxford University Press, 2005),

Schüssler Fiorenza, Elisabeth, 'The Apostleship of Women in Early Christianity', in Swidler and Swidler (eds.), *Women Priests*, pp. 135-40.

———. *The Book of Revelation: Justice and Judgement* (Minneapolis: Fortress Press, 1998).

———. *Bread Not Stone, The Challenge of Feminist Biblical Interpretation* (Boston: Beacon, 2002).

———. *But She Said: Feminist Practices of Biblical Interpretation* (Boston: Beacon, 1992).

———. *Discipleship of Equals: A Critical Feminist Ekklesia-logy of Liberation* (Crossroad: New York, 1993).

———. 'Text and Reality—Reality as Text: The Problem of a Feminist Historical and Social Reconstruction Based on Texts', *Studia Theologica* 43 (1989), pp. 19-34.

———. 'The Twelve', in Swidler and Swidler (eds.), *Women Priests*, pp. 114-22.

Schwartz, Daniel R., *2 Maccabees* (CEJL; Berlin: W. de Gruyter, 2008).

———. 'Doing Like Jews or Becoming a Jew? Josephus on Women Converts to Judaism', in Jörg Frey, Daniel R. Schwartz and Stephanie Gripentrog (eds.), *Jewish Identity in the Greco-Roman World* (Ancient Judaism and Early Christianity 71; Leiden: Brill, 2007), pp. 93-110.

———. 'Yannai and Pella, Josephus and Circumcision', *Dead Sea Discoveries* 18 (2011), pp. 339-59.

Schwartz, Seth, 'Conversion to Judaism in the Second Temple Period: A Functional Approach', in Shaye J. D. Cohen and Joshua J. Schwartz (eds.), *Studies in Josephus and the Varieties of Ancient Judaism: Louis H. Feldman Jubilee Volume* (Ancient Judaism and Early Christianity 67; Leiden: Brill, 2007), pp. 223-36.

———. 'Euergetism in Josephus and the Epigraphic Culture of First-Century Jerusalem', in Hannah Cotton *et al.* (eds.), *From Hellenism to Islam: Cultural and Linguistic Change in the Roman Near East* (Cambridge: Cambridge University Press, 2009), pp. 75-92.

Schweizer, Eduard, *The Good News According to Matthew* (London: SPCK, 1976).

Scott, James M., *On Earth as in Heaven: The Restoration of Sacred Time and Sacred Space in the Book of Jubilees* (JSJSup 91; Leiden: Brill, 2005).

Sedgwick, Colin, 'Healed, Restored, Forgiven', *ET* 118 (2007), pp. 261-66.

Sedgwick, E. K., *Epistemology of the Closet* (Berkeley: University of California Press, 1990).

Segal, Alan, *Paul the Convert: The Apostolate and Apostasy and of Saul the Pharisee* (New Haven: Yale University Press, 1990).

Segal, Robert A., *The Myth and Ritual Theory: An Anthology* (Oxford: Blackwell, 1998).

Selvidge, Marla J., 'Powerful and Powerless Women in the Apocalypse', *Neotestamentica* 26 (1992), pp. 157-67.

Shelley, Mary Wollstonecraft, *Frankenstein or The Modern Prometheus* (ed. Maurice Hindle; rev. ed.; London: Penguin Books, 2003).

Sherwood, Yvonne M., 'Prophetic Scatology: Prophecy and the Art of Sensation', *Semeia* 82 (1998).

Shidlo, Ariel, Michael Schroeder and Jack Drescher, *Sexual Conversion Therapy: Ethical, Clinical, and Research Perspectives* (New York: Haworth Medical Press, 2001).

Singer, Isidor (ed.), *The Jewish Encyclopedia*, vol. 4 (London: Funk & Wagnalls, 1925).

Skinner, Marylyn B., *Sexuality in Greek and Roman Culture* (Oxford: Blackwell, 2005).

Skolnik, Fred (ed.), *Encyclopaedia Judaica*, vol. 4 (2d ed.; New York: Macmillan Reference USA, 2007).

Smit, E. J., 'The Concepts of Obliteration in Ezek. 5.1-4', *JNES* 1 (1971), pp. 46-50.

Smith, Morton, *Jesus the Magician* (New York: Harper & Row, 1978).

Smith, Robert Payne, *A Syriac English Dictionary* (Oxford: Clarendon Press, 1903).

Spittler, Janet E., *Animals in the Apocryphal Acts of the Apostles* (Tübingen: Mohr Seibeck, 2008).

Stein, Siegfried, 'The Concept of the "Fence": Observations on Its Origin and Development', in Siegfried Stein and Raphael Loewe (eds.), *Studies in Jewish Religious and Intellectual History: Presented to Alexander Altmann on the Occasion of His Seventieth Birthday* (Alabama: Published in Association with the Institute of Jewish Studies, London, by the University of Alabama Press, 1979), pp. 301-29.

Stern, Menahem, *Greek and Latin Authors on Jews and Judaism* (3 vols.; Jerusalem: Israel Academy of Sciences and Humanities, 1974–80).

Stolper, Mathew W., 'Inscribed in Egyptian', in Maria Brosius and Amélie Kuhrt (eds.), *Studies in Persian History: Essays in Memory of David M. Lewis* (Achaemenid History 11; Leiden: Nederlands Instituut voor het Nabije Oosten, 1998), pp. 133-43.

———. 'Registration and Taxation of Sale Slaves in Achaemenid Babylonia', *ZA* 79 (1989), pp. 80-101.

Stone, Michael E., *Features of the Eschatology of IV Ezra* (HSS; Atlanta: Scholars Press, 1989).

———. *Fourth Ezra: A Commentary on the Book of Fourth Ezra* (Hermeneia; Minneapolis: Fortress Press, 1990).

Strauss, David F., *Das Leben Jesu kritisch bearbeitet* (2 vols.; Tübingen: Osiander, 1935–36). Published in English as *The Life of Jesus, Critically Examined* (3 vols.; trans. George Eliot; London: Chapman Brothers, 1846).

Streete, Gail P. C., *Redeemed Bodies, Women Martyrs in Early Christianity* (Louisville: Westminster John Knox Press, 2009).

Strine, Casey A., 'Ezekiel's Image Problem: The Mesopotamian Cult Statue Induction Ritual and the *Imago Dei* Anthropology in the Book of Ezekiel', *CBQ* (2014), pp. 252-72.

———. *Sworn Enemies: The Divine Oath, the Book of Ezekiel, and the Polemics of Exile* (BZAW 436; Berlin: W. de Gruyter, 2013).

Stuckenbruck, Loren T., *1 Enoch 91–108* (CEJL; Berlin: W. de Gruyter, 2007).

Sutherland, John, 'How Does Victor Make His Monsters?', in *Is Heathcliff a Murderer? Great Puzzles in Nineteenth-Century Fiction* (Oxford: Oxford University Press, 1998), pp. 24-34.

Swan, Laura, *The Forgotten Desert Mothers: Sayings, Lives and Stories of Early Christian Women* (Mahwah: Paulist Press, 2001).

Swidler, Leonard, and Arlene Swidler (eds.), *Women Priests: A Catholic Commentary on the Vatican Declaration* (New York: Paulist Press, 1977).

Tabory, Joseph, *JPS Commentary on the Haggadah* (Philadelphia: Jewish Publication Society, 2008).

Taylor, Joan E., *The Immerser: John the Baptist within Second Temple Judaism* (Grand Rapids: Eerdmans, 1997).

———. *Jewish Women Philosophers in First-Century Alexandria: Philo's 'Therapeutae' Reconsidered* (Oxford: Oxford University Press, 2003).

———. 'Missing Magdala and the Name of Mary "Magdalene"', *Palestine Exploration Quarterly* (forthcoming).

———. 'The Name Iskarioth (Iscariot)', *JBL* 129 (2010), pp. 369-85.

———. 'Women, Children and Celibate Men in the *Serekh* Texts', *HTR* 104 (2011), pp. 171-90.

Taylor, Joan E., and Federico Adinolfi, 'John the Baptist and Jesus the Baptist: A Narrative Critical Approach', *Journal for the Study of the Historical Jesus* 10 (2012), pp. 247-84.

Theissen, Gerd, *The Gospels in Context: Social and Political Tradition in the Synoptic Tradition* (Edinburgh: T. & T. Clark, 1992).

Theissen, Gerd, and Annette Merz, *The Historical Jesus: A Comprehensive Guide* (London: SCM Press, 1998).

Thiessen, Matthew, *Contesting Conversion: Genealogy, Circumcision, and Identity in Ancient Judaism and Christianity* (Oxford scholarship online; New York: Oxford University Press, 2011).

Thiselton, Antony C., *The First Epistle to the Corinthians: Commentary on the Greek Text* (Grand Rapids: Eerdmans, 2000).

Thorley, John, 'Junia, a Woman Apostle', *Novum Testamentum* 38 (1996), pp. 18-19.

Thurston, Bonnie Bowman, *The Widows: A Woman's Ministry in the Early Church* (Minneapolis: Fortress Press, 1989), pp. 30-34.

Tigay, Jeffery H., *Torah Commentary: Deuteronomy* (JPS Torah Commentary; Philadelphia: Jewish Publication Society, 1996).

Tigchelaar, Eibert J. C., and Florentino García Martínez (eds.), *The Dead Sea Scrolls Study Edition* (2 vols.; Leiden: Brill, 1997–98).

Trexler, Richard, *Sex and Conquest: Gendered Violence, Political Order and the European Conquest of the Americas* (Ithaca: Cornell University Press, 1995).

Trible, Phyllis, *Texts of Terror: Literary-Feminist Readings of Biblical Narratives* (Philadelphia: Fortress Press, 1984).

Tromp, Johannes, 'Can these Bones Live? Ezekiel 37:1-14 and Eschatological Resurrec-tion', in Henk Jan de Jonge and Johannes Tromp (eds.), *The Book of Ezekiel and Its Influence* (Aldershot: Ashgate, 2007), pp. 61-78.

Turner, Bryan S., 'The Body in Western society: Social Theory and Its Perspectives', in Coakley (ed.), *Religion and the Body*, pp. 15-41.

Turner, Victor, *The Ritual Process: Structure and Anti-Structure* (New Brunswick: Aldine Transaction, 1969).

Tur-Sinai, Naftali H., 'קעקע תכבת', in *Enṣiqlopedya Miqra'it* 4:378–80 (Hebrew).

Twelftree, Graham H., *Jesus the Exorcist* (Tübingen: Mohr Siebeck, 1993).

———. *Jesus the Miracle Worker: A Historical and Theological Study* (Downer's Grove: InterVarsity Press, 1999).

Twigg, Julia, *The Body in Health and Social Care* (Basingstoke: Palgrave Macmillan, 2006).

Tzoref, Shani, 'The Use of Scripture in the Community Rule', in Matthias Henze (ed.), *A Companion to Biblical Interpretation in Early Judaism* (Grand Rapids: Eerdmans, 2012), pp. 203-34.

Valantasis, Richard, 'The Question of Early Christian Identity: Three Strategies Exploring a Third Genos', in Levine (eds.), *New Testament Apocrypha*, pp. 60-76.

van Gennep, Arnold, *The Rites of Passage* (trans. Monika B. Vizedom and Gabrielle L. Caffee; Chicago: University of Chicago Press, 1960).

Van Hoof, Anton J. L., *From Autothanasia to Suicide: Self Killing in Classical Antiquity* (London: Routledge: 1990).

Van Kooten, Geurt H., *Paul's Anthropology in Context: The Image of God, Assimilation to God, and Tripartite Man in Ancient Judaism, Ancient Philosophy and Early Christianity* (WUNT 232; Tübingen: Mohr Siebeck, 2008).

Vander Stichele, Caroline, 'Re-membering the Whore: The Fate of Babylon According to Revelation 17.16', in Levine (ed.), *Apocalypse of John*, pp. 106-20.

Vanderhooft, David S., ' *'el-mĕdînâ ûmĕdînâ kiktābāh*: Scribes and Scripts in Yehud and in Achaemenid Transeuphratene', in Oded Lipschits, Gary N. Knoppers and Manfred Oeming (eds.), *Judah and the Judeans in the Achaemenid Period: Negotiating Identity in an International Context* (Winona Lake: Eisenbrauns, 2011), pp. 529-44.

———. 'New Evidence Pertaining to the Transition from Neo-Babylonian to Achaemenid Administration in Palestine', in Rainer Albertz and Bob Becking (eds.), *Yahwism After the Exile: Perspectives on Israelite Religion in the Persian Era: Papers Read at the First Meeting of the European Association for Biblical Studies, Utrecht, 6–9 August 2000* (Assen: Royal van Gorcum, 2003), pp. 219-35.

Vanhoye, Albert, 'L'utilisation du livre d'Ezechiel dans L'Apocalypse', *Biblica* 43 (1962), pp. 436-70.

Vedeler, Harold T., 'Reconstructing Meaning in Deuteronomy 22:5: Gender, Society, and Transvestitism in Israel and the Ancient near East', *JBL* 127 (2008), pp.459-76.

Vermes, Geza, *Jesus the Jew: A Historian's Reading of the Gospels* (London: Collins, 1973).

———. 'Leviticus 18.21 in Ancient Jewish Bible Exegesis', in J. J. Petuchowski and E. Fleischer (eds.), *Studies in Aggadah, Targum and Jewish Liturgy in Memory of Joseph Heinemann* (Jerusalem: Magnes Press, 1981), pp. 108-24.

———. *The Passion* (London: Penguin Books, 2005).

———. *The Religion of Jesus the Jew* (London: SCM Press, 1993).

Wainwright, Elaine, *Women Healing/Healing Women: The Genderization of Healing in Early Christianity* (London: Equinox, 2006).

Walker, Christopher, and Michael B. Dick, *The Induction of the Cult Image in Ancient Mesopotamia: The Mesopotamian Mīs Pî Ritual: Transliteration, Translation, and Commentary* (State Archives of Assyria Literary Texts; Helsinki: The Neo-Assyrian Text Corpus Project, 2001).

Walsh, Jerome T., 'Leviticus 18:22 and 20:13: Who Is Doing What to Whom?', *JBL* 120 (2001), pp. 201-9.

Walters, Jonathan, 'Invading the Roman Body: Manliness and Impenetrability in Roman Thought', in Judith P. Hallett and Marilyn B. Skinner (eds.), *Roman Sexualities* (Princeton: Princeton University Press, 1997), pp. 29-43.

Watts, James W., *Ritual and Rhetoric in Leviticus: From Sacrifice to Scripture* (Cambridge: Cambridge University Press, 2007).

Wellhausen, Julius, *Einleitung in den drei ersten Evangelien* (Berlin: Georg Reimer, 1911).

Werblowsky, R. J. Zwi, and Geoffrey Wigoder (eds.), *The Encyclopedia of the Jewish Religion* (New York: Holt, Rinehart & Winston, 1965).

Westermann, Claus, *Genesis 1–11: A Continental Commentary* (trans. John J. Scullion; Minneapolis: Fortress Press, 1994).

White, Hayden, 'The Value of Narrativity in the Representation of Reality', in W. J. T. Mitchell (ed.), *On Narrative* (Berkeley: University of Chicago Press, 1981), pp. 1-23,

Wilker, Julia, *Für Rom und Jerusalem: die herodianische Dynastie im 1. Jahrhundert n.Chr.* (Studien zur alten Geschichte 5; Frankfurt am Main: Verlag Antike, 2007).

Wilkinson, John, *The Bible and Healing: A Medical and Theological Commentary* (Edinburgh: Handsel, 1998).

———. *Egeria's Travels* (rev ed.; Warminster: Aris & Philips, 1981).

Willett, Tom W., *Eschatology in the Theodicies of 2 Baruch and 4 Ezra* (JSPSup 4; Sheffield: Sheffield Academic Press, 1989).

Williams, Sam K., *Jesus' Death as a Saving Event: The Background and Origin of a Concept* (Missoula: Scholars Press, 1975).

Wills, Lawrence, *The Jewish Novel in the Ancient World* (Ithaca: Cornell University Press, 1995).

Wilson, A. N., *Paul: The Mind of the Apostle* (London: W. W. Norton & Co., 1997).

Wilson, Robert R., 'An Interpretation of Ezekiel's Dumbness', *VT* 22 (1972), pp. 91-104.

Wilson-Kastner, Patricia, 'Macrina: Virgin and Teacher', *Andrews University Seminary Studies* 17 (1979), pp. 105-17.

Wiseman, Donald J., 'Medicine in the Old Testament World', in Bernard Palmer (ed.), *Medicine and the Bible* (Exeter: Paternoster Press, 1986), pp. 15-42.

Wood, Mitchel J., 'The Gay Male Gaze', *Journal of Gay and Lesbian Social Services* 17 (2004), pp. 43-62.

Wright, N. T., *The Resurrection of the Son of God: Christian Origins and the Question of God* (London: SPCK, 2003).

———. *Surprised by Hope* (London: SPCK, 2007).

Wunsch, Cornelia, *Judeans by the Waters of Babylon: New Historical Evidence in Sources from Rural Babylonia: Texts from the Schoyen Collection* (Dresden: Islet Verlag, forthcoming).

———. 'Sklave, Sklaverei', in Michael P. Streck (ed.), *Reallexion des Assyriologie II* (Berlin: W. de Gruyter, 2011), p. 593.

Yamauchi, Edwin M., 'The Eastern Jewish Diaspora Under the Babylonians', in Mark Chavelas (ed.), *Mesopotamia and the Bible: Comparative Explorations* (JSOTSup 341; London: Sheffield Academic Press, 2002), pp. 356-77.

Yarbro Collins, Adela, *Crisis and Catharsis: The Power of the Apocalypse* (Philadelphia: Westminster Press, 1984).

———. 'Feminine Symbolism in the Book of Revelation', in Levine (ed.), *Apocalypse of John*, pp. 121-30.

Yardeni, Ada, 'Remarks on the Priestly Blessing on Two Ancient Amulets from Jerusalem', *VT* 41 (1991), pp. 176-85.

Yoreh, Tzemah, Aubrey Glazer and Justin Lewis (eds.), *Vixens Disturbing Vineyards: Embarrassment and Embracement of Scriptures: Festschrift in Honor of Harry Fox* (Boston: Academic Studies Press, 2010).

Zellentin, Holger, *Rabbinic Parodies of Jewish and Christian Literature* (Tübingen: Mohr Siebeck, 2011).

Zerwick, Max, and Mary Grosvenor, *A Grammatical Analysis of the Greek New Testament* (3d rev. ed.; Rome: Editrice Pontificio Istituto Biblico, 1988).

Zimmerli, Walter, *Ezekiel: A Commentary on the Book of the Prophet Ezekiel, Chapters 1–24* (trans. R. E. Clements; Hermeneia 1; Philadelphia: Fortress Press, 1979).

Zimmerli, Walther, *Ezekiel: A Commentary on the Book of the Prophet of Ezekiel, Chapters 25–48* (trans. James D. Martin; Hermeneia 2; Philadelphia: Fortress, 1983).

Zimmermann, Johannes, *Messianische Texte aus Qumran: Königliche, Priesterliche und Prophetische Messiasvorstellungen in den Schriftfunden von Qumran* (WUNT 104; Tübingen: Mohr Siebeck, 1998).

INDICES

INDEX OF REFERENCES

INDEX OF AUTHORS

INDEX OF SUBJECTS

Lightning Source UK Ltd.
Milton Keynes UK
UKOW06f0225101215

264402UK00006B/83/P